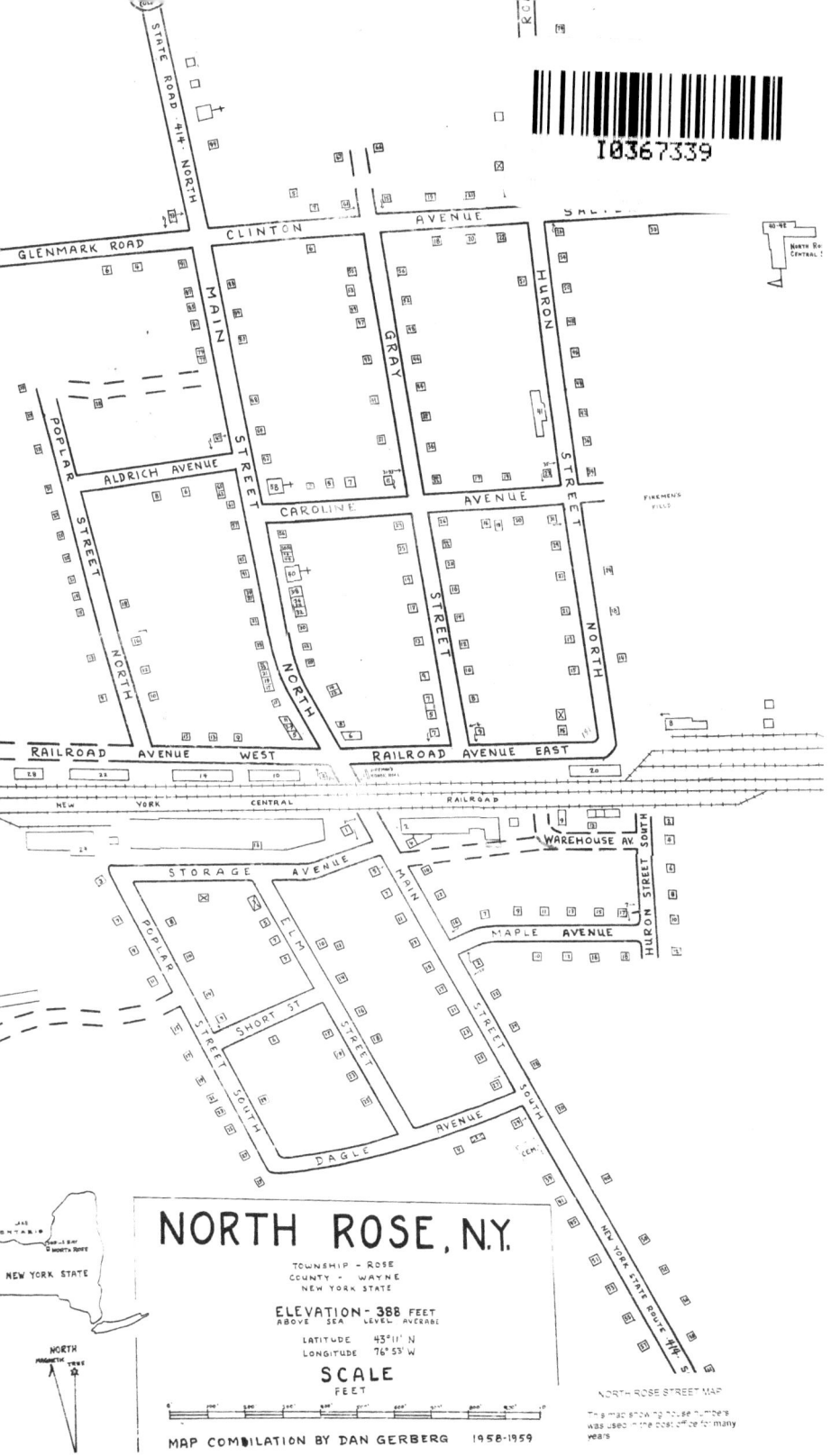

North Rose 1940

The 192 Families Who Created a Vibrant
Community in the Apple Capital of New York State

ALEXANDER G. SKUTT

BOOKS
NORTH COUNTRY BOOKS
Essex, Connecticut

BOOKS
NORTH COUNTRY BOOKS

An imprint of The Globe Pequot Publishing Group, Inc.
64 South Main Street
Essex, CT 06426
www.globepequot.com

Distributed by NATIONAL BOOK NETWORK

Copyright © 2025 by Alexander G. Skutt

All rights reserved. No part of this book may be reproduced in any form or by any electronic or mechanical means, including information storage and retrieval systems, without written permission from the publisher, except by a reviewer who may quote passages in a review.

ISBN 9781493093342 (paperback)

Dedication

This book is dedicated to the memory of my sister,
Marilyn Skutt Roberts (1936–2023),
who was a lifetime member of the Rose Historical Society.

Aerial photo of North Rose circa 1950s from the Rose Historical Society Farnsworth Museum archives, photographer unknown

Illustrated maps of the towns surrounding North Rose in Wayne County (this page) and of the hamlet of North Rose (opposite page) by Olena Merjievska

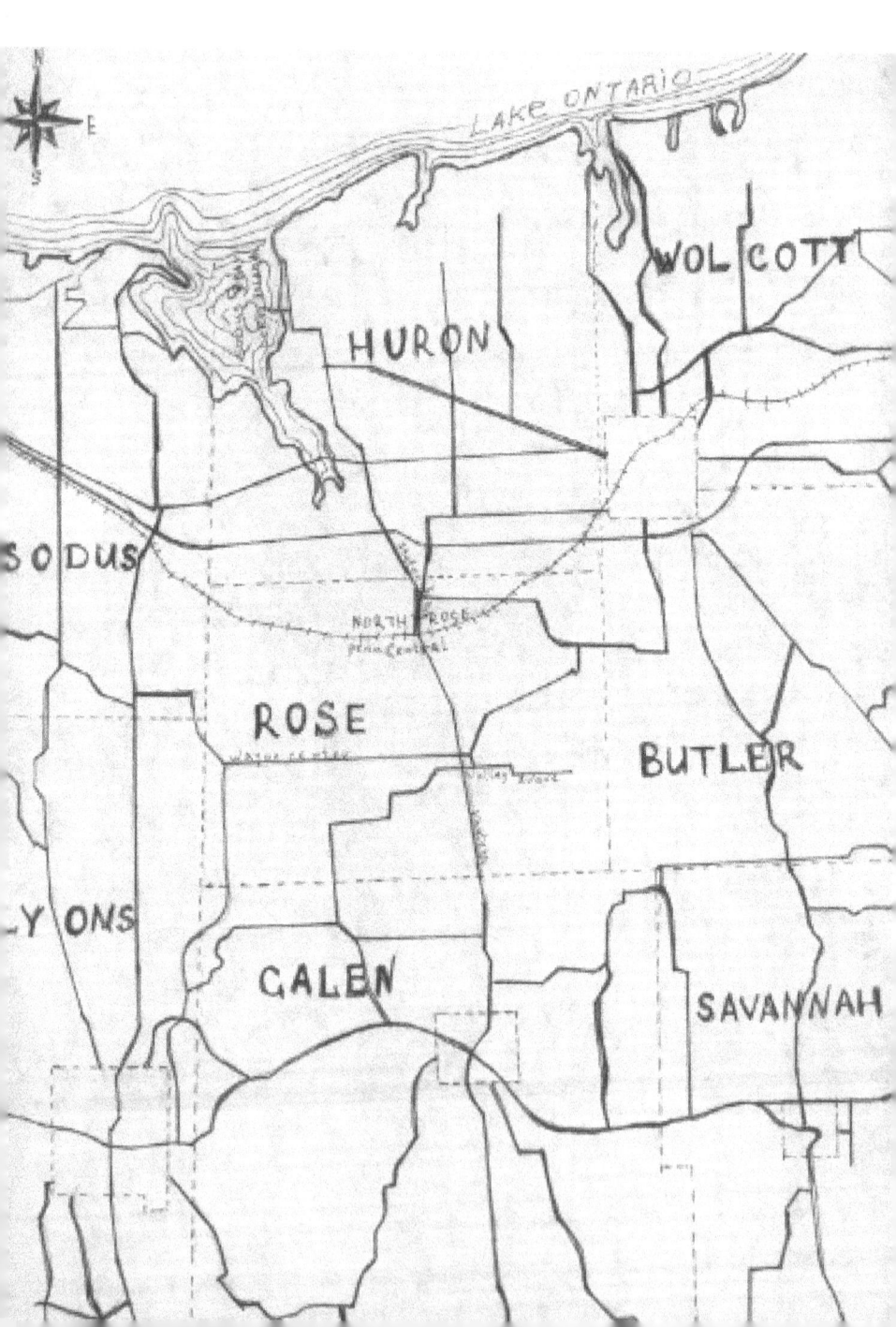

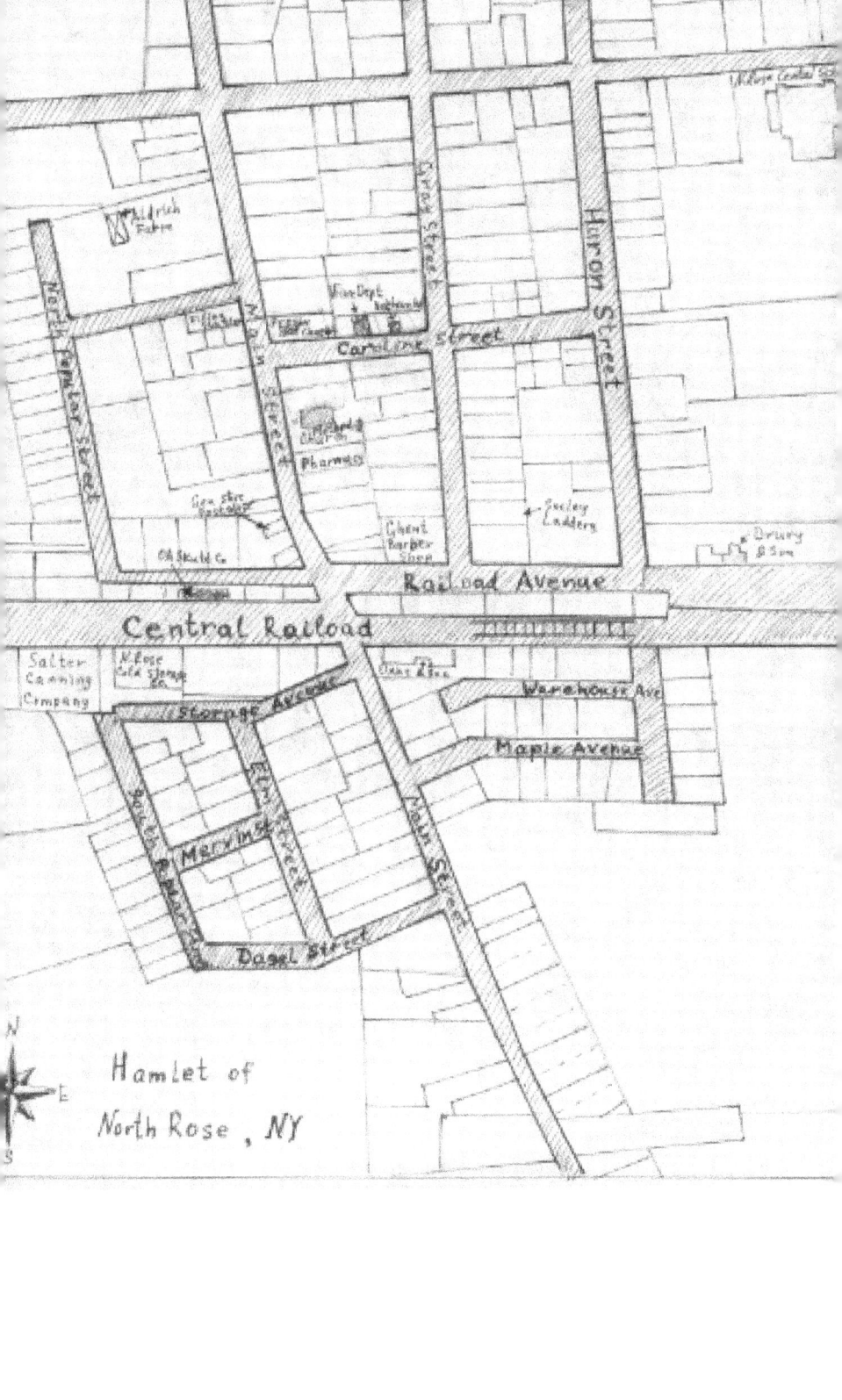

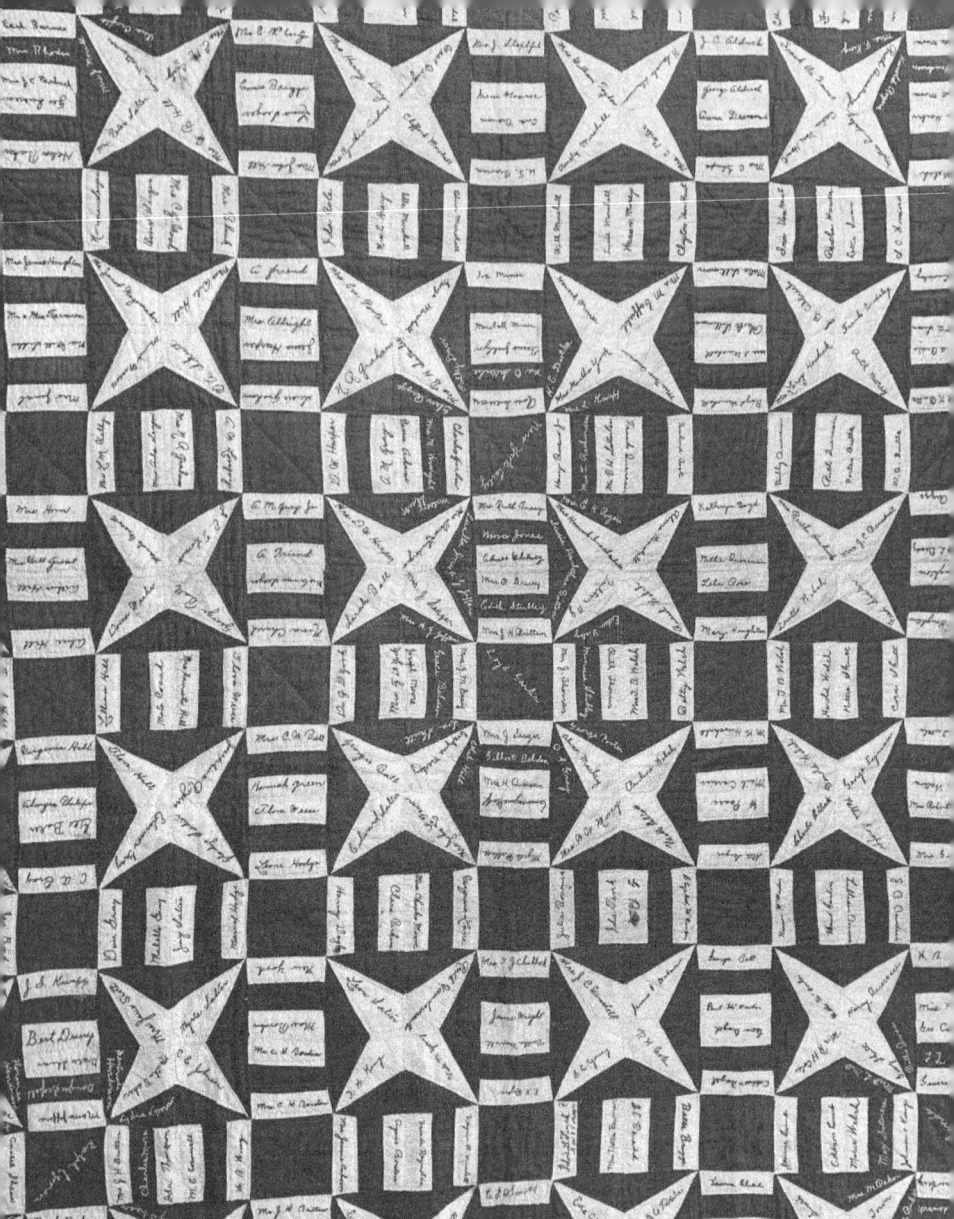

The Quilt

FOR GENERATIONS, sewing circles have brought people together to enjoy each other's company, to share stories, and, often, to create bedspreads that are both useful and beautiful. In the first half of the twentieth century, the women of North Rose, New York, often gathered to make quilts for fundraisers. Quilt showers were thrown for those about to get married.

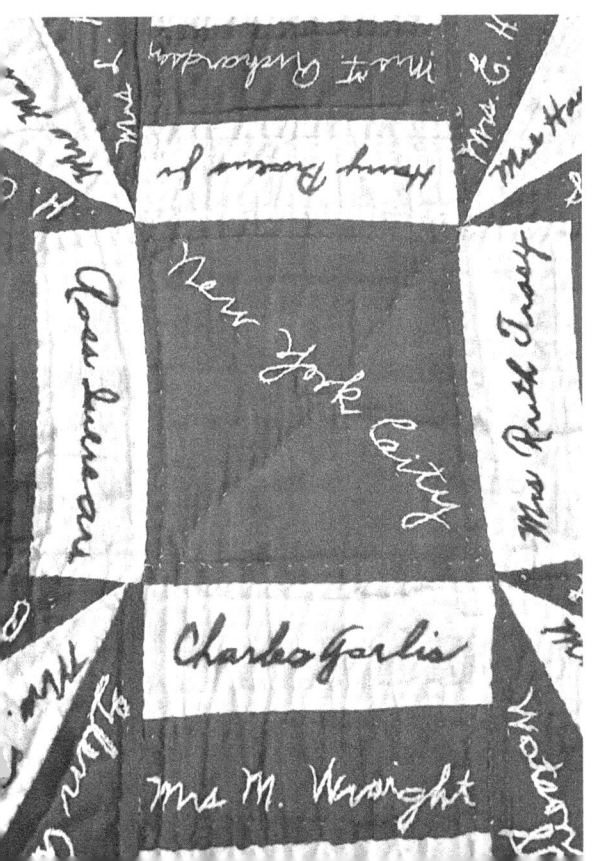

The quilt shown here was made in the mid-1920s for my father, A. Gray Skutt, on the occasion of his graduation from Cornell University and his imminent move to New York City to work in finance. (The color scheme is red and white, which are Cornell's school colors.) The names of many people in *North Rose 1940* appear on the quilt; you'll see close-ups of some of them in the Families section of this book.

The quilt has been and continues to be a treasured Skutt family heirloom.

—*Alex Skutt, January 2025*

North Rose 1940

NORTH ROSE, NEW YORK, is now a small, quiet hamlet east of Rochester. It is located in the Wayne County apple-growing country, near the southern shore of Lake Ontario. I spent the first eight years of my life in North Rose, and I love it dearly. However, I must admit the North Rose that I really love isn't the North Rose of today. The North Rose that holds my deep affection is the town of my earliest memories.

When I was a child in the early 1950s, North Rose still had most of the vigor that it displayed throughout the first half of the 20th century—the time of my parents and grandparents. My North Rose had two hardware stores, a general store, two barbershops, and a meat market. It had the North Rose Central School (NRCS) for grades K through 12, three churches, a florist, a few gas stations, a pharmacy, and a strange amalgam of a furniture store and a funeral parlor. There was also a formidable array of civic, recreational, fraternal, and religious organizations—ranging from the elaborate (and mysterious) Masons and (the women's auxiliary) Order of the Eastern Star to the informal and lighthearted Contract Bridge Club, Thursday's Club, and Anniversary Club.

The Rebekahs, the Women's Auxiliary of the Odd Fellows.

Returning to the array of North Rose businesses, none was more important than the New York Central Railroad. It was an oft-repeated story that North Rose swiftly outgrew the hamlet that North Rose's name referenced—Rose, New York—because the tracks of the Rochester/Oswego branch of the New York Central were laid through the center of North Rose.

The Cold Storage, the Canning Factory, the Bean House, the coal and feed company, and other wholesale and retail concerns were accessible to townsfolk, allowing them to feed their families and keep their farms running. These economic exchanges between the family farmers and the businesses they traded with in town were the reasons that North Rose and many hundreds of other farm towns throughout the United States were such lively places in the first half of the 20th century.

Interpersonal connections were robust. Visiting and hosting friends were extremely popular activities in these pre-television days. Three newspapers that covered North Rose news—*The Lyons Republican*, *The Lake Shore News* (published in Wolcott), and *The Wayne County Herald Eagle* (published in Clyde)—included the minutiae of residents' daily lives. A separate column appeared for each town, village, and hamlet the newspaper covered. For example, "Mr. and Mrs. Clinton Smith entertained Mr. and Mrs. William Jones, of Huron, at their cottage on LeRoy Island last Sunday" was a typical announcement in a North Rose column. Occasionally citizens of North Rose would travel to New York City or Canada or some other distant spot, but remarkably often they simply visited friends—and especially relatives—in nearby towns and, of course, in North Rose itself.

I take pride in the Skutt family's role in the history of North Rose. As I grow older, I also take comfort in my memories of a time when farms and other businesses operated on a more human scale, when many people (including myself) lived in friendly, tight-knit, small communities where each person had an important part to play in the history of a little hamlet.

This book is an attempt to capture a town and its people at a particular moment in time. It is commonly known that, according to the United States Constitution, a national census must be conducted every 10 years. Less well known is the law that keeps individual census information private for 72 years after it is collected, although statistical summaries of census data are released as soon as they are compiled. It is easy to understand that people might not want to reveal personal data—such as their income, the amount of rent they pay, or even their age—to their contemporaries. Therefore, that data is intentionally unavailable for a long time.

I chose to write about North Rose in 1940 because the 1940 census was the latest available as I began to write this and because people like my sister, Marilyn S. Roberts, and friends Janet Clingerman and Suzanne McQueen Polvino, who were four years old in 1940, were able to provide me with first-person accounts of the period. It was also the last census preceding my own birth and arrival in North Rose in 1948.

A page from the 1940 census of North Rose, New York.

In this book, each household which existed in the hamlet of North Rose (as defined by the Census Bureau) has its own section. Each section begins with specific data from the census about the members of that household in 1940. The remainder of each section gives more information about the household members before and after 1940 and expands the reporting to include close relatives of the 1940 North Rose residents, especially their spouses, children, and grandchildren.

Stories of North Rose

NORTH ROSE OWED ITS PERIOD of most significant growth and commercial success to four factors. The first two were a superb fruit-growing climate and the Rome, Watertown, and Ogdensburg Railroad, which was well placed to ship crops to urban markets. (In 1914 this railroad was integrated into the New York Central system.) The third factor was a skilled, industrious group of fruit farmers; the fourth, their workers, consisting of local year-round laborers and the migrants who showed up in the early summer to pick the fruit.

The hamlet is near the southern edge of a stretch of agricultural land that is ideal for growing apples. Although winters are cold and snowy, Lake Ontario's great mass (deep for a Great Lake) has never wholly frozen since meteorologists began to keep records over a century ago. This huge body of water (393.5 cubic miles) moderates the air temperatures to which the trees are exposed. The low-flowing air across the lake's center should be at a temperature close to 32 degrees. That is the temperature of fresh water mixed with ice. Because of Lake Ontario, apple trees survive harsh Upstate New York winters. Lake Michigan is the only other Great Lake that has never completely frozen over in modern times.

For well over one hundred years, Wayne County, especially the area around North Rose, has produced excellent apples. In the late 19th and early 20th centuries, apples were stored for use in the winter months by drying or evaporating them. Apples were sliced and placed in fire-heated units (some constructed in Wolcott). In the 1920s apple preservation switched to cold storage compartments of large, specialized buildings with a controlled atmosphere which minimized the oxygen and maximized nitrogen. One of the most significant changes to the technique of apple growing was to suspend apples from wires like grapes. This allowed for machine harvesting of apples and bringing new species to market in only a few years. The apples that were grown by either the traditional ladder climbing method or the grapevine-like suspension were used for eating by hand, cooking, or juicing. Many seasons brought new favorite varieties to North Rose area orchards. By approximately 1940, Wayne County was the fourth largest producer of apples in the nation. Today, if Wayne County seceded from New York to become the 51st state, agricultural statisticians would rank this small county as the fourth largest apple-producing state in the nation.

From Lamb's Corners to North Rose

ISAAC D. LAMB (1776–1862) and his wife, Sarah "Sally" Stanley (1777–1846), were the first European "permanent" residents of North Rose—then about to be called Lamb's Corners—according to Alfred S. Roe (*Rose Neighborhood Sketches*, 1893). Isaac, who was my great-great-great-grandfather, was born in Montgomery County to John William Lamb (1739–1819) and Elizabeth Hopner Lamb (1738–1810). In 1804 Isaac married Sally Stanley. When he bushwhacked into Wayne

County and reached the swift-flowing Thomas Creek, he thought he had found a great place to construct a sawmill, which he did in nearby Glenmark. He built a home uphill to the east, and he and his wife gave their surnames to the settlement—Lamb's Corners.

The Lambs themselves contributed to the growing population of the new village—they had 10 children: seven daughters and three sons. Lamb's Corners existed until 1874 when the railroad came through. At that time, the largest settlement in the Town of Rose was Rose Valley, now simply called Rose. (This was two miles south of Lamb's Corners, which was still small and quiet. Even out-of-the-way Glenmark, about two miles west of North Rose, was a livelier settlement than Lamb's Corners.) Glenmark was an early success because of the waterpower generated from the rapid descent of Thomas Creek—the most significant feeder stream coming from the south that flows into Sodus Bay. Thomas Creek's official name has been Sodus Creek since about the 1940s. It often has been informally called Glenmark Creek. (Conversation with Lucinda Collier and email from New York State Library, September 2020.)

According to Lucinda Collier in *Cures and Remedies from a Glenmark Store Ledger*, published in 2019: "During the mid-1800s, Glenmark was the site of the Converse Hotel, a tavern, a rural school (District School Number 1), two grocery stores, a blacksmith shop, several sawmills (including Isaac Lamb's), a water-powered carding machine, [and] two gristmills." Lamb's Corners, largely residential, featured several family homes and a post office. The small crossroads community called Lamb's Corners grew around the crossing of the Clyde–Port Glasgow Road (the north-south road) and the drive that came east from Glenmark. (Port Glasgow is now Resort.) This north-south road was a privately owned plank road that ran from Clyde to the Huron town line and eventually became North Rose's Main Street.

The owners of this road collected fees from their roadway users by manually operated turnpikes, which blocked the road until the users paid the toll. It was the first in Wayne County chosen as a county road and the first that received an appointment as a state highway—eventually becoming a portion of NYS 89 and then NYS 414. A surveyor carefully charted the north-south route in 1812. The west-to-east road from Glenmark to Lamb's Corners—and slightly beyond—was completed by the surveyor two years later. About one hundred years passed until, in 1910 and 1911, road crews rebuilt these roads as "improved roads." Improved roads have hard surfaces and were crowned in the center so that rainwater would drain off the sides. Some improved roads even had curbing along the edges.

The Railroad

UPON THE RAILROAD'S ARRIVAL, there was some confusion about the train station's name and location. Many people had expected that this new lakeshore-hugging train route—inexplicably nicknamed the "Hojack" line (see page 311)—would pass through either Rose Valley or Sodus.

There had been a reason why most thought that one of those two communities would be getting the boost of business generated by the railroad: In that era, a municipality would show appreciation for getting service from a railroad by issuing municipal bonds to help pay for the newly arriving rail line. That kind of encouragement (or bribe) did not seem to be illegal. In this instance, neither Rose Valley nor Sodus stepped up to the plate with a cash offer for the rail line. The RW&O Railroad headed equidistant from the two early contenders that the railroad expected to attract, so neither Rose Valley nor Sodus would benefit from being close to the tracks.

This "equidistant route" placed the roadbed about one-half mile south of Lamb's Corners. Perhaps the deciding factor for changing the station's name from Rose (which was what the railroad first intended, rather than Lamb's Corners) was that the freight timetables and tags were already printed as "Rose" by the railroad. They thought it would be confusing to railroad shippers and freight handlers to remember that "Rose" on railroad paperwork meant Lamb's Corners. Everyone (except maybe the Lamb family members) thought it would make more sense to change the name of the railway station to "North Rose" and to use up the existing Rose preprinted forms (labels, tags, and tables). The fast-growing hamlet would also change its name to

North Rose so that the settlement would have the same name as the railroad station.

With a railroad station and a new name, North Rose quickly surpassed

R. R. STATION, North Rose, N. Y.

its neighbor, Glenmark, in terms of activity. By the early 1900s there was a post office, two cold storage plants (that eventually merged), a Methodist church, a Presbyterian church, a Masonic temple, the Garlick general store, a school, separate stations for freight and passenger trains, two hotels (Pimms and Cottage), thriving apple and peach orchards, upland and downland crops depending on whether they were planted on a hill or in a valley, and an eight- or ten-story building called the hops barn. (The hops barn was the only eight- to 10-story building the town ever saw and it burned to the ground within 10 years of its construction.)

North Rose residents were very community minded. They were frequently invited to each other's houses for meals, visits, or small celebrations. They attended numerous meetings of fraternal organizations and religious groups. They fished and swam in Sodus Bay and went hunting in the Adirondacks (where deer were still plentiful). They had performances including concerts, plays, and exhibitions—an 1891 program for the North Rose School exhibition featured performances by the schoolchildren and teachers with music provided by the Gardner Family Parlor Orchestra. There were baseball games where the North Rose team would play against other towns.

North Rose was a dry town. Huron and Sodus were not, so that's where people went to drink and dance. There was a hardware store in Clyde that had pool tables in the back, where gambling and illicit boxing matches took place. (At age 6 I knew I wasn't supposed to go in and watch, so I didn't even try.) A legendary unregulated boxing match also occurred in nearby Port Glasgow. There was a father/son combination of corner man and fighter, and midway through the match, the son was getting the worst of it. The story goes that he had a knife hidden in his waistband and when he was in the corner, taking his one-minute break between rounds, his father looked at the opponent and said to his son: "Cut his heart out." The fighter cut off his opponent's ear instead of his heart, but the police were called and the fighter was sentenced to two months in jail. His opponent, on the other hand, was sentenced to one ear for the rest of his life.

The Great North Rose Fire of 1917

ON JANUARY 17, 1917, A FIRE broke out in the rear of the second floor of the four-story M. E. Newberry's chain department store. (M. E. Newberry's department store was a separate business from the J. J. Newberry's 5¢ &10¢ store chain.) The fire rapidly grew, in spite of all efforts by the community to stop it, destroying what was the Quereau Block: Harry Quereau's residence, the new Harris & Winchell Meat Market, the post office, the office building of Skutt, Welch, & Aldrich, and the Calkins barbershop. The North Rose Fire Department attempted to stand firmly at Charles Garlick's general store, but the flames took the building.

The post office and Garlick's general store on the west side of Main Street before the fire.

One of the witnesses of the fire was Henrietta Quereau Collier, who was 6 at the time and lived with her parents and older sister above the Quereau family general store. Her experience was captured by her daughter-in-law Lucinda Hance Collier in the book *The Voices of Wayne County*. An excerpt from her story is as follows:

    Late on the night of January 17th . . . panicked voices awakened Henrietta, ordering her to get up. . . . She was taken down the stairs and outside. A fire had broken out down the street and anticipating that it would take the Quereau building as well, townspeople frantically carried Quereau store goods and upstairs apartment possessions out of the building into the freezing night, throwing them in piles in the middle of the graveled street as they tried to save what they could.

    Henrietta was placed on the growing pile of their belongings, terrified, but doing as she was told. She watched as the firemen poured water on the rapidly growing inferno. She watched as water was brought in from elsewhere to supply the fire hoses, and fire companies from other towns arrived to try and help halt the flames. She watched as the Quereau building caught fire and moved on to her grandparents' house, consuming both buildings. She even watched a few people help themselves to some of her family's belongings from the piles. . . . When the fire had finally burned itself out, all the stores on the west side of the street and her grandparents' house were gone.

    With the arrival of the Rose, Wolcott, Clyde, and Sodus Volunteer Fire Companies, the Gray Brothers' hardware store was the last building lost to the fire. The locomotive engineer was the hero of the day. He alerted the neighboring fire companies of the need for help in North Rose. The combined fire departments stopped the spreading flames and saved the J. B. Frey storehouse occupied by J. C. Benedict. Fortunately, the fire did not jump to the east side of Main Street. Still, authorities estimated the damage to be $150,000 or over $3 million in today's currency. No lives were lost in the fire. The Quereaus took what was left and rebuilt their building, and the store continued to operate until 1963. You can see some of the charred floor beams in the building's cellar, which is still in use today.

The Minstrel Show

THE NORTH ROSE MASONS and the NRCS minstrel shows presented the "Laffalot" Minstrel Show performed at The North Rose School Auditorium in March 1950. The organizers of these old-time performances were North Rose dwellers who shared the prevailing racial views of the time.

These residents produced shows of music and comedy usually performed by white men in "blackface"—dark makeup that allowed them to pretend to be people of color. These black characters were often held up to ridicule. They behaved like fools and confirmed the stereotypes that whites expected of blacks. The interlocutor was the master of ceremonies. He frequently carried on conversations with the other performers. The original Jim Crow was a stock character in minstrel shows. White comedian Thomas Rice created Jim Crow as the butt of much tomfoolery. Besides being a comic character in many minstrel performances, Jim Crow gave his name to the segregation laws passed by most southern states after Reconstruction.

With its military enforcement of civil rights and voting freedom for men of color, the Reconstruction Era ended with the Compromise of 1877. In an exceptionally close election, the Rutherford B. Hayes (R) vs. Samuel J. Tilden (D) decision on who had won shifted from the Electoral College to the House of Representatives.

Enough Democrats agreed to throw their support to Hayes to give him the win if the Republicans agreed to withdraw Union occupation troops to leave the Democratic South to its own devices. This absence of Union troops in the southern states left the south in the thrall of the Jim Crow laws for the better part of a century. It is surprising to see this racist show, which brought many respected members of the community onstage, held in the NRCS auditorium as recently as 1950.

The War

THE WORLD WAS ALREADY AT WAR when enumerators fanned out across the United States in April 1940 to take the United States Census. The census would show a North Rose population of 580. The United States was still in a depression: The national 1940 unemployment rate was 14.6 percent. As the economy continued to stagnate, the world situation was becoming increasingly dangerous. In May, Germany invaded and conquered France. The summer of 1940 brought The Blitz—the German bombing of English cities.

President Franklin Roosevelt campaigned to victory in the 1940 election by promising to keep America out of war. (Wayne County, solidly Republican as usual, gave his Republican opponent Wendell Wilkie 72 percent of the vote.) But FDR also began a dramatic military buildup with legislation adding ships to the Navy and planes to the Army Air Corps. In September Congress authorized a peacetime draft, and conscripts began entering military service in December.

One in 11 people in North Rose went off to fight in World War II, a statistic that mirrored almost exactly the percentage of people who went off nationally to fight in the war. At home in North Rose, the war effort was felt everywhere: Victory gardens—providing nutritious food for families so they wouldn't take food away from the soldiers—were in nearly every backyard. At Red Cross meetings held in church basements, women folded sterile bandages to provide comfort to wounded soldiers overseas. Some supplies—cooking oil, meat, and gasoline among them—were so important to the war effort that they were rationed. The war was also kept alive by the placard located at the corner of Main Street and Railroad Avenue that listed the participants in the war—soldiers, sailors, and marines—by name.

There were a few North Rose war stories that stand out to me. In September 1945 two service members from the hamlet of North Rose were awarded the Distinguished Service Cross, an acknowledgment of heroism second only to the Congressional Medal of Honor.

The two men were Corporal Nolan Powell and Lieutenant Richard Drury, who lived within a stone's throw of each other in North Rose. Powell had already been awarded a Purple Heart when, as a paratrooper, he suffered two arm wounds from a German sniper. According to the Rochester Times Union in February, he wrote to his parents shortly afterward telling them not to worry. He was enjoying the clean hospital beds and the three "squares" a day. He received the Distinguished Service Cross from a battle near Grosetto, Italy, in 1945, when Powell and a sergeant broke from their platoon and under heavy fire silenced a machine gun, returning to Allied lines with five German prisoners. After being momentarily pinned down by more bullets, he and the sergeant returned to the field of battle and ordered the enemy to surrender. They did. Through these acts of bravery,

Private Powell made possible the capture of 19 German prisoners and the killing or wounding of 10 more while protecting his own platoon. (Powell later became a teacher at North Rose Central School and was my sister's favorite.)

The second incidence of extreme heroism was on the part of Lieutenant Richard Drury (who received his title as a battlefield commission). He received the Distinguished Service Cross for heroic action in the Battle of Tunisia after he and a companion held a forward position, firing a trench mortar to cover the withdrawal of Allied tanks. Later he received a Silver Star medal for gallantry in action and disregard for personal safety in Belgium in 1945. He was wounded and captured by the Germans in April 1945 during a counterattack at Badetz and taken to the Altengrabow in Germany—liberated in May. There's a memorable story about the medal presentation to Richard Drury. After the announcement came out that he had won this prestigious award, he was due to be flown in to meet with Dwight D. Eisenhower, general of the armies in Italy. But bad weather grounded Eisenhower's plane, forcing General Patton to step in. When it was time to present the award, Patton searched through his pockets and realized he didn't have the pin to give the young lieutenant, so he unpinned his own Distinguished Service Cross from his army blouse and pinned it on Drury's uniform.

Lieutenant Richard Drury, 1945.

Names of the War Heroes

FOR SEVERAL DECADES these names were listed on a wooden monument in North Rose at the corner of the railroad tracks and Main Street. In my mind, the placard was also associated with the noon whistle, which signaled to several businesses that it was time for their employees to break for lunch. Unfortunately, the monument was removed a decade or two ago. It's rumored to be in the basement of the Rose elementary school building.

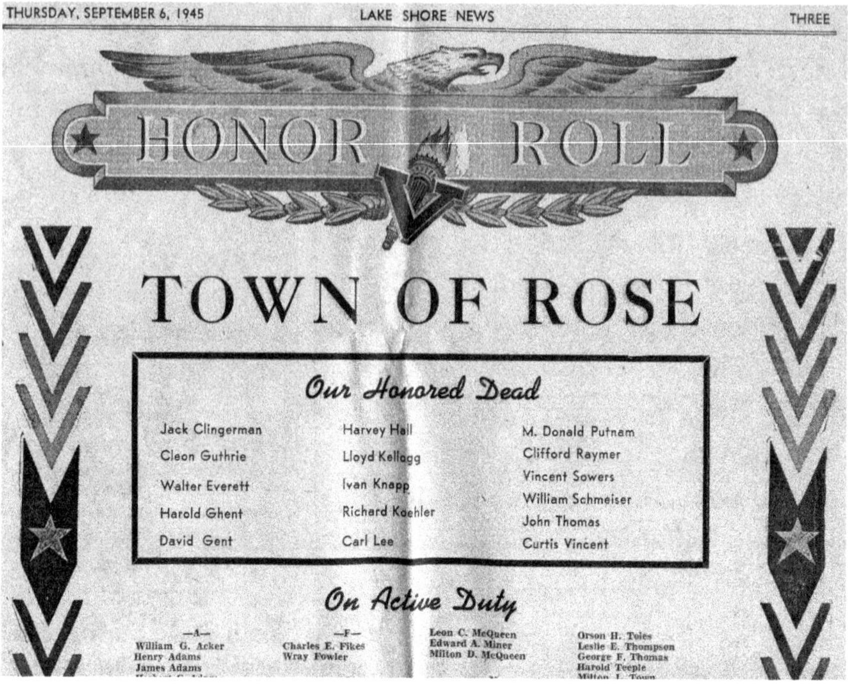
THURSDAY, SEPTEMBER 6, 1945 LAKE SHORE NEWS THREE

HONOR ROLL

TOWN OF ROSE

Our Honored Dead

Jack Clingerman	Harvey Hall	M. Donald Putnam
Cleon Guthrie	Lloyd Kellogg	Clifford Raymer
Walter Everett	Ivan Knapp	Vincent Sowers
Harold Ghent	Richard Koehler	William Schmeiser
David Gent	Carl Lee	John Thomas
		Curtis Vincent

On Active Duty

—A—
William G. Acker
Henry Adams
James Adams

—F—
Charles E. Fikes
Wray Fowler

Leon C. McQueen
Edward A. Miner
Milton D. McQueen

Orson H. Toles
Leslie E. Thompson
George F. Thomas
Harold Teeple

The volunteer fire departments of Rose and North Rose sponsored a full-page listing in the *Lake Shore News* of those from both towns who served in World War II.

Below are the 215 men and women from the town of Rose and the hamlet of North Rose who served in our nation's armed forces during WWII. Capitalized names indicate people who lost their lives in the war.

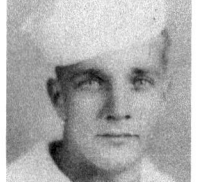

William G. Acker

Henry Adams

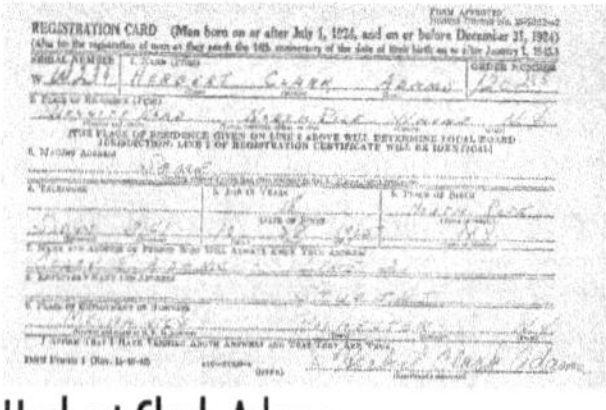
REGISTRATION CARD (Men born on or after July 1, 1924, and on or before December 31, 1924)

Herbert Clark Adams

James Adams

William G. Austin

Carlton Baker

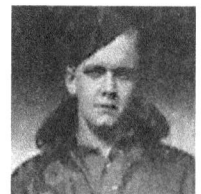

Milton G. Ball
(also George Milton Ball)

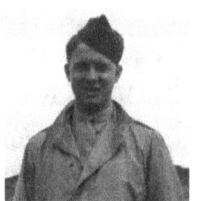

Richard Edward Ball

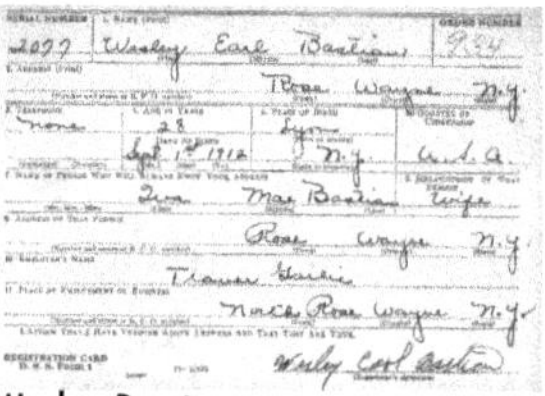
Wesley Earl Bastian
Rose Wayne N.Y.
REGISTRATION CARD

Wesley Bastian

Kenneth R. Blauvelt

Walter Blauvelt

Charles A. Brandes

James D. Brewster

Keith C. Brewster

Eddie Briggs

John Brockhuisen
(also Broekhuizen)

William Brockhuisen

George Brown

Edwin Bullock

Edgar G. Camp

Fred A. Case

Charles Castor

Howard Castor

B. Joseph Catchpole

Nancy A. Catchpole

JACK CLINGERMAN

Walter Clingerman

Wayne Clingerman

Glenn Clum

Everett Cohoon

James A. Colburn

Charles E. Converse

Ernest E. Converse

John E. Converse

Seth Converse

Dennis Coonrod

Robert M. Cotton

Deleon Day

Leslie Dean

Leland DeKing

Donald DeVall

Richard Drury

Harry L. Edwards

Warren G. Edwards

Kenneth R. Ellinwood

John H. Everett

WALTER EVERETT

Charles E. Fikes

Wray Fowler

DAVID GENT

HAROLD GENT
(also Howard Ghent)

John Gilder

James Gill

Valentine Godkin

Lloyd Goodsell

Merrial Goodsell

Albion Gray

George Gray

Leo Green

David Groat

Floyd Groat

CLEON GUTHRIE

Gerald Guthrie

Lyle Guthrie

Glenwood Haleus

HARVEY HALL

Calvin Hamm

Norman Haviland
Barton Hayes
Betty Henecke
Lincoln S. K. Horn
Frederick Hubbard
Glen Hutchings
George E. Kalbfliesch
Bertha Kellogg
LLOYD KELLOGG
Donald Kester
Mary Kinny
Leonard Kise
IVAN KNAPP
Earl G. Knepka
RICHARD KOEHLER
Asher M. Lape
Homer Lape
Mahlon Lape
Gordon Lapp
Bruce R. LaVere

CARL LEE

David Loveless
Elnathan J. Loveless
Emil J. Ludwig
Charles Lyman

Joel C. Marsh
Edwin E. Marshall
Betty Jane Maunder
Donald McCarthy
Paul McComber
Leon C. McQueen
Milton D. McQueen
Glenn Mills
Edward A. Miner
Allan Mitchell
John Morgan
Frederick R. Murray
John Murray
Ruthmary Murray
Howard F. Niles
Albert Norris
Charles O. Norris
E.F. Norris
Thomas Norris
Earl Pankratz
Charles Powell
Gray D. Powell
Nolan L. Powell
Harry Proseus

M. DONALD PUTNAM

Charles Ransley

CLIFFORD RAYMER
William A. Reed
Donald Richardson
Edwin Rings
Frederick D. Robinson
Merrill J. Roney
John D. Rotach
Richard Rotach
Harold Satterlee
Russell Satterlee
WILLIAM SCHMEISER
Raymond E. Scullion
Lawrence Sears
James W. Sebring
William A. Seely
Leaon N. Schuyler
Earl Shading
Donald Sherman
Arthur Sidler
George Sidler

Lawrence Sidler
Emery Skinkle
Grant Skinkle
VINCENT SOWER
(also spelled Sowers)
Frederick L. Spade

Leo Spade

Marion Spade

Chester R. Smith
Donald Smith
Frank Smith
Harold Smith
Irving Smith
Ralph Smith
Wilbur L. Smith
William C. Straut
Chester W. Taft
Clifford Taft

Weldon Taft
Harold Teeple
Laurence E. Thayer
George F. Thomas
JOHN THOMAS

Leslie E. Thompson

Orson H. Toles
Eugene Town
Milton L. Town
Carlton E. Towne
Franklin Turner

Carl C. Van Hoff

James J. VanPatten
CURTIS VINCENT
Fred Vincent
Ralph Waldorf
Richard Weed
Charles Wilson
Hayes Wilson
Richard Wilson
Charles D. Wirth
Arden T. Wood
Donald B. Yancey
LeRoy B. Yates

A FINAL NOTE: As this book was being written, John Thomas, a World War II flyer, was given a ceremonial burial in Rose cemetery. Thomas, who was 23 and had recently become engaged when he left Cornell University to fight in the war, was one of 660 airmen who died in a perilous mission: flying low to evade radar and take out an enormous fuel depot in Ploiesti, Romania, known as "Hitler's gas station." He was buried by Romanians in an unidentified grave in a cemetery in Ploiesti, moved to Belgium at the end of the war, and then exhumed in 2017. A

Mass card from John Thomas's 2023 burial

DNA sample taken from his nephew Edward Thomas in 2018 helped officially identify the remains in 2022. In May of 2023, they were brought home to the town of Rose. As his coffin made its way through town, hundreds of Rose and North Rose residents lined the streets to honor the fallen soldier. He is currently resting in the Rose cemetery next to his twin brother, George.

The Rochester Connection

WHILE NORTH ROSE was almost equidistant from Rochester and Syracuse, Rochester was the city people turned to for such things as university educations, cultural and sports events, fine clothes, hospital care, and factory employment. Rochester was born as a Genesee River mill town and was neither located on the coast nor a major river connected to the coast, and yet, due to the Erie Canal, it was a major trading center—in the first 10 days of the Erie Canal operating, 3,600 tons of flour were shipped from Rochester to the Hudson.

Interestingly, although the grain mills gave the city its first nickname, "Flour City," they employed relatively few people. Many people, however, were employed by the industries that grew up around the mills, including barrel-making and canalboat building. From there, due to successive waves of immigrants, Rochester transformed into a cosmopolitan Flower City when it had the world's largest seed company, The Ellwanger & Barry nursery, known for its outstanding fruit and ornamental plant seeds. It also had an emerging clothing industry, fueled by the German Jewish immigrants whose skill in millinery and dressmaking was rapidly making a name for itself. By the late 1800s, it had become a cultural center supported by major employers like Eastman Kodak, Bausch and Lomb, and Gleason Works, a gear manufacturer set in a stylishly designed building. Hickock, a leather company famous for their belts, was also a draw. Its ceremonial "Hickock Belt" was awarded each year to the outstanding athlete in any sport. This custom remains active to this day.

If cities help to shape the small towns that emerge and thrive nearby, I would say that North Rose mirrored Rochester more than it did Syracuse. Syracuse didn't have the emphasis on food distribution, and it didn't have the same kind of successful industrialists bringing in culture.

In the same way that Rochester was a small town until the development of the Erie Canal, North Rose profited from the railroads. It became a hub for nearby towns that didn't have much in the way of business centers. (Huron, for example, had a plethora of apples but it didn't have the apple dryers or storage, including cold storage.) And as Rochester did in its mill-town days, North Rose benefitted from the grit and honest labor of its populace. There was equality in North Rose between employers and employees—it was not unusual for workers in cold storage or warehouses to own a boat and a cottage or to go hunting and fishing with their employers.

Unlike Rochester, North Rose was a dry town, and there was almost no manufacturing industry—they had Seelye Ladder because ladders were used for picking apples, but that was about it. They didn't offer a quality secondary education—at the turn of the century if you wanted to continue your education past grammar school in North Rose, you had to go to the Leavenworth Academy in Wolcott. For those interested in pursuing higher education, nearby there were the University of Rochester and the Rochester Athenaeum and Mechanic's Institute, which became the Rochester Institute of Technology (RIT) in 1944.

To the people of North Rose, Rochester was "the city." If someone wanted to buy a new dress or a suit, they didn't go to Macy's on 34th Street in Manhattan, they went to Sibley, Lindsey and Kerr on East Main Street in Rochester. The park system was designed by Frederick Law Olmsted of Central Park fame. Due to the largesse of George Eastman, Rochester had a symphony orchestra and a large theater. Eastman was also a major financier of the great medical center founded in 1925–1926 under the auspices of the University of Rochester. Other monies came from the daughters of Eastman's late partner Henry Alvah Strong. The hospital provided extraordinary medical care along with employment opportunities for the people of North Rose.

Here are some examples of the people from North Rose who later had Rochester connections:

• George Ball Jr., born Rufus Rogers, was an orphan from Rochester. He reportedly rode the "orphan train" across Upstate New York before being adopted by George H. Ball Sr. and Maude Garton Ball. The Children's Aid Society, founded by Charles Loring Brace in New York City in 1854, relocated approximately 200,000 children to hopefully loving homes in rural areas. Orphan trains continued to run until 1929. The adoption of Rufus Rogers to George Ball was a success. However, some children were used as free labor, treated poorly, and ran away.

• Jean Boughton worked at the Hickock belt factory and later moved to Rochester. (Eventually she returned and became the secretary to my father at O. A. Skutt Company.) Several of her contemporaries—Anna Baldridge, Marion Edwards, and Louise Ziegler—were also working in Rochester at that time.

• Iva Betts moved to Rochester and worked at Lincoln Alliance Bank.

• Floyd Groat moved from North Rose to Rochester to work for Clapp's Baby Foods.

• Russell Groat attended the Mechanic's Institute.

Finally, like many people on our street, we had the *Rochester Democrat and Chronicle* (a Republican paper) delivered to our front porch each morning.

North Rose Businesses, Circa 1940

Dean's Service Station, Railroad Avenue—Charles Dean. Gasoline, oil, auto service.

Clinton D. Dillingham Insurance, Clinton Avenue—Fire, liability, auto, life, hail insurance.

Drury and Son, Huron Street & Railroad Avenue—Bert Drury and son, Paul Drury. Coal, oil, feed, and cement.

Farnsworth and Son Funeral Directors, North Main Street—John Farnsworth and son, Bernard Farnsworth. Funeral directors, furniture sales.

General Storage and Ice Co. ("The Cold Storage"), Storage Avenue—Lloyd Marshall (a director and manager). Cold storage of fruits and vegetables at a choice of temperature and atmospheres; ice production—particularly for refrigerated railroad cars. The founders in June 1922 were I. Laverne Wilson and Edward Hay of Rose, Irving Colburn of Clyde, and Orin A. Skutt of North Rose.

Joseph H. Ghent Barber Shop, North Main Street (east side)—Haircuts and shaves.

Gray Brothers Hardware, North Main Street—Charles and John Gray. Hardware items, appliances, fishing tackle, garden seeds, spraying materials and orchard supplies, paints, plumbing and heating, sinks and cabinets.

Hoff's Service Station, North Main Street—Grant Hoff. Gulf gasoline and lubricants, tires, spark plugs, and general auto repair.

Latham's Pharmacy, North Main Street—William A. Latham. Prescriptions, complete drug supplies, veterinarian's supplies, baby needs, health and surgical supplies.

Market Basket, North Main Street—Samuel Wise. Groceries.

Meat Market, North Main Street—Marvin W. Winchell. Fresh, custom-cut retail meat sales.

Caroline Moore's Beauty Shop—Women's hair styling.

New York Central Railroad—Formerly the Rome, Watertown & Ogdensburg. In 1940 it was called the "Hojack Line" of the New York Central, Ontario Division.

North Rose Cold Storage Company, Storage Avenue—Don Welch, Manager. Extended storage of fruits and vegetables, especially apples. Founded in the 1890s by M.C. Hall, John Hill, Frank Hill, Thomas Welch, and A. Weed. After World War II, General Storage and Ice purchased North Rose Cold Storage. The buildings were adjacent and operated as a single business. In May 1962, Sodus Cold Storage Company purchased General Storage and Ice. William Bishop currently operates both Sodus and North Rose cold storage facilities under the Sodus Cold Storage name.

North Rose Supply Company, North Main Street—Henry Lawrence. Tractors and farm implements, hardware, toys, housewares.

Frank Noyes—Coal and feed.

Oaks and Son, South Main Street—Charles Oaks and son, Seth Oaks. Lumber, fertilizer, oil, and paint.

Harry Quereau General Store, North Main Street—Harry Quereau. Frozen foods, groceries, candy, footwear, school supplies, stationery, men's, women's, and children's clothing.

Salter Canning Company ("The Canning Factory"), Storage Avenue & Railroad Avenue—Edward A. Salter and son, Leon Jay Salter. Canners of fruits and vegetables.

Seelye Ladder Co., Gray Street—Frank Seelye and sons, Dorr and Carson Seelye. Manufacturers of wooden ladders.

Pete Skinner Barber Shop, North Main Street—Haircuts and shaves.

O. A. Skutt Company ("The Bean House"), Railroad Avenue—A. Gray Skutt. Wholesale sales of grains and red kidney beans.

Wells Dodds Nursery, North Poplar Street—Wells Dodds. Flowers, bulbs, evergreens, and general nursery stock.

B. A. Yancy, North Main Street—General auto repairs, body and fender work, and G.E. appliances.

Marshall Farm—William Gilman Marshall (1917–2011) founded the company that increased in size so much from its modest start in 1939, it has become the largest firm with a North Rose postal address at the time of this book's publication. That business is Marshall BioResources, headquartered in Huron, between North Rose and Sodus Bay, but it has overseas facilities in Lyon, France; Hull, East Yorkshire, U.K.; Beijing, China; and Tsukuba Ibaraki, Japan.

Gilman was the son of William M. Marshall (1874–1955), a stagecoach driver, and Susan M. Fisher Marshall (1877–1965). Gilman married Ina Stevens (1919–2011) just one year before Gilman turned his hobby of raising ferrets as pets into a business. Ina worked with Gilman to raise ferrets on which the pharmaceutical industry could test vaccines.

In 1942 it became the usual practice to test new medical discoveries on dogs as a useful step between testing on rodents and humans. The Marshalls established a colony of beagles for that task. The Marshalls placed a priority on the animals' health, and they expanded to supply to the medical trade in addition to ferrets and beagles: minipigs, mice, rats, guinea pigs, and chicken eggs. Since ferrets react to airborne Covid-19 viruses similarly to the way people react, the Marshall staff believes that ferrets could play an important role in developing new vaccines for Covid-19.

Of course, many animal rights activists are opposed to performing experiments on animals in the name of science. In Italy the Marshall facility was shut down by the authorities over the alleged mistreatment of dogs. "To produce the most accurate and sturdy data, the dogs needed to be healthy and well-acclimated." It had a hundred dogs seized and given to volunteer families as pets. Now one of Gilman and Ina's grandsons, Scott Marshall, heads the company.

The Marshalls donated to the local community an attractive sports complex on Fifth Road, just north of North Rose. Members of the Marshall family have purchased real estate in North Rose and elsewhere in the Town of Rose.

Incidentally, the Marshalls owned the cottage next door to the Skutt cottage on LeRoy Island in Sodus Bay.

Glossary of Organizations

IN HIS INSIGHTFUL 2000 book *Bowling Alone: The Collapse and Revival of American Community*, Robert Putnam, a Harvard sociologist, presents a frightening portrait of the collapse of civil society in the United States. Church attendance is down, fewer people vote or attend public meetings. Americans move to new homes frequently and they have less empathy and contact with their neighbors.

Sixty years earlier, in North Rose, the lifestyle was diametrically opposed to that book's dire portrait. In the days before vastly diverse incomes, television, the internet, long commutes to work, and two-or-more-job households, people participated in a plethora of community organizations. There were patriotic, service, religious, and recreational groups galore—and their meetings were regularly and enthusiastically attended. Many people saw participation in these groups as a routine activity or even a societal duty.

In the 21st century, many of these organizations still exist, but they are much less familiar to the reader. Here is a list of some of the groups in the North Rose area that are frequently mentioned in this work.

Churches and Church-Affiliated Organizations

Baptist Missionary Society—A Christian mission organization, working in many countries around the world. It was involved in establishing churches, economic development, disaster relief, education, and healthcare.

Epworth League Institute (Young People's Institute)—Methodist young adult association for members aged 18 to 35. It encouraged community building, missions, and spiritual growth.

The Glad Tidings Church—An Evangelical, Pentecostal Church established in North Rose in the 1950s.

Home and Foreign Missionary Society—Organization that supported Presbyterian missionaries, foreign aid, and Bible distribution.

Kappa Phi—Methodist study group that met in congregants' homes.

Ladies' Aid Society—Early organization supporting missionaries, schools, church building projects, and other charitable endeavors.

Ladies' Guild—Raised money to support the Church, sponsored children overseas, provided food for the hungry.

Methodist Youth Fellowship—Organization for Methodist youth between the sixth and twelfth grades.

North Rose Methodist Church—The Methodist Church was an extremely popular English and American Protestant denomination founded by John Wesley in the 18th century. Charles Wesley, his brother, is still remembered for writing nearly a thousand hymns. (They were good ones too.) This church gradually separated from the "mother" Anglican or Episcopal Church. Circuit riders preached the Methodist gospel, reaching countless cities, villages, and crossroads throughout young America. Religious practices often included outdoor preaching and personal testimonials. The denomination was popular with the growing middle class through the 19th century.

In 1939 the Methodist Episcopal Church; the Methodist Episcopal Church, South; and the Methodist Protestant Church merged to form the Methodist Church.

In North Rose the church changed from the Methodist-Episcopal Church to the Methodist Church. During the 1900s, the Methodist Church was the largest church in North Rose.

Outside the North Rose Methodist Church in the 1950s. Bottom left: Elizabeth and Horace Putnam, Mary Ann Wilson, Ella Marshall. Bottom right: Sue and Diane Thomas, Ginny Collier, Reva Thomas, Henrietta Collier, Dorr Seelye, Claude Collier. Back row: Doug Ball, two unknown women, Mary Closs, Leonard Hackney, Harold Pierson, unknown, Sam Wise, Frank Noyes, unknown. Front row: Mary Moore (Dunham), Ellen Seelye, Ellen Closs, Katie Collier, Steve Boyer, unknown.

Presbyterian Church—North Rose Presbyterian Church was the other long-established church in North Rose. Nationally, the Presby-

terian Church was one of the largest Protestant denominations. Presbyterianism was descended from the early teachings of John Calvin, one of the key figures in the Protestant Reformation. In style and teachings, the Presbyterian Church fell between the Methodist and Episcopal Churches. It was less evangelical than the former and more liberal and modern than the latter. Presbyterian churches were governed by elders elected by the congregations. There were multiple levels of authority between the individual church and the national body.

The North Rose Presbyterian Church had a smaller congregation than the North Rose Methodist Church and eventually had to rely on lay (nonprofessional) clergy instead of ordained ministers.

Rosary Society—A service organization of women supporting the needs of St. Mary Magdalene Catholic Church.

Rose Baptist Church

Sigma Society—Met in homes of congregants. Speakers sparked discussions of timely issues.

Sodus Church of the Epiphany—Roman Catholic.

Wolcott St. Mary Magdalene Catholic Church

Women's Society of Christian Service—A union of Methodist women's groups established in 1929. Supported women's rights in the Methodist church, domestic and foreign missions, aid for women employed outside the home, and racial equality.

Fraternal and Service Organizations

The American Legion—chartered by Congress in 1919 as a patriotic wartime veterans organization devoted to mutual helpfulness. Among their programs were the sponsorship of American Legion baseball leagues for older teenagers, the advocacy for veterans' rights in federal legislation, services for veterans, and the conduct of social activities for veterans and their families. Miner-Youngs, NY Post 582 (North Rose); Wolcott, NY Post 881.

The American Red Cross—The American Red Cross had five major functions: disaster relief, supporting military families, collecting and distributing blood, health and safety services, international services. The Auxiliary was particularly active during wartime when the need for blood drives and fundraising for the Red Cross was especially intense. The local arms of the Red Cross: American Red Cross Auxiliary, Red Cross Committee, and Red Cross War Fund.

The Federation of Home Bureaus—A statewide organization whose purpose was to enrich and improve housekeeping and the community of homemakers. It was founded in 1919 and organized by county throughout the state. Meetings centered around instruction in housekeeping skills. Originally the Home Bureau was an extension program of Cornell University and was supported by tax dollars. In 1956 the Home Bureau became a private organization and was no longer tax supported. The local arms were: North Rose Home Bureau and Savannah Home Bureau.

The Independent Order of Odd Fellows—A service organization that visited the sick, helped the elderly and dying, cared for survivors of members, helped youth, and were active in the field of eye health. The two local organizations were Bay Shore Lodge No. 606, and Ontario Shore Lodge, Wolcott. Abbreviated as IOOF in this book.

The Masons—The origin of Freemasonry dates back to guilds of medieval stone masons. Many of the stories of early Masonry are lost in myth. Freemasonry is a secret society in the sense that many of its practices are meant to be known only by members. The modern history of Freemasonry dates from the establishment of the first lodge in London in 1717. In the 19th century, Masons were, in some places around the world, quite active in politics. In France in 1871, the Masons attempted to negotiate a last-minute peace between the

French government and the anarchists of the Paris Commune. When the French monarchy rejected the peacemaking effort, the Freemasons threw in their numbers at the barricades with the doomed Paris Commune.

The American Anti-Masonic movement got its start upstate, after William Morgan from Batavia disappeared in 1826 and was suspected of being murdered by Masons. Thurlow Weed, editor of the *Rochester Telegraph*, became a—maybe *the*—key builder of the movement. More recently Masons operate somewhat similarly to other fraternal societies, although they had more elaborate and secret rituals.

In addition to the North Rose Masonic Lodge was the Arbor Vitae Chapter, No. 577, of the Order of the Eastern Star—the women's auxiliary to the Masons.

National Grange of the Order of Patrons of Husbandry— Known commonly as "The Grange," it was the major organization of farmers and small-town people associated with agriculture. They were advocates for farmers and farm families. In addition to the Rose Grange No. 1051, many North Rose residents were members of the Wolcott Grange No. 348.

North Rose Chemical Company No. 1—The oldest firefighting group in the hamlet. It was called a "Chemical" company because the fire apparatus consisted of a large soda/acid fire extinguisher. Until the 1950s North Rose lacked a water system and therefore had no fire hydrants.

The North Rose Hook and Ladder Company—Only existed from 1917 to 1919.

The North Rose Fire Department—Formed when the North Rose Chemical Company No. 1 and North Rose Hook and Ladder Company merged in 1919.

The Public Health Committee—This organization raised money to combat illnesses and loaned equipment that was important for ill people to have at their disposal.

Rebekah Utopia Lodge No. 400—The Rebekahs were members of the women's auxiliary to the Odd Fellows.

Salter Hose and Chemical (Fire) Company—This second North Rose fire company was presumably funded by the Salter family, the owners of the Canning Factory. The presence of the word "hose" implies that their equipment included a water pump that could spray water from a well or pond through a fire hose onto a burning building. Though they existed simultaneously with the North Rose Fire Department, eventually the two merged.

Social Organizations

I have not been able to find accurate descriptions of all of these clubs. I imagine most were formed to provide additional opportunities for North Rose citizens to socialize.

Contract Bridge Club—A group of players of the most popular card game of the 1930s and 1940s. The site of the game rotated among club members. Probably the card game was supplemented by coffee and dessert.

Bridge Club, 1950. Standing, from left: Ella Marshall, Carrie Fisher, Ethel O'Loughlyn, Dora Chapin, Lena Quereau, Flora Hill, Lena Gray, Olive Welch, Myrta Salter. Seated: Sabra Smith and Gertie Boyd. Whoever wrote the key to this photo omitted a person but also remarked on the Easter lily blooming in October!

Literary Club—A very long-lived book club for both men and women. The site of meetings rotated among the homes of members. A lecture, usually about a book read by all the club members, was followed by discussion and refreshments.

Luncheon Club

Saturday Night Club

Sew-and-Sew Club—A needlework club.

Starlight Club

Thursday Club—A women's club that met for a luncheon or dinner on one Thursday each month.

Young Married Couples Anniversary Club—Held dinners to celebrate the wedding anniversaries of one or more of the participating couples.

The Families

THE CRITERION USED FOR DECIDING whether people were North Rosers was whether or not they were listed in the Federal Decennial Census of 1940, mandated by the Constitution of the United States.

The population of North Rose decreased at the time of the land rush to Michigan in the 1800s. The 1940 census recorded 640 persons residing in North Rose at the time. The illustrations in this book contain photographs of the people listed in the 1940 census, as well as some of their close relatives. When possible, the photographs show the actual appearance of these people near the time of the census. In a few cases, persons listed as residents did not actually live in North Rose; several of our fact-checkers lived outside the geographical area and we have included their families, marked with an asterisk: Dennis, Frank & Corinne; Harper, Roscoe & Louise; and Mitchell, George & Josephine. Also included are the two Salter households—Salter, Edward & Myrta and Salter, Leon & Thelma—because of the economic impact their Salter Canning Factory had on North Rose.

One unusual feature of the photographs on the following pages is the presence of sections of a quilt embroidered with the signatures of the residents of North Rose, given to A. Gray Skutt, the author's father, following his graduation from Cornell University and upon his move to New York City to work in the financial district. This quilt, a tribute to one of North Rose's favorite sons, remains in the possession of the Skutt family.

Unfortunately, for some households we were unable to obtain more than the cursory information provided by the census. If you have photographs or other information about the families, including people who were renting in North Rose at the time, please send it via email to alex@northroseny.com.

We plan to publish subsequent editions with new information as it becomes available. We will continue to keep the website (www.northroseny.com) updated.

Abbott, Foster & Edith

Gray Street. Estimated value in 1940: $2,000.
Foster Henry Abbott (1877–1943), 62, head of household, laborer (fruit packing house), 13 weeks for $250.
Francis Edith Abbott (1867–1943), 73, wife, homemaker.

FOSTER, A FARM LABORER most of his life, was the son of Nelson Abbott of Huron (1849–1937) and Ella Goss (1859–1939). He married Edith Riggs in April 1930 at the Free Methodist parsonage. An article in the *Lake Shore News* announced their plans to reside on Gray Street. Both Foster and Edith completed eight years of school.

Edith was Miss Frances Edith Riggs when she married Foster at age 63, but she was born Frances Edith Garlick, the twin sister of Franklin Garlick (which could explain why she used her middle name as her first name). Her parents were Henry and Sally Garlick of Rose, and they were in their 40s when she and her brother were born.

She married her first husband, another Frank, Frank Riggs (1867–), in Rose in 1888. They had one child, Glenn David Riggs (1893–1973). It is unclear what happened to Frank Riggs. In the 1915 census, he and Edith were still living together and married, but then he mysteriously disappeared, and she married Foster in 1930. It was a late-in-life marriage—Foster was 52 and Edith was 63. It was a second marriage for Edith and a third for Foster, who first married Maude Torrey (1882–1973) in Huron in 1900. Maude was the daughter of George D. Torrey and Annah L. Torrey of Sodus Point. The marriage did not last long; Maude remarried in 1908 to Frederick Stimers and in 1910 was living in Sodus. But Foster and Maude did have a child in 1903: Edward Abbott. In 1905 Foster married Jennie M. McLaury in Fulton, but on the 1910 census he was single again, living in Huron and working as a farm laborer.

Edith was a lively member of the Abbott family and was frequently mentioned in the pages of the *Lake Shore News*. In 1930 she participated in creating a lavish dinner to celebrate Foster's father Nelson's 82nd birthday with her sister-in-law Lena Kimpland of North Syracuse.

The table was centered with a huge pyramid cake topped with pink and white candles. In 1931 she and her husband traveled with Mr. and Mrs. Nelson Abbott to Ann Arbor, Flint, and Munro, Michigan, and Toledo, Ohio.

There was less in the papers about Foster, although he did earn an entire item in *The Clyde Herald* in April 1933: "The Pied Piper has little on Foster Abbott, who killed 70 rats in his hen house in two hours one-day last week."

Edith's health began to fade in 1939, and in 1943 she suffered a "shock" that landed her in Barber Hospital. She died shortly after that at age 77. She was survived by Foster, her son Glenn Riggs of California, and her twin brother, Frank Garlick. Foster followed soon after, with a claim by his dependent survivors on his Social Security card in 1943.

Acker, William & Kate

Beehive apartments on Gray Street. 1940 monthly rent: $8.
William Henry Acker (1878–1944), 62, head of household, farm laborer, 20 weeks for $250.
Kate Satterlee Acker (1885–1964), 53, wife, bean picker, 42 weeks for $350.
William Gordon Acker (1922–2001), 17, son, student.

WILLIAM AND KATE EACH HAD completed eight years of school. William was a farm laborer, and Kate was a "bean picker" at the O. A. Skutt Company Bean House. (What the census calls a "bean picker" was someone who sorted out irregular beans and foreign material.) Their son Gordon Acker attended school.

William was a native of the Town of Rose. His parents were Herbert J. Acker (1856–), a day laborer, and Jane "Jennie" Johnson Acker (1850–1913), a homemaker. In 1900 William lived with his grandfather David Johnson, a farmer. William was a slim man: six feet tall and 145 pounds. In 1910 William was living with his mother, Jennie Burch, who had taken the name of her second husband, Charles

Burch. In October and November, William and Lloyd Marshall spent the apple-evaporating season of 1912 working in Genesee County. William married Kate Satterlee of Branch (Ulster County) in August 1915. The next year William and Kate had a daughter named Edna (1916–2007). In November 1916 the Ackers bought the Chapin farm, east of Rose. In March 1918 they moved into the Charles Osborn house. William and Kate had a second child named Gordon in 1922. By 1930, the Ackers lived at 5 South Main Street in North Rose. Their home was the first house south of the railroad tracks—on the southwest corner of Main Street and Storage Avenue.

Kate grew up in Shandaken (Ulster County). She was the youngest child of Uriah Satterlee (1837–1917) and Delia Wright Satterlee (1845–1905). Uriah was a carpenter and farmer and a veteran of the Civil War. (For more information about Kate's family, see the section featuring her brother: "Satterlee, Gene & Mae.")

In May 1930 Harry and Mary Earle and their son William were weekend guests of William and Kate. The Earles repeated this visit many times. In the late spring of 1931, the Ackers were victims of a house fire, which destroyed much of their home furnishings. In a separate incident that month, Edna required hospitalization with a burn.

In July 1935 Edna went camping near Canandaigua Lake with other members of the North Rose Central School (NRCS) girls' basketball team. In 1936 Edna worked first in Syracuse then in Rochester. In 1940 Edna was a student nurse at Bellevue Hospital in New York City. She graduated from the nursing program at the State Institution in Poughkeepsie in September 1940. Her mother Kate attended the ceremony.

Edna married Raymond Francis Downing (1913–2011). Raymond, a graduate of Bard College, had been teaching at a private school in Tivoli (Dutchess County). Raymond enlisted in the armed services in 1941. In September 1942 Carole Arlene was born to Edna and Cpl. Raymond Downing. The Downing family left North Rose to move to the Washington, D.C., area in March 1945.

Raymond visited his parents in Madalin (Dutchess County) in June 1945 when the Army granted him a short leave. Raymond received his discharge in December 1945. Upon his completion of active duty, the U.S. Army War College offered him a position. In February 1947 Edna and her daughter Carole visited Kate in North Rose for two weeks. The Downings were living in Alexandria, Virginia. The three Downings visited Raymond's parents in Millsport (Chemung County) in August 1947. Raymond traveled to Europe where he served as an employee of the U.S. government from 1949 to 1951.

Gordon Acker graduated from NRCS in 1942. During World War II, he served in the U.S. Navy. In September 1944 Gordon returned to North Rose on a furlough. The Navy transferred him to the Seabees in November 1944. In 1945 he took part in retaking the Philippines from the Japanese. In May 1946 Gordon received his honorable discharge and returned home from the Pacific.

At the North Rose Methodist Church in June 1946, Gordon Acker married Elizabeth Lucille "Betty Lou" Dillingham, daughter of Clinton and Elizabeth Dillingham of North Rose. In November 1946 Gordon and Betty Lou spent the weekend in Rochester. They attended the basketball game between the Chicago American Gears and the Rochester Royals in the Sports Arena at Edgerton Park. (These teams played in the National Basketball League. The Gears featured early basketball superstar George Mikan who stood 6'10" tall and carried the moniker "Mr. Basketball." He wore thick-lensed glasses. Mikan gave basketball fans a taste of a style of basketball that would develop decades later, centered around a "big man" who would block shots, get rebounds, and sink baskets with ambidextrous hook shots. In 1949 the NBL merged with the Basketball Association of America to form today's NBA.)

In April 1947 daughter Loral Frances "Lorie" Acker was born to Gordon and Betty Lou. On Christmas Day 1947, Gordon and Betty Lou entertained a group of people for dinner: Gordon's mother, Kate; Betty Lou's parents, Clinton and Sadie; Mary Godkin and daughter Claire; Carrie Fisher; and George and Millie Aldrich with children John and Linda. In May 1948 Gordon and Betty Lou had a son, Clinton Gordon "Clint" Acker. The Ackers were joined by a second daughter, Darlene, in July 1950. Gordon Acker was a member of the

Wolcott Post 881 of the American Legion and the IOOF. (For more information about Gordon Acker's and Clinton Dillingham's families, see their respective sections of this book.)

Adams, Harry

Renter.
Harry J. Adams (1914–1978), 25, head of household, laborer at the Canning Factory, 25 weeks, unemployed.
Henry Adams (1922–1982), 17, brother, unemployed.

HARRY JAMES ADAMS AND James Henry Adams were the children of Fred Adams (1872–1930) and Nina Belle Penner (1884–1938). Fred and Nina were married in Ontario in 1908. They had three children, Harry, Henry, and Charles, who was born in 1919 and did not live through his first year. Harry was born in Manchester (Ontario County) but by 1920 the family was living in North Rose.

In 1940 the two Adams boys were orphans, their father and mother having died in 1930 and 1938 respectively. They were on their own together, renting in North Rose. Harry, who was working at the Canning Factory, completed eight years of grammar school, while Henry, unemployed in 1940, had completed one year of high school. The brothers were socially active in North Rose, Henry being mentioned as being the "Right Scene Supporter" at a meeting of the IOOF Bay Shore Lodge in 1942. They also enjoyed fishing at Star Lake where they went with M. L. Briggs and his son Maynard.

Henry Adams married Teresa Mary Jane DeSanto (1917–2010). Harry J. Adams got married in North Rose, December 25, 1940, and died in Rochester in 1978.

Aldrich, George & Millie

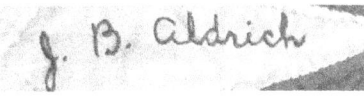

77–79 North Main Street, now 5101 North Main—Built in 1833. Estimated value in 1940: $2,600.
George Delos Aldrich (1903–1957), 36, head of household, farmer,

52 weeks, self-employed.
Mildred Cornelia Collier "Millie" Aldrich (1908–1982), 31, wife, homemaker.

GEORGE ALDRICH MARRIED MILLIE COLLIER in Rochester in November 1934. At the time of the 1940 census, George had completed one year of college and was working the family farm next to his home. Millie was a high school graduate who worked as a homemaker.

George's family were pioneers in the Town of Rose. George's great-grandfather Amos Aldrich (1793–1885), hailing from Ontario, bought, between 1832 and 1861, much of the land on which North Rose would grow. At that time, North Rose was called Lamb's Corners, named for the first settler, Isaac Lamb. He built a sawmill west of his home that operated for 60 years. Lamb's Corners consisted of the homes built around the crossroads of Glenmark Road and the main north-south road, later dubbed Main Street.

Amos Aldrich purchased the land on both sides of the north-south road from Glenmark Road south to what is now Railroad Avenue. He first lived in a sod house and then in a log cabin, which—over the years—was rebuilt in stages into the familiar Aldrich home on North Main Street, according to Frank Dennis in "Century Farm—The Aldrich Farm," in the Town of Rose Historical Society Newsletter in 2002. Ken and Karen Weiss, distant relations of the Aldrich family, now own the sprawling Aldrich home.

Aldrich Land

Since they owned a large farm right in the center of what was becoming the northern half of North Rose, the Aldriches seem like the pioneers of North Rose. However, they weren't the first family to own the Aldrich land, where many of North Rose's homes and businesses were built—during the railroad-induced construction boom. Isaac Lamb Jr., son of the original pioneer who founded Lamb's Corners, Isaac Gillett (1786–1829), married Sally Sellick

(1789–1863) while living in Vermont. The couple and Isaac Gillett's father, John Gillett (1748–1819), moved from Vermont to Lamb's Corners in 1813. Isaac Gillett looked after his family's property for several years, until he began thinking about the rich Michigan soil and was tempted away after he received the standard 160 acres per family from the Land Commission. President Martin Van Buren signed the document.

The responsibility for the Lamb's Corners property then fell upon the shoulders of John Gillett. John Gillett was a cousin of two well-known residents, Dr. Asahel Gillett and Harvey Gillett. Peter Lamb, a brother of Isaac Lamb, next took over the large plot of land (upon John Gillett's death) that included a wide swath from the future railroad tracks on the south side to Glenmark Road eastern extensions through Lamb's Corners on the north side. So the Aldrich land was previously owned by Lambs and Gilletts.

In 1833, the land was purchased by Amos Aldrich (1793–1885), the first of several generations of Aldriches who owned or sold portions of this land: George W. Aldrich; John Clarence Aldrich; Clarence's widow Carrie; George D. Aldrich (the son of Clarence and Carrie); Millie (the widow of George D. Aldrich); John and his sister Linda (the children of George D. and Millie). After Linda's death, John sold the homestead to distant relatives Ken and Karen Weiss.

Aldrich land was important in the late 19th and early 20th centuries when it was in high demand for the wholesale produce warehouses that commodity traders built along the railroad tracks. It was also conveniently located for the homes of the people who gained jobs working for the fruit and other produce dealers.

The Aldriches were not the only people who prospered by converting some of their orchards to building lots. The

Jonathan Briggs family also subdivided some of their farmland into housing sites.

Once the railroad arrived, commerce alongside the tracks and the need for conveniently located homes burgeoned. Amos's son Benjamin laid out Aldrich Avenue, Poplar Street, and Caroline Avenue. Another son, George W. Aldrich (1833–1910), remained on the family homestead. The railroad caused a business boom in North Rose and resulted in that hamlet replacing Rose Valley as the commercial center of the Town of Rose. George served terms as justice of the peace and inspector of elections. He gave the Methodist Church its original building site on Gray Street. Many years later, after a new church arose on Main Street, this building was remodeled into the "Beehive" apartments.

John Clarence Aldrich (1871–1918), a teacher and farmer, was the son of George W. Aldrich and Ellen J. Carrier Aldrich (1844–1903).

Clarence and Carrie Dillingham Aldrich (1876–1959) were the parents of George D. Aldrich. George D., the grandson of George W. Aldrich, was the family member who ran the farm in 1940. The farm was legally the property of his mother since she inherited it upon the death of Clarence. Clarence and Carrie married in January 1894. The wedding took place in South Lyons at the home of the bride's parents, Delos W. Dillingham (1846–1917), a farmer, and Elizabeth Stanton Dillingham (1844–1917). Delos and Elizabeth had five children, including Clinton D. Dillingham (1883–1958), who moved to North Rose ca. 1918 and became the region's leading insurance agent. (See "Dillingham, Clinton & Elizabeth.")

Clarence, while he was a 21-year-old schoolteacher in 1893, faced trial for arson. Allegedly, he had set fire to Delos's barns. Clarence was boarding at the Dillinghams' farm and had taken a liking to their daughter Carrie. At his arson trial, the prosecution theorized that he anticipated rescuing Carrie when the fire reached the house. Then he would win Carrie's hand for his heroism. Another theory was that when Delos told Clarence—five years Carrie's senior—to wait a year before courting Carrie, Clarence was furious at Delos and ignited the barns for revenge. Detective Mervin M. Compson, the primary witness for the prosecution, could not attend the trial due to illness. The proceedings were postponed several times. A host of defense witnesses from North Rose testified to Clarence's excellent character, and the Judge found Clarence innocent in October 1893. It is extraordinary that the Dillinghams allowed Carrie to marry Clarence in the same house that he may have sought to set ablaze just six months earlier. Around the turn of the century, Clarence began to operate the Aldrich fruit farm.

Another incident led some to question Clarence's judgment. In October 1911 Clarence took some friends and relatives on an auto ride. He deposited his passengers in the farmhouse yard and drove into the second story of a hillside barn. The car sped through the barn and exited the large doors, a story above the ground. It landed upside down on Clarence. When bystanders lifted the vehicle off Clarence, his friends discovered that he had avoided injury except for bruising. Dr. Winchell examined him and found no sign of internal injuries.

In September 1913 Clarence sold his Rhode Island Greenings for $2.25 per barrel and Baldwins for $2 per barrel. These two old apple varieties were favorites with consumers. Greenings were fine pie apples. The long-lasting Baldwin was good for winter eating. A barrel of apples weighs about 160 pounds. Compare today's retail prices for apples with the wholesale prices that Clarence earned. He received about 1.6¢ per pound of apples. Wegmans charges $6.99 for a plastic bag of about nine medium apples weighing about 48 ounces, or $2.33 per pound. Today's Wegmans price is about 145 times greater than Clarence's by-the-barrel charge.

Clarence died in 1918. In February 1921, the widowed Carrie Aldrich visited the Rochester Automotive Show with John Robert Pepperdine. Carrie married John (1867–1934) later that year. John had held several jobs, including a stint in show business. In 1930 John was the manager of Carrie's "Aldrich" farm in North Rose.

George was a student at the Cazenovia Seminary in 1921. This nonsectarian, coeducational institution traces its origin back to 1824, when it opened as the Seminary of the Genesee Conference.

George's August 1923 marriage to Hilda Anna McMullen was annulled in March 1926. The bride was just 16 at the time of the wedding and did not have parental consent to marry, which was required by New York State if the bride or groom was under 18. In 1923—before their separation—both George and his bride planned to study in Rochester. George entered the Mechanics Institute, and Hilda matriculated at the Rochester Business Institute. That latter school endured many trials and tribulations before it finally locked its doors in April 2015. The Mechanics Institute has developed much more successfully. In 1944 it changed its name to the Rochester Institute of Technology (RIT) and became a full-fledged research university.

George joined the Seventh Division, Third Battalion of the National Guard in January 1927. George was living in Rochester in 1930, and in 1934 he married Millie Collier, who grew up in Marion and later in Rochester. Her father was Henry R. Collier (1883–1962). Henry was a farmer, a salesman in a general store in Williamson, a sign card maker, a "creaser" at Eastman Kodak, and—the position to which he aspired—the manager of a retail grocery store. Leora A. Collier (1885–1918) was Millie's mother.

Both of Millie's grandfathers emigrated from The Netherlands. Leora died in 1918. Henry later married Ethel E. Morey (1888–1963) of Rose. Ethel was a college graduate who worked as a public school teacher. In 1940 Henry was living at the Rochester State (Psychiatric) Hospital but was back in his Rochester home by March 1942.

In about 1935, George Aldrich assumed operation of his mother Carrie's farm in North Rose. Carrie's second husband, John Pepperdine, had been managing the farm but he died in 1934. Carrie married again, in 1938, to William C. "Will" Fisher (1868–1948), a veteran barber whose parents were born in Holland. Will had moved his barbershop from Sodus to Sodus Point around 1904. Carrie had an apartment in the Aldrich home which could be reached from the foyer off the front porch—it had its own street number: 79—but she was living in Sodus at the time of the 1940 census.

On the nearly 250-acre Aldrich farm, fruit was just one of the crops George grew: Wealthy and Road Island Greening apples, sour cherries, and a small acreage of blueberries. (Wealthy apples were developed in Minnesota in the 1860s by Peter Gideon. They were cold-resistant. They were a cross between a traditional early American apple and a Chinese crab apple, and they became one of the top five favorite apple varieties by the early 20th century.) The Aldrich farm's highest revenue in the 1930s and early 1940s came from its livestock: dairy cattle. They required care and occupied two Aldrich barns, but they provided sizable revenue. George discontinued the dairy business in the 1940s. He experimented with growing string beans and cabbage. First, George removed the cherry trees. Then in the 1980s the apple trees came out. The farm eventually produced mostly field corn.

In August 1937 George and Mildred were spending time at their cottage at Bonnie Castle. Mildred volunteered in 1937 to be the Red Cross membership drive chairperson for North Rose. She maintained that position the following year. George was the best man for his brother-in-law Claude Collier of Rochester at his wedding to Henrietta Quereau. The candlelight wedding took place in the Quereau home. George was a dedicated member of the Masons and the Bay Shore Lodge, No. 606, of the IOOF. George and Mildred hosted Reg and Shirley Catchpole and their daughter Lynda; Gray and Jane Skutt and their daughter Marilyn; and Dr. Ray and Theresa Kenan, and their daughter Patsy on the Fourth of July 1940 at Bonnie Castle. In November 1940 Claude Collier and George hunted in the Southern Tier.

Dinner party with cat: George Aldrich, Phoebe Jane Collier, Millie Collier Aldrich, Henrietta Quereau Collier, Claude Collier, ca. 1930s.

George did not display enough caution when a friend of his gave him a tip on combating the nuisance that was prevalent in Wayne County apple orchards: poison ivy! The friend told George that if he chewed and swallowed a quarter leaf of poison ivy periodically, he would become immune to its intense skin-irritating effects. George tried this method and experienced acute swelling in his mouth and throat. He could not speak for several days. He suffered a bad sore throat for over a week, and the Methodist Choir had to do without his strong bass voice for two Sundays.

Millie's brother John Collier of Rochester and her nephew Robert "Bob" Tracy, also of Rochester, visited the Aldriches for a few days in July 1941. Bob was John and Millie's sister's son. Claude and Henrietta Collier visited the State Fair with George and Millie in August 1941. Millie eagerly attended the Contract Bridge Club sessions in the early 1940s. In May 1942 the North Rose Future Farmers of America planted a victory garden on land provided by George. George and Millie hosted their nephew Bob Tracy in North Rose for the summers of 1942 and 1944. John Collier joined George, Millie, and Bob in the summer of 1944. After the summer was over, John enlisted in the Navy. His first stop was the Sampson naval training facility at nearby Seneca Lake.

George and Millie adopted a newborn boy, John Clarence Aldrich (1944–). In March 1947 they adopted a newborn girl, Linda Jane Aldrich (1947–2002). Later that year, Millie was involved in the WSCS. John Collier and George went on a fishing trip to Canada the following September.

In the 1950s the Aldrich family had a shaggy black-and-white cocker spaniel named Lassie. She used to run next door to the back porch of my childhood home after practically every evening meal and scratch on the screen door seeking a bone. For a while, John and Linda had another pet—a small riding horse. Linda and John were my neighbors and were among my first playmates as a boy in North Rose.

After George died in 1957, Alan Anthony worked the Aldrich family farm for Millie. In August of the following year, the large two-story Aldrich barn behind their home on North Main Street burned to the ground. Tommie Cole, who lived on North Poplar Street—behind the barn—was the first person to spot the blaze. He raced to notify his uncle Gerald Guthrie, who called the fire department. It was too late to save the barn.

John Aldrich married Carol Price in 1969. They had two children: Susan and George. Through most of the 1980s, John lived in Mexico (Oswego County), and worked at the Niagara-Mohawk Nine Mile Point nuclear power plant just west of Oswego. He worked his way up to more senior posts until in 1985 and 1986 he had the highly responsible job of supervisor of operations of Unit One. From 1987–1989, John worked at the Corning Glass Canton Plant. He retired to Englewood, Florida.

Linda Aldrich was a perennial member of the honor roll at NRCS. Linda was a piano pupil of Esther Rexer. Linda had two children: Timothy Huhak (who is a doctor of osteopathy in Binghamton) and Andrea (who is a social worker in Wayne County.)

Armstrong, Lellavene

Estimated value in 1940: $1,050.
Lellavene Armstrong (1882–1957), 57, head of household, school teacher (public school), 40 weeks for $1,400.

LELLAVENE ARMSTRONG WAS BORN in Rose in 1882. She was the daughter of Edgar A. Armstrong (1845–1910) and Elizabeth Head Armstrong (1851–1910), both farm laborers who married in 1874. She had a brother named Virgil Sweet Armstrong (1888–1957). Although she and her brother were six years apart, they died the same year.

Lellavene was an independent, very socially active woman who was often in the columns of the *Lake Shore News* and Sodus and Clyde newspapers—sometimes twice on the same page. In one issue of the 1906 *Sodus Record*, she was mentioned for being elected treasurer of the Epworth League, as well as the recipient of "four yards of black silk as a holder of one of the lucky tickets at the Rose Fair." She enjoyed traveling—in one issue of *The Clyde Herald*, she returned home after spending the summer in Illinois and Colorado and was a Labor Day guest at the Seagers'. She was also a member of the North Rose Methodist Church, and the Arbor Vita Chapter, Order of the Eastern Star.

She began her career as a teacher early in the 1900s and was teaching primary school at North Rose Central School by 1904. Both of her parents died in 1910, and around 1917 Lellavene headed west to work at the Cunningham Children's Home in Urbana, Illinois, an orphanage opened in 1895. It was run by the women of the Urbana Methodist Episcopal Church in the mansion left to the church by Judge Joseph O. Cunningham and his wife Mary. Lellavene taught eighth and ninth grades there through the beginning of the 1920s, returning home and spending weekends with friends such as Gertrude Bush and Pauline Porter. In 1917 *The Clyde Herald* reported that "Miss Lellavene Armstrong gave a very interesting talk concerning the Cunningham Home at Urbana, Illinois, and her work in that institution at the Methodist church Sunday evening in place of the usual preaching service."

Lellavene's sense of adventure and desire to help others may have come in part from her father, Edgar. Edgar was the son of James Armstrong, who had fallen in love with the abundance of Rose after fleeing a stern and punitive father in the southern part of the state. He married Mary Eliza Sweet, who came from a family of famous bonesetters from Providence, Rhode Island. One of the most well-known Sweet family stories is of Job Sweet, who healed Theodosia Burr (daughter of Vice President Aaron Burr) of a hip ailment the day before she was scheduled for surgery. Job arrived at the Burr mansion in New York City by carriage, which he mistrusted—he did not like traveling "in a thing" nor did he like being "jostled and tossed about." Sweet put his hands on her hip and told the bedridden Miss Burr to try taking a few steps. She did. The next day a coterie of doctors arrived to perform the surgery, only to find Theodosia up and walking, and Sweet on his way back to Rhode Island on a sloop.

In the late 1920s, Lellavene attended the Oswego Normal School. (Normal School was the name for a Teaching College.) That same year she was also presented with the gift of a Japanese tea set by the Loyalty Class of the Methodist Episcopal Church. She returned to teaching at North Rose Central School in 1929 (third grade), and in 1932 she purchased the LaVerne Terbush bungalow and moved there from the rooms she was renting in the house of Mrs. Josephine Tibbits.

In 1943 she moved to Oswego where she worked for the Oswego Orphan Asylum—the first one in the area. She often returned home to spend time with good friends like the Seagers, fellow teacher Pauline Porter, and Mrs. Valentine. In 1944 she returned to North Rose from Oswego to care for her friend Edna Gage, who had fallen ill.

In November of 1956, she slipped on some icy pavement in front of the Gulf gas station in North Rose and broke her hip. She never fully recovered and died six months later in May 1957 at the Greenacre Restorium in Clyde. She was survived by her niece, Nedra Seelye of North Rose, who married into the Seelye Ladder family.

Baker, William & Millicent

15 South Poplar Street, now 4957 South Poplar—Built in 1920. Estimated value in 1940: $2,500.
William Baker (1898–1974), 41, head of household, grocery store owner, 52 weeks, self-employed.
Millicent Sarah Strong Baker (1899–1994), 40, wife, homemaker.

WILLIAM AND MILLICENT BAKER MARRIED in May 1917. William owned a grocery store in Clyde. He reported working 70 hours the last week of March 1940. Millicent was a homemaker. Both of the Bakers had completed ten years of school.

William was born in Fleming (Cayuga County), but his parents were both born in England. In 1920 William was a farm laborer. William, Millicent, and their first born, Marjorie, lived in a rented home in the Town of Genoa, near King Ferry (Cayuga County). By 1930 the Bakers owned the North Rose home on South Poplar Street, and William was managing the Market Basket grocery store in North Rose. He was also a leader in the IOOF's Bay Shore Lodge.

In August 1931, William filled in as manager at Clyde's Market Basket grocery while its regular manager, LaVerne Terbush, was on vacation. In September 1932, the two Market Basket managers—William and LaVerne—became business partners. They purchased James Costello's Clyde grocery and meat business and renamed it Terbush and Baker. At that time, Samuel Wise from the Weedsport Market Basket became manager of the North Rose store. The Bakers moved to Clyde for a couple of years but returned to North Rose in September 1935. In 1937 Mr. Terbush left the partnership and took over the Clyde Red and White store with a new business partner.

William attended the 1936 World Series in New York with three friends. He was also chosen in July 1940 to be treasurer of the North Rose committee of the Red Cross, where he served for nearly three years. In December 1943 he was nominated for fire chief of the North Rose Fire Department.

Millicent was born in Scipio (Cayuga County). Active in the Rebekah Lodge, she was elected treasurer in October 1929 and held the post for several terms. Millicent was also active in the Kappa Phi class.

William and Millicent Baker had two children: Marjorie Elizabeth Baker (1918–2000) and Paul Baker (1922–1976). They frequently visited Millicent's parents in Scipioville. During the summer, they enjoyed short vacations on LeRoy Island.

Marjorie married Donald Robert Huckle of Clyde—a Cornell University graduate—in North Rose in August 1939. The couple had one daughter and four sons. They lived in western New York: first in Ripley (Chautauqua County), then in Hamburg (Erie County). Donald Huckle was farm director of Buffalo radio station WGR.

Paul married Margery Elizabeth Hill (1922–2015) when he was still a student at NRCS. Paul and Margery moved in with her mother and stepfather. (See "Skinner, Pete & Ethel.") In August 1940 Paul and Margery visited the New York World's Fair. Paul was a member of the North Rose Fire Department. Margery was active in the UPWA (likely the United Presbyterian Women's Association) of the North Rose Presbyterian Church. In 1942 the family moved to West Webster (Monroe County). They had four daughters.

Baldridge, Herbert & Meda

23 North Poplar Street, now 5049 North Poplar—Built in 1900. Estimated value in 1940: $2,500.

Herbert Simpson Baldridge (1889–1973), 50, head of household, carpenter, 30 weeks, self-employed.
Meda M. Moore Baldridge (1887–1973), 52, wife, homemaker.
Warren E. Baldridge (1913–1983), 26, son, apple runner, 32 weeks for $620.
Anna Irene Baldridge (1915–1982), 24, daughter, secretary (started work in 1940).
Eva E. Kitchen Moore (1868–1957), 71, mother-in-law, trimmer, 24 weeks for $270.

HERBERT BALDRIDGE WAS A CARPENTER and an independent building contractor. Meda was a homemaker. Both Herbert and Meda completed the typical eight grades of school. Their two adult children, Warren, and Anna, lived at home with them. Warren, a high school graduate, was an apple runner for an apple packing house. Anna, also a high school graduate, was a secretary at a paper manufacturing company. Also living at the Baldridge home was Meda's mother, Eva E. Moore. Eva completed the eighth grade and worked part-time as a trimmer at the Canning Factory.

In 1892 Herbert lived on his parents' farm in Huron. His parents were William E. Baldridge and Anna Waldron Baldridge. Also living on the farm was Herbert's older brother, Edward (1886–1976). In 1900 Edward and Herbert worked on the family farm. Added to the family was a younger brother, Earl L. Baldridge (1898–1912). In 1910 Herbert was 18 and living on his own in the village of Newark, New York. (All references to "Newark" in this book refer to Newark, New York, a town west of North Rose.) Herbert worked as a carpenter at the Newark State School (which began as the State Custodial Asylum for Feeble-Minded Women before becoming the Newark State School for Mental Defectives; it became the Newark State School in 1927, housed only women until males joined the "inmates" in 1932, and closed in 1991).

Until 1912 Meda lived on her parents' farm in the Town of Huron. Her parents were William H. Moore (1861–1914) and Eva E. Kitchen Moore. Eva's parents, like Herbert's, were Wayne County natives: Matthew Kitchen (1843–1929) and Olive L. Atwater (1844–1884). In 1912 Meda and Herbert married. By 1915 Herbert and Meda lived at 25 North Poplar Street in North Rose, where Meda gave birth to Warren and Anna.

Two of the notable buildings that Herbert constructed during his career were the original structure of the Alton Canning Factory and the Presbyterian Church in Huron. In 1920 the Baldridges lived on Lummisville Road in Huron and rented a farm, on which Herbert worked. The Baldridges lived on Chimney Bluff Road in Huron in 1925. Herbert purchased a lot with a house foundation at 23 North Poplar Street and by 1930, Herbert had completed the house where he would live the rest of his life. In August 1930 the Baldridges camped in the chestnut grove on the Baldridge farm near East Bay. In April 1932 Earl and Iva Maynard of Lyons hosted 20 guests to celebrate Herbert and Meda's 20th anniversary. (Iva was Meda's sister.) Herbert and Meda were active in the Huron Presbyterian Church.

Herbert ventured to Beaver River (Herkimer County) for a week of deer hunting shortly after his son Warren hunted in the same territory in November 1938. Beaver River was a favorite hunting ground of the Baldridges for many years. Herbert and Meda often socialized with Earle W. Canty and his wife, Alta Baldridge Parkhurst Canty, of Rochester and later Wolcott. Alta, Edward's daughter, was Herbert's niece and thus Warren's first cousin. In October 1940 Earl Maynard and Herbert Baldridge visited New York City to see the World's Fair. Herbert's mother, Anna Waldron Baldridge, died in September 1943; she had been caring for her aging husband, W. Edward Baldridge Sr., who died the next month.

In November 1944—running unopposed—Herbert won election as Town of Rose tax collector. He faced a Republican opponent in 1945. Although he lost that contest, he ran well ahead of most of the rest of the Democratic slate. Later, in two other successive elections, he again captured then lost the office. Herbert, Warren, and Merritt

Thomas spent a weekend in November 1949 hunting near Forestport (Oneida County).

Herbert and Meda's children Anna and Warren were both Sunday school teachers. In 1931 Warren journeyed to Washington, D.C., on the annual NRCS Easter Week senior class trip. Warren and Charles Oaks took an eight-week course in Sodus on Boy Scout leadership in March and April 1939. The NRCS Alumni Association elected Warren vice president of the group in June 1940.

Warren married Virginia A. Stone (1919–2004) in April 1941 and honeymooned in Boston. Virginia was the daughter of Earl Lewis Stone (1892–1957), a construction engineer from Springwater (Livingston County), and Alison Connon Green Stone (1891–1977). Virginia had completed a three-year course at Geneseo Normal School (now SUNY Geneseo) before moving to North Rose, where she taught kindergarten for many years. Virginia's brother Earl and his wife, Margaret, of Ithaca (Tompkins County), often exchanged visits with Warren and Virginia. In May 1942 Warren and Virginia moved into their brand-new home in North Rose. Warren built the house at 27 North Poplar Street with help from Herbert. Virginia canvassed door-to-door in March 1944 for the Red Cross Fund Drive. Virginia was also active in the Rose Public Health Committee and the WSCS.

Virginia's parents moved to Tennessee in January 1944. Soon they returned to upstate New York, living in Belgium (Onondaga County). Warren, a longtime firefighter, gained the presidency of the North Rose Fire Company in January 1949. Warren and Virginia became the parents of a son, (Warren) Scott Baldridge. Scott played on the NRCS 1962 varsity baseball team and was valedictorian of the 1963 NRCS graduating class. He earned an AB in geology from Hamilton College and a PhD in geology from Caltech.

Scott has accumulated many academic honors. During the majority of his career, he has been a staff member of the Los Alamos National Laboratory. He is also a full professor on the faculty of San Diego State University. Scott is the author of *Geology of the American*

Warren Scott Baldridge, NRCS Class of 1963.

Southwest, published by Cambridge University Press.

Warren and Virginia welcomed a second son, Mark Steen Baldridge, into the world in December 1946. Mark achieved a BS in art education from State University College at Buffalo and an MFA in 1968 in metalsmithing and jewelry with a minor in design from Cranbrook Academy of Art in Bloomfield Hills, Michigan. After 44 years of full-time teaching art at the college level—mostly at Longwood University in Farmville, Virginia—he is pursuing his own art projects and operating Mark Baldridge Design.

During his tenure as an art professor, Mark had two terms as chairman of the art department. He is currently a professor emeritus at Longwood. Mark's art has been shown in over 150 museums, galleries, art and craft shows, and other exhibitions.

In January 1949 Warren and Virginia became the parents of a third son, Kenan Stone. His parents named Kenan in honor of Dr. Ray Kenan. The Baldridges report that at 9 months old, Mark was very ill with what Dr. Kenan correctly diagnosed as the rare condition called intussusception—which is often fatal if not properly treated. Mark was rushed to the Syracuse hospital along with Dr. Kenan's diagnosis. Mark surprised the hospital staff by recovering after undergoing the corrective procedure that Dr. Kenan ordered. Warren and Virginia honored the man who had saved the life of their second son by naming their third son after him. This generous action had a sad element: Kenan Baldridge's was the last childbirth at which Dr. Kenan assisted before his untimely death the following month.

Kenan earned an AB at Middlebury College, a master's degree at Syracuse University, and a PhD in urban studies and public affairs from the University of Akron. Kenan worked as a paramedic; he is an active firefighter on the North Rose Fire Department's roster. Kenan became an administrator of a regional blood bank and the American Red Cross. He took charge of the Red Cross blood program in one-fifth of New York State and converted that sector from the least productive to the most productive.

Kenan is a progressive Democrat who has four times won election as the supervisor of the Town of Rose. His victories are quite remarkable, considering that enrolled Republicans outnumber enrolled Democrats in the Town of Rose by a tally of 585–296. (Wayne County is one of 16 counties in New York State in which the Town Supervisors perform an executive function in the town and also perform the legislative role in the county. In more than two-thirds of New York's counties, this traditional "Board of Supervisors" system has been replaced by a separately elected County Legislature. Many people believe that the Board of Supervisors system is too burdensome on the Supervisors, giving them two very different roles in local government.)

Kenan also served more than 10 years on the North Rose–Wolcott school board. He was president of the school board for four years. His father Warren had earlier held that same post. Kenan threw his hat in the ring for the office of state senator three times, in 2016, 2018, and 2022. Running in a larger district for a seat in the upper house of the New York State Legislature, he took positions on regional issues. One of Kenan's main platform planks was opposition to large-scale trash incineration and the expansion of the mountainous local landfills that accept the garbage from New York City. The metropolitan area hauls trash to economically challenged parts of the state whose people think they cannot afford to refuse it. He also took strong positions on corruption in state government, education, and women's rights.

Ball, George & Maude

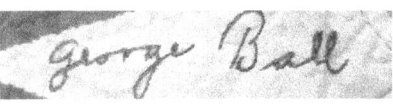

19 Elm Street, now 4943 Elm—Built in 1920. Estimated value in 1940: $2,500.

George H. Ball Jr. (1895–1961), 45, head of household, factory manager, 52 weeks for $48 a week.

Maude Garton Ball (1896–1953), 42, wife, homemaker and paid laborer, 12 weeks for $13 a week.

Richard Ball (1922–1995), 17, son, student and paid laborer, 8 weeks for $9 a week.

(George) Milton Ball (1924–1983), 15, son, student.

GEORGE AND MAUDE BALL WERE living with their sons, Richard and

Milton. Both boys were still in school, but Richard also held a summer job. George was the manager of the Canning Factory. Maude was a homemaker and also worked outside of the home for part of the year. George and Maude had each received an eighth-grade education.

George Ball Jr., born Rufus Rogers, was an orphan from Rochester who reportedly rode the "orphan train" across Upstate New York before being adopted by George H. Ball Sr. and Sarah Seager Ball. George Jr. was a World War I U.S. Navy veteran. In 1930 he was foreman in the Canning Factory. (His sister, Myrta, was married to the owner of the factory, Edward Salter. See "Salter, Edward & Myrta.") In April of that year, he took a 10-day trip to Texas with his wife and four friends. In October the Balls attended the American Legion convention in Texas. Over the years, George attended several canners' conventions—including the one held in Chicago in January 1937.

In December 1938 George and his family helped celebrate his adoptive parents' 60th wedding anniversary at a dinner hosted by his sister, Myrta Sarah Ball Salter (1879–1956). The senior Balls received gifts as well as 150 congratulatory postcards. In 1940 George lost his mother in January and his father in May.

In September 1948, George and Maude drove to California with Myrta. They took a northerly route to California and a southerly route for the return trip. The same trio spent a few weeks in Florida in March 1950.

Maude was active in the Methodist Church Sunday school program, their Kappa Phi class, and the WSCS. She was also a member of both the Rebekah Lodge and the OES, and chaired an October 1945 American Legion Auxiliary Fair held in Wolcott. Tragically, her father, George Garton, perished in March of 1944—after leaving his home for a late-night walk. After an intensive search, his body was located north of the hamlet. He was 82. (For a more detailed description of George Garton's demise, see "Davis, Clifford & Lena"; Lena Davis was Maude's sister).

The Balls' son Richard enlisted in the Army Air Corps in October 1942. For several months he was stationed at Sioux City, Iowa. He married Dorthea Miner, daughter of James Odell Miner and Lillie

Belle Kitchen Miner, at her parents' home in August 1947. Richard's brother, Milton, was his best man. The matron of honor was Dorthea's sister, Ada Ruth Miner Young of Clyde. Dorthea Ball was an active member of the North Rose Methodist Church and worked as a secretary for O. A. Skutt Co.—the wholesale distributor of red kidney beans. The couple had three children: Douglas, Brenda, and Alan.

Milton was in the U.S. Army in the European theatre 1944–1945. He served in the Italian campaign with the 91st Division of the 5th Army in the Northern Apennine Mountains, Rome, Arno and Po Valley. He was awarded three battle stars and a good conduct medal and then was given a monthlong furlough at home. Milton married Dorothy Marie Morey of Clyde in September of 1945 and was honorably discharged as Private First Class in November of that same year. Milton and his wife settled in Rose and were close friends of (Marion) Harry Spade and Leah Grace Mock Spade.

Barnes, Earl & Lillian

57 South Main Street. Estimated value in 1940: $2,500.
Earl Nelson Barnes (1885–1975), 55, head of household, carpenter, self-employed, 30 weeks for $890.
Lillian Elizabeth Barnes (1885–1970), 55, wife, homemaker.

EARL COMPLETED SEVENTH GRADE; Lillian completed one year of high school. Earl's father was Nelson T. Barnes (1854–1926); his mother was Isabel May Coon (1865–1921). Earl had six siblings: Lucy (1884–1919); Arthur (1887–1892), who died in childhood; Frank (1894–1986); Benjamin (1897–1991; see "Dagle, Albert & Minnie"); Linwood (1901–1986; see "Barnes, Linwood & Helen"); and Gladys (1908–1997).

Earl married Lillian Langley in June 1909. In 1920 they were living in her mother's house on North Poplar Avenue. Lillian's parents, Samuel Langley (1830–1915) and Margaret Brisbin Langley (1852–1924), are both buried in the Rose cemetery.

Earl Barnes

In 1952 Lillian moved to Los Angeles (apparently without Earl).

We were unable to obtain much more than the cursory information provided by the census for this household. If you have information about the Barneses, see page 32.

Barnes, Irving

18 North Huron Street, now 5046 North Huron—Built in 1915. Estimated value in 1940: $500.
Irving Barnes (1859–1940), 80, head of household, retired, other income source.

We were unable to obtain more than the cursory information provided by the census for this household. If you have information about Irving Barnes, see page 32.

Barnes, Linwood & Helen

25 South Main Street, now 4947 Main—Built in 1901. Estimated value in 1940: $2,000.
Linwood Walter Barnes (1902–1986), 38, head of household, farm laborer, 52 weeks for $1,000.
Helen Adelia Dagle Barnes (1904–1997), 36, wife, homemaker.
Harvey Linwood Barnes (1938–1998), 1, son.

LINWOOD WAS EARL BARNES's brother (see "Barnes, Earl & Lillian" for information about his family.) Linwood completed four years of high school. He died in Ontario. Helen's parents were Harvey Dagle (1872–1945) and Grace Briggs (1875–). Helen completed two years of high school.

Harvey Linwood Barnes, NRCS Class of 1957.

Harvey married Barbara Ann Black in 1958 when he was a student at the State Agricultural and Technical Institute at Morrisville.

We were unable to obtain much more than the cursory information provided by the census for this household. If you have information about the Barneses, see page 32.

Bastian, Ruth

1940 monthly rent: $7.
Ruth M. Bastian (1891–1956), 49, head of household, bean picker, 40 weeks, $300.
Mary E. Bastian (1923–1991), 17, daughter, student.

RUTH COMPLETED FOUR YEARS of high school. She married Roy G. Bastian (1894–1976) in 1916. In 1950 she lived in Hillsborough, Florida. In 1940 Mary had completed two years of high school.

We were unable to obtain much more than the cursory information provided by the census for this household. If you have information about the Bastians, see page 32.

Beck, Walter & Edith

1940 monthly rent: $20.
Walter Adam Beck (1909–1968), 30, head of household, school teacher, 40 weeks, $1,400.
Edith Elizabeth Weeks Beck (1912–2001), 27, wife, homemaker.
David W. Beck (1938–), 1, son.
Mary E. Beck (1939–), 3 months, daughter.

We were unable to obtain more than the cursory information provided by the census for this household. If you have information about the Becks, see page 32.

Betts, James & Edith

1940 monthly rent: $12.
James H. Betts (1866–1947), 74, head of household, retired, 11 weeks for $250.
Edith L. Chase Betts (1873–1952), 66, wife, homemaker.
Charles "Ivan" Betts (1902–1963), 37, son, apple packer at Cold Storage, 26 weeks for $410.
George Elvin Betts (1902–1961), 37, son, laborer at Cold Storage, 24 weeks for $380.

JAMES AND EDITH MARRIED in 1893. Their adult twin sons, both of whom finished six years of school, were living with them.

Their son George married Cecille Mary Guthrie (1909–1987) and they had three sons: Donald Elvin Betts (1929–1996), James William Betts (1930–1989), and Roy L. Betts (1933–1978). In 1940 Cecille was one of two lodgers in the household of Eleanor T. Driscoll in Oswego (Oswego County) and was working as a telephone operator. She remarried in the 1940s to a widower from Oswego, Frank Benton Cole (1883–1959). They had a son, Thomas Benton Cole (1950–2014). Frank was born in Michigan but grew up in Oswego County, the son of a farmer.

Cecille Guthrie and George Betts

James and Edith's son Ivan married Eva Isabelle Fenk, or Fink (1907–1992), in 1925. Eva was the daughter of Frank and Josephine Fink of North Rose (see "Fink, Frank & Josephine"). In 1930 Ivan was living with Eva and their 4-year-old daughter Iva on Maple Avenue in North Rose. By 1940 all three were living in different households: Ivan had moved back home with his parents; Eva was living in Rochester; and their daughter Iva was living with her grandparents, Frank and Josephine, in North Rose.

We were unable to obtain much more than the cursory information provided by the census for this household. If you have information about the Bettses, see page 32.

Bly, John & Lida

20 North Main Street, now 5030 North Main—Built in 1875. Estimated value in 1940: $3,000.

John W. Bly (1864–1952), 75, head of household, painter, 10 weeks for $200.
Lida May Bly (1869–1942), 71, wife, trimmer, 20 weeks for $235.
Bertha Louisa Fowler Warner (1881–1945), 64, lodger, store clerk, 52 weeks for $730.

John was a freelance painter, and Lida was a homemaker and a trimmer at the Salter Canning Co. They had each completed the standard eight years of grammar school. The Blys married in February 1891. John's father had been born in Europe, likely in Germany. John's mother's birthplace was definitely Germany. Lida was the daughter of Merlin H. Pierse (1851–1918) and Elizabeth W. Pierse (1850–1918). Merlin was a farmer in Huron.

The Blys changed their surname in the 1920s. Before that time, their name was Blycostin. They truncated their name to just one syllable (Bly) so other people could easily remember and spell it. Perhaps Bly sounded more "American" than Blycostin. For legal matters, such as his will, John continued to use his full surname. His siblings kept the Blycostin name for all uses.

In 1880, at the age of only 13, John worked as a farm laborer on Walter Emery's farm in Sodus. In 1902 John was operating an apple evaporator in North Rose. In 1904 John and Lida lived in Resort, a hamlet near the southern tip of Sodus Bay. The Blys had their only child, Gertrude Gladis Bly, in 1906.

In 1908 John bought a farm from M.E. Wright. The Wright farm is one of five farms on the land owned and cleared by North Rose pioneer James Catchpole and his sons. In 1910 John Bly was staying at the sanitarium in Ogdensburg (St. Lawrence County), resting in the fresh air to cure a TB infection. He was there for most of the next 10 years. In March 1913 John Bly bought the Rapp home on Main Street and rented it to Frank Hill. In the late 1920s and early 1930s, John bought and sold several pieces of real estate.

Around 1919 to 1921, Gertrude was very active in the North Rose Methodist Church. She was an officer of the Epworth League. By October 1924 Gertrude had moved from the Town of Rose to Lyons. Gertrude had returned to the Town of Rose by the second month of 1925. After her homecoming, she continued visiting friends in Lyons.

John and Lida's daughter Gertrude (1906–1943) married electrician James Thomas Whalen (1901–1981) in February 1925. James was the son of Mary A. Whalen (1872–1945), a laborer in an enamel factory. This factory most likely produced metal coated with enamel and was manufactured in Newark. At least six companies produced this coated metalware. James's father, the late Thomas Whalen (1874–1920), was a machinist from Canandaigua. The newly married couple lived in Rochester and Akron (Erie County) and Albion (Orleans County). Gertrude and James Whalen had four daughters: Kathleen married Earl James Doyle in 1947 and moved to Richmond, Virginia. They divorced five years later. Anna Mae married William Stolte and moved to Holley (Orleans County). The Stoltes then moved to Rochester. Arleen married Donald Hodom and moved to Barker (Niagara County). Ruth (ca. 1933–2006) in 1956 lived in Rochester and married Albert J. Abbazia. Albert's parents were born in Italy.

In February 1930 and again in May 1930, Kathleen and Anna traveled from Rochester to visit their grandparents, John and Lida. Lida was a member of the Loyalty Class and the Home Missionary Society of the Methodist Church. She was also a member of the Home Bureau. Charles Bly of Chicago was a guest of the North Rose Blys in August 1930. John was so ill in February 1932 that Ruth Briggs accompanied him to Clifton Springs Sanitarium, acting as his private nurse. His granddaughter Anna spent the 1934–35 school year living with her grandparents.

Kathleen and Anna spent part of the summer of 1936 with John and Lida. In September 1941 John and Lida Bly visited Gertrude and her family at their home in Albion (Orleans County). John and Lida's granddaughter Anna Mae Whalen returned to North Rose with the Blys. That same month, William Pierse of Palmyra visited his sister Lida with his wife, Minnie.

Lida died in April 1942. Beginning around September 1942, John endured a five-and-one-half-month stay at the Barber Hospital with a broken leg. Myrtle French took care of him.

In May 1943 the Blys' lodger Bertha accompanied John to Albion, when he rushed there upon the death of his daughter, Gertrude, of influenza. After Gertrude's death, the Whalen family moved to Brockport (Monroe County). James's mother and Gertrude's mother-in-law, Mary A. Whalen, died in the Canandaigua hospital after having her legs severed by a railroad switching engine in December 1945.

In 1951 John Bly spent the winter in Albion with a granddaughter, likely Kathleen. In May 1951 several of his female relatives visited him in North Rose: Kathleen of Albion; Arleen and Arleen's daughter (and John's granddaughter) Lyndia of Barker; and Ruth of Medina.

Living with John and Lida Bly in 1940 was a lodger, Bertha Louisa Fowler Warner. Bertha, the widow of Truman Dare Warner (1876–1935), was a full-time grocery clerk at Quereau's store. The Warners married in December 1899. Bertha was the daughter of William Henry Fowler (1841–1895) and Ann Eliza Sours Fowler (1851–1936). Bertha was a member of the Utopia Rebekah Lodge, the women's auxiliary to the IOOF. Truman was the son of Woodworth Warner (1816–1885) and Esther Ann Bancroft Warner (1834–1903). The fathers of the newlyweds were both farmers.

Bertha and Truman had a daughter, Anna Eliza Warner (1902–1963). Anna married Charles Gerber (1902–1947) and they moved to Boston. In November 1929 Charles and Anna Gerber visited her parents, Truman and Bertha, for a week. By July 1930 Anna and her husband had moved to Philadelphia. Truman died in October 1935. Around that time, the Gerbers moved to Clyde to be closer to Bertha.

Borden, Albert & Hattie
50 North Huron Street, now 5124 North Huron—Built in 1870. Estimated value in 1940: $1,300.
Albert Hiram Borden (1884–1957), 55, head of household, carpenter, 40 weeks for $800.
Harriett (Hattie) Anna McOmber Borden (1885–1976), 54, wife, bean picker, 40 weeks for $350.
Velma Borden (1916–1955), 24, daughter, trimmer at the Canning Factory, 12 weeks for $180.

WHILE ALBERT AND HARRIETT completed eighth grade, Velma was a high school graduate. Albert's parents were John H. Borden (1856–1936) and Jennie Caroline Hamm (ca. 1860–1930), who were buried in the Rose cemetery. Hattie was Albert's third wife; he married Ina

Davenport (1891–1923) in 1914 and Celia M. Lovejoy (1887–1984) in 1925 before marrying Hattie in Florida.

We were unable to obtain much more than the cursory information provided by the census for this household. If you have information about the Bordens, see page 32.

Borden, Raymond & Viola

61 Gray Street, now 5139 Gray—Built in 1900. Estimated value in 1940: $2,000.
Raymond Borden (1895–1971), 45, head of household, carpenter, 40 weeks.
Viola B. Correll Borden (1894–1978), 44, wife, bean picker, O. A. Skutt Company, 38 weeks for $325.
Elizabeth Correll (1860–1944), 80, mother-in-law, retired.

RAYMOND WAS ALBERT BORDEN'S YOUNGER BROTHER. (See "Borden, Albert & Hattie). Their sister, Florence Ida Borden, was married to the local veterinarian, Dr. Jacob Van Hout. Florence and Jacob lived in the Town of Rose, but Jacob's parents lived in North Rose. (See "Van Hout, Lloyd & Elsie.")

Both Raymond and Viola completed the eighth grade. The December 1, 1911, item in the *Democrat and Chronicle* announcing their marriage stated "Groom Sixteen and Bride Fifteen Wed at North Rose."

Viola's parents were Daniel Correll (1840–1913) and Elizabeth Brush Correll (1858–1944). After becoming a widow, Elizabeth lived with Raymond and Viola until her death.

We were unable to obtain much more than the cursory information provided by the census for this household. If you have information about the Bordens, see page 32.

Boughton, Raymond & Kate

19 South Poplar Street, now 4939 South Poplar—Built in 1900. Estimated value in 1940: $1,200.

Raymond W. Boughton (1893–1978), 48, head of household, retailer, 52 weeks, self-employed.
Katherine "Kate" Ziegler Boughton (1889–1960), 50, wife, bean picker, 46 weeks for $8 a week.

RAYMOND AND KATE BOUGHTON were married in Lyons in March 1912. Raymond was the proprietor of a retail lumberyard. Kate was a full-time bean picker at the Bean House. Their only child, Jean K. (1921–1990), was no longer living at home in 1940. Raymond and Kate had, respectively, eight and nine years of schooling. Kate's younger brother, Henry Ziegler, lived two houses to the south. (See "Ziegler, Henry & Mabel.")

In 1918 Raymond was farming his own land in Huron, but by 1920 he was a day laborer and lived with his wife in North Rose. He was not living with his family in the 1930 census but had returned by 1940. He was in charge of feeding the 1,200 attendees of the Lake Shore Volunteer Firefighters convention held in North Rose in July 1935. Kate lost her mother in November 1936 and was living in Resort when she lost her father six months later. Kate was also active in Kappa Phi. In May 1938 the Boughtons and the Farnsworths visited Niagara Falls. In December 1939 Raymond was reelected as a fire commissioner. In March 1946 he was living in Kanona (Steuben County), while Kate remained in North Rose.

The Boughtons' daughter, Jean, took piano lessons from Grace Partrick. She took part in the annual NRCS Class of 1938 trip to Washington, D.C. After graduation, she spent a year in Rochester, returning to North Rose by September 1939. Then she accepted a position at the Hickok Company and moved back to Rochester. Several other young women with North Rose origins were also working in Rochester at the time: Marion Edwards, Anna Baldridge, and Louise Ziegler.

In October 1942 Jean was a patient at Ithaca's Biggs Memorial Hospital—a state tuberculosis sanitarium. Later that year, Jean entered Iola Tuberculosis Sanitarium for treatment. That same year, she moved to Ithaca (Tompkins County), where she remained until at least 1946. By 1950, she had returned to North Rose. She became active in the Order of the Eastern Star and WSCS. She also became the secretary to A. Gray Skutt at O. A. Skutt Company.

Boughton, Wallace & Ida

19 Gray Street, now 5055 Gray—Built in 1910. Estimated value in 1940: $2,500.
Wallace Boughton (1865–1945), 74, head of household, proprietor of a lumber mill, 52 weeks worked, self-employed.
Ida M. Garton Boughton (1869–1946), 72, wife, homemaker.
Emily Jane Boughton Garton (1856–1942), 84, sister, retired.

WALLACE'S PARENTS WERE Alanson Boughton (1828–1904) and Margaret Kellicutt (1830–1884). Ida's parents were George Garton (1820–1875) and Sarah Garton (1826–1892). Wallace, Ida, and Emily each completed six years of school. Wallace and Ida were married in 1887. Wallace's sister Emily married Ida's brother Abram in 1889. Emily resided in Huron until the death of her husband, Abram Garton (1857–1928). Her obituary states that she was living with her nephew William LeFavor when she died from pneumonia on September 9, 1942.

Wallace and Ida's only child, Raymond W. Boughton, also lived in North Rose. (See "Boughton, Raymond & Kate.")

Boyd, Jim & Gertie

58 North Main Street, now 5084 North Main—Built 1890. Estimated value in 1940: $2,500.
James "Jim" Boyd, Jr. (1873–1960), 66, head of household, retired.
Gertrude "Gertie" Bailey Boyd (1872–1965), 67, wife, homemaker.
Huldena Zapf (1870–1951), 70, lodger, self-employed.

JIM AND GERTIE BOYD OWNED a home next to the Presbyterian Church. Jim finished the ninth grade and was a retired blacksmith. Gertie was a homemaker and had completed the eighth grade. Their lodger, Huldena Zapf, was a widow who had six years of schooling.

Jim and his father, James Sr., took up residence in Sodus in July 1894, where they and Jim's brothers opened a blacksmith shop. Jim's father bought Fred Knapp's new barn on Mill Street in Wolcott to open another blacksmith shop with his son Jay in March 1895. Jim was living in Victor in 1895 and took his ill brother Jay's place at the shop in March 1896. For $3 in a feat of daring, agility, and blacksmithing acumen, Jim agreed to scale the extremely tall Wolcott school flagpole to replace the broken pulley at the tip.

Jim enlisted in May 1898 in Co. L, 65th Regiment, U.S. Army. He served briefly in the Spanish-American War, but had been mustered out of the Army and obtained favorable employment in Batavia by November. Jim married Gertie Bailey in November 1899 and the couple was among 300 passengers on the excursion steamer *Arundel* that left Fair Haven for the Thousand Islands in September 1900. Active in the Wayne County Veteran Soldiers' and Sailors' Association, Jim was elected an officer of the Ontario Shore Lodge, Independent Order of Odd Fellows of Wolcott, in June 1903. That October, Jim and his six siblings lost their mother, Dalinda Boyd, to cancer: Minnie Boyd Winchell (1869–1929), J. Wilgar (ca. 1872–), Clayton (ca. 1878–), Effie Boyd Foote (1884–1974), Florence (1887–1969; see "Quereau, Florence"), and Leslie (1893–1959; see "Boyd, Leslie & Marion").

In 1917 Jim was hired to manage the Wolcott grain warehouse established by Skutt and Aldrich. The firm advertised that they were buying beans, wheat, buckwheat, and "practically all kinds of grain." Jim served a term as one of three North Rose fire commissioners.

When a new band was organized in North Rose in June 1924, Jim played tenor trombone. In November of that year, the Boyds were honored at a surprise party for their 25th anniversary and E.A. Salter presented them with a purse of silver. In June 1925 Jim fell off a ladder, breaking both heels. He was elected to a five-year term as fire commissioner a year later. Jim also became a trustee of the North Rose Presbyterian Church.

Gertie was active in the Matinee Whist Club and The Ladies' Guild of the Presbyterian Church. She lost her father, William Bailey, when he suffered a stroke in June 1910 and her mother, Sophronia Bailey, in November 1919. In 1920 Gertrude was elected an officer of the Home and Foreign Missionary Society of the North Rose Presbyterian Church and attended the convention for the Order of the Eastern Star in New York City as a delegate from North Rose. She was elected secretary of the Literary Club in April 1921.

North Rose Literary Club at the Pepperdines', 1924: 1. Ed Salter; 2. Frank Quereau; 3. Minnie Dagle (Mrs. B); 4. Frank Hill; 5. Harry Tellier; 6. Elliott Quereau; 7. Mrs. George Marshall; 8. Lena Rose; 9. Mrs. Edwards; 10. Mertie Salter (Mrs. Ed) 11. Jack Hill; 12. Jim Boyd; 13. Dr. Roney; 14. Gertie Boyd (Mrs. Jim); 15. George Marshall; 16. Prof. Warren Edwards; 17. Mattie Peck; 18. Sabra Smith (Mrs. Herb) 19. Flora Hill (Mrs. Frank); 20. Mrs. Roney; 21. Nell Quereau (Mrs. Frank); 22. Mrs. Catchpole; 23. Charles Gray; 24. Mrs. Romaine Cole; 25. Mrs. Elliott Quereau; 26. Maud Tellier (Mrs. Harry); 27. Mrs. Winchell; 28. George Porter; 29. Ed Catchpole; 30. George Mitchell; 31. Romaine Cole; 32. Mabel Gray (Mrs. Charles); 33. Otis Gray; 34. Lena Gray (Mrs. Otis); 35. Herb Smith; 36. Bert Dagle; 37. Ruth Quereau; 38. Josie Mitchell (Mrs. George); 39. Dr. Winchell.

Gertie's cousin Richard Forgham of Lyons took an 18-month leave of absence from his studies at Rensselaer Polytechnic University to sail around the world on a 79-foot ketch.

Jim and Gertie took a fishing trip to Canada with John and Carrie Pepperdine and Charles and Mabel Gray in August 1926. They spent most winters of the late 1920s and 1930s in Florida. In February 1929 they joined several families from Huron, Wolcott, and North Rose in a Wayne County reunion in Ft. Lauderdale, Florida. In September 1939 the couple took a trip to Quebec and in August 1940 they visited New Jersey, Connecticut, and attended the New York World's Fair with John and Mary Kay Gray. In July 1941 the Boyds left on a monthlong trip. They traveled by train to Seattle, then took a 3,500-mile boat trip to Seward, Alaska, via Ketchikan, Juneau, and Skagway. Additionally, Gertie and her brother William Bailey of Rochester often exchanged visits. Jim's brother Jay and his wife frequently made the trip from Washington, D.C., to visit the Boyds in North Rose.

In December 1948 Gertie suffered a heart attack, but she and Jim celebrated their 50th wedding anniversary in November 1949.

The Boyds' lodger, Huldena Zapf, came to the U.S. from Germany when she was a baby. By 1900 she was married to George H. Zapf, a farmer, and they lived in Darien (Genesee County). In 1920 she was operating a rooming house and her children all lived with her: Wallace managed a lumber company, Florence was a bookkeeper, and Irene was a student. Though Huldena called herself a widow, it is possible that she may have been divorced or separated. In 1925 she was living in Dansville with her daughter Florence, a homemaking teacher. In 1930 Florence was married to Willis Knapp; the couple had a 1-year-old son and her mother was living with her family. By 1940 the Knapps and Huldena had separate living arrangements all in North Rose. Huldena died in Batavia. (See "Knapp, Florence.")

Boyd, Leslie & Marion

Rented for $12.
Leslie K. Boyd (1893–1959), 46, head of household, laborer, the Canning Factory, 30 weeks for $450.
Marion Boyd (1895–1977), 44, wife, secretary, public school, 50 weeks for $700.
Mary Ellen Boyd (1921–1987), 19, daughter, unemployed.

LESLIE WAS A MUCH YOUNGER BROTHER of Jim Boyd. (For details about Leslie's parents and siblings, see "Boyd, Jim & Gertie.") Leslie completed ninth grade; both Marion and their daughter Mary Ellen were high school graduates.

A North Rose contingent traveled to St. Monica's Church in Rochester for the October 26, 1946, wedding of Mary Ellen to John Lingl:

Leslie and Marion Boyd (the bride's parents), Jim and Gertie Boyd (her uncle and aunt), Florence Quereau (her aunt), Grace Partrick, and Dr. Ray and Theresa Kenan.

We were unable to obtain much more than the cursory information provided by the census for this household. If you have information about the Boyds, see page 32.

Briggs, Cleon & Mary

15 Caroline Avenue, now 10388 Caroline—Built in 1925. Estimated value in 1940: $1,600.
Cleon Laverne Briggs (1893–1963), 46, head of household, blacksmith, 15 weeks, self-employed.
Mary E. Stoutenger Briggs (1896–1963), 44, wife, homemaker.
Ernest "Ernie" Cleon Briggs (1918–1979), 21, son, laborer, 30 weeks for $400.
Bernard R. "Stretch" Briggs (1928–1997), 11, son, student.
Bernice Marie Briggs (ca. 1931–2001), 9, daughter, student.

CLEON OWNED A BLACKSMITH SHOP. He had completed the eighth grade. Mary, a homemaker, had the same amount of education. Three of their four children lived with them: Ernie, a laborer at the Cold Storage who had eight years of schooling behind him; Bernard, who was in the fifth grade; and Bernice, who was in the third grade.

Cleon was the son of Ernest E. Briggs (1870–1935) and Mariam Dowd Briggs (1870–1940). (See "Briggs, Mariam" for more information about Cleon's parents and siblings.) Mary was from The Town of Lysander (Onondaga County). She was the daughter of Joel Stoutenger (1863–1906) and Carrie A. Guernsey Stoutenger (1875–1904). Joel was a day laborer. Since Mary lost both of her parents while she was very young, she lived in the Onondaga County Orphan Home for some time around 1910.

Cleon and Mary's eldest child, Lyman Laverne Briggs (1917–1999), had already left home by 1940. He married Mildred Farnam in April 1934 and soon they had two sons, Bruce and Keith, and a daughter,

Constance. Lyman and Mildred's family lived at 38 Auburn Street in Wolcott. Lyman was an owner/operator of his own trucking business. Mildred was a member of the Wolcott village Home Bureau.

Ernie moved to Newark. In 1941 he enlisted in the Navy. He was on the *USS Sturtevant* when the destroyer either hit a "friendly" mine or was struck by an enemy torpedo in April 1942. Another nearby Navy ship quickly rescued Ernie and the majority of his shipmates before the ship sank. In October 1942, Mary went to the Times-Union building in Syracuse and cut an audio recording of a letter to send to her son Ernie. Ernie happened to meet Sgt. Jack Dodds of North Rose on the street in Oahu, Hawaii.

Ernie Briggs

In January 1962 Ernie married Florence Anna Braun (1913–1979) in Brevard County, Florida. Florence was the daughter of Julius O. Schwab, a waiter born in Germany, and Anna Boll Schwab, a homemaker. Florence's parents lived in Queens, New York.

As a teenager, Bernard R. Briggs was nicknamed "Stretch" because of his height, and was active in the Boy Scouts and 4-H. In April 1942 he accompanied his older brother Lyman to New York City. Bernard was a member of four consecutive varsity basketball squads for NRCS from 1944 to 1947. He also played baseball and soccer. With his friends Herbert Hendershot and Eddie Dean, Bernard attended a Rochester Red Wings baseball game in June 1944. (Rochester was the Triple-A [top] minor league affiliate of the St. Louis Cardinals from 1929 to 1960; the Baltimore Orioles from 1961 to 2002; the Minnesota Twins from 2003 to 2020; and the Washington Nationals from 2021 to the present. The longest professional baseball game ever played was played in Rochester in 1981. The game lasted 33 innings and 8 hours and 25 minutes and was played over three days.)

Bernard was in the U.S. Navy from 1949 to 1951. His ship visited France in January 1950. In September of that year, he married Barbara Marie Farrow of Wolcott. Two days later, he shipped out to Korea. Barbara was the daughter of Jay D. Farrow (1896–1975) and Minnie Lapp Farrow (1892–1964). Jay was a farmer in Huron. Later Bernard and Barbara had sons named Richard, Michael, and Terry and a daughter Judy. Bernard and his family lived in Wolcott. In 1955 Bernard was employed by Gleason's in Rochester—a prominent gear manufacturer. He died in Zephyrhills, Florida, in March 1997.

Bernice attended an event at Casowasco, a newly acquired Methodist summer camp, in July 1946. This was the same year that the church purchased the former Theodore Willard Case estate for a fraction of its value. (See the description of Casowasco on page 323.) In June 1950 she won election as recording secretary of the Ontario County American Legion Auxiliary. Bernice traveled to England to marry Robert McWharf (1931–2017). Robert was overseas with the U.S. Army. His parents were Raymond "Ray" McWharf (1905–1984) and Laura M. O'Donnell McWharf (1909–1997) of Red Creek. By November 1960, Robert and Bernice had both a daughter, Tammie Sue McWharf, and a son, Randy McWharf. The family lived in South Butler and later in Wolcott.

In August 1935 Cleon had an accident in his blacksmith shop, which resulted in several cracked ribs. In May 1941 Lyman and Mildred attended Mildred's brother Stanley's wedding in Rome (Oneida County). Connie and Bruce stayed with their grandparents, Cleon and Mary, during their parents' trip to Rome. In April 1942 Cleon announced that his blacksmith shop would only be open on rainy days. Mary suffered a nervous breakdown in July 1944. She returned from the hospital in September 1944.

Cleon and Mary often exchanged visits with Clyde and Lena Eidman and their daughters of Weedsport (Cayuga County) and with Henry and Blanche Duger of Plainville (Onondaga County).

Cleon was a school bus driver for the last 20 years of his life. He died at the wheel driving a bus filled with children. Fortunately the bus merely backed into a snowbank; none of the children were injured.

Briggs, Jesse & Eunice

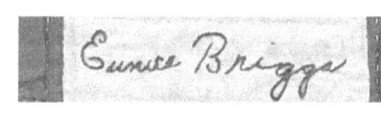

Rented for $14.

Jesse T. Briggs (1875–1955), 64, head of household, tailor, self-employed.

Eunice (Emmie) Briggs (1871–1941), 69, wife, homemaker.

JESSE AND EUNICE completed eight years of school. Jesse's parents were Birney Briggs (1842–1927) and Anna Briggs (1845–1922). Eunice's parents were Barnard Mitchell (1825–1900) and Sally Ann Mitchell (1830–1899). Their son Stephen (1902–1963) had graduated from the University of Rochester and was living in Brighton (Monroe County) in 1940. In 1950 Stephen worked as an x-ray technician and lived in the employees' quarters of Iola Sanitorium in Rochester with his wife, Rose Fulmer Briggs (1910–1967), a registered nurse, and their 6-year-old daughter Deborah. After Eunice's death, Jesse married Mae Satterlee, a widow 20 years his junior. (See "Satterlee, Gene & Mae.")

We were unable to obtain much more than the cursory information provided by the census for this household. If you have information about the Briggses, see page 32.

Briggs, Mariam

25 Gray Street, now 5063 Gray—Built in 1870. Estimated value in 1940: $1,500.
Mariam Irene "Mary" Dowd Briggs (1870–1940), 69, head of household, homemaker.
Magdalene Elizabeth "Lena" Yancey (1897–1994), 42, daughter, apple sorter, 25 weeks for $300.
Joyce Mariam Yancey (1923–2005), 17, granddaughter, student.
Carol Janice Yancey (1924–1982), 15, granddaughter, student.

MARIAM WAS A WIDOWED homemaker who had completed eight years of school. Living with her were her daughter Lena Yancey and two granddaughters, Joyce and Carol Yancey. Lena, who had also completed eight years of school, was an apple sorter at the Cold Storage. Joyce was a senior at NRCS; Carol was a sophomore.

Carol and Joyce Yancey, ca. 1927

Mariam was the daughter of George W. Dowd (1835–1913) and Mary E. Dowd (1845–1895) of Huron. George was a farmer. Mariam was the widow of Ernest E. Briggs (1870–1935); Ernest had also farmed in Huron. He was the son of Lyman Briggs Sr. (1848–1923) and Helen H. Doremus (1853–1917). Ernest and Mariam married in 1890. Ernest died in June 1935, when a horse in its stall trampled him. Paul Marshall and Paul McOmber made courageous but ultimately unsuccessful efforts to save Ernest.

On the Fourth of July 1938, Mariam's two-story barn on Gray Street burned to the ground. The fire damaged a sizable collection of blacksmithing tools. Children playing with fireworks may have started the blaze. John Jensen turned in the alarm. Robert Dickinson dispersed chemicals from his homemade fire truck to help save Mariam's house, which was only 10 feet from the barn at its closest point. North Rose's complete lack of fire hydrants hampered the fire companies that responded to the North Rose alarm. Although the North Rose Fire Department formed in 1915, fire hydrants would have been useless until after the creation of the water district in 1951 that brought municipal water to North Rose.

In March 1940 Mariam entertained Lee H. and "Cassie" Dowd; Lyman, Mildred Briggs and family; Blanche Gilfilian and daughter, Lucille; Irving Smith; Cleon, Mary Briggs and family; and Eva Yancey and her daughter, Paula. Mariam was a member of the North Rose Methodist Church. She died in August 1940.

Mariam and Ernest had four children: Roy, Cleon, Lena, and Eva.

Roy Eugene Briggs (1890–1970) married Ardella Elizabeth Correll (1890–1935) in October 1908. Ardella was the daughter of Daniel and Elizabeth Correll of Huron. Roy and Ardella had four daughters: Bessie B. (1910–2012), Beulah B. (1911–2012), Beatrice Belva (1912–1994), and Irene Elizabeth (1917–1967). Bessie married Kenneth Walter Yates. Beulah married William Edward Yates. (William was Kenneth Yates's brother.) Ardella and Roy also had a son named Harry (1914–1916) who died in infancy. In February 1932 Beatrice suffered a head injury in a fall to the hardwood floor during a basketball game at NRCS. In the spring of 1936, Roy's family moved to the house at the Pepperdine farm. In the 1930s Roy married Ila V. Seager (1894–1977). In February 1944 Roy and Cleon auctioned off the livestock and equipment on their farm southeast of Rose on Finch Road. By 1946 Roy and Ila were active in the Sunnyside Mission church. In November 1947 they moved from Wolcott to Wolcott Street in North Rose. She was a member of the Women's Christian Temperance Union.

Cleon Laverne Briggs (1893–1963) married Mary Stoutenger (1893–1963). They had one daughter, Bernice Marie, and three sons, Ernest, Lyman, and Bernard. (For more information about Cleon Briggs and his family, see "Briggs, Cleon & Mary.")

Magdalena Elizabeth Briggs married Theodore M. Yancey (1890–1944), brother of well-regarded businessman Ben Yancey, in January 1920. Lena Briggs was a laborer in a shoe factory in 1920. Theodore Yancey was a laborer in a store in 1920 and a warehouse in 1930. His parents were Daniel Yancey (1860–1940) and Lena K. Reyne Yancey (1866–1937). In 1930 Lena Briggs was a homemaker. She and Theodore had two daughters, Joyce and Carol. Lena and Theodore separated in the 1930s.

Related to this section is the story of the mysterious death of a young woman named Katie Borys at Dayton's Mills Pond, near Wolcott, in August 1938. Katie disappeared from the home of Daniel Yancey, where she worked as a housekeeper. Daniel Yancey was Theodore Yancey's father. Neighbors had last seen Katie in a small boat on the millpond near Daniel Yancey's home. The boat was still afloat when police searched for the 22-year-old woman. She had neatly stacked her valuables on a seat in the boat. There was no sign of the boat's passenger. An attempt at dragging for Katie's body was not successful. The authorities ordered the millpond partly drained. With the help of a flashlight, a searcher found Katie's body that evening. The coroner ruled the young woman's death a suicide. About the only clue to a motive for Katie's taking her own life was that authorities mentioned that she was "sensitive" and "high-strung." Shortly before her disappearance, people in the vicinity said that Katie "had words" with a member of Daniel's family. One Ancestry.com user theorized that this family member was Theodore; I have no corroboration of that. Katie was from Marengo, a hamlet in the town of Galen, the eldest of 11 children. A Roman Catholic, Katie was buried in St. John's Cemetery in Clyde.

Lena and her daughters moved to Lena's mother Mariam's home in North Rose. Theodore lived in Huron. In the 1940s Lena moved to Rochester and entered a long-term relationship with Russell Dowd Gillette (1898–1965).

Eva Belle Briggs (1899–1993) married Benjamin "Ben" Yancey in 1920. Ben (1898–1992) was originally from Croghan (Lewis County). He was one of Theodore Yancey's brothers. Ben worked as a logger and on the family farm until 1918. He started working in the garage of J.J. Colling in North Rose in 1920, and in 1927 started his own garage and appliance store where he sold G.E. appliances with the help of his sons Donald and Boyce. Ben worked full days at his store into his 80s and appeared much younger than his age, with a head of youthful black hair. Eva and Ben also had two daughters: Phyllis and Paula. Ben and Eva lived to celebrate their 72nd wedding anniversary in the Wayne County Nursing Home in Lyons.

Joyce Mariam Yancey, Lena's daughter, was living in Rochester when she married in April 1947 Richard F. Rotach (1921–1992), the son of Frank (1893–1979) and Mary Rotach (1894–1980) of Avis Street, Rochester. Frank and Mary later lived in Rose. Richard and Joyce Rotach had a son, Darren Duane, who died in infancy; Richard and Joyce's other children were Brian, Keith, Beth, and Sherry Lou.

Carol Janice Yancey graduated from NRCS. Carol was two years younger than her sister Joyce. She worked as a Comptometer (mechanical calculator) operator at Bourjois, Inc.—a French-owned cosmetics company with a factory and offices in Rochester. Carol married John W. Usher (1921–1997) of Rochester. John was the son of Samuel Usher (1896–1980) and Ruth Newbury Usher (1901–1969). Carol and John had three children: William, Joan, and Gloria. John was a longtime employee of the General Railway Signal Company. (This firm is still prospering but has since dropped the word "Railway" from its name. A measure of its diversification is that in recent decades it has purchased eight other companies. Now 20 percent of its revenue is derived from its high-tech operations. It is the third-largest producer of machines for the manufacture of computer chips.)

Brown, Claude & Greta

22–24 Gray Street, now 5060 Gray—Built in 1860. Estimated value in 1940: $1,300.
Claude Erwin Brown (1892–1854), 47, head of household, farmer, 40 weeks, self-employed.
Greta M. Fink Brown (1892–1957), 47, wife, homemaker, bean picker, 28 weeks for $300.

CLAUDE WAS THE SON OF John David Brown (1860–1931) and Ann Janette "Nettie" Miles Brown (1852–1939) from the Baldwinsville area in Onondaga County. John was a woodturner and knife maker and probably worked at the American Knife Works, a prominent Baldwinsville company that remained in business until 1960. Claude had five siblings and three half-siblings. John worked as a farm laborer in 1910.

Greta M. Fink was the daughter of Franklin J. "Frank" Fink (1865–1948) and Josephine Farnsworth Fink (1873–1943) (see "Fink, Frank & Josephine"). Frank was a farm manager and railroad laborer. Greta and Claude, both of whom had completed seventh grade, were married in October 1912, and subsequently lived with Greta's sister, Julia Richardson, and Julia's husband Bert at the site of the old Jeffers farm about two miles west of Rose Valley. Greta worked part-time as a bean picker at the O. A. Skutt Company Bean House.

Claude accepted a position in Boston in December 1917, but he and Greta were back in North Rose in 1919. Claude opened a blacksmith shop in Savannah in that year, and Greta was the matron of honor at the wedding of her sister Edna. In 1920 Claude was working for Jim Boyd, the area's senior blacksmith. While living in North Rose he and Greta became the parents of a baby, Isabel (1920–1997).

In November 1924 Greta became an officer in the North Rose Utopian Rebekah Lodge No. 400 and remained active in the organization for several years. The following year, the family was living on Gray Street and Claude was working as a day laborer. They subsequently lived in Baldwinsville for a short time but then purchased the Fremd house on Main Street in North Rose. Claude moved to Manchester (Ontario County) in April 1928, where he worked at the Salter Canning Company. In early 1930 they lived with Greta's parents on Maple Avenue in North Rose, and Claude was a millwright in a candy factory. (Perhaps this was The Original Candy Kitchen in Williamson, founded in 1890.) They then moved into the Besenfelder house on Gray Street after the Besenfelders had moved to Rome (Oneida County). In August 1930 they hosted the Fink Family reunion there and Frank was elected president of the family group, and the next month Greta entertained the Sigma Society of the North Rose Presbyterian Church.

In March 1933 they purchased the Foster family house at the northern end of Gray Street. In June of that year, Greta served as one of the leaders of the North Rose unit of the Home Bureau. In December 1940 Claude and Bert Richardson attended the canner convention in Buffalo.

By the end of the year, the Browns sold their home to Peter and Ruth Barton. (Peter was the grandson of Ella Dean.) Claude and Greta moved to a new home on the old McCall farm. (The Browns appear to have been making a career of buying and selling real estate in Wayne County.)

In June 1933 Isabel, who had a strong singing voice, performed a solo at the officer induction ceremony of the Utopian Chapter of the Rebekah Lodge. She followed in her mother's footsteps the next year by becoming an officer of the Lodge. She resided in Newark in 1938, and in about 1940 she married Russell Martin McKay (1912–2011) of Rochester, who had a son, Russell Jr. ("Rusty") (1932–2006) from a previous marriage with Ellen J. Lowe, a French Canadian. In May of 1943, Isabel and Russell were living in Buffalo. They had a daughter, Claudia Arlene (1944–2006), and visited Claude and Greta periodically. Another daughter, Linda, followed in November 1948, and

Greta helped care for both her new granddaughter and Isabel. The McKays had moved to Erie County by May of 1950 when they hosted Claude and Greta in their new home in East Aurora.

Brush, Sears & Eunice

41 Gray Street, now 5091 Gray—Built in 1890. Estimated value in 1940: $700.
Knowles Sears Brush (1870–1953), 69, head of household, 6 years of school, retired.
Eunice H. Rounds Brush (1879–1967), wife, 60, 7 years of school, bean picker, O. A. Skutt Company, 37 weeks for $320.
Inez Van Hout, niece, 18, 1 year of high school, unemployed.

SEARS'S PARENTS WERE James N. Brush (1851–1918) and Adeline E. Brush (1847–1912). Eunice H. Brush's parents were James S. Brush (1851–1915) and Emily Adeline McQueen (1847–1912). Sears completed six years of school; Eunice finished seven. They had three children: Laverne Jerome Brush (1894–1938), Grace B. Brush (1894–), and Neta Mary Brush (1896–1897).

We were unable to obtain much more than the cursory information provided by the census for this household. If you have information about the Boyds, see page 32.

Bullock, Herbert & Ethel

1940 monthly rent: $7.
Herbert Rowe Bullock (1896–1966), 43, head of household, laborer, fruit evaporator, 40 weeks for $725.
Ethel Della Ferguson Bullock (1903–1986), 36, wife, homemaker.
Edwin Herbert Bullock (1924–2008), 15, son, student.
Lewis Clark Bullock (1929–1974), 10, son, student.
Doris M. Bullock (1933–2018), 6, daughter, student.
Shirley Ann Bullock (1935–2022), 5, daughter.

HERBERT COMPLETED SEVEN YEARS of school and Ethel completed eight. They were married in 1922. By 1950 the family had moved to Lyons.

Edwin married Betty Willey (1926–2009) and had a son, Stephen.

Lewis married Mary Ann Chadwick (1931–1996) in 1949 in Lyons. They had two sons, Robert and Michael, and one daughter, Brenda.

Doris married Richard DeVay (1931–1985) in Lyons in 1955. They had three daughters and a son.

Shirley married James Austin in 1954. They had one daughter, Andrea. They were divorced in 1981. She married Andrew Joseph Parlantieri on December 24, 1991, in Palm Beach Gardens, Florida.

We were unable to obtain much more than the cursory information provided by the census for this household. If you have information about the Boyds, see page 32.

Burnett, George & Bertha

1940 monthly rent: $10.
George Theodore Burnett (1900–1974), 39, head of household, fruit sorter, fruit packing house, 30 weeks for $450.
Bertha Della Stickles Burnett (1903–1974), 37, wife, trimmer, apple evaporator, 18 weeks for $240.

GEORGE'S PARENTS WERE Franklin H. Burnett (1858–1940) and Mary Benton (1865–1943). George's older sister Addie also lived in North Rose in 1940. (See "Burns, Joe & Addie.")

Bertha's parents were Nelson E. Stickles (1860–1929) and Fidelia A. Stickles (1861–1946). Nelson died instantly after being run over by a snowplow.

George and Bertha married in 1928 in Savannah; they had no children. They were living at 13 Grey Street in North Rose when George died after a long illness in October 1974. Bertha died less than a month later after a short illness; they were both buried in Huron.

We were unable to obtain much more than the cursory information provided by the census for this household. If you have information about the Boyds, see page 32.

Burns, Joe & Addie

46 North Huron Street, now 5106 North Huron—Built in 1917. Estimated value in 1940: $2,000.
Joseph "Joe" John Burns (1886–1965), 55, head of household, apple grader, 40 weeks for $700.
Ada "Addie" Mae Burnett Burns (1886–1973), 54, wife, bean picker, 42 weeks for $360.
Harold "Bing" Joseph Burns (1910–1984), 29, son, laborer, 47 weeks for $800.

JOE BURNS COMPLETED EIGHT YEARS of school—spending his childhood in Auburn (Cayuga County). Joe's parents, Mortimer J. Burns (1857–1928), a laborer, and Margaret Byrne Burns (1855–1923), were both born in Ireland, and he had a twin sister, Margaret F. Burns. Joe was an apple grader at the Cold Storage.

Like her husband, Addie also completed the standard eight years of grammar school. She was born in Michigan, but her family moved to Huron when she was a child. Her parents were Frank H. Burnett (1858–1940) and Mary E. Benton Burnett (1865–1943). Her younger brother George lived in North Rose in 1940. (See "Burnett, George & Bertha.") Addie was a bean picker at O. A. Skutt Company. Joe and Addie married in December 1913 and had three children: Harold "Bing" Joseph (1910–1984), Howard Henry (1914–1993), and Leona Mae (1916–2017).

Addie Mae Burnett Burns

Bing completed high school in North Rose and was a reserve on the North Rose–Clyde baseball team in May 1930. In April 1931 he took part in the traditional NRCS Washington, D.C., senior class trip. In August 1933 Bing was delivering excellent pitching performances for the Clyde team in the Empire League. He had the honor of the hurling assignment against an outstanding African American league team representing the Syracuse area. The traveling African American squad was too good for the local team.

In November 1936 Bing and his friends Bernard Farnsworth and Joseph Catchpole spent some time at the DeVol camp in Wanakena (St. Lawrence County). By 1939 Bing had joined the Masons and the Elks Lodge, both in Wolcott. That same year, he attended a Rochester Red Wings baseball game with Roy Davenport and Peter Barton. In 1940 Bing was living with his parents and working as a laborer at O. A. Skutt Company.

In February 1945 Bing married Luella P. Nesbitt (1909–1983), the daughter of Wallace (1879–1961) and Mae B. Adams Nesbitt (1895–1981) of Albion (Orleans County). In July 1945 Bing and Luella moved from Huron Street to the Favreau house on Main Street. Theirs was one of the first homes in North Rose to have a television set. Terry Catchpole has fond memories of Saturday visits to the Burnses' house with his father, Reg Catchpole, to watch a baseball game with Bing on the early black-and-white set. An all-around sportsman, Bing was an enthusiastic bowler. From 1954 to about 1981, Bing operated the Wolcott Bowling Center.

Two children had left the Burns home before 1940: Howard Henry Burns (1914–1993) and Leona Mae Burns (1916–2017). Howard worked in the Scottish Village at the Golden Gate International Exposition in San Francisco—a World's Fair in March 1939 held to celebrate the completion of the San Francisco–Oakland Bay Bridge in 1936 and Golden Gate Bridge in 1937. Joe and Addie lost touch with Howard for a few years, but in September 1941 they learned that Howard was living in Denver. Howard served in the Army during World War II. He was stationed on Attu in the Aleutian Islands from 1943 to 1945 and was honorably discharged in July 1945. Seventeen months later, Howard married Louise Lucille Ziegler (1920–2006). They lived on Main Street in Wolcott. Howard and Louise had a son, David Howard Burns, and twin daughters, Denise Rebecca Burns and Diane Roberta Burns. Howard was a founding member of the Wolcott Friars' Club in June 1948 and Louise Burns was co-chair of the 1961 March of Dimes fundraising drive.

Leona was a piano student of Estella Roney. (See "Roney, Estella.")

In July 1930 she took part in a four-day Girl Scout camp out on LeRoy Island. Beginning in September 1935, she lived for a time in Niagara Falls with Norris and Florence Chaddock. Leona and three friends escaped unhurt from an auto accident while returning to North Rose from Sodus Point in July 1936. Their car overturned, but the vehicle and its occupants suffered only minor damage. Leona was living in Lyons in November 1936. By July 1937, she was a student nurse at Hudson River State Hospital in Poughkeepsie. Leona graduated in September 1940. She continued her studies at Bellevue Hospital in New York City.

In May 1941 Leona accepted a position at the Barber Hospital in Lyons where she worked for a short time. In May 1942 Leona married Francis Mark Skinner (1913–2002), the son of Francis Marion "Pete" Skinner (1882–1948) and Margaret May Mark Skinner (1895–1924) of North Rose. (See "Skinner, Bud & Virginia"; Bud was Mark's brother and he was part of Bud's household in the 1940 census.) The married couple took up residence at 134 Benton Street in Rochester. Leona was a nurse at Highland Hospital in Rochester. Mark worked at Sargent's lock company, which made ordnance and other items under government contract during the war. Mark and Leona had two sons, Dale and Dean. Leona and Mark visited Russell and Jean Satterlee in Wichita, Kansas, in July 1949. Leona lived in Henrietta (Monroe County) during her later years.

From at least 1910 to 1930, Joe was a laborer, mostly working on farms. In November 1931 a fire that started in the electrical system of Sam Wise's car consumed both Sam's car as well as Joe's. Joe and Addie lived in Seneca Falls in 1942, but they soon returned to North Rose. In August 1950 Joe and Addie traveled with their daughter Leona and her husband Mark to the Thousand Islands. While en route, they witnessed the dedication of the new wing of the Baseball Hall of Fame Museum in Cooperstown (Otsego County). Addie was a member of the Wonder Club and the Rebekah Lodge. In 1940 she visited the meetings of the Rebekah Lodges in other Wayne County communities. The local Rebekah Lodge elected Addie financial secretary in 1943.

Carpenter, Fred & Anna

20 Gray Street, now 5058 Gray—Built in 1860. Estimated value in 1940: $1,300.

Frederick "Fred" Troop Carpenter (1880–1945), 59, head of household, laborer in the Bean House, 44 weeks for $800.

Anna May Walhizer Carpenter (1879–1959), 61, wife, trimmer at the Canning Factory, 19 weeks for $225.

FRED AND ANNA HAD EACH COMPLETED six years of school. Fred worked as a laborer at O. A. Skutt Company. Anna was a homemaker and a part-time trimmer at the Salter Canning Company. Fred was the son of John Carpenter (1859–1908) and Hannah E. Hewson Carpenter (1856–1932); John was born in Orwell (Oswego County). He had earlier married Mary Phillips of Boylston (Oswego County); they had one son, Reuben Eliphant Carpenter (1876–1947). John and Hannah married in 1879 and lived in the Town of Rose. They had three children: Fred, Inez (pronounced IN-ess), (1882–1969), and Nancy (1884–1963).

In 1900 John was a farmer and a minister, and Fred was a farm laborer. Fred won admiration for his feat of paring one hundred bushels of apples in eight hours at the Proteus evaporator in October 1903. In 1905 John and Fred were both farmers. In 1907 Fred Carpenter worked as a carpenter with John Morey. Fred and Anna married in September 1908. Two months later, John died; Hannah moved in with Fred and Anna in the Glenmark area west of North Rose. Fred and Anna spent two days in Williamson at a large gathering of the Wayne County Baptist Association in August 1917.

By 1920 Fred and Anna lived by themselves. Hannah moved to the home of her widowed daughter Inez Carpenter Little. In March 1920 Fred purchased a Ford automobile. Two years later, Inez wed Earl Hilts (see "Hilts, Earl & Inez").

By 1925 Fred and Anna had moved to Gray Street in North Rose, and Fred was still working as a carpenter. In February 1927 Fred took on the job of shingling his mother-in-law's house in Sodus Center. Hannah died in March 1932.

Anna was the daughter of Andrew G. Walhizer (1849–1874) and Elizabeth "Lizzie" Walhizer (1851–1944) of Sodus Center. Andrew was a farmer. Both of his parents were German immigrants.

In October 1932 Anna entertained four women at a dinner at Ship Ahoy restaurant at Sodus Point. The Carpenters were living on Wickham Boulevard in that historic resort village. They moved to North Rose by 1934. In the late 1930s and throughout the 1940s, Anna was an active member and Fred served as a deacon of the Rose Baptist Church. He was an officer of the North Rose Grange.

Lizzie spent the winter of 1940–41 with her daughter and son-in-law. Fred and Anna attended a special New Year's Day dinner in 1944 in honor of Lizzie's 92nd birthday. The hosts were Anna's brother, Earl, and George Washington Walhizer and his wife, Flora Walhizer.

Fred died in 1945. In the 1950s Anna was an energetic member of the Rose Grange. In May 1959 Anna, perhaps depressed, died one day after entering the Young Nursing Home in Sodus Center.

Cashady, Ward & Mabel

37 North Main Street, now 5045 North Main—Built in 1915. Estimated value in 1940: $2,500.
Ward Charles Cashady (1886–1962), 54, head of household, carpenter and operator of retail confectionery, 50 weeks, self-employed.
Mabel H. Johnson Cashady (1883–1942), 56, wife, homemaker.

WARD CASHADY (their surname is pronounced "CASH-a-dee") completed one year of high school and operated an ice cream parlor. Mabel Cashady completed eight years of grammar school and was a homemaker. Ward was born and died in Tioga County—in Spencer and Halsey Valley, respectively. Ward's parents were Guy Cashady (1847–1925) and Aminda E. "Mina" Cook Cashady (1863–1934). Guy was a livestock dealer, then a farmer.

Mabel and Ward married in Buffalo in 1916. The couple lived in that city for the next decade. Ward was a carpenter for the Lehigh Valley Railroad. He worked out of Ashmore, Pennsylvania. In 1925

Ward and Mabel lived at 1030 Genesee Street in Rochester. Ward was a self-employed carpenter. Five years later, the Cashadys lived at 1079 Exchange Street in Rochester.

In May 1930 Ward and Mabel Cashady purchased the Coffee Shoppe in North Rose from Pearl Agnes Hackett Gillette Merz (1896–1983) and Pearl's parents, Darwin and Jeanette Doremus Gillette. The shop was located opposite the Methodist Church on Main Street. Although it was named the Coffee Shoppe, the most popular items on its menu were ice cream cones and milkshakes. Ward wrapped up his remaining Rochester carpentry work. Then, to avoid a long daily commute, the Cashadys moved to North Rose.

Mabel befriended John and Myrtle Farnsworth. In 1931 she participated in the Thursday Club which met for lunch or dinner on one Thursday each month. The Cashadys often hosted friends, who kept in touch with Ward and Mabel since their time living in the Rochester area. In January 1933 Ward underwent an operation at the Newark hospital. Thomas Cashady (Ward's youngest brother) and his wife, Marion Koch Cashady, moved from Rochester to North Rose in April 1933 to help Mabel run the Coffee Shoppe while Ward recovered from his surgery.

Glenn Mills enjoyed Ward's company. They went to the races at the state fair and enjoyed a hunting trip. When Ward was ill in the Rochester hospital in June 1936, Mabel's friend Anna Lewis visited Ward with Mabel. Samuel and Esther Wise also accompanied Mabel on a visit to see Ward. In September 1937 Harry Payne announced that he planned to acquire the Coffee Shoppe from Ward and Mabel, but the sale did not go through. That September, Ward accepted the Democratic Party's nomination for justice of the peace. On Thanksgiving weekend 1938, Ward went hunting with Clarence Juffs, Edward Anthony, and Charles H. Buerman of Rose. Mabel died after a short illness in 1942.

In 1944 Ward married Olive Streitle Preston (1892–1977) in Florida. Olive was the daughter of Benjamin E. Streitle (1866–1935), an upholsterer, and Elizabeth "Eliza" Hoppe Streitle (1870–1963) of Irondequoit (Monroe County). Eliza was born in Germany. Olive had married Roy D. Preston, a farmer from Chili (Monroe County), in April 1916. Ward and Olive lived in Rochester for a short while; they soon moved to North Rose. In 1945 Ward received the Democratic nomination for Rose Town Supervisor but lost by a wide margin. (Rose had a large Republican majority among registered voters, so it was an extraordinary achievement when a Democrat was victorious at the polls. The situation was also true for county-wide elective offices.)

Ward and Olive spent the winter of 1946 in Florida. In 1950 the Cashadys again vacationed in Florida. In August 1953, Ward and Olive moved to Williamson. Thomas (Ward's brother) and Frances Cashady (Thomas's second wife) continued to visit Olive in Williamson in the 1960s and 1970s after Ward's death. Gorman Priest, Esther Cashady Priest, and Chester Cashady of Halsey Valley sometimes accompanied the Thomas Cashadys. Esther and Chester were among Ward's siblings. Gorman was his brother-in-law.

Catchpole, Reg & Shirley

6 Clinton Avenue, now 10352 County Road 257—Built in 1925.
Reginald "Reg" Caldwell Catchpole (1902–1981), 38, head of household, wholesale buyer, $1900 for the year.
Ruth Shirley Hartman (1909–1990), 31, wife, homemaker.
Lynda Catchpole (1936–2014), 3, daughter.

REG'S PARENTS WERE Edwin (1859–1951) and Alice Amanda Rich (1863–1933). The couple lived in the Town of Rose. Edwin's father George was born in England. Edwin was a pioneer in the apple-growing industry, a lifelong Granger, and one of the founders of the State Horticultural Society. He graduated in 1881 from Cornell University. Alice was a homemaker. Shirley's parents were Raymon Hartman (1887–1939) and Lulu Rifenberg (1889–1915), who lived in Palmyra. Raymon was a part owner of a bottling works while Lulu was a homemaker. Raymon was U.S. postmaster for the Town of Palmyra.

Reg was a gifted athlete who played basketball and baseball. He was the most outstanding at baseball. He played catcher for the Clyde

North Rose baseball team, and also coached the high school athletics teams in his 20s. Reg was a champion cherry picker and active in the Boy Scouts. He attended Lake Forest Academy in Lake Forest, Illinois.

Shirley was born in 1909 in Palmyra. She attended Albany State Teachers College, now known as SUNY Albany. She was a Gamma Kappa Phi sorority member. Shirley first taught at Clyde High School and then became a language arts faculty member at Mynderse Academy, a high school in Seneca Falls (Seneca County). She was involved in directing stage plays.

Reg married Ruth Shirley Hartman in 1934. The couple had three children. For most of their early married life, Reg and Shirley rented a house on Clinton Avenue, opposite the Dillingham home. Around 1947, they moved into another rental on South Poplar Street while building a ranch-style home on South Main Street which was completed around 1948.

Reg was a key figure at O. A. Skutt Co. He held several positions and was eventually promoted to bean buyer. Reg was the expert buyer for much of the time that A. Gray Skutt operated O. A. Skutt Co.

Reg was the Master of the Masons of North Rose. Shirley was an active member of the Eastern Star.

Lynda (1936–2014) was their first child. She was a 1954 graduate of North Rose Central School and a close friend of Marilyn Skutt, the author's sister. She was class secretary and was instrumental in organizing the class reunions every five years for 50 years. She received a BS degree from the School of Management of Syracuse University in 1958. Following graduation, she worked for Cigna in West Hartford, Connecticut, and for General Electric in Syracuse.

During her college summers, Lynda worked at a resort on Fourth Lake in the Adirondacks where she met her future husband, Jim Schopfer of Syracuse. They married in 1960 and moved to Bayberry (Onondaga County), a suburb of Syracuse, where they raised their three children. They had season tickets for Syracuse basketball for 39 years. Lynda served terms as secretary and historian of the Bayberry Community Association. In 1973 she went to work for Schopfer Bros. Agency Inc., an independent insurance agency in Syracuse that was established by Jim's father and uncle. Following the death of her husband in 1994, she assumed the presidency of the agency and ran it until selling it to Ellis, Moreland & Ellis Insurance Agency in May 2013. She continued to be employed by EME until 2014. She is a past director of the Independent Insurance Agents and Brokers Association of Onondaga County.

Lynda was a longtime active member of the First Presbyterian Church in Liverpool, where she was an ordained elder and deacon and served as a trustee. She was also a member of the Holy Stitchers and Elsie O'Neill Circle.

J. Terry Catchpole (1941–) was their second child. He was a first-class Boy Scout. Terry has fond memories of Saturday visits to the Burnses' house with his father to watch baseball games on an early black-and-white television set with his father's coworker Bing Burns.

Terry was sports editor of *The Scanner*, a publication of the junior class of NRCS. He was an avid table tennis player, as well as a soccer, basketball, and baseball player in high school. He participated in the senior play *Home Sweet Homicide* at NRCS. He headed to Florida for college, attending the University of Miami, where he received his BA in English in 1963. Terry's professional life is divided into two segments: publishing and public relations.

Out of college, Terry worked as a staff editor at *Human Events*, a political publication in Washington, D.C., and was then a freelance writer. He wrote three books and contributed articles to numerous publications, including humor pieces for *National Lampoon*. He then became a staff editor, spending five years in Chicago with *Playboy*, and then served as editor-in-chief of *Boston Magazine*, *Business Computer Systems* magazine, and *Computerworld* newspaper.

In 1988 Terry and his wife, Catherine, formed a public relations firm, The Catchpole Corporation, which specialized in the management of speaker programs for client companies in multiple professions. The firm was extremely successful for 30 years, at its peak having more than 40 clients and employing more than 20 staff members, with offices in Boston's Financial District. Terry is now retired, living in Wellesley, Massachusetts.

Robert "Bobby" Catchpole (1945–2022) was a lifetime baseball fan. Bobby was a star shortstop and second baseman on his Mynderse Academy high school baseball squad. He helped the Seneca Falls nine win the 1961 Section 5 Class A state championship in Rochester's Red Wings stadium. They finished as runner-up in 1962. His exploits did not stop on the field, as he caught Roger Maris's 52nd home run ball in Yankee Stadium in September 1961. He and his parents were there celebrating his 16th birthday.

Bobby headed south to Florida for college, graduating from the University of Miami. He later joined the U.S. Army and was stationed at Fort Gordon, Georgia, where he met his future wife, Yvonne (1947–2019). The couple had two daughters, Belinda and Amy. In 1970 they settled in Miami, where they lived for 14 years. He returned to his alma mater to join the Miami Hurricanes' athletic department as assistant director for sports information, and later became recreation director for the City of South Miami. He was a pioneer of slow-pitch softball in South Dade County and was a charter member of the Homestead, Florida, Umpires' Association.

He began his 42-year career with the Postal Service in 1977 and served as president of the local American Postal Workers' Union. He and Yvonne moved in 1984 to Augusta, Georgia, where he continued his career as a mail carrier.

Catchpole, Vic & Kay

South Main Street—rented for $18.

Victor Caldwell "Vic" Catchpole (1906–1983), 33, head of household, farmer, 50 weeks for $700.

Kathryn Elizabeth "Kay" Bonney Catchpole (1910–2015), 29, wife, hairdresser, 50 weeks, self-employed.

Nancy Alyssa "Alice" Rich Catchpole (1933–), 6, daughter, student.

Charles M. "Chuck" Catchpole (1936–), 3, son.

Edwin Watson Catchpole (1893–1963), 47, brother, fruit salesman, 20 weeks, self-employed.

Vic was a farmer who had completed three years of high school. Kay was a hairdresser who was a high school graduate. She conducted a hairdressing business from her home.

Vic was the eighth of nine children of a prominent North Rose fruit grower, Edwin W. Catchpole (1859–1951) and Alice R. Catchpole (1863–1933). (For more information on Edwin and Alice, see "Catchpole, Reg & Shirley"; Reg was one of Vic's older brothers.) In 1929 Vic lived in Rochester. The next year he returned to North Rose, where he lived with his parents and two of his brothers in a Main Street home. That year he was a farm laborer.

Kay, from Mexico (Oswego County), was the daughter of Charles C. Bonney (1887–1936) and Eva May Sommer Bonney (1911–1946). After living in Mexico, Kay lived in Williamson and then in Sodus before settling in North Rose. When the Bonney family moved to Wayne County, Charles became a superintendent of the Salter Canning Co. Vic and Kay married in February 1932. They set up house at the Pitcher Apartments in Sodus. In June 1932 the couple opened an insurance office on Main Street in North Rose. Their first child was Alice, born in 1933.

One of Vic's older brothers also lived with the family: Edwin Catchpole had divorced; he had completed two years of college. Edwin had his own business selling fruit to the public at retail prices. Edwin had sold his share in the family's orchard holdings to his younger brother, R. Hayes Catchpole, and used the money to travel extensively in the western United States.

In June 1932 Vic and Kay entertained Ruth Shirley Hartman, of Palmyra (later to marry Reg Catchpole); Olga Catchpole, of Poughkeepsie; Ruth Fowler, Reg Catchpole, and Joseph Catchpole. Vic and Kay spent Christmas 1935 with the Bonney family in Alton. In April 1936 Vic and Kay moved to the Eidman house on South Main Street in North Rose. That month, they became parents of their second child, Charles. Vic went hunting with friends in the Adirondacks in November 1937. A third child was born to Vic and Kay in 1948: Elizabeth Caldwell "Betsy" Catchpole.

After she married Vic in February 1932 and settled in North Rose,

Kay was active in the Arbor Vitae chapter of the Order of the Eastern Star. She also enjoyed her memberships in the Contract Bridge Club, the Missionary Society of the Presbyterian Church, and the Home Bureau, Unit 2. In November 1936 Kay and her family rushed to Alton because of the sudden death of her father, Charles Bonney. Evelyn Bonney of Syracuse exchanged visits with her sister, Kay. In November 1947 Kay Catchpole, children Alice and Charles, and Shirley Catchpole and her daughter, Lynda, spent a weekend in Poughkeepsie visiting Vic's sisters Olga and Doris Catchpole. Vic and Kay attended the Rochester Fruit Show for a few days during January 1949. Vic joined the North Rose Fire Department.

Kay won election as president of the board of directors of the Wayne County Girl Scout Council in May 1950.

As did many North Rose children, Alice learned to play the piano under the guidance of Estella Roney (see "Roney, Estella"). In August 1940 Alice visited her aunt Doris Catchpole in Poughkeepsie. Lynda Catchpole spent the week with her cousins Alice and Charles in May 1944. During July 1944 Alice visited her cousin Erminie Catchpole Ferkes, her husband James, and their daughter in Tiverton, Rhode Island. (Alice's cousin's given name was pronounced "ER-my-nee.") Alice won the election for treasurer of her freshman class in September 1947. Two years later she gained a position on the squad of NRCS varsity cheerleaders.

Alice graduated from Pennsylvania State University in 1955, majoring in political science. In December 1954 Alice married Robert K. Hall (1934–), son of Robert E. and Helen Hall of Lock Berlin (Town of Galen). The bridegroom followed a pre-med curriculum at Hamilton College. The bride and groom returned to their respective schools after their honeymoon in Lake Placid. Robert received an MA from the University of Buffalo, served a residency in psychiatry at Letterman Hospital in San Francisco, and became a major in the U.S. Army Medical Corps. He became an ordained Buddhist priest and a meditation teacher. Robert and Alice divorced in March 1973 in Santa Cruz, California. (Alice subsequently used her actual first name: Alyssa.)

Charles Catchpole studied piano with Estella Roney. In August 1948 Charles attended the Boy Scout Camp at Babcock-Hovey near Ovid (Seneca County). The next month, Charles visited his aunts Doris and Olga in Poughkeepsie. Charles earned the assignment as den chief for a new Cub Scout pack in March 1950. (Den chiefs are scouts who assist the den leader of a Cub Scout pack.) Charles Catchpole was a JV basketball player for NRCS in the 1951 season, then moved up to the varsity in 1952. Vic sued NRCS after Charles injured his arm when a lighting fixture fell on him during halftime in the men's bathroom that doubled as a locker room.

At the Stardust Ball in May 1954, Charles was crowned king of the ball. (Suzanne McQueen was queen.) Charles attended Cornell University. He married Esther Virginia Bohrer (1938–) in Sodus in July 1956. Esther selected Sheila Cromback of Marion as maid of honor. Donald Hartley was the best man. Esther's parents were Walter (1910–1987) and Virginia Albert Bohrer (1915–2008) of Sodus Point. Charles and Esther had four children. In recent years the couple lived in Sodus Point.

Edwin Catchpole Jr., one of Vic's older brothers, lived with Vic and Kay in 1940. Edwin had served in the Army in World War I. He enlisted in July 1917 and served overseas in Co. C of the 26th Engineers from March 1918 to March 1919. Edwin was a small man weighing 105 pounds and standing 5'3" tall. In April 1938 Edwin took over management of the North Rose poolroom. In 1942 Edwin was—along with George and Florence Morris of Canandaigua, George and Doris Catchpole and their daughter Nancy—a Christmas Day guest of his brother Reg Catchpole, Shirley Catchpole, and their children: Lynda and Terry Catchpole. By July 1949 Edwin had left North Rose, but he returned to visit his father and his brothers. Edwin remarried in 1943 and then moved to Pittsburgh.

Claus, George & Mabel
34 North Huron Street, now 5084 North Huron—Built in 1915. Estimated value in 1940: $1,400.

George Earl Claus (1885–1953), 55, head of household, farm laborer, 12 weeks for $75.
Mabel E. Baxter Claus (1888–1983), 52, wife, bean picker at the Bean House, 42 weeks for $500.
Dorothy L. Claus (1923–2000), 16, daughter, student.

GEORGE AND MABEL CLAUS (rhymes with "moss") each completed the sixth grade. George was a farm laborer who aspired to work as a carpenter. Mabel was a bean picker at the Bean House and a popular babysitter. George, a slim man weighing 110 lb. and 5'5" tall, was the son of Daniel E. Claus (ca. 1860–1910), a shoemaker, and Clara A. Davenport Claus (1863–1887); they married in May 1883.

Mabel was the daughter of Orselah Williba Baxter (1846–1896), a farmer, and Mary Ruffino Otto Baxter (1854–1940). In December 1914 George and Mabel married; they lived with Mabel's mother in Huron. Mabel was a dressmaker when she married. George farmed. By 1920, George and Mabel had moved to Lyons. They had a 5-year-old daughter, Thelma Mabel Claus (1915–1996). George worked as a house carpenter. Around 1923, a second daughter, Dorothy L., joined the Claus family. The family had moved to Wolcott; George continued to work as a carpenter. By 1930 the Clauses had moved to Huron. They took in a boarder, Frank J. Grove, who was an electrician for the Postal Telegraph. George operated a truck farm in 1930.

In October 1943, George fell from a scaffold and suffered a concussion. Mabel was active in the Kappa Phi class of the Methodist Church. In October 1954 John and Verda Briggs of Calgary, Alberta, Canada, visited Mabel after George's death in 1953.

Thelma married Leon Vernoy (1918–2005) in June 1939. Leon's parents were Hugh Vernoy (ca. 1896–1930) and Alta Candace Seager Vernoy (1893–1979). (See "Vernoy, Leon & Thelma.") Dorothy married Howard M. "Dick" Mierke (ca. 1916–1982) in 1946. Howard was the son of Lewis and Minnie Mierke of Lyons. A decade earlier, Howard had had an exceptional high school basketball career. In the 1934 season, the Lyons team was 22-and-0 going into the sectionals at the University of Rochester. They lost in the semifinals. The next season Howard won a spot as a forward on the second *Rochester Democrat and Chronicle* all-sectional hardwood squad.

Howard worked at the John L. Klug Corporation of Rochester from 1938 to 1978. That company designed and built factories. In March 1949 Dorothy lived in Niagara Falls and Howard lived in Palmyra. In May 1949 George, Mabel, and Dorothy went on a month-long trip to San Francisco. The Mierkes lived in Charleroi, Pennsylvania, in 1950. In 1954 the Mierkes lived in Corning. That December both the Vernoys and the Mierkes visited Mabel, who had been widowed the year before. In July 1958 Mabel married Albert Day. (See "Day, Albert & Maude.") Albert moved into the Claus home.

Clingerman, Ralph & Madeline

Gray Street, likely the "Beehive" apartment building. 1940 monthly rent: $7.
Ralph W. I. Clingerman (1910–1968), 29, head of household, automobile salesman, 50 weeks for $1,200.
Madeline B. Foisia Clingerman (1911–1993), 28, wife, homemaker and apple sorter, 12 weeks for $175.
Lenard Carlton Clingerman (1929–1998), 10, son, student. (Lenard sometimes used the surname of his stepfather, Ralph, though his last name was actually Foisia.)

RALPH COMPLETED EIGHT YEARS of school and worked as an automobile salesman. Madeline likewise completed the standard eight years of grammar school and worked part-time as an apple sorter at the Cold Storage. She was seeking a better job in 1940. Madeline was the daughter of Jay Charles Foisia (1884–1934), a house painter, and Francis "Fannie" Sarah Kirky Foisia (1889–1933).

Ralph was born in Maryland in April 1910. Ralph's mother was Agnes Virginia Clingerman (1883–1974); his father, Thomas Clingerman (1875–1930), was a laborer at a fruit farm. Thomas and Agnes Clingerman were half-first cousins, meaning they had one grandparent in common. It is legal for half-cousins to marry throughout the

United States. However, they were not as closely related as it would seem because their fathers were half-brothers. Agnes and Thomas had a daughter, Rosa May, who passed away in 1909 at age 2. Agnes and her sister, Maggie Ellen Clingerman, both lived in Bedford County, Pennsylvania. Maggie died in 1914, and soon after, Agnes ran off to Ohio with her late sister's husband, Edmond Franklin Smith (1887–1928). Meanwhile, Maggie's brother and sister-in-law took over the responsibility of raising Edmond and Maggie's two young daughters. Edmond and Agnes had a daughter, Thelma Grace Smith (1915–1991). Agnes's other children—Roy Cecil (1900–1971), Millard Harrison (1902–1966), and Emma Pleasant Virginia (1904–1979), and Ralph—searched for their mother for years. Around 1975 they found their half-sister, Thelma, living in Cleveland, Ohio, but Agnes had passed by then, as had Roy.

In 1916 Thomas wed Frances "Effie" Foreback Clingerman (1893–1983) in Morgantown, West Virginia. In 1920 Ralph lived in Hagerstown, Maryland, with his father, Thomas; his stepmother, Effie; his brother, Roy Cecil; his half-sister, Helen (1917–1991); and his half-brother, Jacob. Jacob died in France during the last year of the Second World War.

By 1924 the family had moved to North Rose, and it was in that year that Ralph, then 14, shot himself through the hand while playing with a gun. Dr. Roney treated the wound, which he deemed "not serious." In August 1929 Ralph was in a car accident in Butler. He swore out a warrant against Ernest Loveless, charging him with reckless driving, driving while intoxicated, and subsequent assault. Loveless paid a $15 fine plus the cost of damages. The *Lake Shore News* noted about the Town of Butler, "It is said the Federal authorities are now looking into the Butler speakeasy, and trouble is brewing for their proprietors."

In 1930 Ralph lived with his older brother Roy Clingerman and his family in Huron. Roy was a farmer; Ralph was unemployed for a period of time before working for Charles Faye Lunkenheimer at his auto repair garage in Red Creek. He then gained work as a car salesman for Zonneville Motors in Williamson and, afterward, Clyde Auto Sales. During his time at Zonneville Motors, Ralph sold a 1952 truck to the Mitchell family. The family kept the truck until the 1990s, when they sold it to Rick Patchen, who still uses it today. The Clingermans were one of the first of many families to move from the Mason-Dixon Line area (the counties near the Pennsylvania-Maryland border, especially Bedford County, Pennsylvania) to the North Rose region. Some of the other such productive immigrants bore the names Caldwell, Carnell, Divelbliss, Hartley, Hendershot, Poole, and Spade.

Madeline's mother, Fannie Foisia, died in May 1933 at the age of 44. Ralph, Madeline, and Ralph's aunt and uncle, Helen and Marion Clingerman, visited Ralph's grandmother Emma Smith Clingerman (1862–1949) in Niagara Falls in November 1942. Emma, who was born in Bedford County, Pennsylvania, was living in Niagara Falls with her youngest daughter, Flora Mae Monroe. Marion and Helen owned much of the property on the Bonnie Castle shoreline located on the southeastern side of Sodus Bay.

In February 1945 Madeline received a visit from her brother Lyle Foisia, who was stationed with the Navy on Treasure Island, San Francisco. Lenard Clingerman joined the Army in 1949. After completing basic training, he spent a furlough with his parents in April.

In July 1950 local firefighters chose Ralph to be the chairman of the annual North Rose Fireman's Field Days at which thousands were expected to attend. Ralph opened a used car sales business and garage in Red Creek in 1958 called Ralph Clingerman's New and Used Car Service. In April 1959 Ralph won election as president of the Rose Chamber of Commerce.

Dagle, Albert & Minnie

88 North Main Street, now 5124 North Main—Built in 1860. Estimated value in 1940: $2,000.

Albert Dagle (1866–1955), 74, head of household, retired.
Minnie A. Lamb Dagle (1871–1960), 69, wife, homemaker.
Benjamin Samuel Barnes (1897–1991), 42, son-in-law, plumber, hardware store, 52 weeks for $1,300.
Ola B. Dagle Barnes (1896–1978), 43, daughter, unemployed.

Minnie's parents were Myron John Lamb (1843–1914) and Dorcas Anna Weeks (1845–1927). Albert's parents were Charles Dagle (1821–1894) and Anna D. Lamo (1846–). Albert and Minnie married in 1892. Two of Benjamin's brothers, Earl and Linwood, also lived in North Rose in 1940. (See "Barnes, Earl & Lillian" for more information about his family.)

We were unable to obtain much more than the cursory information provided by the census for this household. If you have information about the Dagles, see page 32.

Dagle, Cora

64 North Main Street, now 5094 North Main—Built in 1900. Estimated value in 1940: $2,000.
Cora J. Lamb Dagle (1872–1968), 67, head of household, homemaker.
(Henry) Addison J. Lamb (1850–1941), 89, father, retired farmer.

Cora Dagle, a homemaker and a widow, shared a home with her elderly father, Addison Lamb. Cora had completed eight years of school, while her father attended six. She was a member of the North Rose Methodist Church, where she participated in the Women's Home Missionary Society, the Loyalty Class, the WSCS, and in Sunday School administration. In 1892 she married Addison Dagle (1864–1939), and four years later they had a son, Mervin Lewis Dagle (see "Dagle, Mervin and Esther"). (Both Cora's husband and father had the given name Addison.)

Cora's late husband Addison was the child of immigrants. His father (Charles) was born in France and his mother in Ireland. He lived in Clyde in 1870 and Lyons in 1880. He worked on his father's farm in Huron in 1892. In 1900 Addison worked his own farm in Huron, but the Dagle family lived on a different farm in Rose in 1910.

By 1920, the Dagles were living on South Main Street. In August 1936, Clyde Lamb and Helen Cornelia Vanatta Lamb of Detroit visited the Dagles at their cottage on LeRoy Island.

Addison Dagle died in June 1939 at the age of 74. Their granddaughter Virginia spent a week with her grandmother Cora the following September and often visited her grandmother and great-grandfather thereafter. In 1942 Cora visited Cygnet, Ohio, and Detroit.

(Henry) Addison Lamb grew up on a farm and was a grandson of Isaac Lamb, for whom Lamb's Corners (later, North Rose) was named. In December 1871 he married Eliza Jenna "Jennie" McQueen (1853–1933). Cora was their only child.

(Henry) Addison Lamb's occupation was "farm laborer" in the 1900 census, "farmer" in the 1910 census, and he was still farming in 1930—at the age of 79—though he and his wife had moved to North Main Street in North Rose. That year he picked a remarkable 306 pounds of cherries in one day in the orchard of his niece, Luna Seager. And he attended the lavish 60th wedding anniversary celebration of George and Maude Ball hosted by their daughter Myrta Salter in December 1938. Addison died in 1941.

This family confounds historians by the inconsistent spelling of their surname. About half the mentions of their surname are spelled "Dagel" and the other half "Dagle."

Dagle, Mervin & Esther

4940 Main Street. 1940 monthly rent: $16.
Mervin Merrion Lewis Dagle (1896–1978), 44, head of household, farmer, self-employed, 52 weeks for $1,500.
Esther Louise Seager Wagner Dagle (1901–1999), 37, wife, homemaker.
Lorraine Wagner (1925–2022), 14, stepdaughter, student.

THE ONLY SON OF ADDISON AND CORA DAGLE (see "Dagle, Cora"), Mervin purchased a home shortly before marrying Harriet Katherine DeNeef (1899–) of Sodus in January 1920. The couple had one daughter, Virginia H. Dagle (1921–2016). In 1938 Mervin married a second time, to Esther Louise Seager Wagner (1902–1999). who had a daughter, Lorraine Wagner. This was a second marriage for Esther as well. Her first husband was Earl Frederick Henry Wagner (1904–1944); their daughter, Lorraine Wagner, was living with Mervin and Esther in 1940. Esther's parents were Alvie B. Seager (1875–1902) and Pearl R. Knox (1879–1970). (See "Davenport, Roy & Pearl.")

Virginia was living in Sodus by July 1940, and had married Bruce Morton of Sodus by October of the following year. Lorraine married Charlie Wilson in 1946. By 1950 Mervin was a florist.

We were unable to obtain much more than the cursory information provided by the census for this household. If you have information about this family, see page 32.

Darling, Mildred

1940 monthly rent: $8.
Mildred Riesdorph Darling (1914–2000), 25, head of household, homemaker, trimmer at the canning factory, 12 weeks for $200.
Theresa Mildred Darling (1936–2008), 3, daughter.

JOURNALISTS FIRST TURNED THEIR ATTENTION to Mildred Riesdorph at the 1915 Flower Festival held by the Ladies Aid Society of the Junius Presbyterian Church. (Junius is in Seneca County.) The fun included a "baby show." Mildred, aged about 1, triumphed in the "most noisy" competition.

Mildred attended school in Waterloo. She had completed two years of high school and worked part-time at the Salter Canning Company. Mildred married William Darling (1914–2002) in March 1934. Mildred was the daughter of Carl A. Riesdorph (1884–1960) and Josephine C. Bulson Riesdorph (1894–1938). Carl was a farmer in Junius. William's parents were Arthur W. Darling (1889–1954) and Grace B. Washburn Darling (1894–1962). Arthur was a road worker in Huron and later a farmer.

Mildred and William had a daughter, Theresa, in 1936, but soon the parents were living apart. After separating from Mildred, William lived in Sodus. Selective Service drafted William into the armed forces in May 1942.

Mildred lived in Newark in 1941. That year she visited Paul and Julia Richardson in North Rose and on another outing visited Paul and Charlotte Marshall. In April 1945 Mildred married Jefferson Albert Sherman (1905–1971), son of Orin Henry Sherman (1866–1932) and Caroline "Carrie" Isabelle Beam Sherman (1868–1932). Orin was a farmer who also served Wayne County as its sheriff. Mildred was active in the Rebekah Lodge in North Rose. She worked her way up to deputy director of the Rebekahs for Wayne County.

When Mildred's brother John Riesdorph received an honorable discharge from the Army in June 1945, he lived with Mildred, Theresa, and Jefferson. The next month the foursome moved from the Marshall farm to the Bly house on North Main Street. Mildred became a Home Bureau leader. In 1945 John moved to Cuba (Allegany County). In January 1946, while driving to visit his sister's family, John ran his car into a pole near the Clyde school. John escaped injury, but his car was a wreck.

In July 1947 Mildred was the chairman of the Red Cross swimming course. On the Labor Day holiday in 1947, Jefferson and Mildred vacationed in Ocean Grove, New Jersey, with James and Barbara Campbell. Jefferson was a machinist at Gleason Works in Rochester, but the couple lived in Palmyra. (Gleason's was a prominent manufacturer of gears and other mechanical parts.)

In December 1948, the Shermans were in a one-car accident on Marion-Newark Road. The Sherman family did not suffer a scratch, although the car rolled over twice. The vehicle sustained only slight damage. Jefferson and Mildred raised two foster daughters: Lois Patricia Johnson and Carol Ann Johnson. Lois married Raymond Smith and lived in Manchester (Ontario County). Carol Ann married Lawrence Wahl and lived in Sodus. In August 1950 Mildred visited her father, who was ill at the Waterloo Hospital.

In 1951 Theresa spent a week in Cuba, New York, with John and Darlene Riesdorph and their family. Mildred, Jefferson, and Theresa later moved to Newark. Theresa graduated from Marion High School in 1956. She was an enthusiastic bowler and baker. Theresa found work in the food preparation department of the Newark State School.

After Jefferson's death, Mildred moved to Sodus.

Davenport, Roy & Pearl

46 Gray Street, now 5102 Gray Street—Built in 1870. Estimated value in 1940: $1,400.
Leroy "Roy" F. Davenport (1885–1949), 55, head of household, foreman, Bean House, O. A. Skutt Company, 50 weeks for $1,250.
Pearl R. Knox Davenport (1879–1970), 59, wife, homemaker.

ROY DAVENPORT AND PEARL KNOX were married in Sodus 1908. Both had completed the typical eight years of school. It was a second marriage for Pearl; she had married Alvie Seager (1875–1902) in 1897 but was widowed in 1902, just a year after the birth of their daughter, Esther Louise Seager (1901–1999). In 1940 Esther was living in North Rose with her second husband. (See "Dagle, Mervin & Esther.")

We were unable to obtain much more than the cursory information provided by the census for this household. If you have information about this family, see page 32.

Davis, Clifford & Lena

6 Merwin Street, now 10336 Short Street—Built in 1927. Estimated value in 1940: $1,500.
Clifford Lewis Davis (1904–1979), 36, head of household, night watchman, 30 weeks for $800.
Lena B. Garton Davis (1903–1972), 36, wife, factory laborer, 24 weeks for $275.
Elizabeth "Betty Jane" Davis (ca. 1926–), 13, daughter, student.
William "Billy" Davis (1935–2022), 5, son.

Betty Davis, NRCS Class of 1946

CLIFFORD AND LENA DAVIS were married in May 1926. Clifford was the night watchman at the Canning Factory, but he was looking for a better job. Lena worked seasonally as a laborer at the Canning

Factory, but she was also looking for better work. Clifford's maternal grandfather was born in Germany. In 1930 Clifford had been a farm laborer and Lena was a homemaker. Clifford finished eighth grade and Lena completed the ninth.

The Davises had two children, Elizabeth and William. Betty Davis graduated from NRCS in the class of 1946. She married Henry Hoad in October 1949 and gave birth to a daughter in September 1950. Betty's brother Billy is the current owner of their parents' former home.

Lena Davis, Jessie Hutchings and her son Glenn, Charlotte Alice McOmber-Marshall, and Harriet Anna Harris McOmber took a day trip to Rochester to see the world-famous, fairy-tale-inspired dollhouse that Colleen Moore—a hugely famous silent film star—spent nearly $500,000 building. The actress ultimately used the dollhouse to raise more than $650,000 for children's charities during the Depression. Currently valued at more than $7 million, the dollhouse is a fairy castle approximately the size of an eight-foot cube. It contains more than 1,500 miniatures, including handmade tapestries, a miniature library of more than 100 real books (including an 1840 Bible that was the smallest ever printed), numerous historic relics including a 4,000-year-old Syrian vase and a 2,500-year-old Roman bust, and even chandeliers made of gold and decorated with precious gems. In 1949 Ms. Moore donated the castle to the Chicago's Museum of Science and Industry, where it is still on display. For more information and to see pictures of the castle, search for Colleen Moore at msichicago.org.

In January 1941, Clifford, Lena, and Lena's sister, Dorothy Garton, hosted a surprise birthday party for Lena's father, George Garton, and 35 of his friends. That December, Lena and Clifford were attendants at Dorothy's wedding to Roy Sherman of Huron. In January 1943 the *Lake Shore News* noted that George was spending some time with his daughter Lena and her husband.

In March 1944 the 82-year-old George disappeared after he was spotted walking along the road late at night. The family offered a reward for locating him, and Frank Quereau found George's body in his cherry orchard. George had died of exposure. It's not known why he decided to visit the orchard in the middle of night, but he might have been drawn there because it was the place where his only son, Ross, had lost his life when a dynamite blast, set to clear the land where the future orchard would be planted, had startled a horse that Ross had been leading.

In addition to Lena, George was survived by three other daughters: Maude Ball of North Rose (see "Ball, George & Maude"), Mattie Garton of Rochester, and Dorothy Sherman of Sodus.

Davis, John & Jessie

"Beehive" Apartments, Gray Street—Monthly 1940 rent: $8.
John Heck Davis (1907–1986), 32, head of household, laborer in the Canning Factory, 25 weeks for $350.
Jessie M. Shortsleeve Davis (1910–1979), 29, wife, homemaker, bean picker, 24 weeks for $250.
Dorothy Jean Davis (1929–2005), 10, daughter, student.

Dorothy Davis, NRCS Class of 1946

JOHN AND JESSIE HAD EACH COMPLETED eight years of grammar school. John worked as a laborer at the Salter Canning Co.; Jessie was a bean picker in the O. A. Skutt Co. Bean House. John and Jessie married in August 1928. Their only child, Dorothy, was born the next year. Two years later, John was a day laborer and Jessie was a homemaker.

John grew up in Huron. His parents were Lewis Hiram Davis (1864–1934) and Margaret "Maggie" C. Heck Davis (1871–1940). Lewis was a farmer. Jessie was also from Huron. Her father, Henry Shortsleeve (1883–1969), was a farm laborer. Her mother, Lucy Day Shortsleeve (1888–1924), was a homemaker. In April 1954 Jessie helped care for her father, who had suffered a heart attack. He lived in Lummisville, a hamlet southeast of Wolcott.

In the summer of 1947, Dorothy was living in Rochester. That July, at the North Rose Methodist Church, Dorothy married Raymond Kelley Jr. (1928–1988), son of Raymond G. Kelley (1902–1959) and Ruth M. Curtis Kelley (1902–1951) of Wolcott. Dorothy and Raymond lived on Wright Street in Wolcott. In November 1947 they had a daughter named Diane Elaine Kelley. Their marriage ended in divorce. Raymond Kelley Jr. remarried and had two sons by 1956. He lived in Hannibal (Oswego County). Later his family moved to Wolcott where his parents lived.

Dorothy's second marriage in 1951 was to Anthony Rossario Comella (1920–2008), son of Phillip Comella (1888–1971), a papermaker, and Maria "Mary" Comella (1891–1971) of Arcadia. Both Phillip and Mary were born in Italy. (They died just a few days apart.) Anthony served as a staff sergeant in the Army Air Corps. He fought in China, Burma, and India. After he completed his Army service, Anthony worked for over 49 years for Billota Enterprises as an amusement machine repairman. Anthony and his brother Joseph J. Comella were partners in the fruit and vegetable company Comella Brothers.

Dorothy and Anthony had a son, Philip John Comella (1953–1994). Dorothy and her husband Anthony retired to Florida in 1994.

Dorothy's daughter Diane Kelley visited her grandparents, John and Jessie, in February 1951 and May 1954. John and Jessie Davis and Diane Kelley paid a visit to Jessie's brother Ted Shortsleeve and his family in Ontario in February 1951. Diane lived in Chicago in 1967. She visited Dorothy and Anthony on Mother's Day of that year. Diane married Jerold Goldstein.

Day, Albert & Maude

6 Gray Street, now 5020 Gray—Built in 1850. Estimated value in 1940: $1,000.

Albert Henry Day (1879–1973), 60, head of household, retired.
Maude M. Lapp Day (1887–1957), 52, wife, bean picker at the Bean House, 40 weeks for $400.

ALBERT COMPLETED EIGHT YEARS of school. He was a large man, standing 6 feet tall and weighing 240 pounds. Maude also completed eight years of school and was a picker at O. A. Skutt Company. Albert and Maude married in October 1901. Albert was a native of Huron. His parents were James Day (1817–1880) and Lucretia Matilda Pettit Day

(1840–1892). James was a farm laborer, Matilda a homemaker.

In 1900 Maude was a housekeeper at age 13 in the Orsen and Mabel Gillett home in Huron. She was the daughter of Mathias Elias Lapp Sr. (1854–1906) and Samantha Wood Lapp (1858–1919). Mathias and Samantha married in Wayne County in 1872.

Mathias Lapp Sr. (Maude's father) and his son (Maude's eldest brother) Mathias Lapp Jr. were, before Christmas 1893, arrested in Port Glasgow, a Huron hamlet now called Resort. In the illicit, regular Sunday boxing matches, the son was getting the worst of a bout and—with his father's encouragement—introduced a knife or other sharp object into the contest. Mathias Lapp Sr. shouted instructions to his son, "Cut his heart out." Mathias Lapp Jr. cut his opponent less lethally—on his ear. Police arrested both Lapps. The prosecutor soon dropped charges against the father, but the law landed harder on the son. He served 60 days in the Monroe County Penitentiary upon his conviction for assault in the third degree. (Reports do not specify whether these unregulated fights were bare-knuckle or gloved.)

In 1905, Albert, Maude, and their 2-year-old daughter, Katherine Maude Day (1904–1989), lived in Huron. Albert was a day laborer. In 1915, the three Days lived in the Town of Sodus. Albert was a farm laborer. By 1920, Albert, Maude, and Katherine lived on Lake Bluff Road in Huron. Albert was a farmer. In 1925 Albert and Maude lived in North Rose. Albert served as a constable. In 1930 Albert and Maude lived in Huron, and Albert was again a laborer. Albert and Maude lived in Helen Munson's home while she spent the winter of 1930–31 in Sodus.

Edward Lapp, Maude's brother, committed suicide on his Huron farm in April 1936—perhaps in despair about his wife's health. Albert, along with Ralph Chase, discovered Edward's body. Mr. Lapp's dog led Albert and Ralph to the deceased man. Albert and Maude's house burned to the ground after a lightning strike in August 1936. In March 1938 the Days purchased a home and lot—formerly owned by the late Wellington Pond—in Huron near the East Bay "Short Bridge." Albert and Maude moved to their home on Gray Street less than two years later.

Katherine married James Ross Thompson (1891–2002) and had a son, Richard Day Thompson (1921–2002). Ross was the son of Frank and Anna Thompson of Hanover (Chautauqua County). He was a machinist, then a partner molder at a factory. In 1929, Katherine, Ross, and Richard lived in Silver Creek (Chautauqua County). Ross and Richard visited Katherine's parents for Christmas. After the holiday Katherine moved westward, and all local references to her dry up after that year. She died in Dayton, Ohio, in 1989.

In 1930 Ross married 19-year-old Clara B. Householder of Huron, who then moved to Silver Creek with Ross and Richard. Ross and Clara had a daughter, Mary Jane, ca. 1934. Clara gained work as a seamstress. She lived to be a 63-year member of the Order of the Eastern Star. Ross worked as a millwright in a shovel factory.

In August 1942 Albert and Maude visited their grandson Richard before he joined the Army. The Days purchased the Charles and Anna Leaird (pronounced "laird") home on Aldrich Avenue. The Leairds were moving to Wolcott Street in Rose. In July 1944 the Days visited their grandson Tech. Sgt. Richard Thompson on furlough at his parents' home in Silver Creek. Richard later received his discharge after three-and-one-half years of Army service. He visited his grandparents in North Rose in January 1946. The Days sold their house on Aldrich Avenue in March 1946 to Lloyd and Ruth Porter.

Albert and Maude attended their grandson's wedding to June Washburn in Silver Creek in April 1948. Albert purchased his brother Martin Day's home in Alton in December 1948. This purchase followed Martin's wife's death. Martin's wife, Lydia "Lida" Lapp Day, was also Maude's sister. Albert and Maude moved to Alton in April 1949. Then they returned to North Rose in April 1957—purchasing the Frank Thompson house on South Main Street.

Around 1962 Richard married a second time, to Yasu Kashiwada (1931–1998). Richard retired as an international specialist at Frederick Electronics in Frederick, Maryland.

Deady, Charles

4987 South Main Street. 1940 monthly rent: $11.
Charles Swift Deady (1857–1945), 82, head of household, retired carpenter, builder, and home designer, self-employed.
Gertrude "Gertie" L. Gilfilian (1881–1960), 57, lodger, housekeeper.

CHARLES WAS A RETIRED CARPENTER who completed one year of college. Gertrude completed eight years of school. She worked as a homemaker—perhaps for room and board.

Charles grew up on a large farm in Huron. He was the son of James W. Deady (1823–1910) and Caroline "Carrie" Swift Deady (1834–1918). In July 1878 Charles purchased a beautiful top buggy in Lyons. (A top buggy was a horse-drawn conveyance with a convertible roof and a single wide seat that could fit three people abreast.) In October 1879 Charles married Phoebe V. Lake (1862–1938), and he farmed in Huron. Phoebe was the daughter of David Lake (1835–1911), a farmer, and Laura Louisa Merrell Lake (1834–1897).

Charles lost a full hop house—with a $2,000 harvest inside—to fire in November 1880. (Hops are an ingredient used in beer-making. They add flavor, bitterness, and stability to the brew.) Charles had purchased insurance for only about 25 percent of the crop's value. Revenue from a healthy onion crop helped Charles pay his bills.

In February 1883 the congregation of the Huron Presbyterian Church threw a surprise party for Phoebe. They gave Phoebe, their longtime organist, a couch, a rocker, and a hanging lamp. Phoebe and Charles divorced in Larimer County in 1886. Charles married again—a bit early to conform with the law if these dates are correct—in October 1885. That marriage to Ida Bell Lansing-Phillipson, like his first, was short-lived. Ida moved to her parents' home. Her father and mother were George H. Lansing (1850–1925) and Josephine Emma E. Osborn Lansing (1853–1936). They lived in Wolcott and then in Canandaigua.

In December 1889 Charles was elected to the post of trustee of Rose School District, No. 5. In this era many school districts consisted of one school—often a one-room schoolhouse. In his first year as a trustee, Charles was the defendant in a lawsuit by Lucy E. Hand. He refused to pay Lucy a teacher's salary of $10 per week that she anticipated receiving for her contract to teach at Rose School No. 5 for a 16-week semester.

Charles's position was that the contract Miss Hand signed with the late David L. Benjamin was invalid because his election was illegal. Benjamin had attended a public meeting to choose a trustee. An inebriated friend nominated him as the trustee. Not waiting for other nominees, Benjamin rallied a quick vote. Only one person responded in the affirmative. Benjamin did not ask for nays and declared himself to be the winner. Most people attending the meeting took his actions as a jest. The meeting came to order and, after following standard procedures, James E. Benjamin was elected trustee. (The two Benjamins do not seem to be closely related.) However, a few days after the meeting, David visited James and intimidated him with threats until he surrendered the district books. David negotiated a teaching contract with Miss Hand. The acting trustee of the district, William James, would not permit Hand to carry out the contract. David died before Hand sued to get the money that she expected to earn. Hand won in a justice court trial. Charles appealed the verdict, and at a County Court proceeding, the jury hung, thereby indicating that she would not receive her pay. Hand appealed to the State Supreme Court. (In New York State, the lowest state court is called the Supreme Court.) The final decision was in Hand's favor and she recovered $142 and court costs.

By 1900 Charles lived as a boarder in Sodus and worked as a carpenter. In 1902 Charles acquired a new, fast naphtha-fueled launch which he sold that very same year. (A launch was a large speedboat.) The following year Charles built a sizable workshop on land he purchased near his home on Main Street in North Rose. In March 1904 Charles moved to Rose Valley and lived with his widowed mother Caroline, his sister Theresa, and his brother William.

In the spring of 1904 Charles built a boathouse on LeRoy Island for J.M. Decker. In April 1906 Charles and John Correll had begun building a North Rose home for Leonard Worden. Charles and Allan Proseus built and donated the pulpit to the First Presbyterian Church of North Rose. They were gratefully recognized at the first service held at the church in November of that year. By the summer of 1907, Charles built a 22-foot motorboat to pilot on Sodus Bay.

In January 1912 Charles sold a house he had recently built to Mr. Ever Chase of North Huron. Charles planned another project when he purchased a building lot from Addison Dagle later that month.

In October 1921 Charles injured his eye with a board while he was working on a sawmill. In June 1930 Charles hurt three fingers on his planing mill.

Charles's lodger Gertie grew up in the Town of Rose. She worked as a servant by age 18. Her father, William J. Gilfilian (1846–1931), was a Civil War veteran who worked as a farm laborer. William was born in Canada and immigrated to the United States in 1857. Gertie's mother was Sedate E. Corey Gilfilian (1848–1922). She was born in Pinckney Corners (Lewis County). Gertie lived with her sister Nellie and Nellie's husband, George Howes, in Rochester in the 1910s. She worked as a laundress in Rochester.

In October 1918, after Charles's mother died, Gertie and her mother moved to North Rose from Rochester to keep house for Charles. By April 1926 Gertie seemed to have become a part of the Deady family. She shopped in Rochester with Charles's nieces, Eva (1890–1968) and Alice Deady (1896–1964).

Four Gilfilians—Gertie, her brother Henry, her sister Nellie Howes, and their niece Kathleen Manion—traveled together to Canada to visit relatives. Gertie attended Kathleen's graduation from the Practical School of Nursing in Rochester. Gertrude temporarily moved to Rochester in August 1957. After spending the winter with Vincent and Gertrude Quinlan, Gertie Gilfilian returned to North Rose. She died in the Monroe County Infirmary in August 1960. Her funeral was in North Rose.

At the time of his death in 1945, Charles had been a member of the Odd Fellows for 53 years. That organization conducted the burial service.

Dean, Charlie & Anna

5023 Gray Street—Estimated 1940 value: $1,500.
Charles "Charlie" Edwin Dean (1891–1963), 48, head of household, proprietor, 52 weeks, self-employed.
Anna Edna Dickinson Dean (1893–1968), 47, wife, homemaker.
Ella Adelaide Parslow Dean (1861–1946), 78, mother, homemaker.
Ruth Irene Dean Barton (1913–2000), 27, daughter, bean picker, 40 weeks for $400.
Marian E. Dean (1921–1978), 19, daughter, apple picker, 8 weeks for $75.
Robert Edgar "Eddie" Dean (1928–2010), 11, son, student.
Mary Ruth Louise Barton (1932–1945), 7, granddaughter, student.
James Nelson Dean (1935–2004), 4, son.
Doris J. Barton (1936–), 3, granddaughter.

FOUR GENERATIONS OF THE DEAN FAMILY lived in this household. Although Ella was the owner of the home, her son, being male, was considered by the census enumerator to be head of the household.

Ella was a homemaker with six years of formal education. She was the widow of Edgar W. Dean (1857–1918), a farm laborer. Edgar and Ella had married in 1881. Their only son, Charlie, operated a garage in the lot just south of the Dean home at the southwest corner of Gray Street and Railroad Avenue. Alan Mitchell remembers the gas station as being a hangout for the locals and recalls that his father always picked up his copy of the Sunday *Rochester Democrat and Chronicle* there. The gas station had a soda pop machine that Alan frequented.

Charlie's wife was Anna Dickinson Dean, who had nine years of school. In 1911, as a teenager, Anna Dickinson worked in the North Rose telephone office. The following year she worked at the local bakery and began working in the North Rose post office. (For more about Anna's family, see "Dickinson, Robert & Emma.")

Four of Charlie and Anna's five children lived with them in Ella's house. Their eldest, Ruth Barton, was a bean picker at O. A. Skutt Company. Ruth completed three years of high school. Her two young daughters, Mary and Doris Barton, were also part of the large household. Ruth's husband, Peter Raymond Barton (1909–1980), was not living in the multigenerational home during the time of the April 1940 census but soon reunited with Ruth and their two daughters.

Charlie and Anna's second daughter, Hazel Maude Dean (1915–1997) was a nurse at Highland Hospital in Rochester so was not living in North Rose. In September 1941 Hazel married Leslie Raymond Balch (1914–1982) at the Asbury Methodist Church in Rochester. Charlie and Anna's third daughter, Marian, completed eight years of school and was a seasonal apple picker. Charlie and Anna also had two young sons: Eddie, who was in the sixth grade, and James, who was too young to attend school. The age difference between the eldest and youngest child in the Dean family was an impressive 23 years.

Ella found satisfaction in her work with the Missionary Society of the Presbyterian Church. In April 1921 she won election as the treasurer of the Ladies' Guild of her church. Ella, Charlie, Marian, and Eddie drove to Muskegon, Michigan, to call on Ella's brother George Parslow in September 1942. Ella died in March 1946.

Charlie completed the standard eight years of school. He became ill with the flu during the pandemic of 1918. Upon his recovery he opened the aforementioned gas station. Charlie won election as first assistant chief of the Salter Hose and Chemical Fire Company. He also became a school bus driver. Anna was a leader of the Home and Foreign Missionary Society of the North Rose Presbyterian Church.

Ruth married Peter Barton of Utica in November 1930. In March 1932, Peter and Ruth moved into the North Rose home formerly occupied by William and Fannie Marriott. The Bartons moved to the Detroit area in January 1937. Ruth and her two daughters, Mary and Doris, left Detroit to spend a month with Charlie and Anna in July 1937. The Barton family returned to North Rose in April 1938. They moved into the house on the corner of Gray and Caroline Streets in February 1939. In July 1940 the Bartons bought, from Claude Brown, a home on the northern end of Gray Street. In September 1941 Ruth held a bridal shower for her sister Hazel. Peter was in the Army by September 1943. The Bartons sold their home to William and Edna

Hoad in February 1946. The next month Mary was on the honor roll in the sixth grade. She was a Girl Scout. Mary died in August 1945 at 13 years old after being ill for only 10 days. Peter was a sergeant stationed in Germany when his daughter died. He returned home from Europe in October 1945. The Bartons' second daughter, Doris, was on the North Rose Honor Roll in April 1950. She switched schools and won a place on the Clyde junior varsity cheerleading squad in November 1950.

In May 1946, Anna, Marian, and Eddie traveled to Detroit to visit Ruth and Peter Barton and their daughter, Doris. (Ruth and Peter's daughter Mary died in 1945.) The group also visited auto factories. In February 1947 Anna visited Ruth, Peter, and Doris in Willow Run, Michigan. In July 1947, Charlie and Anna Dean entertained at a family picnic where much of their family was together for the first time in some years. Present were PFC Robert E. Dean, Ruth and Peter Barton and daughter Doris, Hazel and Leslie Balch, and Marian and her beau, Frank O'Keefe.

Charlie and Anna's daughter Hazel Dean was a piano student of Estella Roney (see "Roney, Estella"). Hazel found summer work in Canandaigua in 1932. In September 1933 Hazel gained a job with the Iona Sanatorium in Rochester for the coming year. Hazel received a high school diploma in 1934. She studied nursing at the Park Avenue Hospital in Rochester, starting in January 1935. She graduated as a registered nurse in June 1937. Several family members attended the graduation ceremonies. Hazel spent six months in further study at Fordham Hospital in New York City. Although Hazel soon worked at the Genesee County Hospital in Rochester, she often found time to pay visits to her parents in North Rose.

After marrying in 1941, Hazel and Leslie installed a large swimming pool in their backyard in Rochester. Home swimming pools were a rare luxury before the post-World War II period of prosperity. Leslie had been an outstanding swimmer in high school. That may have influenced their pool purchase decision. Leslie served in the Marine Corps from May 1944 to June 1946. In his civilian career, he was a salesman. By 1950, Leslie and Hazel had divorced and Leslie was living with his mother in her house in Rochester. Leslie married Helen Mary Reilly (1920–2011) in September 1956.

Hazel opened a nursing home in Clyde in 1950 in rented space—the former Helen Glen house—on West Genesee Street. Charlie and Anna and others in their family moved from North Rose to Clyde. Later Hazel married James Raney (1915–1969). It was the second marriage for James as well as for Hazel. He had a daughter from his first marriage, Nancy Raney (1936–1995). James and Hazel lived in Rochester. Hazel retired to Chandler, Arizona, after James's death. On Hazel's grave marker at Southside Cemetery in Red Creek, she is designated "Captain U.S. Army Korea." It seems likely that she was an officer in the Army Nursing Corps.

Charlie and Anna's daughter Marian spent nine weeks in the Iola Sanitarium in Rochester in 1932 following a complicated operation on her leg. Marian spent the winter of 1939–1940 in Florida. In December 1940 she accepted a job in Newark. Her boyfriend Frank O'Keefe enlisted in the armed forces in April 1942. Marian substituted for Mrs. Finch while she was taking a two-week break from operating the Finch Bakery in Clyde. Marian was active in the Rebekah Lodge. Frank worked as a substitute instructor at NRCS while the regular teacher, William Lundergun, was recuperating from an illness. Marian and Frank O'Keefe (1914–1983) married in January 1950.

Charlie and Anna's son Eddie was active in the Boy Scouts and spent a week in August 1942 at Camp Babcock-Hovey. He advanced to Boy Scout second class in December 1942. Eddie earned a baseball letter for the NRCS 1944 team. He also earned a letter in soccer in 1945–1946. He played a third sport, basketball, during the 1944–1945 NRCS academic year.

Eddie joined the Army in October 1946 and became a

In the 1945-46 school year, Eddie Dean (third from left) was the top scorer for the North Rose Central School basketball team, with 208 points.

member of the Signal Corps. He served in the Korean War. In December 1950 he wed Anna M. Priebe, daughter of Charles M. Priebe Sr. and Florence Priebe of 502 Vienna Street, Wolcott. Both the bride and the groom worked at the Newark State School. They lived in Wolcott and had a son named Robert E. Dean Jr.

James Dean, the youngest of Charlie and Anna's children, was also an active member of the Boy Scouts. In March 1949 James fell off his bicycle and broke his arm in three places.

Anna's father, Robert D. Dickinson (1869–1957), an early resident of North Rose—a carpenter and a garage operator—died in June 1957 at 88. He was the first fire chief of the North Rose Fire Department.

DeBack, Lawrence & Inez

North Main Street. 1940 monthly rent: $20.
Lawrence Harold DeBack (1901–1998), 38, head of household, utility representative, 52 weeks for $1,980.
Inez B. VanDerzell DeBack (1904–1994), 35, wife, homemaker.
Molly Rita DeBack (1934–), 5, daughter.

LAWRENCE HAD COMPLETED THE EIGHTH GRADE and worked as a rural representative for the Rochester Gas and Electric Company. Inez had completed one year of high school and worked as a homemaker. They married in August 1923.

Lawrence was a toddler when the DeBack family moved from Sodus to Penfield (Monroe County). In 1920 he lived and worked on the family farm on Fairport-Webster Road. His parents were Paul DeBack (1886–1932) and Jennie May DeCook DeBack (1877–1943). They married in 1898. Lawrence had a brother and two sisters.

In 1925 Lawrence and Inez lived with Inez's family, headed by her mother, Margaret S. Havert VanDerzell (1882–1978), a laundress who was born in The Netherlands. Inez's father, Frank VanDerzell (1877–1913), a teamster at a flour mill, had died when Inez was 9 years old. Also living in Margaret's house on Rochester Road in Penfield were Inez's sister Pearl (1908–2005) and her brother Raymond (1912–1972). Lawrence was an electrician, and Inez was a timekeeper. Inez taught church school at the Penfield Baptist Church in 1933. Their daughter Molly was born in 1934.

The DeBacks moved to North Rose in July 1937, with the plan of shifting to Wolcott when a suitable house was available. Inez was active in Unit 2 of the Village Home Bureau. By 1939 Lawrence had become the Rochester Gas and Electric farm service representative for the Sodus, Marion, and Wolcott areas. In January 1941 the DeBacks bought the Palmer house from Laverne Olmsted in preparation for a move to Wolcott. In November 1941 Inez entertained the Kappa Phi class of the North Rose Methodist Church. Soon, she was a member of the Wolcott Civic Club and led the junior choir at the Wolcott Baptist Church. Lawrence and Inez hosted a Fresh Air Fund child in July 1942. One year later, Lawrence was the 4-H Club agent for Wayne County. In September 1943 Inez headed the Public Health Committee of Wolcott, Huron, and Butler. As chairman of the Wolcott Salvage Committee, Lawrence led the scrap paper and tin can drives to support the war effort in the summer of 1944. In August 1945 Lawrence announced his candidacy for the Republican caucus's choice for Butler Town Council, but he failed to get the nomination. In February 1947 Inez became secretary for the newly formed Wayne County branch of the American Cancer Society. Lawrence served as Wolcott water commissioner in 1964 and 1965.

Molly attended 4-H camp with her future husband, Grady Youngman. Molly played on the Wolcott girls' basketball team in their 14–11 squeaker over North Rose. She graduated from Elmira College in 1956. That summer Molly was hired as a second-grade teacher in the new Red Creek elementary school.

In 1957 Molly married Graydon Allen Youngman (1933–2021), the son of William Abraham Arthur Youngman (1897–1983), a farmer, and Maria Frances VanLare Youngman (1899–1993) of Sodus and Wolcott. Grady secured a position as the industrial arts teacher at Dundee Central School in 1956. Initially Grady and Molly lived in Lakemont (Yates County). Molly and Grady were residing in Penn

Yan when they had their first child, Julia, who was commonly called Julie, in 1959. In November 1960 Molly and Grady had a baby boy, David (1960–).

In 1961 Lawrence was elected as Wolcott village trustee. He also expected to serve as a commissioner of parks, public buildings, sidewalks, and street lighting. He resigned from these posts when he and his wife moved to Dundee (Yates County) to be closer to their daughter and her family. Shortly after their move, in February 1962, Molly and Grady had another child, James (1962–). Grady took a one-year leave of absence from his teaching duties in the 1962–63 school year. Bruce (1964–) was Molly and Grady's youngest child.

Grady played in a charity basketball game in December 1965 that pitted the Dundee alumni vs. the Dundee faculty. Grady suited up for the faculty. Although the Youngmans lived on a grape farm, Grady and Molly continued to work as schoolteachers. Molly taught kindergarten and Grady continued to teach industrial arts. In 1973 Molly was granted tenure.

DeNeef, John & Annie

1940 monthly rent: $16.
John C. DeNeef (1875–1956), 64, head of household, real estate salesman, 52 weeks for $150.
Anna "Annie" W. Cottrell DeNeef (1879–1964), 60, wife, homemaker.

JOHN AND ANNIE HAD EACH COMPLETED six years of school. Both of John's parents were born in The Netherlands. ("DeNeef" was sometimes spelled "DeNeff.")

Annie Cottrell was born in Pultneyville in the Town of Williamson. Her parents were Libanus H. Cottrell (1851–1892) and Marna "Mary" Dinah Wemelsfelder Cottrell (1848–1925). Mary's parents were also both born in The Netherlands. Libanus was a wagon maker.

John and Annie married in 1895 and they had a daughter, Bertha Mae Cottrell (1902–1974) in June 1902. In 1915 and 1920 John was a farmer. Bertha used her mother's maiden name before she married Glen E. Phelps (1895–) in December 1919. The couple were living with Glen's parents in Marion in 1920. In June 1930, while they were living in Walworth with Glen's mother, Bertha and Glen had a son, Earl William Phelps (1930–2020).

Annie's mother lived with John and Annie for most of her life after Libanus's death in 1892. The DeNeefs settled in Pultneyville.

Dennis, Frank & Corinne*
Town of Rose. Estimated 1940 value: $1,000.
Frank George Dennis (1893–1965), 46, head of household, farmer, 52 weeks at $500.
Corinne Isabel Smith Dennis (1892–1992), 47, wife, homemaker.
Jean A. Dennis (1924–2010), 15, daughter, student.
Carol L. Dennis (1929–), 10, daughter, student.
Frank George Dennis Jr. (1932–), 8, son, student.
Alice Smith (1861–1952), 79, mother-in-law, retired.

FRANK AND CORINNE DENNIS LIVED with their three children and Corinne's widowed mother on a fruit and vegetable farm just south of Rose. Frank was born in Hornell (Steuben County) and lived his adult life in Rose. Corrine lived most of her 100 years in Rose; she lived a short time in Clyde.

The early education of the three Dennis children unfolded at Rose Union School until the consolidation with North Rose Central School, prompting their transfer to Clyde Central School.

Jean Dennis graduated from Clyde High School at 16, worked as a secretary at Sampson Army Base (Seneca County), then continued her education at Rochester Institute of Technology. She wed Lee Edmonds Jr. (1925–2014), an NRCS graduate, and managed the Dennis family fruit farm near Wayne Center in the Town of Rose. Jean and Lee had five children. She worked for many years at Cornell Extension in Alton. Jean's last job before retiring was at Wayne County Mental Health Services in Lyons.

Carol Dennis met her future husband, Walter Agnew (1926–2019), when they were both students at the University of Rochester. Carol balanced a nursing career with raising their three children.

After winning honors at Clyde High School, Frank transferred to NRCS for his last two years. He sang in the November 1947 all-state chorus. Basketball at NRCS was his favorite team sport, but he was active in soccer, baseball, and tennis as well. His tennis prowess notably led the team to victory, securing the banner for C schools in Wayne County in 1949 and 1950. He served as secretary of the student council in his last two years in high school. Frank's academic achievements were equally noteworthy: He was elected president of the senior class and emerged as the valedictorian of the NRCS class of 1950; he achieved a grade point average of 96.00.

Frank Dennis, NRCS Class of 1950

After high school, Frank pursued higher education at the College of Agriculture at Cornell, specializing in pomology. During his time at Cornell, he exhibited leadership as the president of the freshman class, participated in various extracurricular activities including the Glee Club, and joined Alpha Gamma Rho fraternity.

His academic journey was briefly interrupted when his father fell seriously ill in 1953. Frank took a leave of absence to support his family's farm. In 1954 he married Katharine Merrell (1933–) after her graduation from Cornell with a BS in home economics. Frank eventually completed his BS degree in 1955.

Frank's father's fruit farm achieved a disappointing degree of success, so Frank studied pomology to see what his father had overlooked. (Frank decided that his father's orchards were planted in valleys that did not take advantage of the moderating effect of the warmer lake air moving through trees.)

Katharine came from a musical family. Their collective musical interest was evident when three Merrells were in the Wolcott Central School Orchestra. One year Katherine played the string bass. Katharine achieved a master's degree in home economics. She taught home economics in the Clyde school system.

Frank had a 28-year career teaching and doing research at Michigan State University. (For more information about Frank Dennis Jr., see the Acknowledgments section. Though his family did not live in North Rose, Frank was a co-author of this book as well as a fact-checker, which is why his family is included here.)

Frank remained in East Lansing, Michigan, after retirement and edited the Town of Rose Historical Society Newsletter from afar.

DeRuischer, Isaac & Adriana
(Surname is pronounced "da-ROO-shur")
Eastern North Rose. 1940 monthly rent: $10.
Isaac DeRuischer (1870–1958), 70, head of household, self-employed farm laborer, 40 weeks.
Adriana DeJong DeRuischer (1896–1978), 45, wife, homemaker.
Mary Jane Broekhuizen (1924–1953), 17, stepdaughter, student.
Ida J. DeRuischer (1927–2013), 12, daughter, student.
Kathleen J. DeRuischer (1930–1990), 9, daughter, student.
Isaac "Ike" DeRuischer Jr. (1933–), 6, son, student.

ISAAC DERUISCHER SR. WAS A FARM LABORER, and Adriana was a homemaker. They were both born in The Netherlands. Each spouse completed eight years of school. They lived with their three children, plus Adriana's daughter from her first marriage.

The family was a recent arrival in North Rose. In 1935 they had lived in rural Oswego County. Adriana immigrated in 1916. The same year that she came to the United States, she married Willem Broekhuizen (1889–1924). Willem's parents, Teunis Broekhuizen and Maria de Kreij Broekhuizen, were Dutch, and they remained in Holland. Adriana and Willem had five children; they moved to North Dakota before the birth of the first: Anthony "Tony" Broekhuizen (1917–1994). William M. (1919–1988), John A. (1920–1952), Adrian "Dutch" (1922–), and Mary Jane (1924–1953) followed.

Willem died in 1924 and Adriana married Isaac DeRuischer in 1925. They had three children: Ida, Kathleen, and Ike Jr. Mary

Jane, Willem's daughter, lived with Isaac and Adriana in 1940. Mary Jane married John P. DeLisio (1922–2001), son of Joseph DeLisio and Mary DiSanto DeLisio. John and Mary Jane lived in Clyde and had four children: Randolph "Randy" James, Lorena Jean, Lauralea Paula, and Elena Marie. Mary Jane died at 29.

Ida DeRuischer, NRCS Class of 1945

Ida DeRuischer won election as secretary of her senior class at NRCS. She graduated in June 1945. In May 1947 Ida married Melvin Stanley Shippers (1924–2004), son of Isaac J. and Elizabeth Hermenet Shippers of South Butler. The wedding took place in Rose. Ida and Melvin set up their home in Butler Center. In December 1961 Melvin volunteered to organize a squadron of the Sons of the American Legion in Wolcott.

Kathleen DeRuischer worked at the Newark State School. She married Joseph Stanley and, in 1988, lived in North Syracuse.

Ike DeRuischer married Eleanor Burnett in 1953. They had three children: Audrey, Isaac ("Jim"), and Jan Michael. In September 1963 Ike and Eleanor's Wolcott home suffered $3,000 in fire damage. The blaze originated in a faulty lighting fixture in a second-story bedroom. Ike and Eleanor moved to California and later divorced.

Dickinson, Robert & Emma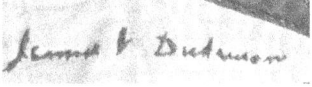

12 Elm Street, now 4966–4968 Elm—Built in 1900. Estimated 1940 value: $2,500.
Robert D. Dickinson (1869–1957), 70, head of household, proprietor, auto repair shop, self-employed.
Emeline "Emma" Briggs Dickinson (1870–1964), 69, wife, homemaker.
Jennie V. Dickinson Adams (1908–1999), 31, daughter, part-time apple packer, 16 weeks for $10 a week.
Clark Everett Adams (1899–1996), 40, son-in-law, auto mechanic, 52 weeks for $19 a week.
H. Clark Adams (ca. 1925–1942), 14, grandson, student.
John "Jay" Adams (1929–2002), 10, grandson, student.

Ralph Everett Adams (ca. 1932–1992), 7, grandson, student.
Robert K. Adams (ca. 1933–1988), 6, grandson, student.
Janet Adams (1936–2020), 3, granddaughter.
Luella Nesbitt Marriott (1915–1970), 25, lodger, bean sorter, 42 weeks at $8 a week.
Ronald Marriott (1933–2020), 6, Luella's son, lodger, student.

ROBERT AND EMMA DICKINSON HAD been married for 52 years. They shared a large home with two lodgers, their daughter Jennie, her husband Everett Adams, and the Adams's five children. The lodgers were Luella Marriott and her son, Ronald. In the back of the house, Robert ran an auto repair shop that employed Everett as a mechanic. Jennie was working part-time as an apple packer but was looking for other work. Jennie and Luella had finished the eleventh grade, Everett made it through the ninth, and Robert and Emma had completed eight years of school.

In addition to Jennie, the Dickinsons had two other children: Anna (1893–1968) and Jay (1905–1970). Jay Dickinson married and moved to Palmyra. Anna married a native of Rose Township—Charles Dean (1891–1963)—and the couple lived in North Rose in 1940. (See "Dean, Charlie & Anna.")

The head of the household, Robert Dickinson, was raised on a farm in the Town of Rose. In March 1888 he married Emeline Delia Briggs, daughter of Birney Briggs (1842–1927) and Anna Terry Briggs (1845–1922), in her parents' North Rose home. Robert worked as a carpenter and builder.

By 1915 the Dickinsons lived in a house on Elm Street. That year Robert was chosen to be the first fire chief of the North Rose Chemical Company No. 1. Two years later he was elected to a second term. Early North Rose firefighters battled blazes with "chemicals" (probably using a large soda-acid extinguisher) rather than water, because the hamlet didn't have a municipal water system until the 1950s.

By 1920 the family lived in a house they owned on South Poplar Street. By 1925 the Dickinsons had purchased a home on Elm Street, Robert had opened his auto repair garage, and the family had taken in a boarder—Everett Adams, recently of Wolcott. Jennie married Everett in July of that year and the couple soon had their first child. Emma's elderly father, Birney, was also living with them at that time.

After Birney's death in 1927, Emma and Robert were living alone. In 1930 Emma's sister-in-law, (Eunice) Mae Briggs of Rochester, moved in for the summer. She and her husband, Jesse T. Briggs, had purchased the former Charles Moore house, south of North Rose, and were renovating it prior to moving in. In October 1935 Robert was building an addition to his house. Dickinson was master of ceremonies at the spontaneous V-J Day North Rose celebration at the Honor Roll Board Park on August 14, 1945. The Dickinsons celebrated their 60th wedding anniversary by holding an open house in March 1948. And in 1950 the couple vacationed in Florida with daughters Anna and Jennie, and Jennie's family. After Robert passed away, Emma spent the last seven years of her life in St. Petersburg, Florida. She died in March 1964 at the age of 93.

In 1918 Everett worked on his father's farm in Albion (Orleans County). While Everett was living in North Rose, his parents, Herbert "Bert" Adams and Luella V. Brown were living in the "Plank Road" area of Butler. Everett and Jennie Adams frequently visited with Paul and Inez Drury. The Adamses purchased the Worden farm on Wolcott Road from Frank Hill. Everett and Jennie retired to St. Petersburg and lived into their nineties—just as Jennie's mother had done.

H. Clark Adams (Everett and Jennie's eldest son) represented NRCS in a 1939 regional spelling bee. He moved to Rochester as an adult, served in the Navy during World War II, and married Etta Armstrong at the Grace Presbyterian Church in Wolcott in November 1946. In 1950 he and his wife had a daughter.

Jay Adams, NRCS Class of 1947

Jay Adams spent time at the Boy Scouts' Camp Babcock Kovey in August 1942. He was vice president of his NRCS freshman class and lettered on the 1945 soccer team. Jay lettered in both soccer and basketball his senior year. He married and had two daughters: Ann Marie was born in October 1947, and Norma Jean in October 1949. The family later moved to Clyde.

Ralph Adams,
NRCS Class of 1950

Ralph Adams was president of his eighth grade class, raised rabbits during his teen years, and attended Boy Scout camp during the summers. Ralph had perfect school attendance during the 1947–1948 school year and was the salutatorian of the NRCS Class of 1950. He was active in band, basketball, baseball, and soccer during all four years of high school. He and his wife, Suzette Lenihan, raised their seven children in Geneseo (Livingston County).

Robert Adams,
NRCS Class of 1951

Robert Adams had a grade point average of 91.59 in his senior year. He was president and valedictorian of NRCS's class of 1951, served as secretary of the student council, and was active in basketball, baseball, and soccer.

Janet Adams was listed on the sixth and seventh grade honor roll all four quarters of 1947–1948 and 1948–1949 and was active in the Intermediate Troop of the Girl Scouts. She married Bill Triska and was living in Florida in 2002.

As a teenager, lodger Luella Marriott lived in Rose. Her father, Wallace Nesbitt (1880–1961), was a farm laborer whose father was born in Ireland and whose mother was born in Canada. Her mother, Mary Belle Adams (1895–1981), lived in Orleans County until the Nesbitts moved to Rose in the early 1920s. In 1933 Luella married Orlo "Bud" Marriott (1912–1999), who also lived in Rose as a teenager. There's no trace of Bud in the 1940 census, although Luella's marital status that year was married. Bud remarried in 1946, to Ellen Louise Kistner (1917–1995); they settled in Webster. Luella also married a second time, to Harold Joseph Burns (1910–1984). In 1950 he worked as a foreman at the Bean House.

Luella's son Ronald Marriott attended the district Boy Scout Camp on Seneca Lake near Ovid in August 1946. Although he was a lodger, he had plenty of family in North Rose—two of his father's sisters married McOmber brothers who lived in town. (See "McOmber, Donald & Doris" and "McOmber, Paul & Margaret.")A graduate of NRCS, he joined the Navy and served aboard the *USS Yosemite* from 1952 to 1956. He worked for General Electric for more than 30 years.

Dillingham, Clinton & Elizabeth

7 Clinton Avenue, now 10391 Clinton—Built in 1860. Estimated 1940 value: $2,300.
Clinton Delos Dillingham (1883–1958), 57, head of household, insurance salesman, 52 weeks for $4,200.
Elizabeth Frances Van Pelt Dillingham (1896–1964), 43, wife, stenographer at insurance office, 52 weeks.
Elizabeth Lucille Dillingham (1927–1984), daughter, 13, student.

Clinton Dillingham, ca. 1920s

CLINTON DILLINGHAM'S PARENTS were Delos Waldorf Dillingham (1846–1917) and Elizabeth Hannah Stanton (1844–1921). Clinton married Sarah "Sadie" Elizabeth Armitage (1884–1982) in 1905. They had a daughter, Hilda Jane Dillingham (1907–2000), in April 1907 in Lyons. Clinton divorced Sadie in 1925, and then married Elizabeth Van Pelt Godkin, a widow with a 10-year-old son, in Cuyahoga County, Ohio, in 1926. Elizabeth was a high school graduate. Their daughter, Elizabeth Lucille ("Betty Lou"), married William Gordon Acker, a Navy veteran, in 1946.

Betty Lou Dillingham, NRCS Class of 1945

The elder Elizabeth's parents were Frank Valentine (1853–1901) and Ida May Abbott (1869–1924). She also had adopted parents John Grove Van Pelt (1848–1913) and Elizabeth R. Crawford (1860–1909). In 1914 she married Ward Godkin (1897–1917). Ward died a year after the birth of their son, Valentine Grove Godkin (1916–1963). (Ward's mother lived in North Rose in 1940; see "Weiland, Albert & Ella.")

Clinton Dillingham was in the insurance business for 44 years. He was a member of the Elks of Lyons, a member of the Rose Lodge Masons, Bayshore Lodge Odd Fellows, the Grange Fire Co., Rebekahs, and the Rose Township Chamber of Commerce. He was supervisor of the Town of Rose for 10 consecutive terms, being elected in 1933. In 1941 he was elected as councilman for the Town of Rose and served for 12 years. Both his son-in-law, William Acker, and his stepson, Valentine Godkin, followed him into the insurance business. Valentine Godkin died at 46 of a heart attack at his home in Wolcott.

Dodds, Wells & Margaret

31 North Poplar Street, now 5075 North Poplar—Built in 1911.
Wells Munson Dodds (1895–1984), 44, head of household, nursery and greenhouse proprietor, 52 weeks, self-employed.
Margaret Bertha Langford Dodds (1896–1987), 43, wife, homemaker.
John "Jack" F. Dodds (1919–1986), 20, son, laborer, 30 weeks, $450.
Donald "Don" Gilbert Dodds (1925–2010), 14, son, student.

WELLS DODDS WAS THE SON of Fred J. (1874–1919) and Harriet Seager Dodds (1874–1964) and lived in Lyons as a young child. Fred lived as a lodger in Rochester in 1910. He worked in manufacturing film at a camera works—likely Eastman Kodak—and later moved to Detroit, where he worked in a restaurant. They parted company between 1910 and 1916, at which point Harriet married a Huron farmer, Gilbert B. Hill (1875–1961); by 1920 they lived on South Poplar Street in North Rose, where Harriet established a millinery shop. (See "Hill, Gilbert & Harriet.")

Wells married Margaret Langford in June 1916 in the North Rose Presbyterian parsonage. Margaret's parents were Rev. John Cosyn Langford (1851–1940), who conducted the ceremony, and Frances L. Langford (1867–1913), who was a native of Vermont. John was born in England and was a Presbyterian pastor for 65 years and an interim pastor for three more. He served the Presbyterian Church in Rose and later the one in North Rose. Rev. Langford died in March 1940. He spent the last few years of his life living with Margaret and Wells. Both Wells and Margaret attended two years of high school and their sons lived with them. Jack had graduated from high school and worked as a laborer in the Salter Canning Co. Don was a student who had completed the eighth grade.

Wells began operating a nursery in 1919. He joined the Masonic Lodge 590 in 1924 and became a member of the Odd Fellows and a ruling elder of the Presbyterian Church. In November 1929 he went hunting with his stepfather near Fine (St. Lawrence County). The North Rose Grange held a debate in March 1931 on the question "Resolved that installment buying is beneficial to rural communities," with Charles Oaks taking the affirmative and Wells taking the negative. Wells won by a margin of two votes. In May 1937 Wells and his mother were driving their new Hudson Terraplane car when they collided with a deer on NYS Rte. 104 near Ontario High School. Wells and Harriet were unhurt, although the vehicle suffered significant damage and the deer was killed. (The Terraplane was a handsome, powerful, and reasonably inexpensive car made by the Hudson Motor Car Company, which made autos until 1957.)

Wells and Margaret were members of the Literary Club. In October 1941, the Republican caucus selected Wells to be a Town of Rose Republican committeeman, and he joined the Wolcott Chamber of Commerce and the Wolcott Rotary Club. In November 1945 Wells sold his Wolcott greenhouse property to B.C. Reed and Son, an Allis Chalmers farm equipment dealer, and Wells merged his business at his nursery in North Rose. In September 1946 Wells and his family helped celebrate the 91st birthday of his grandmother, Emma Seager, at Harriet and Gilbert Hill's cottage on LeRoy Island. In the 1960s he wrote a gardening column which appeared in regional newspapers. The North Rose/Rose Masonic Lodge awarded Wells a 50-year medal in February 1975.

Margaret was a charter member of the Arbor Vitae Chapter of the Order of the Eastern Star, and was active in the Missionary Society, the Sigma Society, and the United Presbyterian Women's Association, all three sponsored by the North Rose Presbyterian Church. She hosted a Fresh Air child from New York in August 1944, and in February 1948 was elected president of the North Rose Presbyterian Church Women's Organization.

In December 1937, Jack sang in the All-State Choir, which convened at the Ithaca School of Music (now Ithaca College). He enlisted in the Army after the start of World War II; by that time, he was 6'2" tall. In June 1942 he was stationed at Fort Niagara, and in December he was a staff sergeant in Oregon. Later he required hospital treatment when he came down with pneumonia. In March 1943 he was in Pine Camp near Watertown, later named Fort Drum, where his parents could visit him. Later that year he faced the Japanese in combat in the Aleutian Islands. In July 1944 two North Rose servicemen, Jack and Ernest Briggs, USN, met by chance on the street in Oahu, Hawaii. In early 1945 Jack was back in a hospital—this time in New Guinea. By March 1945 he had returned to the United States and was assigned to Camp Dix, New Jersey. Jack took a short leave to visit his parents.

After his discharge from the Army, Jack married Norma Weed (1919–1973), daughter of Oscar (1889–1952) and Alice Hebert Weed (1886–1974) of North Rose. In March 1946 Norma was elected as an officer of the Presbyterian Missionary Society of North Rose. In April that year, Jack was starting shortstop on the Wolcott Merchants baseball team; he later switched to outfield. In June 1950 Jack was elected vice president of the NRCS Alumni Association.

Their first son, Brian John Dodds (1946–2018), became a program analyst with Xerox Corporation and married Grace Scalzo. He died on September 15, 2018, leaving behind three sons: Christopher Zane, Phillip Brian, and Eric Martin. Norma and Jack's second son died in infancy; Martin John Dodds lived from only 1950 to 1951, according to the Rose cemetery. Norma and Jack also had a daughter, Jacqueline "Jackie" Ann (1952–). Jackie married twice. Her first marriage produced two sons, Dan and Matt Bacon; she and her second husband, Ron Hoyez, were most recently living in Neosho, Missouri.

In June 1942 Don Dodds was 17 years of age and organized a softball team of 16- to 19-year-olds and challenged all comers. In December he sang a solo, "O Wondrous Night," at a Christmas program presented by NRCS. He also took voice lessons at the Eastman School of Music. In June 1945, during a stretch of only two weeks, Don was the best man at two weddings. In October of that year he married Pearl Frances Hoppel (1927–), daughter of Frederick "Fred" and

Christina Klein Hoppel of Rose. Pearl was valedictorian and president of the NRCS Class of 1944. In the summer of 1946, Don taught junior boys Sunday school at the North Rose Presbyterian Church. Upon completion of a BS in science education from the Agricultural College at Cornell University in 1953, he moved to Newfoundland, Canada, where he worked as a wildlife biologist until 1960. During that time, he also served as a teaching associate and research associate at Cornell while completing an MS in 1955 and PhD in 1960. He and Pearl became the parents of two daughters, Tracey and Kathleen.

Don joined the wildlife division of the Nova Scotia Department of Lands & Forests in 1960 and worked as a big game biologist and assistant and acting director of the division. In 1964 he began a long association with Acadia University in Wolfville, Nova Scotia. From 1964 to 1987, he moved up the academic ladder from professorships to the dean of sciences. He helped to set up the Acadia University wildlife program. Graduates of this program have filled key positions in wildlife management agencies in Canada and the United States. Don's areas of research included reproduction in the snowshoe hare, wildlife forest relationships, and the brain worm parasite in moose and deer. In 1966 he spent a year in Zambia, where he worked on wildlife and land-use issues.

In addition to doing research, publishing scientific articles, and teaching, Don created a consulting business. Among the topics on which he worked were wildlife policy in Ethiopia, organization and animal protection legislation in Trinidad, and impact studies throughout the Atlantic region. The United Nations Development Program and the Food and Agricultural Organization of the United Nations sponsored several of these projects. On finishing his professional career, he had 42 publications to his credit.

Drury, Evelyn & Mary

North Poplar Street. 1940 monthly rent: $10.
Evelyn Drury (1907–1987), 32, head of household, laborer, 26 weeks for $450.

Mary J. Messenger Kepner Drury (1912–1960), 28, wife, homemaker.
Eugene Alexander Kepner (1929–2001), 10, stepson, student.
Ida June Kepner (1932–), 8, stepdaughter, student.
Mary Lou Kepner (1936–), 4, stepdaughter.
Alyce Harriet Drury (1938–2004), 2, daughter.

EVELYN AND MARY DRURY RENTED a home on North Poplar Street. With them were the three children from Mary's earlier marriage to Harvey W. Kepner of Montoursville, Pennsylvania—Eugene, June, and Mary Lou Kepner—and Evelyn and Mary's daughter, Alyce. A son, Lynn G. Drury (1941–2018), soon followed.

Evelyn was a laborer at the Cold Storage. Mary was a homemaker. She was the daughter of Walter Messenger and Ida Seager Messenger. (See "Ghent, Joe & Hazel"; Ida was their lodger.) Evelyn completed the seventh grade; Mary completed the eighth grade. (There was another Mary Drury in North Rose at the same time as this Mary Drury. The other Mary Drury was a single woman in 1940—she married later. She was an avid horsewoman, and she worked at the post office.)

In 1915 Evelyn had lived with his father, Frank Drury (1844–1921), and his grandparents, Benjamin F. and Harriett L. Moore Drury (1845–1933), on Welch Street (an alternate name for Railroad Avenue) in North Rose. Evelyn's mother, Bessie Grinnels Drury (1884–1941), and father, Frank, had separated. In 1920, Benjamin, Harriett, Frank, and Evelyn lived in a home on Gray Street. By 1925, Benjamin had died and Harriett was living on Railroad Street, while Frank, who worked as a cooper, and Evelyn, who worked as a laborer and later as a carpenter, shared a home on North Poplar Street.

June Kepner, NRCS Class of 1949

June married Lee R. Blake in the North Rose Methodist Church in July 1950. Lee's parents were Robert James Blake (1907–1993), a truck driver, and Lois Olive Engel Blake (1910–1999) of Geneva. Lee and June were living in Phelps (Ontario County) in 1951 when June gave birth to a daughter. June and Lee also had a son, Brent, who was born in 1960.

Drury, Paul & Inez

Paul Drury (1913–1985) 26, head of household, truck driver/retail store assistant manager, 52 weeks for $20 a week.
Inez Furman Drury (1915–2007), 25, wife, homemaker.
Lucille Anne Drury (1938–2019), 2, daughter.

PAUL AND INEZ DRURY HAD A 2-year-old daughter, Lucille. Paul worked long hours as a truck driver and as an assistant manager for his father's retail coal and feed business; he had completed the ninth grade. Inez graduated from Clyde High School in 1932, attended college for two years, and was a homemaker. Her parents, Leland (1887–1968) and Mathilda Rothang Furman (1885–1966), both grew up in the Rochester area and married in 1908.

In April 1938 Paul and Inez moved into the Frank Chalupa house vacated by the McOmbers. Their daughter was born the next month. Paul Drury attended the feed dealers' banquet at the Powers Hotel in Rochester with Harry Payne and Jerry Guthrie in February 1939. The Drurys often socialized with Inez's brother Norris Furman, his wife, Dorothy, and their family. In August 1939 Paul and Inez visited Inlet (Hamilton County) with Graydon and Freda Guthrie. (Inlet serves as an entrance to the Adirondack Mountain wilderness.) Leland and Mathilda Furman, Bert and Theresa Drury, and Mary Drury spent Thanksgiving 1939 with Paul and Inez.

In January 1940 Inez substitute taught in the small Spunk School in the Town of Rose when the usual teacher Laura Pitcher Harris Wayne was confined to her home by illness. Inez was a member of the Sew and Sew Club. The Drurys were members of the Anniversary Club. In August 1940 the Drurys returned to Inlet—this time with Everett and Jennie Adams. In May 1941 they visited Pine Camp with Harry Payne and Laura Pitcher Harris Wayne. (Pine Camp was a precursor to the U.S. Army's Fort Drum.)

In March 1942 the Drury family moved to a new home on Caroline Street. In April of the next year, Paul and his father, Bert, bought out Harry Payne's interest in their coal and feed business, and the company's name was changed to Drury & Son. The Drurys and their daughter, Lucille, spent Christmas Day with Wilbur and Mary Furman of Clyde. In July 1944, they spent a week on LeRoy Island with the family of Inez's brother Nelson Furman and his wife, Winona, of Savannah.

By March 1945 Paul and Inez were members of the Saturday Night Club. In May 1946 Inez headed the local fundraising campaign for the Fresh Air Fund. In July she was elected treasurer of the Public Heath Committee. She remained active with this group for 30 years. In July 1947 Paul and Inez vacationed at Black Lake and other spots in the St. Lawrence River region with Nelson and Winona Furman. During this trip, Lucille stayed with her paternal grandparents, Bert and Theresa Drury. (See "Drury, Bert & Theresa.")

The Drury family attended a surprise party in honor of Norris Furman and family, who were about to move to Florida. In March 1948 Paul Drury attended a two-day conference of feed dealers at Langwell Hotel in Elmira (Chemung County). In July of that year the Drurys, along with Norris and Dorothy Furman, attended the 52nd Furman reunion Sunday at the home of Dr. and Mrs. Charles Harris in East Rochester.

In August 1948, Paul, Inez, and daughter Lucille, along with Raymond and Kathryn Albina Washburn MacDougall and their son, Donnie, spent a week at Goose Bay (Jefferson County.) In January of the next year, Nelson and Winona Furman departed with the Drurys for a monthlong trip to Florida. Then, in September, the Furmans and the Drurys spent a week at the Drury cottage at Sodus Point.

Lucille Drury, NRCS Class of 1956

Lucille Drury received her first holy communion at St. Mary Magdalene Church in Wolcott in May 1946 and was confirmed at the Church of the Epiphany in Sodus in October 1949. She was active in the Girl Scouts and often visited her cousins Jeanne and Marilyn Furman in Savannah. In March 1950 Lucille entertained Nancy Raney, Lynda Catchpole, Carolyn Poole, Eva Harrison, and Mary Horton at a St. Patrick's Day party. She graduated from the Morrisville School of Nursing and married Gilbert DeVay of North Rose in July 1960 at St. Mary Magdalene Church in Wolcott. Lucille and Gilbert had a daughter, Susan, and a son, Dale. Lucille married a second time, to Olen Wayne Poole (1932–1996), whose first wife died in 1980.

Drury, Bert & Theresa

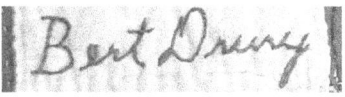

Owned a home in eastern North Rose—Estimated 1940 value: $3,000.
Bert Lewis Drury (1881–1962), 59, head of household, retailer, 52 weeks for $26 a week.
Theresa M. Lundergun Drury (1886–1961), 54, wife, homemaker, trimmer, 6 weeks for $16.50 a week.
Mary T. Drury (1916–2009), 23, daughter, telephone operator, 49 weeks for $12 a week.

IN 1940 BERT WAS THE PROPRIETOR of a retail coal and feed company and Theresa was a homemaker—she also worked occasionally as a trimmer for an apple evaporator. Both had eight years of education and they had two children: Paul (1913–1985) and Mary. Paul had established his own household in North Rose (see "Drury, Paul & Inez"). Mary was a high school graduate, was still living with her parents, and had been a telephone operator since March 1937. During the week that the census surveyed, Bert worked 70 hours and Mary clocked in for 44.

Bert was already working on George Colvin's farm in Butler by the time he was 15, and he was a farm laborer when he married Theresa Lundergun in February 1909. The newlyweds lived in the Town of Rose. In 1920 he was manufacturing apple barrels, and by 1930 he had opened a coal and feed company. Bert was also the Democratic candidate for Rose Town Supervisor in 1937.

Bert's brother Claude died in an elevator accident while working in the Wolcott (apple) Co-op in February 1930. Bert bought Lloyd Marshall's home on South Main Street that June—in anticipation of Marshall's August move to Texas—and Mr. and Mrs. Clyde Edelman purchased the Drurys' home shortly thereafter.

Theresa's parents were born in Ireland and her two brothers also lived in North Rose. (See "Lundergun, Jim & Kittie" for details about Theresa's family.) She was a member of the Thursday Club, the Home Bureau, and the Altar and Rosary Society of St. Mary Magdalene Catholic Church of Wolcott. The Drurys were members of the Anniversary Club, supporters of the Democratic Party, and parishioners of the Roman Catholic Church of the Epiphany in Sodus.

Mary provided piano accompaniment to a vocalist in an Auburn radio broadcast in May 1936, was the maid of honor at her brother Paul's wedding in October 1937, and visited Florida with her parents. In February 1939 Mary moved to Sodus, where she worked in the telephone office. In 1945 Mary vacationed with friends in Canada and the Thousand Islands in June and resigned from the telephone company in July. After a short break, she began working at the North Rose post office, then bought the "Romp-In" Cottage at Sodus Point in October. A lifelong love of horses led her to spend a week in September 1947 with her friend Mrs. Yvonne Bates at the Dude Ranch in Chesterton (Warren County).

By 1954 Mary owned a cottage on LeRoy Island. She met New Jersey native Robert Elsworth Jaqui (1915–1972) at a Clyde Grange dance and married him in 1968. He had been a guard at Clyde's World War Two POW facility. After Robert's death, Mary married (Michael) Frank Griffin (1913–2007), formerly of Pittsford. It was a second marriage for both of them. Frank moved to Webster before his death. Mary lived to be 92 years old. She lived at 4936 South Main Street in North Rose, the former home of her uncle Will Lundergun.

Edwards, Donald & Frances
1940 monthly rent: $12.
Donald Edward Edwards (1911–1985), 28, head of household, laborer, 52 weeks for $900.
Frances Marian Dapolito Edwards (1916–2000), 23, wife, homemaker/trimmer, 10 weeks for $150.
Ronald "Ron" W. Edwards (1934–2019), 5, son, student.
Donald "Don" Philip Edwards (1936–2000), 4, son.

Donald Edwards completed three years of college and worked as a laborer at the Cold Storage. Frances completed one year of high school and was a homemaker. She also worked part-time as a trimmer at the Canning Factory. Donald and Frances had two young sons, Ron and Don.

Donald was the third child of Warren Llewellyn Edwards (1878–1961) and Margaret Mae Barrett (1883–1964), who married in April 1907. Donald's parents lived in Seneca Falls (Seneca County) and then in Cicero (Onondaga County) before settling in North Rose about the time that Donald was born. Warren had come to North Rose when he was offered the post of high school principal there. (See "Edwards, Warren & Margaret" for more information about Donald's forebears.)

Frances's parents, Phillip Antonio Dapolito (1884–1963) and Antonia Santoli (ca. 1878–1962), were both born in Italy and had both been widowed when they married in Clyde in December 1910 or January 1911. Phillip came to the U.S. in 1893; Antonia in 1908. Phillip had two children by his first wife. He was a day laborer, then worked for the New York Central Railroad.

Donald received several honor grades on his New York State Regents exams while he was attending NRCS and was valedictorian in 1929. In November 1932 Donald was living in Rochester. He married Frances in November 1933. Their son Ron was born in 1934 and Don was born in 1936. That same year, Donald taught adult education classes in shorthand, typing, and recreation in North Rose and Red Creek. Donald, Frances, and their sons moved to Clyde when Donald accepted a position at Beacon Milling in Cayuga (Cayuga County). Beacon was one of the largest animal feed companies in the country. In July 1943 the family moved from Clyde to Auburn. Frances and Donald became the parents of twins in June 1944: Sandra Kay Edwards (1944–) and Dennis Alan Edwards (1944–2012). Frances and Donald exchanged visits with Elery and Leona Mills of North Rose.

Frances married a second time, to William C. Bartley (1926–2002). Donald also married a second time, to Irene Elizabeth Briggs (1916–1999), in July 1954. Irene's father, Roy, worked as a farm laborer for decades in various parts of Wayne County. Irene was first married to Leroy Yates (1915–1999).

Ron was elected as vice president of the Clyde Central School Student Council in May 1949. He played on the undefeated 1949 Clyde football team that won the Wayne County and Tri-County championships. In April 1950, Ronald was on the basketball team representing Clyde in the annual Rome Rotary Club Tournament. Ron attended Siena College in Loudonville (Albany County). Ron married Jean Brown (1936–2004) of Clyde in 1956 and settled in Seneca Falls (Seneca County), where he had a successful career working for John Deere and enjoyed golfing at the Seneca Falls Country Club. Ron and Jean had three sons: Paul, Peter, and Mark. They retired in 1986 to Sarasota, Florida, where Ron joined the Rolling Green Golf Club.

Don served in the Marine Corps from 1953 to 1956. He married Beverly Wiltsie (1939–) in August 1960 at St. John's Church in Clyde. Don and Beverly had a daughter, Tracy, who married Donald Gary of Clyde, and a son, Thomas Edwards (1961–2021), who married Wende L. Cahill, and also lived in Clyde, working for 37 years for the Wayne County Department of Social Services. Don worked at Wegmans Supermarket in Newark from 1973 to 1999. Beverly married a second time, to Thomas Sozio (ca. 1948–2003).

Dennis A. Edwards (1944–2012), Donald and Frances's third son, married and had four children: Dennis (wife, Gloria) of West Monroe (Oswego County); Troy of Lake Wales, Florida, Kim (husband, Robin Ryan) of Houston, Texas and Derrick of Missoula, Montana. Dennis moved to Lake Wales and then to West Monroe.

Sandra married Richard Hume (1940–2016) and lived in Plymouth, Minnesota, a suburb of Minneapolis.

Edwards, Warren & Margaret

4 Glenmark Road, now 10308 Glenmark—Built in 1905. Estimated 1940 value: $3,000.

Warren Llewellyn Edwards (1878–1961), 62, head of household, high school principal, 42 weeks for $3,800.

Margaret Mae Barrett Edwards (1883–1964), 57, wife, homemaker.
Clarence Everett Edwards (1913–2006), 26, son, bookkeeper, fruit packing house, 50 weeks for $1,200.
Warren Grant Edwards (1915–1971), 24, son, laborer, fruit packing house, 40 weeks for $650.
Marion Ruth Edwards (1917–1996), 22, daughter, unemployed.
Harry Lauder Edwards (1919–1996), 21, son, laborer, fruit packing house, 40 weeks for $600.
Peter Barrett (1853–1943), 87, father-in-law, retired.

WELL-EDUCATED FOR THEIR TIME, Warren Edwards had completed two years of college and Margaret Barrett was a college graduate when they married in April 1907. Warren's parents were Myron Adelbert Edwards (1854–1943) and Helen Agnes Shepherd Edwards (1853–1944). Born and raised in Cortland County, Adelbert was a mail carrier in Freetown (Cortland County) in 1880, a stage coach driver in Sherburne (Chenango County) in 1900, owned a dairy farm in Homer (Cortland County) in 1910, and owned a truck farm in Onondaga (Onondaga County) in 1920. By 1930 he'd retired and Adelbert and Helen were living with Warren and Margaret in their Glenmark Road home in North Rose.

Margaret was born in Seneca Falls (Seneca County) to Peter L. Barrett (1853–1943) and Anna M. Brace Barrett (1859–1932). Peter and his two younger sisters were born in the U.S., but he had five older siblings who were born in Canada before his family settled in Seneca Falls. Both Peter and his father were commercial painters. After Anna's death, Peter lived in North Rose with Warren and Margaret.

In 1910 Warren and Margaret lived in Cicero (Onondaga County), where Warren was a schoolteacher. The eldest two of their seven children were born in Onondaga County; the others, starting with Donald in 1911, were born in North Rose.

Though the youngest four of Margaret and Warren's children were adults, they were still living with them in North Rose.

Clarence Edwards was a college graduate and was working as a bookkeeper. He married Jennie Elodie Vandewinckel (1915–2006), whose parents and two older siblings had immigrated to the U.S. from Belgium in 1912. In 1950 they had two children: William (ca. 1944–) and Dianne (ca. 1949–). They had another son and another daughter, Joan Kathleen (1952–1952), who died just shy of 9 months old. Clarence and Jennie lived most of their adult lives in Clyde but died months apart in Shepherdstown, West Virginia.

Warren and Margaret's son Warren Grant Edwards was a high school graduate working at a fruit packing house. He married Grace Mable Benedict (1920–1995) in July 1949. It was a second marriage for Grace, whose teenaged sons, Richard and Thomas Cotton, were living with them in Rochester in 1950.

Marion, a high school graduate, was the only child of Warren and Margaret still living at home in 1950. She was secretary to the school principal in Wolcott. She married Sidney Chandler (1903–1995) in 1951. The wedding was in Warren and Margaret's home.

Harry, at 21, had graduated from high school and, like his brother Warren, was working at a fruit packing house. He then worked as a tool grinder for the General Railway Signal Company before entering the Army Air Forces in July 1942. The January 22, 1945, edition of the *Democrat and Chronicle* published the following brief: "Staff Sgt. Harry L. Edwards, 25, North Rose, entered the aerial offensive against Germany recently when he flew a mission to bomb the marshalling yards at Andernach, a short distance back of the German lines. He is the radio operator-gunner on an Eighth Air Force B-17 Flying Fortress." On August 26, 1945, Harry married Ruth M. Bagshaw (1929–2001) of Manchester (Ontario County). They had two sons: Mark and Keith. Harry must have continued his education because he worked as a chemical engineer for Eastman Kodak and retired to central Florida in 1983. He died at 77 in Deltona, Florida.

Warren and Margaret's three eldest children had left the family home by 1940. Lois Margaret Edwards (1908–1982) married Edward William Anthony (1909–1975), who was a farmer in Rose. Lois and Edward had four sons and three daughters. Lois died at 73 at her home on Miner Road in North Rose.

Mildred Anna Edwards (1910–1975) married Robert Lester Van Deusen (1905–1990) in January 1933 and moved to Rochester. Robert was a chef at a restaurant in 1940 and Mildred was a homemaker with two small boys, Richard C. Van Deusen (1935–2022), 5, and Lawrence R. Van Deusen (1936–2010), 3. By 1950, with the boys in their early teens, Robert owned his own restaurant and both he and Mildred were working there 40 hours a week. Mildred was living in Manchester (Ontario County) when she died at 64.

Donald Edward Edwards (1911–1985) was the head of his own household in North Rose in the 1940 census. (See "Edwards, Donald & Frances.")

Farnsworth, Bernie & Virginia

56 North Main Street, now 5066 North Main—Built in 1905. Estimated 1940 value: $1,500.
Bernard "Tommy" "Bernie" C. Farnsworth (1909–1995), 31, head of household, undertaker.
Virginia Jewell Farnsworth (1907–1996), 31, wife, schoolteacher, 40 weeks for $1,000.

BERNARD (WHICH WAS PRONOUNCED "BUR-nurd," not "bur-NARD") had completed three years of college and worked as an undertaker in the family business started by his father. Besides the funeral home, the company included furniture sales. Bernie was the son of John William (1881–1977) and Myrtle J. Brown Farnsworth (1881–1948). (See "Farnsworth, John & Myrtie.")

Virginia graduated from NRCS in 1927 and worked as a schoolteacher. She began her teaching career on Long Island and then taught at Rose Union School and NRCS until 1971. She was the daughter of Charles J. (1875–1961) and Blanche McHuron Jewell (1882–1963). In 1910 Virginia lived with her parents and her older brother Edwin E. Jewell (1905–1982) in Manlius (Onondaga County), where Charles practiced dentistry from a home office. In December 1914 the Jewell family increased to three children with the birth of Dorothy (1914–1997). Before Dorothy's arrival, the Jewells moved to the Town of Rose. Charles beat his dental tools into plowshares. The 1915 New York State Census enumerator described him as a "general" farmer. The Jewells' farmhouse was on Lyons Road in the Town of Rose. Edwin worked as a "garage man"—a contemporary term for "auto mechanic." In 1930 Charles was still farming on Lyons Road. Edwin had moved away from home. In 1947 Edwin lived in Ithaca (Tompkins County).

In January 1933 Harold and Maude DeVol accompanied Bernie to the Rochester auto show. In July 1934 George and Ellen Burch visited the Chicago World's Fair with Bernie and Virginia. Virginia attended a teachers' conference in Rochester in October 1938 and was an adult Girl Scout organizer. Virginia married Bernie in May 1939 and moved to North Rose from a rural section of the Town of Rose. In November 1943 Bernie and Virginia had a son, Craig A. Farnsworth (1943–).

Charles Jewell retired from farming by 1940. Blanche and Charles's youngest child, Dorothy, ran a hairdressing shop. Later, Dorothy married Charles Benjamin Williams (1911–1978) and relocated to Findlay, Ohio. After several years they moved back to North Rose with their son, Jeffrey (1944–2019). Another son, Kent Barry Williams, died in infancy. Jeff and Dorothy opened a fabric shop. Jeff was a 1962 graduate of NRCS.

When the Masons converted the North Rose bank building into the North Rose Masonic Temple, Bernie was the leader of the North Rose Masons—holding the title of master of the lodge. This was in November 1938 when Bernie was just 30 years old, remarkably young to lead a group of 110 men. He was a member of the Rose Masonic Lodge for 64 years. (A distant cousin of Bernard Farnsworth's with the same name was also an undertaker in Wayne County but was a generation younger than Bernard. The Newark doppelganger had the middle initial "J"; he perished in a San Diego traffic accident in 1963.) Bernard held the office of Faithful Captain in the Knights of Columbus in February 1957, when the Knights of Columbus 4th Degree Assembly held its semiformal dinner-dance at the Gardenier

Hotel in Newark in honor of George Washington's birthday. (The Knights of Columbus was the nation's largest Roman Catholic fraternal organization.) In April 1958 Bernard was an adult leader in Cub Scouting; he was elected treasurer of Cub Pack 218 headquartered in Newark. In November 1959 Bernard spent a week visiting Harold and Maude DeVol in Wanakena (St. Lawrence County). Bernard was the first ham radio operator in the area. He had the call letters W20WZ. He was also a member of the Lions Club. One of the long-term charitable projects of the Lions Club has been helping the visually handicapped. Bernard and Virginia trained a young Labrador dog in 1975 and 1976 to be a guide for a blind person.

The Town of Rose Historical Society Museum began as a project of the Lions Club in 1972. Initially, the museum was in the Rose Town Hall (the former North Rose Presbyterian Church) and later in the Old Rose School. More recently, the museum moved into the North Rose bank building and has most likely found its permanent home there. It is officially called the Farnsworth Museum—named after Bernard—who donated many of the first items in the collection. Other early acquisitions were Otis A. Gray's carpentry tools and Frank Seelye's Native American artifacts. The Town of Rose Historical Society now operates the museum, but it retains Bernard's name.

In August 1953 Gary Weed spent a week with Bernie & Virginia's son Craig at the Farnsworth cottage on Sodus Bay. In June 1961 Craig earned a dramatics club award at the NRCS student banquet. As an adult, Craig became a piloting enthusiast. He is the owner of a 2,600-foot grass airstrip on Salter Road, just east of the hamlet. He flew to such pleasant vacation destinations as Florida, the Bahamas, New Orleans, and Boston.

During the Vietnam War, Craig served in an Army grave registration unit processing the bodies of Americans killed in combat.

Besides being a pilot, Craig is a boater. He picked up a boat in France in 1999 and cruised across the Atlantic. He was president of Farnsworth and Son, Inc. funeral directors. Craig followed his father into the Lions Club and like Bernard, Craig became a ham radio operator. In 1978 Craig was the proprietor of Farnsworth's Olde Colonial House. This was a furniture store that specialized in traditional and early American style furniture. Craig was a member of the North Rose Fire Department. Keysor Funeral Home purchased his funeral practice. Craig retired to Brunswick, Georgia.

Craig wed Mary Camilla Farnsworth, a biologist and science teacher at North Rose-Wolcott High School, originally from Lyons. Craig and Mary have become craftspeople in their retirement. Craig is a woodworker and Mary is a basket weaver.

Farnsworth, John & Myrtie

30–32 Gray Street, now 5082 Gray—Built in 1850. Estimated 1940 value: $2,200.
John William Farnsworth (1882–1977), 58, head of household, self-employed (proprietor, furniture store), 52 weeks.
Myrtle "Myrtie" Josephine Brown Farnsworth (1881–1948), 58, wife, homemaker.
Anna Lenora Lewis (1921–1990), 19, lodger, unemployed.

MYRTIE AND JOHN WERE MARRIED on March 8, 1905, in Port Gibson (Ontario County). John had completed six years of school; Myrtie had completed eight. They had a son, Bernard C. Farnsworth (1909–1995). (See "Farnsworth, Bernie & Virginia.") John's father was William D. Farnsworth (1850–1917); his mother was Sylvia Demaris Farnsworth (1853–1934). John and Bernie ran Farnsworth and Son Funeral Directors in North Rose, which also housed a furniture sales business.

Anna Lewis completed two years of high school. Her father was Lloyd Byron Lewis (1873–1947), a farmer in the Town of Rose, and her mother was Maude L. Silliman (1885–1960). She was married twice—first to C. Eugene Towne and then to John A. Winters. She was survived by one son, Norris E. Towne, NRCS class of 1964.

We were unable to obtain much more than the cursory information provided by the census for this household. If you have more information, see page 32.

Favreau, Caroline

16 Maple Avenue, now 10410 Maple—Built in 1890. Estimated 1940 value: $2,500.
Caroline L. Brecht Favreau (ca. 1864–1948), 76, head of household, homemaker.

CAROLINE WAS A WIDOW AND a homemaker and had attended school through the ninth grade. Her parents were born in Germany. Her late husband, Ernest E. Favreau (ca. 1862–ca. 1916), had been an accomplished musician and was born in French Canada. The couple had two children: Ernest H. (ca. 1883–1964), who lived next door (see "Favreau, Ernest & Carrie"), and Alice (1887–1940). Before moving to North Rose, Caroline and her husband lived in Oswego, where Ernest was a music teacher and band leader. In May 1912 Caroline visited Montreal with her daughter, Alice.

Alice married Howard L. Harder (1890–1967) in September 1919. Howard had been a widower for one year and had two children, Richard and Arlene. Caroline was living with Alice's family on their farm in the Town of Butler by 1920. In October 1923, Alice's brother, Ernest H. Favreau bought the Harder family farm at a foreclosure sale for $4,550. At some point in the early 1920s Alice and Howard separated because in 1924 Alice was living with her mother in Wolcott and Howard remarried in 1926. Caroline and Alice moved to Maple Avenue in North Rose.

In May 1930 Caroline hosted her brother and sister-in-law from Oswego, Mr. and Mrs. Aubrecht. (Note: Caroline and her brother used different surnames. Caroline's maiden name was Brecht while her brother went by Aubrecht.) Alice was a bookkeeper for her brother's wholesale produce business and enjoyed playing bridge. Caroline and her daughter often visited family and friends in Oswego—especially Caroline's sister, Mrs. Belle Murdock. Belle passed away in September 1935. Alice died in March 1940. Caroline, her son Ernest, his wife Carrie, and their son Ernest Jr. visited Mr. and Mrs. Edmond Favreau in Montreal in July 1940.

In June 1943 Mr. and Mrs. Edward Closs moved into Caroline's

Maple Avenue home. In July of 1945, Mr. and Mrs. Harold Burns moved into the house from Huron Street.

Caroline spent her final days in Wolcott. She passed away in September 1948.

Favreau, Ernest & Carrie

18 Maple Avenue, now 10416 Maple—Built in 1875. Estimated 1940 value: $5,000.
Ernest H. Favreau (1883–1964), 56, head of household, owner of privately held corporation, self-employed.
Carrie E. Favreau (1888–1963), 51, wife, homemaker.
Ernest H. Favreau Jr. (1916–1999), 23, son, unemployed.

ERNEST AND CARRIE WERE MARRIED in June 1911. Their adult son, Ernest H. Jr., had limitations on his ability to work and was living with them. Ernest (Sr.) was a high school graduate and owned E.H. Favreau Co., Inc., a wholesale produce business with a warehouse. Although he had incorporated the business in 1917, he reported no occupation, industry, or hours worked to the 1940 census worker. Carrie was a homemaker, had worked as a bookkeeper in Rochester during the 1920s, and had completed two years of high school. Ernest Jr. had attended Nazareth Hall School in Rochester and had completed the sixth grade.

Ernest and Carrie not only named their son Ernest, but they also shared the same first names with his parents—Ernest and Caroline, or "Carrie." Their daughter, Harriet Alice (Ernest's sister's name was Alice), was born in 1919 and took dancing lessons with Mrs. Ralph Hotchkiss of Lyons. Tragically Harriet died of appendicitis in 1930, when she was only 11. In 1931 Ernest (Sr.) was a member of the committee that attempted to reorganize the North Rose bank.

Carrie was a member of the Catholic Daughters of America. The family spent the winter of 1937 in Rochester. In December 1939 Carrie and Ernest Jr. were cut and bruised in an auto accident on Ridge Road when a car skidded and struck their vehicle. For many years, the

Favreaus enjoyed vacationing in the Adirondacks at their cottage at Mrs. George Smith's camps in Wilmington (Essex County). In 1950 Ernest and Carrie bought a new Buick. In 1961 they celebrated their golden wedding anniversary.

Ernest H. Favreau Jr. was living in Sodus before he died in 1999.

Fink, Frank & Josephine

10 Maple Avenue, now 10400 Maple—Built in 1890. Estimated 1940 value: $1,500.

Franklin "Frank" J. Fink (1865–1948), 74, head of household, farm laborer, 20 weeks at $15 a week.

Josephine Farnsworth Fink (1873–1943), 66, wife, bean picker, 32 weeks at $11 a week.

Iva Mae Betts (ca. 1926–), 14, granddaughter, student.

FRANKLIN AND JOSEPHINE FINK WERE MARRIED in 1889. In 1940 they were taking care of their granddaughter Iva Betts. Frank completed the fourth grade. He was still employed as a laborer at 74, and was also looking for another job. The highest level of education that Josephine completed was the fifth grade. She was a bean picker in the Bean House.

None of the Finks' four daughters were living with their parents in 1940. Their names were: Julia (1890–1969), Greta (1892–1957), Edna (1899–1958), and Eva J. (1907–1992), who was Iva's mother.

Frank's parents were German immigrants, and although Frank and Josephine lived in Huron around 1900–1910, Frank lived in the Town of Rose for most of his life. In 1910 Frank was working as a farm manager, but by 1920 the Finks had moved to North Rose and Frank was working as a laborer on the railroad.

By 1930 Frank had returned to farm labor. The Finks were living on Maple Street along with their daughter Greta, their son-in-law Claude Brown (a millwright), and their granddaughter Isabelle (see "Brown, Claude & Greta.")

In June 1939, for Frank and Josephine's golden wedding anniversary, their children threw them a surprise party. Their children entertained, and Greta and Claude hosted the party in their home.

Josephine and her father were born in English-speaking Canada, while her mother was born in New York State. Josephine was an active member of the North Rose Presbyterian Church, and—along with her daughter, Greta—a member of The Rebekah Utopia Lodge No. 400.

The Finks' daughter Julia married Albert "Bert" Richardson (1892–1987) of Rose in 1911 and had two children, Franklin and Lloyd. The Richardsons lived on the Jeffers farm in Sodus and later in Huron. Bert operated a small canning factory. Julia was active in the Presbyterian Church and the Home Bureau. In April 1939 she was elected president of the Sigma Society of the Presbyterian Church. Bert was very active in the Wolcott Grange. (At one time, the Wolcott Grange was the largest in the state.) In August 1943 the couple hosted a "Fenk" family picnic, with 47 guests, at their home. (Some family members went by the name "Fink," some by "Fenk," and others used the names interchangeably.) Julia joined the American Legion Auxiliary in Clyde after her son's service in World War II and raised chickens on quite a large scale.

Julia's son Lloyd Richardson married Doris Helen Chalupa in October 1939. The couple initially lived with Lloyd's parents. Their daughter, Catherine Pauline Richardson, was born in February 1941. Lloyd enlisted in the Navy in October 1942. In June 1947 Doris began advertising Doris's Dress Shop, operating out of her new home on Wolcott Street. Doris was also active in the Home Bureau and the Rebekah Lodge. Lloyd and Doris Richardson, Bert and Julia Richardson, and Ward and Ruth Buhlmann attended a canners' convention in Buffalo in December 1950.

Julia's son Franklin Richardson married Ethel Marie Ross in March 1941. The couple lived in Earlville (on the border of Madison and Chenango counties) in March 1943. They lost their 1-year-old son, Maynard Leo Richardson, in October 1945. In 1946 they had a second son, Eugene, and by that November were living in Lyons.

Frank and Josephine's daughter Greta Fink married Claude Brown of Baldwinsville (Onondaga County) in October 1913. They had a daughter, (Greta) Isabelle. They lived with the Richardsons (Greta's sister Julia's family) shortly after their marriage, and lived with Greta's parents (the Finks) for a part of 1930. The Browns moved into the Besenfelder house on Gray Street in July of 1930 and hosted the first annual Fink family reunion there in August.

Greta's father, Frank Fink, was elected president of the reunion organization. In September 1930 Greta entertained the Sigma Society. The Browns attended the canners' banquet at the Hotel Seneca, in Geneva, with the Richardsons in December 1938. Claude bought the Foster house on the northern end of Gray Street. In December 1940 Claude attended the canners' convention in Buffalo with his brother-in-law Bert. Peter and Ruth Barton purchased Claude's Gray Street house. In October 1941 Claude and Greta moved to the old McCall farm. In the latter part of the 1940s, Claude was actively buying and selling real estate in Wayne County.

Frank and Josephine's granddaughter Isabelle Brown married Russell McKay of Rochester in about 1940 and had a son, Russell Jr., who was known as "Rusty." By May 1943 the McKays had moved to Buffalo. Their daughter, Claudia Arlene, was born the following December.

Frank and Josephine's daughter Edna Fink married George Rosa. They lived in Monroe County and had a son named Kenneth, born in about 1922.

Frank and Josephine's daughter Eva married Charles Ivan Betts, son of Mr. and Mrs. James Betts of North Rose (see "Betts, James & Edith"). Eva and Ivan lived in Huron, and then moved to Frank Hill's house on Fifth Road. Their daughter Iva lived with Frank and Josephine in the early 1940s. At this time, Eva Betts lived alone in Rochester, and Ivan—an apple packer at the Cold Storage—lived with his parents on the west side of South Main Street in North Rose.

Iva was a member of the Girl Scouts. In July 1942 she attended the Young People's Institute at Keuka. She graduated from NRCS in 1944—lettering in cheerleading. That July Iva moved to Rochester to live with her mother, and accepted a position in the Lincoln Alliance

Bank there. Iva often returned to North Rose on the weekends to visit her grandfather.

She married Wilmer C. Hall (1921–1985) in October 1946 and gave birth to their first son, David (1947–2015), the following May. In 1950 they lived in Rochester and Wilmer was a brakeman for the railroad; he and Iva had four more children: Lance, Kathleen, Audrey, and Beta. David Hall served in the Vietnam War with the U.S. Marines and was awarded a Purple Heart.

In 2024, at 98 years old, Iva was living in Monroe, North Carolina.

Fink, George

7 Gray Street, now 5043 Gray—Built in 1900. Estimated 1940 value: $1,500.

George Harrison Fink (or Fenk) (1870–1949), 70, head of household, railroad laborer, 35 weeks for $625.

GEORGE MARRIED IDA BELLE WOLF (1874–1939) in 1891 and they had two children: name unknown, born 1892, and Grace Lorena Fenk (1894–1983). George finished eight years of school. Two of his brothers lived in North Rose, one recently deceased. (See "Fink, Frank & Josephine" and "Fink, Nettie.")

George's parents were Christopher Christian Fenk (1830–1900), and Franziska Catherine Kate Homeman (1841–1919).

Grace married Charles David Pitcher (1892–1956) in 1912. Their second child, a son, died in infancy in 1917. They had three daughters: Marjorie Elizabeth Pitcher (1913–1999), Frances Belle Pitcher (1919–1995), and Jean Eloise Pitcher (1923–2013).

We were unable to obtain much more than the cursory information provided by the census for this household. If you have more information, see page 32.

Fink, Nettie

228 Main Street. Estimated 1940 value: $2,500.

Nettie Mae Hart Fink (1886–1963), head of household, 55, farmer.

NETTIE'S HUSBAND, HENRY FINK (1876–1939), died a year before the 1940 census. Henry had more than a dozen siblings; two of his brothers, Frank and George, lived in North Rose in 1940 (see "Fink, George," and "Fink, Frank & Josephine"). Henry was first married to Maud Miner (1878–1910). By 1897 they had four children: Hazel M. Fink, Donald C. Fink, Mildred Fink, and Harold Fink. After being widowed, he married Nettie, who had completed eight years of school, and she gave birth to Gilman H. Fink (1921–1941). The 1940 census had Gilman listed as an "inmate" at the "Craig Colony (for Epileptics)" in Sonyea (Livingston County). Gilman died the following year.

Nettie remarried, to Frank E. Loveless (1884–1951), and outlived him as well. She died in Barber Hospital in Lyons at 79, a few weeks after breaking her hip.

Fowler, Charles and Etta

7 Caroline Street, now 10391 Caroline—Built in 1927. Estimated 1940 value: $1,400.

Charles Gillett Fowler (1881–1949), 58, head of household, manager at the gas station, 32 weeks for $700

Etta E. Bargy Fowler (1882–1952), 58, wife, bean picker at O. A. Skutt Company, 33 weeks for $250.

CHARLES AND ETTA BOTH completed eight years of school. They married in 1905 and had three children: Kenneth Charles Fowler (1907–1935), Ruth E. Fowler (1909–2003), and Floyd Edward Fowler (1910–1957). Charles's parents were Dewitt Clinton Fowler Sr. (1844–1920) and Phoebe M. Gillett (1853–1915). Etta's parents were Peter Bargy (1845–1929) and Mary Elizabeth Rowe (1849–1929).

We were unable to obtain much more than the cursory information provided by the census for this household. If you have more information, see page 32.

Fox, Bert & Maude

13 South Main Street, now 4975 South Main—Built in 1900. Estimated 1940 value: $1,800.
Albert "Bert" Henry Fox (1880–1970), 59, head of household, apple runner, the Cold Storage, 36 weeks for $500.
Maude M. Baker Fox (1879–1965), 60, wife, bean picker at O. A. Skutt, 2 weeks for $20.

BERT'S PARENTS WERE Charles Fox (1850–1931) and May Mary Lincks (1846–1931). Maude's parents were Marcus M. Baker (1847–1939) and Mary D. Genung Baker (1851–1936). Bert and Maude got married in 1905 and soon had a son, Albert Leo Fox (1907–1960).

A. Leo Fox graduated from Syracuse University in 1931. He taught science and coached basketball at Brighton High School (Monroe County) from 1931 to 1936. He coached the RIT basketball team for 15 years, with a winning record for 13 of those 15 and an undefeated season in 1955–1956, after which he retired.

We were unable to obtain much more than the cursory information provided by the census for this household. If you have more information, see page 32.

Fox, Belle

1940 monthly rent: $8.
Arloa Belle Powell Fox (1887–1975), 52, head of household, bean picker at O. A. Skutt, 40 weeks for $350.

BELLE WAS MARRIED TO GEORGE WASHINGTON FOX (1873–1930), a widower 15 years her senior with three grown children, in 1927. The marriage lasted only a few years before Belle became a widow.

George's parents were Lewis Fox (1845–1916) and Mary Goetzman (1853–1914). George and Bert Fox were first cousins (see "Fox, Bert & Maude"). Belle's parents were James H. Powell (1858–1940) and Emma Belle Bullock Powell (1861–1919). She had a brother who lived in North Rose. (See "Powell, George & Lulu.")

We were unable to obtain much more than the cursory information provided by the census for this household. If you have more information, see page 32.

Fox, Dora

44 North Huron Street—Built in 1916. Estimated 1940 value: $1,100.
Dora Kelly Perkins Fox (1867–1942), 72, homemaker.

DORA COMPLETED SIX YEARS of school. She was a widow, but she lived alone well before the death of her late husband. Dora grew up in the Town of Sodus with her parents, George H. Perkins (1832–1899), a farmer, and Martha York Perkins (1833–1916), and Dora's brother John Perkins (1870–1943). Martha's parents were from Maine. George and Martha lost a young daughter, Sarah (1859–1861), before Dora was born. By 1892 George's mother, Sarah Weatherly (1808–1899), widow of George "Harvey" Perkins (1816–1865), had joined the household.

Dora married Clark M. Fox (ca. 1864–1910) of Alton, a farmer, in March 1893. The wedding took place in Wayne County, Michigan. Clark was the son of George H. Fox and Rebecca R. Meyers Fox of Alton; Clark had already married once, in 1890, to Minnie Cutting (1863–1924). In September 1899 Clark attended the Newark Fair with Fred Fox, Harry Fowler, and Fred Davenport.

By 1900 Dora lived alone in Sodus. By May 1903 Dora had moved to Alton. Clark lived in York Settlement in Huron, south of Ridge Road. Dora lived on Preemption Road in Sodus in 1905. (The small settlement arrayed along this road sometimes went by the name of Preemption or Sodus-Preemption.)

Preemption Road

Several different Preemption Roads in different counties run along the old western boundary of New York State. Massachusetts once owned the land to the west of this line, although it was not contiguous with that state. In the 1780s, the country west of the Preemption Line was "aboriginal land" (i.e., occupied by Native Americans). The Treaty of Hartford (1786) settled this boundary. The Preemption Line or borderline ran straight south from Sodus Bay, narrowly missing Geneva, and continuing to the Pennsylvania border. The word preemption refers to the pre-emptive right that Massachusetts received to negotiate with the native sovereign tribes—pre-empting New York State. It also referred to the pre-emptive rights of the two state governments above that of individuals who could not negotiate with tribes without first securing a patent from the respective legislature. Because, by chance, the Preemption Line pointed at the newly created District of Columbia, some people thought that alignment had some special significance. It didn't. Incidentally, the survey had to be repeated because the first survey line pointed toward the magnetic north pole instead of the geographical pole.

In December 1905 Dora visited friends in Syracuse and New York City. Dora's former husband, Clark Fox, died in Syracuse in June 1910 after living outside of Wayne County for several years. From about 1910 to 1916, Dora lived with her mother, Martha Perkins, on Preemption Road in Sodus. In June 1916 Martha died at her daughter Dora's home. By 1920 Dora had moved to North Rose, where she would live the rest of her life.

(There was another Dora Fox afoot in North Rose around this time. A Dora Fox stayed at the home of Benjamin F. Pitcher in North Rose until April 1912. Then she returned with her mother, Mrs. A.J. Ticknor, to her home in Fond du Lac, Wisconsin.)

French, Mark & Elizabeth
25 North Poplar Street, now 5055 North Poplar—Built in 1910. Estimated 1940 value: $2,800.

Mark Leonard French (1888–1944), 51, head of household, printer, 34 weeks, self-employed.
Elizabeth van de Putte French (1890–1984), 49, wife, homemaker.
Elizabeth Neufligier van Eden (1860–1951), 79, mother-in-law, retired.
Myrtle Dobbin (1921–1949), 18, lodger, student.

MARK FRENCH HAD COMPLETED eight years of school and owned his own "job printing" business. Elizabeth had completed seven years of school and was a homemaker. Elizabeth French's mother, Elizabeth van Eden, shared the Frenches' home. So did a lodger, Myrtle Dobbin, a student who had completed two years of high school. Elizabeth French's parents were both natives of The Netherlands. Her father was Abraham van de Putte (1860–1923). Her mother was Elizabeth Neufligier van de Putte; she had not attended school. She was the same woman who was later known as Elizabeth van Eden.

Mark French's parents were Rev. Frank B. French (1854–1899), a schoolteacher, and Celia V. Foster French (1861–1927). They married around 1879. Mark was born in Summerhill (Cayuga County) in 1888. (President Millard Fillmore was also a native of Summerhill.) Mark's father died in 1899, when Mark was 10 and his younger sister Ruth was not yet 1. In 1900 Celia was living with Mark and Ruth; her 17-year-old daughter Myrtle (1882–1945) was living and working as a domestic in a separate Summerhill household. The following year, Ruth died of pneumonia, age 2½.

Mark's mother, Celia, married John J. Miner (1855–1929) around 1901. John was a farmer from Michigan who bought the Bender farm in the Town of Rose from Charles Garlick in April 1902. As a young man, Mark lived and worked on the Miner farm for several years. Mark married Elizabeth van de Putte in March 1913; the newlyweds lived in North Rose.

In 1919 Mark and Elizabeth lived in a rented home at 50 Turpin Street in Rochester with their 5-year-old daughter, Celia Elizabeth French (1913–2000). Mark worked as a tile maker. The next year he worked as a machinist in a machine shop. In the early 1920s, Mark and his family returned to North Rose. Initially they lived at 7 South Poplar Street. In October 1929 Mark gained the Democratic Party's nomination for tax collector for the Town of Rose. He won the election. By that time, Mark had also started a printing business.

The Frenches were members of the Free Methodist Church of Rose—the denomination formed in Pekin (Niagara County) in 1860. Some members of the Methodist Episcopal Church were expelled from the congregation because their beliefs struck the mainstream Methodists as "extreme." The worshipers who were expelled organized themselves as the Free Methodists. The Free Methodists believed that they were adhering to the original teachings of church founders John Wesley and his brother Charles Wesley. The Free Methodist church emphasized personal faith and good works. They were "Free" because they were abolitionists and because their church pews were free of rent. Free Methodists were evangelical and unpretentious. The Frenches adopted simple clothing. The denomination grew as like-minded people established churches in other communities, including Rose.

In September 1935 many church friends from Rose celebrated a surprise birthday party for Elizabeth. In March 1939 Mark and Elizabeth hosted several family friends and relatives for a birthday dinner in honor of Elizabeth's mother, Elizabeth Van Eden. Mark gained the Republican nomination for assessor (two-year term) in October 1939. He won the election. Mark received bipartisan support in the Town of Rose. In November 1940 Elizabeth won election as vice president of the local Women's Christian Temperance Union. Mark died in January 1944 after a month's illness.

Elizabeth French hosted evening prayer meetings at her home associated with the Rose Free Methodist Church. Often Elizabeth helped in the A. Gray Skutt home, doing laundry and household tasks and taking care of young Marilyn Skutt. Marilyn remembers her as a kind caregiver.

Mark and Elizabeth's daughter Celia was one of four girls in the NRCS Class of 1932 who traveled to Washington, D.C., on the customary senior trip. Celia attended Chesbrough Junior College in

North Chili (now Roberts Wesleyan College, in Monroe County), Houghton College in Houghton (Allegany County) in 1936, and Geneseo Normal School (now SUNY Geneseo) in 1938 for a librarian course. Celia taught French in Greenwood (Steuben County) for a semester starting in January 1940. The next school year, she taught and was the high school librarian at Avoca Central School (also Steuben County).

By 1943, Celia had returned to North Rose. She became a favorite high school teacher at NRCS. She taught English and Latin and directed school plays.

In late 1946 Celia underwent two surgeries at the Cortland Hospital. After an extended hospital stay, she convalesced at the home of her uncle in Homer under the care of her mother, Elizabeth French. Celia returned to North Rose in February 1947. Elizabeth Lawrence substituted for her, teaching English in her absence. Celia resumed her pedagogical duties at NRCS by the fall of 1947. In July 1949 the NRCS Alumni Association elected Celia as their president.

Celia French Sattler

Celia French got married late in life, to widower Charles L. Sattler (1910–1997). Charles, a muck farmer, married his first wife, Alberta M. Norris Sattler (1910–1967), in November 1930. That earlier marriage resulted in one son, John Charles Sattler (1932–1983).

The eldest member of the French household in 1940 was Elizabeth French's mother, Elizabeth van Eden. She was born in The Netherlands and immigrated to the U.S. around 1884. Her maiden name was Elizabeth Neufligier. Abraham Van de Putte (1852–) was her first husband. Elizabeth and Abraham had three children, including Elizabeth in 1890 and William (1892–1981). The family lived in Union Hill (on the border of Wayne and Monroe Counties). William moved to Rochester, where he worked as a machinist and married Clara C. Latosky in August 1912. The couple next moved to Williamson. Elizabeth became a naturalized citizen in 1900. Elizabeth van de Putte's second husband was Adrian VandenBrook (1861–1926). (His birth name in Holland was Adriaan van den Broek.) They married about 1907. He had immigrated to the United States in about 1889 and became a naturalized citizen in 1900. In 1910 Elizabeth and Adrian lived in Chili (Monroe County). In 1913 Adrian bought property in Williamson.

Also, from Holland was Elizabeth's third husband, Jacob van Eden (1860–1935). Jacob and his first wife, Cora Hollebrandt (1854–1927) had immigrated to the United States from The Netherlands in 1890. He became a naturalized citizen in Rochester in 1911. Jacob and Cora van Eden lived in Williamson in 1925. Jacob was a farmer.

Elizabeth VandenBrook married Jacob van Eden in October 1928 in her home in Williamson, where they took up residence. Jacob soon retired. After Jacob's death in 1935, Elizabeth van Eden began to spend more time in North Rose with her daughter Elizabeth French and son-in-law Mark French. She spent the entire winter and early spring of 1940 with the Frenches—returning to Williamson at the end of April. She was still living with the Frenches when the census enumerator visited, so she was counted as living in North Rose instead of Williamson. In 1949 Elizabeth van Eden again spent part of the year living in North Rose with the Frenches.

Although the 1940 census form lists Myrtle C. Dobbin as a "lodger," she was likely treated as a foster daughter. In 1930 Myrtle lived with her widowed grandmother Catherine M. Wood and her uncle Wallace K. Wood in the Town of Rose. She attended the Stewart's Corners rural school and was active in the 4-H club. By 1935 Myrtle lived with the Frenches. In December 1940 the newly formed Youth Temperance organization at the Rose Methodist Church elected Myrtle secretary.

In February 1941 at a Valentine's Day dinner party, Myrtle announced her engagement to Charles Powell (ca. 1919–1949) of Rose. Charles was the son of Luther and Cora Powell, who moved their family to Rose from rural Fulton County, Pennsylvania, in the 1930s. Myrtle and Charles's wedding took place in August 1941 at the Frenches' home. The newlyweds began their married life in a house on North Poplar Street. In June 1942 Charles and Myrtle moved to the Moore house on Huron Street. Charles's fellow workers at Hickok Manufacturing presented him with a monetary gift when he received his draft notice from the armed services. In February 1944 Charles advanced to the rank of corporal and won a medal for marksmanship. While her husband was in the service, Myrtle moved back to the French home. In January 1946 Charles returned to North Rose after receiving an honorable discharge from the Army. By May 1947 Charles and Myrtle were parents of a daughter, Celia Powell.

In February 1950 Celia French accepted guardianship for young Celia Powell after her parents perished in a three-vehicle accident on Route 104 east of Sodus. The accident occurred just two days before Christmas of 1949. Because of multiple injuries she sustained in the crash, Celia Powell recovered in the hospital for nearly two months. Upon her recovery, Celia French took Celia Powell into the French home and raised her as her daughter. Celia Powell's deceased mother, Myrtle, was the same person as the young "lodger" who had lived in the French home 10 years earlier.

In 2024 Celia Powell was living in the house on North Poplar Street.

Gage, Harold & Lydia

1940 monthly rent: $18
Harold John Gage (1905–1976), 35, head of household, farmer, 52 weeks for $150.
Lydia Jane Syron Gage (1911–1996), 28, wife, public schoolteacher, 40 weeks for $1,375.
Virginia Stone (1919–2004), 21, lodger, public schoolteacher, 40 weeks for $900.

Lydia Gage, in the 1962 NRCS yearbook

HAROLD AND LYDIA WERE MARRIED on June 30, 1934, in the rectory of St. John's Catholic Church in Clyde. Harold's parents were Frederick William Gage (1880–1940) and Margaret M. Dawson (1880–1917). Lydia's were Roy Sloan Syron (1885–1932) and Myrtle Susan Bond (1890–1962). Harold had completed the standard eight years of school, while Lydia and their lodger, Virginia, had each completed three years of college.

Virginia soon married Warren Baldridge and by 1950 she was no longer teaching school; she was a homemaker with three young sons: Scott, Mark, and Kenan. (See "Baldridge, Herbert & Meda.")

We were unable to obtain much more than the cursory information provided by the census for this household. If you have information about the Gages, see page 32.

Gage, Henry & Hattie

85 North Main Street, now 5117 North Main—Built in 1900. Estimated 1940 value: $3,000.
Henry M. Gage (1878–1968), 61, head of household, bus driver and groundskeeper, 52 weeks for $1,190.
Hattie Davis Gage (1880–1968), 59, wife, trimmer, 22 weeks for $250.

HENRY AND HATTIE COMPLETED eight years of school. Henry worked as a groundskeeper and school bus driver for NRCS. Hattie worked part-time as a trimmer at the Canning Factory. The Gages married in June 1899.

When his parents named Henry, they gave him a middle initial: M, but not an actual middle name. As a young child, Henry lived on his parents' farm in Wolcott. He was the son of Edwin J. Gage (1854–1899) and Ida Miller Gage (1856–1931). Henry's parents separated around 1915.

Hattie Gage's parents were Caleb U. Davis (1833–1921) and Frances Jane Church Davis (1837–1906). They had a large family—Hattie was the youngest of 11. Caleb farmed in the Town of Ulysses (Tompkins County), and then in Huron.

In 1900 Henry and Hattie lived in the Town of Rose. Henry worked as a farm laborer. The Gages lived in the Town of Galen in 1910. They took two boarders into their home. Their daughter Dorothy H. Gage (1911–2004) was born after the Gages moved to Rose. In 1914 Henry worked for George Marshall. In June 1917 Henry and Hattie saw the Ringling Bros. Circus in Rochester with a couple of friends. (Two years later that classic traveling show merged with the

Barnum and Bailey Circus.)

By 1918 the Gages had moved to North Rose. In March 1918 Henry sold his car to George Lyman. Henry worked as a farm manager for Orin A. Skutt. In April 1920 Henry moved from the O. A. Skutt farm to the Oaks farm. Later that year, the Gages lived on Clyde-Resort Road. Henry was again working as a farm laborer. Henry, Hattie, and Bert and Maude Fox spent part of July 1925 in the Morey cottage on LeRoy Island.

In January 1926 Hattie substituted for the ill D.P. Mitchell at the North Rose Post Office. Henry broke his foot while descending the cellar stairs in 1929. The next year, the three Gages lived on Wolcott Road in North Rose. Henry was driving a school bus for the North Rose School District and Dorothy was still attending school. Hattie was active in the Methodist Episcopal Church Kappa Phi Sunday school class.

In August 1935, Thorne Button, Peter Barton, Eugene Towne, Mark Skinner, and Henry Gage went to Syracuse to watch the Sunday baseball games. Most likely, it was a doubleheader hosted by the Syracuse Chiefs. That season, the Chiefs were the top farm club of the Boston Red Sox.

Hattie was an active member of the Thursday Club from about 1928 to 1933. In April 1936 Henry and Hattie bought the Garlic house at 85 North Main Street. Henry, Hattie, and Dorothy spent a week at Sodus Point in the Desmond cottage in August 1936. Later that month, the three Gages and Norris Seelye Towne took an auto trip to Philadelphia, Atlantic City, and New York. In March 1944 Henry retired from a 17-year stint as an NRCS bus driver. Hattie helped canvass North Rose for the American Red Cross Fund. The Gages celebrated their 50th wedding anniversary in Rochester in June 1949. In 1951 Hattie was active in the Chaloux Circle (a women's group affiliated with the North Rose Methodist Church). The Gages took a few-weeks-long trip to Florida with Bert and Media W. Pierson in February 1955.

At a party at her home, Henry and Hattie's daughter Dorothy announced her engagement to Norris Seelye "Red" Towne (1910–1967) of Rochester, son of Norris Eugene Towne (1876–1933) and Charlotte H. "Lottie" Towne (1881–1951) of North Rose. The wedding took place in October 1939. Jane Gilmore was Dorothy's attendant. Eugene Towne stood as his brother's best man. The couple honeymooned in New York City. The bride was the chief clerk of the Rochester Gas and Electric in Wolcott. Eastman Kodak employed the groom. They established a home at 4269 Culver Road in Rochester.

Most Talkative
Dottie Towne Phil Palermo

Dottie Towne in her high school yearbook

In October 1944 they became the parents of Dorothy Lee "Dottie" Towne. In January 1950 Dorothy and Seelye had a son, Lynne Seelye Towne (1950–2007). In July of that year Dottie spent a week with her grandparents. The 1962 yearbook for Rochester's East High School named Dottie the "most talkative" in her senior class.

In May 1967 Dottie married Rodney Taylor of Webster (Monroe County). The following month Seelye had a fatal heart attack at his camp on Eagle Bay (Herkimer County) in the Adirondacks. After being told by his physician that he needed rest, Seelye had gone to his wilderness retreat for an extended period.

Galloway, Vincent & Elizabeth

60 Fifth Road, now 5146 Fifth—Built 1915. 1940 monthly rent: $12.
Russell Vincent Galloway (1908–2005), 31, head of household, truck driver, 40 weeks for $1,100.

Betty Galloway, NRCS
Class of 1952

Elizabeth Mae Countryman Galloway (1913–1992) 25, wife, homemaker.
Betty Jean Galloway (1935–2004), 5, daughter.

VINCENT AND ELIZABETH MARRIED in December 1933. Vincent had finished one year of high school. Elizabeth's parents were Ralph "Obee" Countryman

(1897–1970) and Eunice Carrie Stickles (1896–1942).

Betty Jean married Robert L. Atkins in 1953; they made their home in Clyde. A daughter, Cheryl Lynne, was born in 1957.

We were unable to obtain much more than the cursory information provided by the census for this household. If you have more information, see page 32.

Gardner, Floyd

Main Street. 1940 monthly rent: $6.
Floyd Gardner (1902–1987), 36, head of household, farm laborer, 9 weeks for $120.

FLOYD GARDNER WAS ONE OF three children born to Grace Sherman (1877–1928) and William Gardner (1876–1928). Floyd had completed four years of school. Floyd had two brothers: Carl Gardner, born in 1907, and Henry Gardner, born in 1912.

We were unable to obtain much more than the cursory information provided by the census for this household. If you have information about the Gardners, see page 32.

Garlic, Traver & Ruth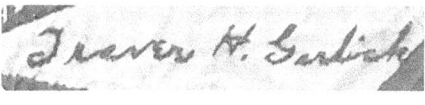

17 Maple Avenue, now 10413 Maple—Built in 1900. Estimated 1940 value: $3,000.
Traver Henry Garlic (1893–1958), 47, head of household, wholesaler, self-employed.
Ruth Thomas Garlic (1894–1968), 44, wife, homemaker.
Jane Alice Gilmore (1912–1981), 27, lodger, schoolteacher, 40 weeks for $34 a week.

MARRIED IN 1923, TRAVER AND RUTH GARLIC shared their home with Jane Gilmore, a lodger. Traver was the proprietor of a fruit-packing house and Ruth was a homemaker. The Garlics were high school graduates and Ms. Gilmore had completed four years of college.

The Garlics had a varied social life. In August 1930 the couple and Lawrence and Mildred Putney Fox spent their summer vacation in the Adirondacks at the Tellier camp in Croghan; the couple often returned to Croghan in subsequent years. Traver enjoyed fishing and hunting in that area with Oscar Weed, George Catchpole, and other friends. In September 1936 Traver was fishing in Sodus Bay when he caught a huge pickerel—33 inches long and weighing $7\frac{1}{2}$ pounds! The Garlics were members of the Literary Club and were frequent guests at Lloyd Marshall's cottage. In June 1948 Hayes and Frances Green Catchpole entertained in honor of the Garlics 25th wedding anniversary.

Traver was a native of North Rose and a graduate of Wolcott High School's Class of 1913. In 1915 he worked as a bookkeeper in Geneva, but he soon returned to North Rose and obtained a manager's position with Skutt, Welch & Aldrich, bean and grain storage and wholesaler. He was appointed the North Rose Postmaster in March 1927, reappointed in March 1932, and resigned in January 1936.

Like his neighbor Frank Noyes, Traver was very involved in the community. He was a member of a group who attempted to reorganize the "suspended" First National Bank of North Rose at a meeting held in November 1931, and was an officer of the Salter Hose and Chemical (Fire) Company—where he also served as treasurer in 1936. At the start of 1937, Traver was one of several prominent citizens who tried to convince the WPA to contribute to installing a municipal water system in the Town of Rose. They proposed that the system should include a standpipe, filtration system, and water mains, and that the water source would be natural springs. The project, without the help of the WPA, finally reached fruition in the 1950s. In June 1940 Traver became chairman of the local Red Cross committee. In December 1941 he was appointed both as War Relief Director of North Rose and as the treasurer of the Rose Lodge, No. 590 of the Free and Accepted Masons.

In August 1942 Traver attended the apple shippers' convention in Buffalo with A. Gray Skutt. From the summer of 1945 until early December of that year, Traver lived and worked in Albany. In February

1946 he sold his spray business to his neighbor, Frank Noyes, but the business continued to operate out of the Weed, Garlic & Wilson warehouse. Traver went to work for the Duffy Mott Company in Hamlin (Monroe County) and was transferred to Holley (Orleans County) in May 1947.

Traver's wife, Ruth, had two older brothers, Fred and William, and was a native of the Town of Huron. She was a member of the Luncheon Club and the Arbor Vitae chapter of the Order of the Eastern Star and was active in the Wayne County Women's Republican Club. She had a beautiful singing voice, and often entertained at weddings and community functions. After Ruth's father, John Thomas, died in January 1931, the Garlics rented out their Main Street home to Mr. and Mrs. Claude Gillette and moved into the Maple Avenue house with Ruth's mother, Katherine Oaks Thomas. Ruth lost her mother in November of the following year.

By December 1936 Ruth was an active member of the Kappa Phi society of the Methodist Episcopal Church and a member of the Bridge Club. In the mid-1940s, she began to attend meetings of the Lookup-Catchpole Club because her grandmother was a Catchpole. In May 1946 Ruth and four other women from North Rose attended a WSCS meeting in Waterloo. In May 1948 she was elected to the board of directors of the Wayne County Girl Scout Council. After Traver's death in the 1960s, Ruth resided in the Town of Butler.

The Garlics' lodger, Jane Gilmore, was from East Bloomfield (Ontario County). A college graduate, Jane began teaching mathematics at NRCS in the 1935–1936 school year. By 1939 her annual salary was $1,370.

Jane attended summer school with Lillian Hill at St. Lawrence University in Canton (St. Lawrence County), prior to September 1937 when she joined with a group of other young teachers—Grace Bowell, Miriam McHugh, Margaret Johnston, and Mildred Hetzke—to rent the Garlics' previous home on Main Street, with Mrs. Katherine Proseus as their housekeeper. Subsequent to this, she ended up renting a room in the Garlics' new home on Maple Avenue, which is where she was living in 1940.

Jane was a member of the Literary Club and the Arbor Vitae chapter of the Order of the Eastern Star. She sang at her friend Alyce Hill's wedding. Jane chaperoned the senior class trips to Washington, D.C., in 1938, 1939, and 1944. In 1939 she joined a bowling league and was attendant to the bride at Dorothy Gage's October wedding.

Jane's father, John Alexander Gilmore, died when Jane was about 8 years old. In September 1941 Jane's mother, Mrs. (Elizabeth) Mae Gilmore, moved to North Rose to be closer to her daughter for a year. In 1944 Jane attended summer school at the University of Rochester. That July, she was maid of honor at Helen Lucy McQueen's wedding. Jane was also close friends with Mr. and Mrs. Donald Lawrence and they camped and fished together.

Jane left NRCS after the 1944–1945 school year, accepting a position in guidance and mathematics at the Alfred–Almond Central School (Allegany County). This was the same area of the state where her brother John Elton Gilmore lived with his family.

Jane was living in Canandaigua when she married widower James Dean Baxter (1897–1967) on September 1, 1949; Jane's mother died later that month. The Baxters lived in Rochester in 1950 and afterwards lived in Palmyra. Their daughter, Jeanne Alice, was born on Valentine's Day 1953 in Clifton Springs (Ontario County) and baptized at Zion Church in Palmyra. Jane acquired two adult stepsons, James and George, from Mr. Baxter's previous marriage to Julianna Mikeltish (1893–1944). Jane died in 1981 in Oak Park, Illinois, just west of Chicago.

Ghent, Joe & Hazel

12 South Huron Street, now 4998 South Huron—Built in 1900. Estimated 1940 value: $1,800.

Joseph Ghent (1890–1965), 49, head of household, proprietor of barbershop, 52 weeks, self-employed.

Hazel Mae Steitler Ghent (1892–1971), 47, wife, homemaker.

Harold S. Ghent (1920–1943), 19, son, truck driver, 30 weeks at $8 a week.

Ida J. Messenger (1873–1953), 66, lodger.

Joe and Hazel married in 1918. They shared their home with their adult son, Harold, and a widowed lodger, Ida Messenger. Joe worked long hours in his barbershop, Hazel was a homemaker, Harold was a part-time local trucker, and Ida Messenger wasn't employed outside of the home. Joe had attended one year of college, his wife and son had both completed the eleventh grade, and Ida Messenger had finished the eighth grade.

Joe's parents were both born in England, but he was born in Sodus and lived most of his life in North Rose. He was on the board of deacons of the Rose Baptist Church. In 1933, while he was attending church in Rose, someone stole $40 worth of barbering instruments from his car. In August 1940 Joe moved his North Rose barbershop across Main Street to the Lawrence Building next to the Masonic Temple. He had worked out of the Quereau Block on the west side of the street for 22 years. Recently the town of Rose Historical Society purchased the Joseph Ghent barbershop.

Hazel was active in the Baptist Missionary Society and the Baptist Sunday School in Rose. In 1936 she supervised the Cradle Roll children's outreach of the Rose Baptist Church. In 1942 the Ghents and George Lee visited relatives in Pennsylvania and Maryland. In September 1947 Hazel was chosen secretary of the Ladies Auxiliary of the Rose American Legion.

As a child, Harold was a piano pupil of Mrs. Estella Roney. (See "Roney, Estella.") When he enlisted in the Army—in Rochester, on July 17, 1942—he was assigned to the engineers' corps. He died near Mukden, China, when two ships collided on February 12, 1943. Nine days before his death he had been promoted from Private to Technician Fifth Grade. T/5 Ghent's remains, initially buried in Bermuda, were brought back to North Rose for interment in December 1947.

After their son's death, Joe and Hazel called upon and aided patients at the Canandaigua Veterans' Hospital. Hazel became active in the Gold Star Mothers, an organization open to mothers whose sons were killed in the war. The Ghents also lost a nephew in the war—Robert Klippel of Rochester. In October 1950, at the United Congregational Church in Rochester, they attended the unveiling and dedication of a memorial painting honoring Klippel and another church member who had also died in the war.

The Ghents' lodger, Ida Messenger, was the widow of Walter L. Messenger (1873–1938). The Messengers had three daughters: Lula, Bertha, and Mary.

Lula (1896–1983) married George Powell and was living in North Rose in 1940. (See "Powell, George & Lula.")

Bertha (1899–1987) worked as a telephone operator in North Rose and Palmyra. She married Homer Pulver, a Palmyra policeman.

Mary (1911–1960) married Harvey Kepner (1910–1936) and lived in Montoursville, Pennsylvania. They had three children before Harvey died at 26. Mary had two more children with her second husband, Evelyn Drury. (See "Drury, Evelyn & Mary.")

Ida Messenger was hospitalized at Barber Hospital in Lyons in April 1950. Upon release, she stayed with her daughter Mary. In May 1953 Ida Messenger lost her grandson, Lula's 36-year-old son, Gerald Powell. Gerald had served in the South Pacific during World War II.

Gillette, Claude & Frieda

1940 monthly rent: $22.
Claude Coe Gillette (1905–1987), 34 head of household, schoolteacher, 48 weeks for $2,700.
Frieda Louise Machholz Gillette (1907–1997), 33, wife, homemaker.
Richard Gillette (1934–), 6, son, student.
Marjory Gillette (1937–), 3, daughter.

Richard Gillette, NRCS Class of 1952

CLAUDE GRADUATED FROM Bacon Academy in Colchester, Connecticut, in 1924 and Connecticut Agricultural College in 1928. Frieda was a high school graduate. Claude and Frieda were married in September 1929, and he received a master's degree in entomology from Cornell in 1930.

Claude Gillette from the NRCS 1967 yearbook

Claude taught vocational agriculture in North Rose, before retiring in 1967 to run his own farm in Traer, Iowa. From his obituary: "An agricultural award to further education of a student in North Rose, NY, is being established c/o the Rose Grange, North Rose, NY."

We were unable to obtain much more than the cursory information provided by the census for this household. If you have information about the Gillettes, see page 32.

Graham, Susie

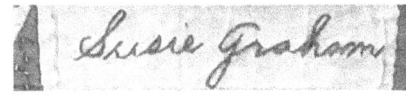

21 South Main Street, now 4957 South Main—Estimated 1940 value: $5,000.
Susan Graham (1895–1964), 46, head of household, bookkeeper.

SUSAN E. GRAHAM WAS A HIGH SCHOOL GRADUATE who worked as a bookkeeper for the Cold Storage. Susie was single. She was the daughter of Nelson Graham (1845–1927) and Florence Lovejoy Graham (1866–1933). Nelson was a farmer in the Town of Rose. He had retired by 1910. In 1930 Florence and Susie lived together after Nelson's death.

At 9, in 1905, Susie was the associate editor of the "North Rose Union School Column," which appeared as a subsection of the North Rose column in *The Record* (Sodus). Susie was a member of the Class of 1913 at Wolcott High School. That fall, she began further studies at the Mechanics Institute of Rochester. This school grew over the years and in 1944 was renamed the Rochester Institute of Technology. Susie left the school after only one year.

In 1915 she worked as a bookkeeper. Susie traveled to Washington, D.C., with Olga Catchpole and Ralph Jeffers in April 1914. In February 1917, Susie took a short sabbatical from her bookkeeping duties when she pinch-hit teaching sixth and seventh grades in the North Rose School in the absence of Grace Keeler, who had appendicitis.

She assisted at the Hawley Bank in Red Creek in June 1917. In 1920 she was a bank accountant. In the early 1920s, Susie enjoyed outings to The Evergreens, the popular restaurant in Sodus Center. Susie and her longtime friend Ruth Marshall relaxed at Wilmington (Essex County) in July 1924 in the Whiteface Mountain district of the Adirondacks. In August 1925 Susie assisted in the opening of the Savannah First National Bank.

Susie returned to the Mechanics Institute in the 1920s to complete her college education. She received a degree in homemaking in 1926. In August 1929 Susie took a trip through the Catskills with Earl and Lillian Barnes and Harry E. Partrick. Later that month, she assisted at the Savannah Bank. In October 1929 Susie and Lillian Barnes attended a Grand Army of the Republic (GAR) event in Watertown. The GAR was the preeminent veterans' association of Civil War Union Soldiers and their descendants.

In December 1929 Susie was selected to be the treasurer of the Methodist Episcopal Sunday school; she was also active in the Kappa Phi class. She was a member of the Luncheon Club, a group of women that met at a restaurant, and some of the members provided entertainment. Arch Graham of Utica spent two weeks visiting his niece Susie and her mother, Florence, in July and August 1931.

Susie was a sociable person and often organized shopping trips and meals with her circle of acquaintances, with frequent trips to Rochester. Shopping companions often included Evelyn Salter, Sarah Ball, Florence Graham (Susie's mother), and Martha Peck. Florence and Susie spent Christmas 1932 in Rochester with Alfred and Anna James and their family. In July 1934 Susie took a trip through the Adirondacks with Earl and Lillian Barnes and Harry and Grace Partrick. In December 1937 Joseph Keefe lost control of his truck at night on Dagle hill on South Main Street and struck Susie's house and the home of George Ball. Susie vacationed two weeks during the summer of 1938 at Henderson Harbor (Jefferson County).

In February 1940 Susie was a member of the bridge club. She had been an ardent bridge player since her school days. Susie spent Christmas 1940 in Rochester with Alfred and Nellie Jones. In March 1942 Susie attended the Wolcott Business Women's meeting; within a few years she became the president of the group. Susie was active in the Women's Society of Christian Service. In the mid-1940s Susie was the Red Cross chairperson in North Rose. She and Ruth Marshall vacationed in Florida for five weeks in February and March 1949.

Gray, Charles & Mabel

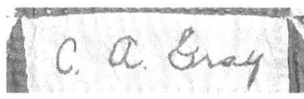

81 North Main Street, now 5111 North Main—Built in 1903. Estimated 1940 value: $3,200.
Charles Andrew Gray (1875–1958), 64, head of household, proprietor of a retail hardware store, 52 weeks, self-employed.
Mabel M. Campbell Gray (1876–1967), 63, wife, homemaker.

CHARLES COMPLETED EIGHT YEARS of school and was co-proprietor of Gray Bros. Hardware. Mabel completed two years of high school. She was a homemaker. Charles was born in New Jersey, but his family moved to North Rose by 1877. His father, Albion Mintonye Gray (1853–1945), a carpenter, was born in Maine. His mother, Sarah Elizabeth Smalley (1853–1920), was born in Fairfield, New Jersey. Albion and Sarah lived in New Jersey after their 1874 marriage, then moved to North Rose. After Elizabeth's death, Albion moved to his brother-in-law's home in Caldwell, New Jersey.

Mabel was the daughter of Isaac George Campbell (1838–1912), a farmer, and Josephine Minot Campbell (1848–1899), and was a lifelong resident of the Town of Rose.

Charles and Mabel Gray had three daughters: Marian, Eleanor, and Doris. Marian Gray (1900–1900) died in infancy.

Eleanor Gray (1902–1985) married George E. Hoffman (1898–1957) of Clyde in July 1924. George was a veteran of World War I who owned a dry cleaners. He was the son of Seymour Horatio Hoffman (1850–1938) and Julia Exter (1857–1939). Eleanor and George had a son named Gray and a daughter named Darleen. They lived in Canandaigua and, later, in Syracuse. In 1958, after George's death, Eleanor married Charles E. Roth of North Main Street, North Rose.

Doris Gray was pursuing nursing studies at Geneva City Hospital in September 1924. In 1925 she married Lynn O. Wright of Wolcott. Lynn was a college graduate and gained a job with a dairy products firm. Lynn's father was Charles Wright, who would win election as the sheriff of Wayne County for multiple terms in the 1930s and '40s. Lynn and Doris became the parents of two sons: Brendon and James.

Charles Gray was the eldest of Albion and Elizabeth's five children. In 1940 Charles and his two surviving brothers lived in North Rose (see "Gray, John & Mary" and "Gray, Ote & Lena"). Their youngest brother, Alvin M. Gray (1884–1921), also lived in North Rose until his death at 36. Their only sister, Elizabeth "Lizzie" Gray (1880–1897), died at 16 of spinal meningitis.

Charles began his career as a carpenter and then later joined his brother John in the retail hardware business. Their enterprise was appropriately called Gray Bros. Hardware. The store sat in the central business block of North Rose on the west side of Main Street, alongside businesses such as Quereau's Dry Goods Store and Winchell's Butcher Shop, and just half a block north of the railroad tracks. Ote was a locally prominent carpenter and builder. Alvin was also a carpenter and homebuilder, though he later operated a coal yard.

Charles received the Republican nomination for Tax Collector at their October 1903 caucus for the Town of Rose. He was victorious in the general election the following month. In December 1904 Charles and Mabel sold their house to George Fenk (a.k.a. George Fink). At about the same time, Charles built a new home on Main Street. In December 1905 Charles severely injured his wrist while working with a chisel. Charles led the Independence Day parade in 1922. Over 5,000 people crowded North Rose. Among the highlights of the show were marching Civil War veterans.

Charles, Mabel, Florence Desmond (Mabel's sister), and Charles Desmond (Florence's husband) took an auto trip through New England in August 1929. In June 1930 Elizabeth Gray and her son Albion were guests of Charles and Mabel at their LeRoy Island cottage.

In September 1930 Mabel became president of the Home Missionary Society. In October 1930 she attended the annual convention of the Grand Chapter of the Order of the Eastern Star. Mabel was an active member of the Ladies' Aid Society of the Methodist Episcopal Church. In 1939 the various Methodist women's home and foreign missionary societies consolidated as the Woman's Society of Christian Service. Mabel was also a member of the Bridge Club.

In February 1932 Charles was on the committee of stockholders and depositors who attempted to reopen the First National Bank of North Rose, which failed in the depths of the Depression on October 26, 1931. Lacking the necessary $100,000, the committee was unsuccessful in its endeavor.

In September 1934 Mabel, Lena Gray (her sister-in-law), Watson Skutt, and Ruth Towne attended the World's Fair in Chicago. In July 1935 Charles served as grand marshall for the Lake Shore Volunteer Firemen's Association convention held in North Rose, and a parade of 1,200 firefighters. Charles owned a farm in the Lower Lake Avenue region of Wolcott. He and Mabel visited Charles's father, Albion, and other relatives in New Jersey in August 1936. Mabel won the election to be the president of the Ladies' Aid Society in September 1938. In April 1939 Charles and Mabel visited Bermuda with Doris and Lynn Wright. Charles and Mabel gave a talk on their Bermuda trip at the May Grange meeting. That year found Mabel an active member of the Loyalty class, a Methodist women's group.

In August 1940 Charles and Mabel traveled with James and Gertie Boyd to Connecticut, New Jersey, and on to the New York World's Fair. In February 1941 Mabel and her daughter Eleanor took a three-week trip to California. Mabel was co-chairperson of a Red Cross group making surgical dressings for the armed services in 1942. In November 1944 Charles and Ote Gray brought their father, Albion, to North Rose. In January 1945 Charles and Mabel joined George, Eleanor, and Darlene Hoffman on a visit to Fort Knox, Kentucky, to visit George and Eleanor's grandson, Pvt. Gray Hoffman. Albion Gray died in April 1945 at the age of 94. Charles and Mabel traveled to Florida with Frank and Nellie Quereau in February 1949. In May 1950 Gertie Boyd spent the month with the Grays.

Gray, John & Mary

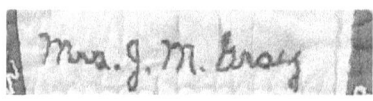

41 South Main Street, now 4915 South Main—Built in 1910. Estimated 1940 value: $2,400.
John Martin Gray (1877–1968), 63, head of household, proprietor of retail hardware store, self-employed.
Mary Belle Quereau Gray (1871–1941), 68, wife, homemaker.

JOHN GRAY RAN GRAY BROS. HARDWARE along with his brother Charles. (See "Gray, Charles & Mabel" for more about John's family.) John graduated from high school and Mary completed three years of college. John and Mary had two children: George Otis Gray (1906–2003) and John Russell Gray (1909–2006).

The author remembers a cylindrical cistern in John and Mary's backyard that had large goldfish, perhaps koi.

We were unable to obtain much more than the cursory information provided by the census for this household. If you have information about the Grays, see page 32.

Gray, Ote & Lena

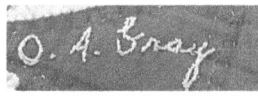

15 Clinton Avenue, now 10375 Clinton—Built in 1888. Estimated 1940 value: $4,800.

A current photo of the Grays' house on Clinton Avenue

Otis "Ote" Albion Gray (1882–1970), 58, head of household, contractor-builder and landlord, self-employed.
Sarah Selena "Lena" Shaver (1876–1962), 64, homemaker.

OTE'S BROTHERS Charles and John also lived in North Rose in 1940.

(See "Gray, Charles & Mabel" for more about Ote's family.) Lena's parents were Cassius Martin Shaver (1846–1905) and Charlotte Rebecca Beckett (1850–1888). Ote and Lena both completed their second year of high school.

In 1900 Lena was a housekeeper for a farm laborer, George Stubley. She was later housekeeper to Ote's father, Albion Gray, which is how she and Ote met. The two were married December 21, 1920, and honeymooned in Florida for two months following their wedding. They attended the World's Fair in Chicago together in 1933. The couple cared for the author's sister Marilyn during his birth.

As a contractor, Ote built houses for rental purposes—five in total. They included, for example, 35 North Poplar Street, 6 Clinton Avenue, and 53 Gray Street. He commissioned homes for local families. Earl Van Patten purchased a new house on Poplar Street built by Ote. Ote also built the First National Bank building.

In 1940 Ote purchased the Ball House on Main Street. He had an extensive workshop with a fine collection of hand woodworking tools. The author remembers going to his great-uncle Ote's workshop and being shown how different planes generated different spiral shavings. Some of Ote's tools were early donations to the Town of Rose History Museum.

The First National Bank building on Main Street in North Rose was built by Ote Gray.

As a hobby he was a wood whittler. He made remarkable wooden sculptures, many with moving pieces carved from a single piece of wood. Ote had a drawer in his rolltop desk that always had a pack of Black Jack gum from which he would give sticks away to young visitors. Clint Acker and Gordon Hoople (son of Dr. Howard Hoople and Phyllis) often visited Uncle Ote. They thought he was the author's grandfather but he was in fact the author's great-uncle: Ote's wife, Lena, was a sister of Arloa Shaver Skutt, the author's grandmother.

Unlike his Skutt relations, Ote was an ardent Republican and especially disliked the New Deal policies of Franklin Roosevelt.

Lena was an exceptional gardener and had a large vegetable and flower garden from which the author recalls picking green beans.

Groat, William & Maude

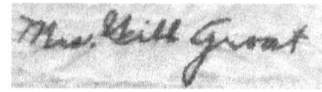

23 Elm Street, now 4939 Elm—Built in 1920. 1940 monthly rent: $14.
William N. Groat (1872–1953), 67, head of household, processor, 52 weeks at $39 a week.
Maude Milliman Groat (1880–1964), 59, wife, homemaker and wage earner, 18 weeks, $12 a week.
William Raymond Groat (1903–1965), 36, son, census enumerator, 8 weeks at $25 a week.
Floyd J. Groat (1907–1977), 32, son, laborer, 32 weeks at $17 a week.
David N. Groat (1915–1958), 25, son, billiard room proprietor, 40 weeks, self-employed.
Russell Jerry Groat (1917–1977), 22, son, laborer, 26 weeks for $17 a week.

WILLIAM AND MAUDE GROAT married in 1900. They had seven children over the following 18 years. Four of those adult children were living at home: William, Floyd, David, and Russell. Gladys (39), Paul (34), and Elaine (19) no longer lived with their parents. William earned $2,000 as a full-time processor at the Canning Factory. Maude was a homemaker but also worked several weeks a year outside of the home. The combined income of the household exceeded $3,500; their rent was only $14 per month, or less than 5 percent of their gross wages. William and Maude, respectively, had sixth- and eighth-grade educations. All four of the sons living at home were high school graduates. William had also attended one year of college.

The Groats moved to North Rose from Perinton in southeastern Monroe County in 1913, not long after William began working in the Salter Canning Factory. By 1930 he was a foreman there and regularly attended the canners' conventions in Buffalo—sometimes with George Ball, the canning factory manager.

Maude was active in Kappa Phi and the Missionary Society. In January 1938 she was elected historian of the Arbor Vitae chapter, No. 577, of the Order of the Eastern Star. She was also active in the Women's Society of Christian Service. The couple often entertained their Rochester-based children's families for Christmas. In February 1950 the Groats celebrated their 50th wedding anniversary.

The Groats' daughter Gladys (1900–1976) spent the last two years of her schooling in North Rose and was valedictorian of the 1915 graduating class. In 1926 she married Roy Schultz (1901–1970) and moved to Rochester. In 1930 Roy was a draftsman and Gladys was a supervisor at a telegraph company. They had one son, George Lee Schultz (1939–2016)

In 1930 William was working as a bank clerk and boarding in a widow's home in LeRoy (Genesee County). He was named the manager of a produce concern just purchased by an out-of-town company in 1938. He wasn't regularly employed in 1939–1940 but found a job as an enumerator for the 1940 census. That November he began working as clerk for the Wayne County Draft Board. He married Karolyn DeLeys in her parents' home in Sodus in July 1945. His brother Russell—a recently liberated POW—served as best man. Karolyn was a graduate of Brockport Normal School and a teacher in the Irondequoit Public Schools.

Paul (1905–1978) married Loretta Johnston in 1924, moved to Rochester, and had three children—Marian (1925–2005), Grace (1926–1976), and Erwin (1929–1963).

Floyd broke an ankle and lacerated his face in an auto accident near Sodus in October 1934. He worked as a laborer in the Canning Factory for most of 1939. And, like William, he worked as a census enumerator in 1940 with a territory comprising the western half of the Town of Rose. In November 1940 he moved to Rochester and began working for Clapp's Baby Foods. On September 9, 1942, Floyd enlisted in the Army and was promoted to corporal by May 1943. He returned to his family after being discharged in July of 1945. In May 1949 Floyd and David were operating the North Rose lunchroom and gas station formerly run by Bill Baker.

David Groat (right) with Dick Ball

David Groat was the proprietor of a local billiard parlor. He enlisted in the Army in February 1941 and by October was stationed in Fort Sill, Oklahoma. He returned home in October 1945. He married Mary Fischette (1912–2005) in July 1946 and moved to Clyde.

Russell graduated from NRCS in 1937 and took part in the customary class trip to Washington, D.C. In February 1938 he registered as a postgraduate at Leavenworth School in Wolcott. In September he matriculated at Rochester's Mechanics Institute—which became RIT. Although Russell worked part of 1939 as a laborer in the Canning Factory, he and his brother Floyd were both seeking other employment.

Russell left for Buffalo to be inducted into the Army in February 1942. That spring, he married Anna C. Buttaccio of Clyde. The couple was able to live together while Russell was stationed at Fort Jackson, South Carolina, and in Sioux Falls, South Dakota. In October 1943 Russell was promoted from PFC to Corporal and was transferred to Las Vegas. He received a few days' leave for the birth of his first child, Linda Anne, at the Barber Hospital in Lyons. While he was stationed in Nevada, his wife and daughter spent a few months with his parents.

In June 1944 Russell was stationed in England when he crossed paths with his brother Floyd in Cambridge. By this time Russell was a Technical Sergeant in an Army Air Corps bomber squadron—where he worked as both a radio operator and gunner on a B-17 Flying Fortress. Later that month Russell was reported missing. Captured by the Germans and held as a POW for nearly a year, he somehow managed to send his mother a birthday card from the camp. Russell was liberated in the spring of 1945, discharged, and awarded the Distinguished Flying Cross, the Air Medal, and three Oak Leaf Clusters. A cluster is given as a second award of the same type. He rejoined his family in Clyde, and the following February he and his wife had a second daughter, Darlene Marie.

In June 1937 Elaine Groat (1921–1953) attended the Epworth League institute at Keuka College. The institute was an association of persons aged 18 to 35 who were members of the Methodist Church. Elaine was salutatorian of the NRCS Class of 1938. In February 1940 she entered nurse's training at Rochester General Hospital and then went to the Poughkeepsie State Hospital for further training in March 1942. After she completed her nursing education in Rochester in February 1943, she worked at Rochester General Hospital. She spent the winter of 1945 in St. Petersburg, Florida, then moved to White Plains (Westchester County) to do private nursing. She worked as a therapist there until June 1953. She died at 32 at Strong Memorial Hospital in Rochester in August.

Guthrie, Graydon & Freda

11 South Poplar Street, now 4965 South Poplar—Built in 1900. Estimated 1940 value: $1,500.

Graydon Guthrie (1912–1985), 28, head of household, engineer, 52 weeks for $22 a week.

Freda Mae Guthrie (1911–1920), 28, wife, apple packer, 24 weeks for $9 a week.

Lyle Guthrie (1917–1991), 23, brother, laborer, 52 weeks for $18 a week.

GRAYDON AND FREDA GUTHRIE shared a home with Graydon's brother Lyle. All three worked at the Cold Storage and ice plant. Graydon was a full-time engineer there, Freda had been an apple packer but was now seeking other employment, and Lyle worked long hours as a laborer. Freda and Lyle were both high school graduates; Graydon attended nine years of school.

In April 1937 Graydon and Freda were the attendants at Graydon's brother Maurice's North Rose wedding to Lulu Mettler of Spring Lake. The couple settled in Auburn to be close to the spark plug factory where they worked. In August 1938 they traveled to Blue Mountain Lake in the Adirondacks with Mr. and Mrs. George Guthrie. Graydon and Freda visited Owasco Lake Park in June 1939 with Gerald and Alice Powell. The Guthries also drove to Inlet with Paul and Inez Drury.

Freda and Graydon were matron of honor and best man when Alice Guthrie married Ralph Richardson in Newark in August 1941. They were also members of the Starlite Club, the Anniversary Club, and were active in the North Rose Methodist Church.

The Guthries also often visited Edwin and Dorothy Blanchard in North Victory in northern Cayuga County.

Active in both the Red Cross blood and fund drives, Graydon was named co-chairman, along with Frank Noyes, of the blood donor committee for the local Red Cross in February 1943. In 1949 he was chosen to be the financial secretary of the North Rose Fire Department and chaplain of the Masonic Lodge. And in 1956 he was elected chairman of the local Boy Scout troop committee no. 109.

Freda was a member of the Sew and Sew Club and the Arbor Vitae chapter of the Order of the Eastern Star. She eventually moved to Dade City, Florida, where she lived to be 100.

Graydon's brother Lyle moved to Hornell in December 1935 to take the position of assistant manager of a Market Basket store. By 1938 Lyle had moved to Newark. In December 1939 he went hunting in southern New York State with friends George Powell, Gerald Powell, Paul Marshall, Jack Marshall, Gerald Guthrie, Clarence Juffs, Ellery Mills, and Grant Hoff. In August 1940 Lyle and George Ball visited the New York World's Fair. Lyle was also the best man at the wedding of Raymond MacDougall and Katherine Washburn.

Lyle married Beatrice M. Washburn (1920–1989) of Wolcott in February 1941. They made their home in North Rose and moved to the Chalupa house on South Poplar Street in March 1942. In December Lyle was elected vice president of the North Rose Fire Department but began serving in the Army in January 1943. During Lyle's absence, Beatrice lived in Rochester and then with her sister Katheryn MacDougall in North Rose, where she was a member of the Utopia Rebekah Lodge. In January 1945 Beatrice began working for the Sodus Telephone Company. That same year Lyle was awarded the bronze star for bravery in action in the Philippines. Lyle and Beatrice purchased the Hoff house in August 1946, and the Bruce Richardsons moved into the house that the Guthries vacated. Lyle and Beatrice had a son, Larry Cleon Guthrie (1947–2007), in July 1947. In January 1948 Lyle was elected president of the North Rose–Huron Fire Department. Lyle joined the Wolcott-based American Legion post.

Cleon Guthrie (Graydon and Lyle's brother) died while serving in the Navy in the Pacific Theater. Other Guthrie siblings included Cecile, Gerald (also a war veteran), and Alice.

Harper, Chelsea & Mary

55 Gray Street, now 5119 Gray—Built in 1940. Estimated 1940 value: $2,500.
Chelsea Damon Harper (1891–1984), 48, head of household, mail carrier, rural route, 50 weeks for $2,000.
Mary Bethania Cahoon Harper (1894–1982), 45, wife, homemaker.
Lydia Elaine Harper (1925–2006), 15, daughter, student.

MARRIED IN JANUARY 1915, Chelsea and Mary both had completed the typical eight years of grammar school. Chelsea's parents were Albert Fremont Harper (1861–1930) and Mary A. Moore (1864–1948). Mary was a member of the Order of the Eastern Star.

We were unable to obtain much more than the cursory information provided by the census for this household. If you have information about the Harpers, see page 32.

Harper, Marvin & Jessie

7 Elm Street, now 4969 Elm—Built in 1890. Estimated 1940 value: $1,500.
Marvin A. Harper (1896–1975), 43, head of household, laborer, 34 weeks for $20 a week.

Jessie Harper (1895–1963), 45, wife, homemaker.
Marvin David Harper Jr. (1934–1995), 5, son.

MARVIN AND JESSIE HARPER married in June 1921. It was a second marriage for Marvin, whose first wife, Nina Marguerite Sidler, died nine months after their January 31, 1918, wedding. Marvin Jr. was born 13 years later. Marvin Sr. was a highway laborer for the state. Jessie, whose maiden name was also Harper, was a homemaker. Jessie and Marvin both completed the eighth grade.

During the 1920s the couple rented a farm on North Rose-Wolcott Road. Jessie's mother, Anna "Annie" M. Lovejoy Harper (1864–1932), lived with them after her husband, David W. Harper (1864–1929), died. The following year Marvin Sr. lost his father, George Harper 1861–1930).

The Harpers were close friends with Mr. and Mrs. Alfred Jones of Rochester and Susie Graham of North Rose. The family spent the winter of 1935–1936 in Irving Winchell's house while Mr. Winchell passed the season with his daughter in Washington, D.C. And in July 1938, the couple attended the Lovejoy reunion at Cayuga Lake Park with Mr. and Mrs. Alfred Dagle.

Marvin worked for E. W. Catchpole and Sons in 1918. Although Marvin was a native of North Rose, he had also lived in Rochester while working for Eastman Kodak. In April 1938 Marvin was working "on the road" outside of North Rose. In October 1941 Marvin received the Democratic Party nomination for superintendent of highways. He canvassed for the Red Cross War Fund in both March 1944 and 1945. When his mother, Mary Moore Harper, died in March 1948, she was survived by eight children, 29 grandchildren, 30 great-grandchildren, and one great-great-grandchild.

In March 1936 Jessie was driving the Harpers' car when Leon Baylard accidentally struck it with a vehicle that he had "borrowed" as a joke from "Dude" Scott. Baylard was charged with larceny and taken to the Lyons lockup by state troopers. In November 1937, Jessie Harper suffered another misfortune: a dislocated hip. During World War II she knit 98 items for the Red Cross's relief efforts.

Marvin Jr. was a model airplane enthusiast as a boy and played basketball for NRCS in 1951. He married Elaine Sullivan (1940–2019) of Wolcott in 1957, and the couple had four children. Their sons Marvin and Dale were living in North Rose at the time of Elaine's death.

Marvin Harper Jr., NRCS Class of 1954

Harper, Roscoe & Louise*

Roscoe Ladu Harper (1899–1983), 41, head of household, farmer, 52 weeks.
Louise Rebecca Fairbanks Harper (1912–2007), 27, wife, homemaker.
Janet Harper (1936–), 3, daughter.
Dorothy Harper (1937–), 2, daughter.
Cora Permillie "Millie" Welch Harper (1874–1968), 65, mother.
Christina Welch (1848–1950), 91, grandmother.

THE HARPER FAMILY LIVED IN GALEN in 1940; this household is included because Janet Harper Clingerman was one of the fact-checkers for this book; her family has also been very involved in North Rose.

Roscoe and Louise were married on New Year's Day 1936; Janet was born later that year. At the time of the 1940 census, Roscoe's mother and grandmother were part of the household, along with Janet and her sister Dorothy. Janet grew up in the Town of Galen, the eldest of 10, on her parents' farm.

Janet earned a remarkably high grade-point average (second in the county in 1954) at Clyde High School. In November 1957 she married Larry Bruce Clingerman (1938–) in the First Methodist Church of Clyde. Larry was the son of Clarence E. Clingerman (1911–2002) and Shelia Seager Clingerman (1914–1987) of Alton.

When she married Larry, Janet was a senior at the State University Teachers College at Brockport. Soon after her 1958 graduation, she gained a temporary assignment as the fourth-grade teacher at NRCS. After teaching in Rose, Batavia (Genesee County), Bergenin (Genesee

County), and Sodus, Janet taught kindergarten in Clyde from 1956 to 1992. Larry started work as a farmer. After a stretch of illness, he attended SUNY Brockport and achieved a BS in elementary education in three years. Larry then taught fifth grade in Clyde Central School from 1962 to 1970. He next turned to home building, constructing houses for several years. The three Clingerman children are Brenda (1960–), Renee (1963–), and Bruce (1965–). Brenda is a layout designer for the family taxidermy business in North Rose. Renee works as a production planner with Parker-Hannifin in Lyons. Parker, as its employees call it, makes a panoply of products, mostly components for industrial machinery employed in aerospace and other fields. These parts include EMI shielding, filters, separators and purifiers, seals and O-rings, and valves. Bruce and his wife live in Palmyra. He works in GMAC's Rochester division as an engineer. He was an early researcher in the development of hybrid drive autos.

In the 1970s Janet pointed out to Larry that his longtime hobbies of hunting and fishing—and his desire to keep the best examples of the fish and birds that he hunted or fished for on display indefinitely—were resulting in quite a windfall for the area taxidermists. Janet suggested that, as an alternative, Larry learn taxidermy himself. Brenda decided to join her father in his studies. The result was Clingerman Taxidermy, which opened for business in 1978. Larry developed molds for other taxidermists to create fiberglass heads of trout and other fish they were mounting. These proved to be extremely popular with their intended audience. Real fish heads are exceedingly difficult to preserve.

In the 1990s Janet came out of retirement to join Larry and Brenda in the family enterprise. Janet made the first contact between Shi Wen-long, a wealthy Taiwanese industrialist who wanted to create a museum, and Clingerman Taxidermy. Impressed with the skills and versatility of the Clingermans' business, the delegation from Taiwan pre-qualified Larry and Brenda Clingerman for further testing on the Asian island. All that remained was a trip to Taiwan to demonstrate their skills. The directors of the Chimei Museum wanted to surpass similar collections of modern-day animals displayed at the Smithsonian Institution and the New York Museum of Natural History. The principal part of Larry's test was to convert a live duck to a mounted duck in front of a museum panel. The Clingermans won the job. Janet worked with Larry and Brenda on each phase of the project.

In their first of several trips to Africa for the museum in May and June of 1994, their assignment was to obtain a crocodile, a hippo, a giraffe, an elephant, and over 100 other birds, reptiles, and mammals. On their first night in northwest Zimbabwe, they heard a lion and an elephant in a life-and-death struggle. Janet and Larry found the bull elephant the next day. It had liver disease and was old by elephant standards. The Zimbabwe authorities agreed to the culling of this animal by Larry, who shot it. The Zimbabwe government claimed the tusks. The elephant meat went to animal sanctuaries caring for carnivores. The skin of the gigantic elephant—removed all in one piece—weighed two tons before tanning. The elephant was 28 feet long and 12 feet tall and weighed 16 tons.

The rest of their trip resulted in the collection of the skins of 92 animals and 54 birds. This African adventure was just the first of many trips taken by Larry and Janet. Often accompanying them was Hank Walker of Oswego. When the museum opened, it attracted 10,000 visitors per week

The Chimei Museum does not limit its collection to taxidermy-preserved animals; it is so diverse an attraction that in addition to natural history and fossils, it also features fine arts, arms and armor, antiquities and artifacts, and musical instruments. The museum founder Shi Wen-long was especially enamored with stringed instruments; he frequently carried a $2 million Stradivarius with him and owned a $4 million cello. So it's not surprising that the museum has a world-famous collection of stringed instruments, including the Chi-Mei Cultural Foundation collection of violins and bows (said to be the world's largest). Christopher Reuning of Reuning and Sons Violins in Boston (formerly of Ithaca) assembled the collection of outstanding violins and bows.

In a second semi-retirement, Janet is continually active in the Town of Rose Historical Society. She served as a fact-checker for this book.

Larry and Janet sold the taxidermy shop to a key employee. It still operates in the building next to the Clingermans' home on Brick Schoolhouse Road in the Town of Rose. The property contains many ponds and a nine-hole golf course constructed by Larry and his son Bruce. The taxidermy business now operates at a smaller staffing level than was employed at its peak. It is open for business and welcomes visitors.

Harris, Ray & Neva

21 South Poplar Street, now 4941 South Poplar—Built in 1910. Estimated 1940 value: $1,800.

Horatio "Ray" Harris (1881–1963), 58, head of household, apple packer, 28 weeks for $590.

Neva Monroe Harris (1889–1957), 50, wife, bean picker, 44 weeks for $329.

Ray and Neva Harris married in April 1934. Ray was employed as an apple packer at the Cold Storage, and Neva worked as a bean picker at the Bean House. They both had eight years of schooling.

Ray's father was born in England, and Ray spent his childhood in Orleans County. Ray's first wife was Gladys J. Newkirk Harris (1882–1931). Her father had been a blacksmith in Batavia (Genesee County).

In 1920 Ray and Gladys lived in Huron with their 12-year-old son Ralph (1907–1971). During that period, Ray was both a fruit farmer as well as the first "financial secretary" of the North Rose Fire Department—which had formed in 1919 when the North Rose Hook and Ladder Company merged with the North Rose Chemical Company. In 1921 Ray was elected first assistant fire chief. In 1937, as well as on other occasions, Ray substituted for Marvin Winchell at the meat market when Marvin was ill.

In February 1921 Ray's first wife, Gladys, was elected to the visiting committee of the Kappa Phi Sunday school class associated with the North Rose Methodist Church. She was also a member of the Thursday Club and the Rebekah Utopia Lodge. In November 1929 Gladys was suffering from tuberculosis of the throat and entered the Pleasant

Valley Sanitarium in Bath. She died in April 1931.

Ray's second wife, Neva, was a native of North Rose. In January 1904 her father was fatally kicked by a horse when he was trying to free a load of coal stuck in a snowdrift. Neva was living in the Town of Hamlin (Monroe County) in 1910, but by 1911, she had returned to North Rose and had joined the Rebekah Utopia Lodge, No. 400. In April 1921 she was elected president of the Sigma Society of the Presbyterian Church.

Ray and Neva often visited with, or hosted, Neva's sisters: Bertha Satterlee of Niagara Falls and Irene Monroe Rolfe of North Rose. Neva's brother, Emil Monroe, and his wife, Nora (of Savannah), lost their only child, Muriel Monroe, aged 18, in a sailing accident that claimed the lives of four young women in October 1941. The girls were sailing from Toronto.

The Harrises' son, Ralph, married Olive Ruth Eaton in June 1929. They had a daughter, Zaida, and a son, John Watson. The family lived in Lyons.

Harrison, William & Helen
8 South Huron Street, now 4976 South Huron—Built in 1900. 1940 monthly rent: $10.
William Harrison (1896–1968), 43, head of household, laborer, 30 weeks for $18 a week.
Helen L. Kalbfleisch Harrison (1912–1999), 28, wife, homemaker and laborer at the Canning Factory, 10 weeks for $17 a week.
Betty Anne Harrison (1932–2008), 7, daughter, student.
Doris Helen Harrison (1934–2004), 5, daughter, student.
Eva Mae Harrison (1937–2008), 2, daughter.

In November 1931 William and Helen Harrison were married in the Baptist parsonage in Rose. In 1940 they were renting a home in eastern North Rose and had three daughters: Betty, Doris, and Eva. William had completed tenth grade and was working as a laborer on the railroad. Helen had completed the ninth grade and was working both as a homemaker and as a part-time peeler at the Canning Factory.

William's parents lived in Utica, and the couple traveled there multiple times upon the illnesses and deaths of William's parents, who died within a week of each other in April 1936.

William was working for the WPA in July 1936 when he was promoted and his work was shifted to Lyons. Helen was quite ill in November 1936 and again in February 1939. Her older brother, Richard Kalbfleisch, and his family also lived in North Rose. Helen's mother, Myrtle French of Savannah sometimes helped care for the Harrison children. In May 1941 the family moved to Glenmark.

William eventually separated from the family and moved to Batavia (Genesee County).

Betty studied piano under Estella Roney, was secretary of her sophomore class at NRCS, and became an adult adviser to North Rose Methodist Church Youth Fellowship at the same time that her younger sister Eva was vice president of the organization.

Doris was a junior-varsity cheerleader at NRCS and was elected to student council representing her sophomore class in September 1949 and her junior class in September 1950. She graduated from NRCS in 1952. When she married her classmate, Private Donald Robert Pierson, in June of 1953, her sister Eva was the maid of honor. Doris worked for Empire Nurseries in Newark. Donald was in the Marine Corps, stationed at Parris Island, South Carolina. They rented an apartment in North Rose and had two children: Steven and Kristine.

Doris Harrison, NRCS Class of 1952

Eva was a perennial presence on the honor roll. She graduated from NRCS, then moved with her mother to Clyde. In March 1960 she married Ronald K. Miller (1935–2003) of Wolcott. Her sister Doris was matron of honor. Ronald, a graduate of Leavenworth High School, served in the Army and then was employed by Kordite in Macedon. The newlyweds settled in Lyons.

Eva Harrison, NRCS Class of 1956

William and Helen also had a son, William Richard Harrison (1941–2001).

Hendershot, Lester & Dora

13 Railroad Avenue, now 10329 Railroad—Estimated 1940 value: $1,000
Lester Lee Hendershot (1899–1985), 40, head of household, laborer, 40 weeks for $800.
Dora Eva Carnell Hendershot (1907–1983), 32, wife, job not listed, 12 weeks for $155.
Herbert Hendershot (1926–2021), 14, son, student.

LESTER AND DORA HAD EACH completed eight years of school. Lester worked as a laborer, repairing New York State roads. Dora was a homemaker. Herbert was attending seventh grade. The Hendershots were married in August 1924. They and their parents were all natives of Pennsylvania.

Lester was born in Robinsonville, Pennsylvania, the son of Raymon Lee Hendershot (1878–1967) and Susan Smith Hendershot (1876–1912). Raymon led the North Rose brass band for many years. In 1900 Lester lived in Monroe, Pennsylvania. He was the eldest child in his family. By 1910 he had two brothers and four sisters. In 1912 the seven siblings lost their mother. In 1918 Lester worked on his father's farm in Clearville, Pennsylvania. In August 1920 Raymon made a second marriage with Elizabeth "Bess" June Brown (1877–1945) in Robbinsville, Pennsylvania. She was an immigrant to America from England who had lived in Ohio and West Virginia—as well as Pennsylvania—before moving to North Rose. Bess died in January 1945. She had a son and a daughter from a prior marriage.

Lester Hendershot married Dora Eva Carnell in August 1924. Lester was a farm laborer. Lester and Dora's son, Herbert, was born in 1926. The Hendershots moved to North Rose and lived on Glenmark Road in the 1920s. The family shifted between living in Wayne County and Bedford County, Pennsylvania, for the next two decades.

The Hendershots remained in Pennsylvania following Dora's father's death in 1931. Lester and Dora visited friends in Pittsburgh in January 1933. The Hendershots were absent from Wayne County in 1935. Lester lived in Clearville, Pennsylvania, and Dora and Herbert lived in Amaranth, Pennsylvania. In the late 1930s the family reunited and returned to North Rose. Lester was a laborer in the timber business. Dora's mother died in Pennsylvania in 1941. Lester worked for the New York State Highway Department. Lester's stepmother, Elizabeth Hendershot, died in North Rose in January 1945 at 67.

Lester and Dora's son Herbert and two friends attended a June 1944 Rochester Red Wings baseball game. Herbert played varsity basketball for NRCS. He married Kathryn Foster Barnes (1925–2002) at her South Huron home in October 1944. Kathryn was the daughter of Arthur L. Barnes (1902–1984), a farm laborer, and Clara Ferguson Barnes (1903–1964). In 1946 Kathryn was active in the Home Bureau, Unit 2. Herbert and Kathryn became parents of a daughter, Cynthia Hendershot.

Dora spent her childhood on a farm in Union Township in Fulton County, Pennsylvania. Her father, a farmer, was Leonard H. Carnell (1866–1931). Her mother was Elmira Smith Carnell (1868–1942). In July 1937 Lester and Dora visited Elmira in Amaranth. Dora's sister Catherine Blanche Carnell Ward, her husband, George Ward, and the Wards' son Clyde of Hancock, Maryland, visited Lester and Dora in May 1947. In July 1948, Lester, Dora, Sarah Caldwell, Herbert and Kathryn Hendershot, and their daughter, Cynthia, traveled to Amaranth to attend the funeral of Pvt. Homer E. Caldwell, who was killed in October 1944, in the Battle for Brittany, in western France following the D-Day invasion. Homer was Lester and Dora's nephew, the son of Lee Jackson Caldwell and the late Elizabeth "Lizzie" Carnell Caldwell, Dora's sister.

Sarah Caldwell, NRCS Class of 1955

Sarah E. Caldwell (1937–) spent much of her childhood and youth living with her aunt and uncle, Dora and Lester. They treated her as a daughter. In July 1955 Lester and Dora's home in Warfordsburg, Pennsylvania, was the site of a wedding that joined Sarah and Charles E. Divelbliss in marriage. The bride was a 1955 graduate of NRCS. The newly married couple initially made their home with Lester and Dora.

Dora and Lester sold a piece of North Rose property to Samuel

Wise in April 1949. In September 1961 many of Lester's relatives assembled in North Rose in honor of his father Raymon's 85th birthday. (Raymon did not receive the gift of a "d" on the end of his given name.)

Hill, Frank & Flora

Address unclear. Estimated 1940 value: $2,200.
Frank Hill (1878–1942), 61, head of household, self-employed, proprietor of Cold Storage.
Flora Hill (1878–1959), 60, wife, homemaker.
Arthur Hill (1908–1941), 32, son, self-employed farmer.

FRANK HILL HAD FINISHED two years of high school; Flora had finished one. In 1930 Frank and Flora and family were part of the North Rose household of his father, John Hill (1855–1935). John's younger brother William also lived in North Rose. (See "Hill, William.")

We were unable to obtain more than the cursory information provided by the census for this household. If you have information about the Hills, see page 32.

Hill, Gilbert & Hattie

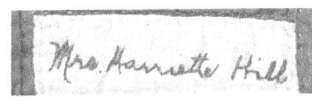

7 South Poplar Street, now 4975 South Poplar—Built in 1914. Estimated 1940 value: $1,500.
Gilbert B. Hill (1875–1961), 64, head of household, carpenter, 32 weeks at $36 a week.
Hattie Cercea Seager Dodds Hill (1874–1964), 63, wife, greenhouse attendant, 52 weeks at $9 a week.
Emma E. Dunbar Seager (1855–1947), 84, mother-in-law.

GILBERT AND HATTIE HILL WERE married in July 1912 and lived with Hattie's mother, Emma Seager. Gilbert was a carpenter and worked for a building contractor. Hattie was a greenhouse attendant. Both of the Hills were high school graduates. Emma completed eight years of school and was also a homemaker.

Gilbert grew up on a farm in the Town of Sodus. He had previously been married to Mattie Allen (1876–1907), who died at 31 of peritonitis; they had a son named Eliott G. Hill (1897–1967), who married Ruth I. Weeks in 1919 in Ontario. In 1930 Eliott and Ruth were living in Sodus with their 8-year-old son Richard. Later in life, Eliott lived in Rochester. He died in Macedon.

In December 1929 the Hills bought a new Chevrolet sedan. The next year, Gilbert was working as a carpenter. In May of that year, he was aiding other boaters in distress when he was thrown from the upper deck of his cruiser into Sodus Bay by heavy seas. His boating companion, George Burnette, helped him back on board. Besides boating, Gilbert enjoyed hunting with his stepson, Wells Dodds, and also with Jack Dodds and other friends.

Hattie had been married previously to Frederick D. Dodds (1874–1919) in 1894, and had one son, Wells Munson Dodds (1895–1984), the well-known nurseryman. (See "Dodds, Wells & Margaret.") In 1920 Hattie was making hats in her home. And by 1930, she owned a millinery shop.

Hattie enjoyed entertaining. Over the years, she frequently entertained members of the Order of the Eastern Star Past Matrons Club and many other groups at her cottage on LeRoy Island. She was elected secretary and treasurer of the Presbyterian Missionary Society in 1931 and treasurer of the Sigma Society of the North Rose Presbyterian Church in 1933. She was appointed USO chairman for the Town of Rose in 1942, chairman of the Red Cross First Aid Committee in 1944, and treasurer of the Arbor Vitae Chapter of the Order of the Eastern Star in 1947—she had been a member for decades. A skilled gardener, Hattie sold dahlia tubers for planting in May. She was also a patient at the Clifton Springs Sanitarium in July of 1952.

Hattie's parents, Emma Dunbar and (David) Munson Seager (1848–1916), were married in July 1872. Munson kept his farm near North Rose while living in Rochester from 1907 to 1909. Emma lived in Syracuse from at least 1925 to 1933 after her husband's death, and was living in North Rose in 1935. Nearer to the end of the decade she was living in the Town of Butler, but by 1940 had rejoined her daughter Hattie in North Rose.

In July 1938 Emma's home was struck by lightning. An electrical surge followed a power cord to her buffet and caught a cloth on fire. She extinguished the blaze herself. In June 1944 Emma visited her daughter Mrs. Fanette "Nettie" Barton at her home in Boston and remained there for some time. Emma celebrated her 90th birthday on September 14, 1945, with an open house at the Hill home. Nettie Barton came from Boston to join in the festivities. In May 1947 Emma fell and broke her hip. As so often used to happen to older people who suffer this accident, it led to her demise.

Hill, William

14 South Poplar Street, now 4962 South Poplar—Built in 1913 and owned by L. Belle Kitchen Miner. Estimated 1940 value: $1,250. 1940 monthly rent: $8.
William B. Hill (1863–1955), 76, head of household, retired.

WILLIAM HILL WAS A RETIRED WIDOWER who had five years of education. His parents emigrated from Ireland (his mother was Scotch-Irish), but he was born in New York, the youngest of eight. His father farmed in Huron. At the age of 16, he and an older brother Thomas were day laborers and boarded with Myron and Mary Harrington in the Town of Rose. In December 1885 William married Lydia J. Doremus (1864–1936). Their daughter, Arlo B. Hill, was born in 1895 and died in 1979. By 1900 William was working as a house painter.

In 1919 William had changed careers and was a department head in a wholesale fruit business in Syracuse. He was also a member of the Huron Grange. By 1930 he had returned to house painting and to North Rose. He and Lydia rented a house on North Main Street. In 1936, on his own after Lydia's death in May, William spent Thanksgiving, Christmas, and New Year's with his daughter, then Arlo Wardwell, and her family, in Hatboro, Pennsylvania—a Philadelphia suburb. In February 1937 William was painting the interior woodwork for the Yancey house—recently vacated by Mr. Barber. In June 1950 his daughter and son-in-law visited him while he was seriously ill at Barber Hospital.

William's brother John Hill (1855–1935) built the North Rose Cold Storage plant. John's son Frank Hill, William's nephew, built eight cold storage facilities and passed away in April 1942. (See "Hill, Frank and Flora.")

Arlo had a fine singing voice and sang a solo at the 1910 dedication of the new Methodist Episcopal Church at Resort. In August 1912 Arlo visited her friend Eleanore Albright in Detroit. In January 1920 Arlo was a salesperson in a Syracuse dry goods store.

In June 1920 Arlo Hill married aviation engineer Horace M. Wardwell (1894–1971) of Ledyard (Cayuga County), then of Syracuse. They lived in Ithaca (Tompkins County), then in various places in Pennsylvania: Philadelphia, Hatboro (ca. 1936–1940), Montgomery, and Ambler. They had two daughters, Maxine and Marilyn, and five grandchildren. In 1940 Horace was a factory superintendent for A.G.A. General Aviation. Arlo later lived in Somers Point, New Jersey.

Hilts, Earl & Inez

27 South Poplar Street, now 4935 South Poplar—Built in 1915. Estimated 1940 value: $1,100.

Earl F. Hilts (1889–1981), 50, head of household, laborer, 52 weeks at $18 a week.
Inez Carpenter Little Hilts (1882–1969), 57, wife, homemaker,
Catherine Joyce Little (1931–2023), 8, granddaughter, not in school.
James Little (1934–2016), 5, grandson, not in school.

EARL AND INEZ HILTS WERE RAISING two of Inez's grandchildren: Catherine and James Little. Earl spent six years in school and was a laborer at the Cold Storage plant. Inez completed eight years of school and was a homemaker.

Earl fought in World War I. In 1950 he belatedly received a medal inscribed with "The American Troops operating victoriously in the S. Mihiel Secteur broke the resistance of the enemy and captured 13,300 prisoners" for his service on September 12 and 13, 1918. Earl was a member of the American Legion, Bay Shore lodge, No. 606, Odd Fellows, Rose Grange, and Glad Tidings Church. The Hilts family hosted a reunion of the Abbott family in August 1945, and put their home up for sale in September 1947.

Earl was Inez's second husband. Her first marriage was to Fletcher N. Little (1885–1917) in January 1905. The couple lived in Butler and had three children: Gladys Thelma (1908–1995), Russell Elvin (1909–1955), and Willis Ray (1913–1983). Inez and her children moved in with her mother, Hannah Carpenter, after Fletcher's death from appendicitis in 1917. Inez worked from her mother's North Rose home as a dressmaker.

In the early 1920s Inez married Earl Hilts and the couple moved into the house on South Poplar Street with Inez's mother and children. In 1930 Inez's sons Russell and Ray were working as laborers in a coal yard and still living in the house, and the couple also had taken in a retired 74-year-old boarder, William Smart.

Gladys Thelma Little married William H. "Bill" Adams (1909–1994) in 1928. William and Gladys had two sons, William F. and Earl Herbert (1936–1993). The Adamses lived in Wolcott, then moved to Webster (Monroe County), where Bill worked as a mix maker in an ice cream factory. In 1950 Gladys lived in Rochester with her two sons and was working as a hairdresser. Although the census that year listed her as widowed, Bill was living in his new wife's parents' household in Rochester. His second wife, Elizabeth "Betty" LeVal, was also a hairdresser. In October 1951 Gladys married again, to Edward William Schmidt (1898–1986).

Inez's son Russell married Sylvia Monteith (1908–1937) in August 1930. The couple had three children, Catherine Joyce (born in May 1931), James, and Jane Louise. Catherine and James went to live on Poplar Street with their grandparents, Earl and Inez, after a June 1937 car accident killed both their mother and 3-week-old sister.

Russell and Sylvia lived in Red Creek at the time of the accident.

In 1940 Russell was a farm laborer. He rented a house in Williamson which he shared with his housekeeper Emma Wood and her 14- and 6-year-old daughters Pauline and Marion. In 1950 Russell was a farmer in Rose. Emma and Marion were lodgers, as were Emma's mother, Louise Saner (1882–1954), a native of Berne, Switzerland, and an 8-year-old boy, Barry Lee Baker. Russell died in 1955.

Inez's son Ray married Iona Mae Van Amburg (1918–1991) in 1936; they were renting a house on North Poplar Street in 1940. (See "Little, Ray and Iona.")

Inez and Nancy Worden attended the Western Assembly of the Gospel Tabernacle at Silver Creek in August 1944. Inez was operating a boarding house in Rose in 1949. A former boarder, William Halterman of West Virginia, who returned to the boarding house, was later arrested for stealing $250 from Inez.

Inez's granddaughter Catherine Little married Raymond Wigfield (1933–2022) of Rose in April 1951. The Wigfields lived in Lyons before returning to North Rose. Catherine played the piano and organ at the Rose Free Methodist Church for many years. The Wigfields had three children—Richard (1954–), Ronnie, and Joyce—and in 2024 their family still owned Earl and Inez's house on South Poplar.

In March 1948 James Little (Inez's grandson) was a charter member of a model airplane club. James served in the Army from 1957 to 1959 and was a member of the Wolcott American Legion. He married and had a son (Richard James Little) and stepchildren. He lived in Wolcott and worked as a truck driver.

The Hilts' boarder, William Smart, was driven by his stepdaughter Bertha Satterlee to her home in Niagara Falls for a visit in November 1931. In September 1936 Mr. and Mrs. William Rolfe called on Mr. Smart at the Lyons hospital. In January 1937 Mr. Smart died after a long illness. His daughter, Mrs. Frank Quereau; granddaughter, Ruth McQueen; and a great-granddaughter, Suzanne McQueen, survived him.

Hoff, Grant & Mary

1940 monthly rent: $15
Grant Hoff (1899–1967), 40, head of household, self-employed, proprietor of gas station.
Mary Hoff (1905–2005), 34, wife, homemaker.
Mary C. Hoff (1932–), 7, daughter, student.
Helen H. Hoff (1934–2019), 5, daughter, student.

We were unable to obtain more than the cursory information provided by the census for this household. If you have information about the Hoffs, see page 32.

Horn, Earl & Grace

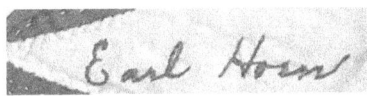

24 South Popular Street, now 4938 South Poplar—Built in 1915. Estimated 1940 value: $2,500.

Earl R. Horn (1895–1959), 44, head of household, repair mechanic, 52 weeks at $29 a week.
Elsie "Grace" Anderson Horn (1895–1975), 44, wife, apple packer, 16 weeks at $11 a week.
Sarah Annabel "Anne" B. Anderson (1864–1944), 75, mother-in-law.

The 1958 NRCS yearbook was dedicated to Earl Horn for his "cheerfulness and kindness" in his 20 years of service as a bus driver.

EARL AND GRACE HORN SHARED the home with Grace's widowed mother. The Horns were both natives of the Keystone State. Earl was a full-time repair mechanic at NRCS and would also become a bus driver for the school. Grace worked part of 1939 as an apple packer at a wholesale fruit company but was seeking other work. Mrs. Anderson was a homemaker and had completed eight years of school. Earl also completed eight years of school, and Grace had finished two years of high school.

In 1900 and 1910, Mrs. Annabel Anderson, her husband Lincoln C. (1864–1934), and her young daughters Rea N. and Grace were living in Montoursville, Pennsylvania. Lincoln Anderson was working as a traveling salesman for a chemical company. They later moved to a boarding house in Wesleyville, Pennsylvania, where they were living in 1930 while Lincoln worked as a mail clerk. After her husband's death, Anne moved from Waterford, Pennsylvania, to North Rose to live with her daughter and son-in-law. She died in January 1944.

Earl had worked as a plumber and tinsmith in 1917. In 1920 he was a milling machine operator at the Erie Electric Motor Company. The Horns and their son, Lincoln (1918–1985), lived in the Town of Millcreek in Erie County, Pennsylvania.

In March 1930 Earl was working in North Rose as a mechanic at the Eldman garage—a dealer in Oakland and Pontiac automobiles. (The Oakland was a General Motors marque that predates the Pontiac. The Pontiac was introduced to create a brand with a price point above the Chevrolet and below the Oakland.) Clyde Eldman had just bought out the ownership interest of his partner, Mr. Yancey. The Horns had moved to Elm Street in North Rose.

In November 1929 Earl and Grace traveled to Williamsport, Pennsylvania. Grace was active in the Arbor Vitae Chapter, Order of the Eastern Star. In January 1947 Earl was elected Master of the North Rose Masonic Lodge. In early 1947 the Reginald Catchpole family purchased a house from the Horns.

The Horns' son, Lincoln (named after his grandfather), graduated from NRCS in 1937. In 1940 he lived at the YMCA in Rochester and worked as an inspector at Ritter Dental Company. In June 1942 he married Edna May Warren (1914–2001), a native of Williamstown (Oswego County) who had taught school in Wolcott for the previous four years.

Edna's father, Avery Warren (1883–1918), died when she was 2. Avery was manager of the Lyndonville railroad station, part of the Hojack line in Orleans County between Buffalo and Rochester. He died from sepsis after contracting the Spanish flu. In 1920 her 7-year-old brother Paul lived at the Rome State School (established in 1893 as the New York State Custodial Asylum for Un-teachable Idiots); he died later that spring of a skin infection. Edna was 5. She and her mother, Addie Greenwood Warren (1884–1972), moved back to Oswego County. Addie was the manager of the school cafeteria in

Williamstown for many years.

During World War II, Lincoln served in the U.S. Navy in the South Pacific. He was discharged in January 1946. Lincoln and Edna were living in Poughkeepsie in October; Lincoln was working for International Business Machines. In January 1948 they became parents of a daughter, Sharon Lee Horn.

In 1959, when his father Earl died, Lincoln and his family were living in Winchester, Kentucky. (IBM had opened a 386,000-square-foot typewriter plant in nearby Lexington, which employed 1,800 people when it opened in 1956.) That year Lincoln was named director of IBM World Trade Corporation, with offices in Paris, France. The Horns lived in Europe until June 1961.

Lincoln Horn was invited to give the commencement address to the NRCS class of 1963. He was then living in New Canaan, Connecticut, and his title at IBM was corporate director of manufacturing services. His talk was called "The Challenge of Change."

Lincoln had retired to Rogers, Arkansas, when he died in 1985 at the age of 67.

Horn, Lorenzo

29 South Poplar Street, now 4925 South Poplar—Built in 1910. Estimated 1940 value: $1,000.
Lorenzo Horn (1871–1946), 69, head of household, farm laborer, 37 weeks for $15 a week.

LORENZO HORN WAS BORN IN Anthony, Pennsylvania. He worked as a farm laborer and had spent eight years in school.

His mother, Christian Horn, was born in Germany. He married Bertha Alice Reeder (1875–1937) and had a son, Earl (1895–1959), who headed his own North Rose household in 1940. (See "Horn, Earl & Grace.")

In 1910 Lorenzo was farming in Pennsylvania. At that time he was living with his wife, Bertha; his mother, Christian; his son, Earl; and a ward, Helen Louna Aderhold (1904–1961). By 1920 Lorenzo and

Bertha had moved to the Town of Rose along with Helen, who lived with them as their daughter. In June 1926 Lorenzo purchased an Essex Coach automobile.

Bertha entered the Barber Hospital in May 1921 and returned home in June. In late July 1931, she had a serious operation at the Geneva City Hospital. In 1937, Bertha became critically ill and stayed at the home of her son, Earl. Miss Bernice Wilson, a nurse, cared for her. Bertha died at home in August 1937. In January 1945 Lorenzo was a patient in the Barber Hospital in Lyons. He passed away in November 1946.

Helen Aderhold married Marion Clingerman (1900–1961) in 1924. Her bridal shower was held in February, and it was hosted by Helen Dagle and Esther Phillips. The Clingermans had two children, Alice Elizabeth "Betty" (1925–2013) and Robert (1926–1995). In 1930 Marion was a farm laborer and the family rented a house on Poplar Street in North Rose. The Clingermans then moved to Huron, where Marion was a farmer.

Betty married Raymond Cole (1921–2007) of Sodus in November 1946. Raymond was a sergeant in the U.S. Army Air Forces in World War II. The Coles lived in Sodus and had a son, Terry, in late 1947 or early 1948, and a daughter, Sandra Lee, in July 1949.

Robert Clingerman served in the occupation forces in Japan. He married Kathryn Taylor (1919–2014), who grew up in Butler and Wolcott, in 1949. She brought a daughter, Jonnie Kay, to the marriage; they had a son, Robert, in 1949, and a daughter, Pamela, in the early 1950s. Jonnie Kay's last name was listed as Taylor in the 1950 census, but she went by Jonnie Kay Clingerman. In the mid-1970s Robert moved from Wolcott, where he worked as a machinist, to Zephyrhills, Florida, where he died at 69.

Hutchings, Arthur & Jessie

South Poplar Street. 1940 monthly rent: $12.
Arthur Thomas Hutchings (1892–1955), 48, head of household, shipping clerk, 52 weeks for $23 a week.

Jessie Brown Hutchings (1886–1970), 53, wife, historian, 25 weeks for $12 a week

ARTHUR AND JESSIE HUTCHINGS WERE born in England but had become naturalized citizens. In 1911 Arthur worked as a servant in Weston Super Mare, Somerset, England. Arthur and Jessie immigrated to the United States in 1912 and were married about January 1914. Their only child, Glen Frank (1915–1992), was born a year and a half later. Arthur Hutchings worked year-round as a shipping clerk in the Canning Factory. Jessie Hutchings worked seasonally outside the home. Arthur went to school for eight years, Jessie for 10.

In 1917 Arthur worked as a farm laborer for Addison Dagle (see "Dagle, Cora"), and he was a member of the Rose Lodge 590 of the Masons. In December 1929 he was elected chorister (a person who leads the church choir) of the Methodist Episcopal Sunday school. In June 1938 the Hutchingses took an auto trip to Washington, D.C., Virginia, and Tennessee. In September 1939 Arthur and Jessie's oil stove exploded. The fire department was called, but damage was limited to the stove. A year later the Hutchingses took an auto trip to Old Forge (Herkimer County).

In September 1942 Arthur was elected assistant superintendent as well as chorister of the North Rose Methodist Church. In October 1942 he and Jessie, along with George and Maude Ball, Richard Ball, and Miss Dorothy Miner, went to Rochester for dinner and a show. The following May the Hutchingses visited Rochester again with Martha Peck and Marion Phillips. The two men attended the opening game for the Rochester Red Wings. At North Rose's spontaneous V-J Day celebration in 1945, Arthur led the crowd in singing patriotic songs. Jessie suffered a broken wrist and an injured leg when she fell down the stairs at the Wolcott unemployment office in March 1946. In 1947 she was a member of the Home Bureau. By 1948 she was a member of the American Legion Auxiliary.

Arthur and Jessie's son Glen was best man at the wedding of Gerald Powell and Alice Waldorf in January 1936. In May 1936, accompanied on the piano by Mary Drury, Glen sang over the radio from

Auburn. Lincoln Horn was an usher and Inez Drury a bridesmaid at Glen's July 1938 wedding. The groom was a high school graduate; the bride, Helen M. Spink (1915–2002) of Ontario, had three years of college and served as a teacher in the public schools. After they married, they established a home in East Williamson and frequently visited Glen's parents. Glen worked as a shipping clerk at a fruit and vegetable canning factory in 1940 and enlisted in the Army in February 1942. He rose through the ranks to staff sergeant. In 1945 he was stationed in the Pacific and contracted a tropical fever. That October he was hospitalized and his wife and parents visited him in a military hospital on Long Island. He came home on furlough in November 1945 when he was transferred to a hospital in Utica. His wife was living in Ontario at that point.

In August 1947, after his marriage to Helen came to an end, Glen married Edith Everett (1925–) of Wolcott. Edith had 10 siblings. In May 1953 Glen and Edith were living in Auburn and she visited her mother in Wolcott with their two sons. By the 1970 the Hutchingses had moved back to Wolcott; Glen was living there when he passed away in 1992. At 99, Edith was still living in Wolcott, having outlived all of her siblings.

Jacques, Gordon & Nathalie

17 Elm Street, now 4953 Elm. 1940 monthly rent: $12.
G. Gordon Jacques (1905–1972), 34, head of household, wholesaler, 40 weeks for $15 a week.
Martha Nathalie Mitchell Jacques (1907–1990), 32, wife, homemaker and wage earner, 18 weeks for $15 a week.
Eugene L. Jacques (1929–2006), 10, son, student.
John Mitchell Jacques (1933–1999), 7, son, student.

GORDON AND NATHALIE JACQUES (pronounced "Jakes") had two young sons, Eugene and John. Their third son, James G. Jacques (1944–2017), had not yet been born. Gordon was a wholesaler of fruit and produce. Nathalie was a homemaker and also supplemented the family income by working outside the home. The Jacqueses had both attended one year of college.

Gordon was the son of English immigrants. Due to his father's calling as a Methodist minister, Gordon's family moved several times during his childhood. They lived in Cortlandville (Cortland County), the Town of Ulysses (Tompkins County), Horseheads (Chemung County), and Troy, Pennsylvania.

Gordon was one year ahead of Nathalie when the couple met in Troy High School. While at Syracuse University, Gordon pledged with Sigma Chi fraternity. After they wed, the Jacqueses lived in Elmira (Chemung County) and then Hornell (Steuben County) in 1930. Gordon worked as an automobile salesman. Around 1934 the Jacques family moved to North Rose after visiting Gordon's father—the Rev. William Jacques, then a longtime North Rose minister—many times. (See "Jacques, William & Frederica.") In March 1940 the Jacqueses moved to the Skutt rental property on South Poplar Street. In about 1942 the family moved to Lyons, where their son James was born in 1944. In 1950 Gordon worked as a lock operator on the Erie Canal.

Nathalie grew up on her family's farm in Troy, Pennsylvania. She attended Elmira College for one year, was active in the Ladies' Aid Society of the North Rose Methodist Episcopal Church, and was a member of the North Rose Literary Club. In June 1939 Nathalie was elected vice president of the NRCS PTA for the coming school year. After leaving North Rose, she became a longtime resident of Lyons, then moved to Jacksonville, Florida, in 1983.

The Jacqueses' oldest son, Eugene, married and had a son and two daughters. He managed the Lyons National Biscuit Company plant from 1963 until it closed in 1969, then moved to Tonawanda (Erie County) and managed the Milk Bone plant in Buffalo.

Their middle son, John, was a corporal in the U.S. Army during the Korean War. He married and had four children. He lived in Lyons and was a member of Newark Lodge 1249, Elks.

The Jacqueses' youngest son, Jim, was also a U.S. Army veteran. He never married or had children but was devoted to his brothers and their families. He worked as a civil engineer.

Jacques, Malette & Bessy

12 South Main Street, now 4980 South Main—Built in 1880. 1940 monthly rent: $12. Owned by Georgia Jeffers.
(William) Malette Jacques (1901–1991), 38, head of household, laborer, 40 weeks for $7.50 a week.
Bessy Gould Jacques (ca. 1907–1985), 32, wife.
Ronald Jacques (1932–2015), 7, son, student.

MALETTE AND BESSY JACQUES WERE married in June 1931 and had a son, Ronald, who was in the second grade. Malette had attended one year of college and was working as a laborer at a retail coal and feed business. Bessy completed the ninth grade and was a homemaker.

In the 1920s, Malette's family, which at the time included his parents (both immigrants from England) and his two brothers, John and Gordon, moved from Horseheads in Chemung County to North Rose. (See "Jacques, Gordon & Nathalie.")

Harry Partrick, with whom Bessy had lived for several years, gave away the bride. The groom's father, Rev. William Jacques, performed the ceremony. (See "Jacques, William & Frederica.") The newlyweds honeymooned in the Adirondacks and in Montreal. In June 1937 Malette and Bessy moved into the Jeffers house on South Main Street. In September 1938 the Jacqueses, the Partricks, and the Leslie Boyds traveled to Niagara Falls. Bessy was active in the Home Bureau. In March 1940 Bessy filled in the duties of town clerk for Harry Partrick while he vacationed in Florida. In November 1940 Malette and Bessy entertained Raymond and Florence Jacques of Sodus, and Gordon and Nathalie Jacques and family of North Rose. Malette Jacques was active in the Masons. Around 1943 the Jacqueses moved to Rochester, where Bessy worked as a clerk and Malette as a machine operator.

In 1958 Ronald M. Jacques received an AAS degree at SUNY Farmingdale in ornamental horticulture. In July 1978 Ronald ran in the middle of the pack in the Utica Boilermaker 15K run. In August 2002 Ronald sold his house in Palmyra and moved to Lewisville, North Carolina. He died in 2015, leaving his wife Karen and two stepchildren.

Jacques, William & Frederica

15 North Poplar Street, now 5039 North Poplar. 1940 monthly rent: $12.

Rev. William Jacques (1871–1954), 69, head of household, retired minister, self-employed.

S. Frederica Malette Jacques (1871–1947), 69, wife, homemaker.

WILLIAM WAS BORN IN DEAL, County Kent, England, to John Jacques and Anna "Annie" Nicholas Jacques (1841–1910). William became a U.S. citizen in 1893. Frederica was born in Chemung County to William Smith Malette (1837–1910) and Lestina Tanner Malette (1842–1910). She was a high school graduate. William studied at Syracuse University and Boston University, where he earned a PhD. In 1900 the census occurred before William and Frederica married in September of that year. In the decennial enumeration, William was still residing with his mother, Annie, in the Town of Cincinnatus (Cortland County). William was already a clergyman when he immigrated to America from England in 1892. In the United States, he led Methodist flocks in Rutland, Pennsylvania; Cincinnatus; Wellsburg (Chemung County); Watkins Glen (Schuyler County); and McGraw (Cortland County).

In 1910 Rev. Jacques was a Methodist clergyman in Cortland County. William and Frederica lived with their sons—all three were students in McGraw in the town of Cortlandville—William Malette (1901–1991), John Raymond (1903–1981), and George Gordon Jacques (1905–1972). Also living with them was Rev. Jacques's mother, Annie, who died later that year.

In 1918 Rev. Jacques was a Methodist minister in Horseheads (Chemung County). The Jacqueses rented a home on Orchard Street in the Town of Horseheads. It was the practice of the Methodists to examine the church assignment of each minister annually. Often ministers stayed put, but on average the Methodists moved their ministers to another church about every four years. In 1920 the Jacqueses had five children living with them. Malette was a laborer at a store, and the other four attended school: Raymond, Gordon, Montefort

Lloyd (1910–1928), and Jean Malcolm Jacques (1913–1994). In 1924 William was the pastor of the Methodist Episcopal Church at Troy, Pennsylvania. Rev. Jacques secured an appointment as the minister of the North Rose Methodist Episcopal Church in October 1927.

North Rose Methodist Episcopal Church

TO MANY PEOPLE, the Methodist church seems decidedly different from the Episcopal Church. Methodists are in the mainstream of Protestant churches. Methodists look for guidance in the writings of church founders John and Charles Wesley. (Charles wrote over 6,000 hymns.)

The Episcopal Church is closer in its practices to the Roman Catholic Church than other Protestant churches. Its teachings are much like the Anglican Church (The Church of England). After the American Revolution, however, the clergy of the Episcopal Church in the United States no longer swore allegiance to the British monarch as Supreme Governor of the church as did the clergy of the Anglican Church. The Book of Common Prayer is central to Episcopal worship. Since the 1950s the Episcopal Church has adopted much more liberal views. The church now calls for the full legal equality of LGBTQ people, blesses same-sex marriages, welcomes women to the priesthood, and has ordained a gay bishop. The church supported the civil rights movement and opposed the death penalty.

When the Methodist Church split from the Episcopal Church in 1784, the separating body chose the name The Methodist Episcopal Church. ("Episcopal" meaning it had bishops.) Although there were several smaller groups of Methodists, the Methodist Episcopal Church was the largest Methodist denomination until 1939. This is the group to which the North Rose church belonged. The official name of the local church was the North Rose Methodist Episcopal Church until that same year. In 1939 the Methodist Episcopal Church; the Methodist Episcopal Church—South; and the Methodist Protestant Church merged worldwide to form the Methodist Church. In 1968 the Evangelical United Brethren Church and the Methodist Church joined to become the United Methodist Church. (In this book, the Methodist Episcopal Church and the United Methodist Church's names are usually simplified to the Methodist Church.)

In 1930 three Jacques children remained with their parents. Lloyd had died in 1928 while he was a senior at Troy High School in Pennsylvania, and Gordon was working as an automobile salesman and living in Elmira with his wife and young son. Malette was a bookkeeper for a produce dealer; Raymond was a radio service technician; Malcolm attended high school. In October 1930 the congregation honored William and Frederica at a reception which recognized Rev. Jacques's four consecutive years as pastor of the North Rose Church. In August 1932 the Rose Methodist Episcopal Church celebrated its 100th anniversary. Rev. Jacques was one of many speakers at very well-attended celebrations and religious services. In September 1934 Rev. Jacques's brother the Rev. George H.P. Jacques of South Africa visited William in North Rose.

Rev. William Jacques was hospitalized for several months in 1937. The next year Rev. C.T. Winkworth took over the pastoral duties at the North Rose Methodist Church and Rev. Jacques became the interim minister at the Rose Presbyterian Church. In April 1940, just after the 1940 census count that placed the Jacqueses in North Rose, William and Frederica moved to the Presbyterian parsonage in Rose. In September 1940 Clinton Dillingham hosted William and Frederica at the Green Gate restaurant in Camillus in honor of the Jacqueses' 40th wedding anniversary. Rev. Jacques was a patient at the Psychopathic Hospital in Syracuse in September 1941. This hospital opened a decade earlier and specialized in mental illness. William resolved to retire from the pulpit and carry on his spiritual work without the administrative responsibilities of leading a church and a congregation.

Rev. Jacques was healthy enough to return home from the hospital by Christmas 1941. He performed a wedding ceremony in the Rose

Presbyterian Church in February 1942. Despite his stated intention, Rev. Jacques resumed complete duties as the pastor of the Rose Presbyterian Church. Rev. Jacques returned to the hospital from August to October 1942. In July 1943 he preached at one of his past postings, the Brewerton Methodist Church (Onondaga County). In December 1943 Rev. Jacques was back in the Syracuse Psychopathic Hospital. Doctors released William in July 1944, but by October 1945 Rev. Jacques entered Willard State Hospital in Seneca County. In November 1946 Rev. Jacques attended Sunday services at the North Rose Methodist Church.

Frederica was an active participant in the Literary Club and a member of the Women's Missionary Society of the Rose Presbyterian Church. She was a skilled pianist and organist, so she enjoyed entertaining by performing in piano duets. When Frederica's husband returned to the hospital in the fall of 1941, Frederica stayed for a time with her son Malette's family in North Rose. She spent the first few months of 1944 in Florida with Gordon's family.

In June 1931 Malette married Bessy May Gould (1908–1985) of North Rose. (See "Jacques, Malette & Bessy.") The bride had been living with Mr. and Mrs. Harry Partrick for several years. She remained lifelong friends with the Partricks and regularly exchanged visits with them. Henrietta Quereau attended the bride at the wedding while Raymond attended his brother Malette. The couple settled on a home on Maple Avenue in North Rose. Malette and Bessy became the parents of a son, Ronald, in 1932. Malette's love for music led him to a job in the Wurlitzer Music Store in Rochester in January 1937. That year was an auspicious time for the Wurlitzer company. Only two years earlier they developed a compact piano model—the spinet. The spinet received a warm welcome from the piano-buying public. It was much smaller than the traditional upright; it was only 32 inches tall. Despite this sales opportunity, Malette's family returned to North Rose in June 1937 and settled in the Jeffers house on South Main Street. Bessy was diligent in her work for the Home Bureau. Malette was involved in the Masons.

Raymond married Cecile Mae Fowler (1905–1997) in June 1936.

She grew up in Huron and was a sixth-grade teacher at Leavenworth Central School in Wolcott. After a honeymoon, they resided at 72 Lake Avenue, Wolcott. Raymond and Cecile moved into a house they acquired on Orchard Street in Sodus in July 1938. They became the parents of a son, Pieter, in October 1944. Cecile was a third-grade teacher at Sodus Central School in 1959.

In November 1930 Gordon Jacques visited his parents with his wife, Nathalie Mitchell Jacques (1907–1990), and their new son, Eugene. (See "Jacques, Gordon & Nathalie.") The young family lived in Hornell (Steuben County). In less than two years, they moved to Elmira (Chemung County). In January 1933 Gordon and Nathalie celebrated the birth of a second son, John. During the 1930s they moved to North Rose. Near the end of that year, Gordon, Nathalie, and Jon visited Nathalie's parents in Troy, Pennsylvania. Gordon's family moved to the Skutt rental property on South Poplar Street in April 1940. In 1941 the Gordon Jacques family moved to Lyons, where Gordon and Nathalie had a third son, James, in 1944.

Malcolm was elected class president in NRCS in both his junior and senior years. He went on the traditional senior class trip to Washington, D.C. In May 1931 Malcolm attended the Epworth League annual convention at the Geneva Methodist Church. In August 1931 he accompanied Lloyd and Ruth Marshall and daughter Yvonne to their ranch in Mercedes, Texas. An accomplished violinist, Malcolm sometimes played the instrument at church services. He took a course in violin music at the Eastman School of Music in Rochester and played the violin as a member of the Symphony Orchestra in Auburn (Cayuga County). By March 1939 Malcolm was living in Syracuse. In both the 1940 and 1950 censuses, Malcolm was a patient at the Willard State Hospital. Thus, mental illness was a prevalent ailment that affected the Jacques family. His parents visited when Rev. Jacques's health allowed.

When William died at 83 in 1954, he was at Willard, as was Malcolm. Malette was living in Rochester, Raymond in Sodus, and Gordon in Lyons.

Jensen, John & Edra

1940 monthly rent: $8.
John Jensen (1905–1995), 34, head of household, laborer, retail coal, 45 weeks at $550.
Edra Jensen (1909–1996), 30, wife, homemaker.
June Jensen (1929–2003), 10, daughter, student.
Shirley Jensen (1931–2023), 8, daughter, student.
Marvin Jensen (1939–), infant 3 months, son.
Margaret Davis (1871–1940), 68, mother-in-law, retired.

June Jensen, NRCS Class of 1947

Shirley Jensen, NRCS Class of 1949

We were unable to obtain more than the cursory information provided by the census for this household. If you have information about the Jensens, see page 32.

Kemp, R.S. & Edith

1940 monthly rent: $15.
Robert Samuel Kemp (1904–1983), 35, head of household, minister, 52 weeks for $1,100.
Edith Kemp (1909–1993), 30, wife, homemaker.
Dorothy Maria Kemp (1934–2013), 6, daughter.
Grace Irene Kemp (1935–), 4, daughter.
Mary Elizabeth Kemp (1937–), 3, daughter.
Virginia Ruth Kemp (1939–), 8 months, daughter.

We were unable to obtain more than the cursory information provided by the census for this household. If you have information about the Kemps, see page 32.

Kenan, Ray & Theresa

In the eastern half of North Rose. 1940 monthly rent: $22.
Raymond Hadley Kenan (1901–1949), 38, head of household, medical doctor, self-employed.
Theresa Florence O'Donnell Kenan (1908–1961), 31, wife, homemaker.

Patricia Ann "Patsy" Kenan (1937–2023), 2, daughter.

RAY AND THERESA KENAN had two children: Patricia and Thomas Francis (1941–2022). Dr. Kenan spent five years in college, graduating from Syracuse University Medical School in 1928. Because he was a physician in private practice, he was not required to furnish his income to the census, but as North Rose's only doctor, he reported working 52 weeks during the previous year and 80 hours during the week that was surveyed. Theresa was a homemaker and a high school graduate.

Dr. Kenan's short-lived first marriage to college graduate and librarian Mary L. Bowen (ca. 1905–1975) took place in Syracuse in 1926. The couple had one son, Robert C. Kenan (1929–2005), and the family lived in Salina (Onondaga County) in 1930. After Ray and Mary separated, Robert lived with his mother: in 1935 in Montclair, New Jersey, and in 1940 in Bakersfield, California—where Mary was the children's librarian at the public library. In 1942 she was named director of the Muskegon County Library in Michigan. At some point Mary changed her name to Mary Kenan Hadley; she was named the first director of the Prince George's County Memorial Library System in Maryland in 1947. In 1950 she lived in Mount Rainier, Maryland, with her partner, Marguerite Hansen.

This photo of Dr. Ray Kenan appeared in the 1949 NRCS yearbook in a tribute to him.

Dr. Kenan came to North Rose in 1932 after practicing medicine in Syracuse for two years, and hung his shingle outside the former office of Dr. Frank Roney. He also served as Health Officer for the Town of Rose and as the North Rose School physician. He was a member of the professional medical fraternity Alpha Kappa Kappa and enjoyed hunting with friends at Limekiln Lake in Herkimer County.

Theresa, who married Ray in 1933, was an enthusiastic member of the Contract Bridge Club and a member of the Home Bureau, and her parents and sister were frequent visitors from Syracuse. She visited the New York World's Fair with her husband in September 1940. In November 1942 they moved into a new house on Wolcott

Street. Patricia took piano lessons from Mrs. Roney.

Dr. Kenan died after emergency surgery at the Barber Hospital in Lyons during February 1949. Soon after, the Kenan's home was purchased by Dr. Howard Hoople—who started a practice there that June. Theresa and the children moved to Syracuse in September, but she and her daughter sometimes returned to the area to visit Ora Stechow.

Patsy married Thomas Ogden in 1955; they had four sons and a daughter before they divorced in 1966 and she became a single mom. Her children remember her bringing them to various Lake Ontario beaches she'd visited as a child in North Rose. She remarried late in life, to Donald Dimon.

Kimpland, George & Lena

1940 monthly rent: $12.
George Kimpland (ca. 1871–), 69, head of household, retired.
Lena Kimpland (ca. 1873–), 67, wife, retired.

We were unable to obtain more than the cursory information provided by the census for this household. If you have information about the Kimplands, see page 32.

Knapp, Florence

10 South Main Street, now 4986 South Main—Built in 1906. 1940 monthly rent: $18. Owned by Seth Oaks.
Florence Zapf Knapp (1895–1973), 44, head of household, schoolteacher, 16 weeks for $40 a week.
Willis G. Knapp Jr. (1929–), 11, son, student.
Frederick "Fred" C. Knapp (1931–2001), 9, son, student.

FLORENCE KNAPP WAS THE WIDOW of Willis G. Knapp (1882–1937). Her two sons were both in school; Willis had finished fifth grade and Fred had finished third. Florence had five years of college, earned a BS in Home Economics from Cornell University, and was working as a home economics teacher.

In 1920 Florence was a bookkeeper living in Ithaca in her widowed mother's rooming house with her brother, Wallace, and sister, Irene. Wallace was manager of a lumber company, and Irene was unemployed. Next, Florence lived in Dansville in Livingston County (directly south of Monroe County). There, in July 1926, she married Willis G. Knapp (1882–1937), who was 13 years her senior. Knapp cofounded a prominent Dansville insurance agency, Krein & Knapp, and Mrs. Knapp was a homemaker. The couple had two children in Dansville, and Florence's mother, a German immigrant, Huldena Zapf, moved in with them.

NRCS teacher Florence Knapp in the 1958 yearbook

After her husband's death in 1937, Florence got a job as a home economics teacher for NRCS. Her mother joined her in North Rose, lodging with Jim and Gertie Boyd. (See "Boyd, Jim & Gertie.") Florence was the pianist at the North Rose Methodist Church. She was very active in the Grange for decades and also participated in Red Cross activities. Florence, Willis, and Frederick took many two-day bicycle trips from North Rose to Dansville with stops along the way, including Canandaigua Lake. In July 1949 the Knapps moved to the Seeley house on Huron Street. Mrs. Zapf died in Wales Center (Erie County) in December 1951.

Willis G. Knapp, NRCS Class of 1947

Willis Jr. was valedictorian of the NRCS Class of 1947. He attended Cornell University and studied at RIT. He was drafted into the Army and was assigned to duty in Europe in 1952; he returned to civilian life in 1954. In February 1954 he married Beverly Jane Richardson, daughter of Paul and Betty Richardson. Willis's brother, Frederick, was best man at the wedding. The couple settled in Rochester, where Willis was employed at the Camera Works. Later in life he lived in Webster (Monroe County) and in Leesburg, Florida.

As a child, Frederick Knapp was active in the Boy Scouts. In June 1951 he was in the Army and stationed at Fort Dix. Later on, he lived in Sodus. He married Elizabeth "Betty" Furguson (1930–2015) in May 1954. The Knapps had a daughter, Cheryl Ann, in May 1955 and a son, Richard Daley, in June 1957. He died at 70 in Sodus.

Knapp, Leon & Leola

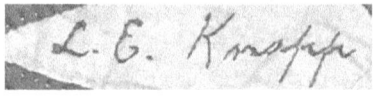

4868 South Main Street. Estimated 1940 value: $2,000. Telephone 3401.
Leon E. Knapp (1882–1947), 58, head of household, farmer and highway superintendent, 50 weeks for $1,500.
Leola Nancy Snyder Knapp (1888–1951), 51, wife, homemaker and trimmer, 13 weeks for $146.

LEON WAS BORN ON New Year's Day 1882. Leon farmed and—for the last 10 years of his life—served as the highway superintendent for the Town of Rose. (That is an elective office in Rose.) His middle initial was "E." It did not stand for any middle name; it was just the letter E. Leon attended one year of high school.

Leon's parents were Carl Knapp (1860–1896) and Addie A. Brown Knapp (1862–1943). They lived in the village of Albion (Orleans County). In 1900 Leon worked on his mother's farm. A younger brother and sister attended school. In 1910 Leon lived with his first wife Nellie B. Watt Knapp (1885–1919) and their son Harold L. Knapp (1901–1987) in the Town of Gaines (Orleans County). Leon was a farmer. In 1915 the three Knapps lived in the Town of Rose. Nellie was a dressmaker besides being a homemaker. Nellie's parents were George Gray Watt Sr. (1858–1943) and Mary Eliza Harris Watt (1861–1925). Nellie died in 1919. In 1920 Leon was a widower who owned a home on North Poplar Street in North Rose, where he lived with his son, Harold Knapp. Leon farmed, and Harold was a farm laborer.

Leola N. Snyder—who later became Leon's wife—completed eight years of school. She was a homemaker, but she worked a portion of the year as a trimmer at an apple evaporator. Her parents were Esbon Blackmer Snyder (1852–1921) and Mary E. Trummonds Snyder (1851–1913). Leola married her first husband, Peter Charles Fraser

(1882–1923), a farmer, around 1905. Their household included their two sons, Harold Fraser (1908–1930) and Arthur Roy Fraser (1914–1971), in the Town of Williamson in 1915. In 1925 Leon married Leola Fraser. Around 1930 they owned a farm on Swamp Road in the Town of Rose. Leon's stepson (Leola's younger son) Roy Fraser worked on the farm with Leon. Harold Knapp proceeded to Medina (Orleans County), Macedon, and then Albion. In 1930 he married Perthena Keller Hall, a Canadian by birth. Perthena had married Charles A. Hall in April 1912. They migrated from Welland, Ontario, Canada, to Albion. The year of their marriage, Charles and Perthena had a daughter, Ruth Edna Hall.

In October 1929 Leon's stepson Harold Fraser married Helen Kalbfleisch, daughter of Mrs. Ernest French. They entered their married life living at Long Acres Dairy Farm. The following May, Harold died in a farming accident. He was adjusting the carburetor on a tractor operated by his stepfather. Harold fell from the moving tractor, and the attached disk harrow passed over both his legs. He was rushed to Dr. Roney's office, where he died. Harold was 22 years old—and a newlywed—when he succumbed in this terrible mishap.

In the early 1930s Helen married William Henry Harrison, who was born in Utica. They had four children. Roy Fraser married Carolyn Marie Converse (1916–1996) in March 1935 and by 1940 had three children: Leon A., Donald H., and Harold R. Fraser. Roy Fraser was a farm operator—renting land as needed.

Leon Knapp was one of four constables of the Town of Rose in 1914–1915. In October 1915 Leon and fellow constable Truman Warner ordered an obstreperous group of hoboes to leave town within two hours. Some hoboes objected, but the ornery wanderers left—much to the relief of the townsfolk. In March 1920 Leon purchased an Essex automobile. Leon and Leola visited the state fair in Syracuse in September 1930. In August 1935 Leon and Leola entertained Earl and Lillian Barnes, Ray and Teresa Kenan, and Susie Graham at Addie's (Leon's mother) cottage, near Albion. A fire of an unknown origin destroyed the barn on Leon's farm west of the hamlet in March 1939. A dozen head of cattle and five horses died. Leon had served

10 years as highway superintendent of the Town of Rose at his death in March 1947. He fell in the line of duty. Leon suffered a stroke after many hours of continuous snow plowing during a heavy storm. He died 13 days later.

Latham, Arthur & Mabelle

5042 Main Street. 1940 monthly rent: $25.
William Arthur Swaby Latham Jr. (1889–1954), 50, head of household, manager, self-employed.
Mabelle Sterling Hubbard Latham (1895–1995), 44, wife, pharmacist, self-employed.

ARTHUR AND MABELLE LATHAM rented the space for their drugstore in the Odd Fellows commercial block just south of the Methodist Church on the east side of North Main Street. They lived behind and above their shop. Arthur and Mabelle were both proprietors of their pharmacy, but Mabelle was the registered pharmacist. Arthur was a high school graduate, while Mabelle was a graduate of the University of Buffalo School of Pharmacy.

Arthur was the son of William Arthur Swaby Latham Sr. (1855–1931) and Alice Alden Hills Latham (1858–1931). Arthur's father was a merchant engaged in businesses selling such things as lumber and coal and, later, dry goods. As a child Arthur Jr. lived in Seneca Falls and as a young adult in Syracuse. Selling was his vocation before entering the drugstore business. He sold automobiles between 1920 and 1925 and gloves in 1930.

Mabelle started working in a drugstore when she was 15. Her parents, Arthur E. Hubbard (1863–1898), a bookkeeper, and Elizabeth "Bessie" Pauline Forbush Hubbard (1866–1898), married in November 1886 and lived in Big Tree Corners in the Town of Hamburg (Erie County). Mabel Hubbard and her four siblings, Bessie P., Alice, Arthur, and Allen—orphaned at young ages—moved from Hamburg to the Buffalo home of their grandmother, Paulina Weston Prince Forbush (1840–1914). In 1920 Mabelle lived with her widowed great-aunt, Charlotte R.S. Prince Church (1849–1929). That year, while attending college, Mabelle served as a drug clerk. Mabelle graduated from the University of Buffalo School of Pharmacy with the highest average (93.3) in the class of 1924. Her senior class comprised eight women and over a hundred men. At the graduation ceremony, she won the William H. Peabody Prize, including a cash gift of $50. In 1925 Mabelle achieved her dream of working as a licensed pharmacist. The next year, Mabelle was superintendent of the local junior branch of the Epworth League, a Methodist organization for the spiritual growth of young people aged 18–25. (Epworth, England, was the birthplace of the founders of the Methodist Church, John and Charles Wesley. In 1939, the year of the major merger which formed the Methodist Church, the Epworth League was renamed the Methodist Youth Fellowship.)

Shortly after that, in September 1928, Arthur and Mabelle married. The Lathams were recent arrivals in North Rose. In 1930 they lived in Syracuse and in 1935 they lived in Cayuga County. Mabelle and Arthur opened Latham's Pharmacy in North Rose by October 1939. Mabelle won election as the corresponding secretary of the Presbyterian Missionary Society in February 1942. The church elders selected Arthur as a trustee of the North Rose Presbyterian Church in April 1942. In October of that year, Mabelle was the teacher of all adult Sunday school classes at the Presbyterian Church. Mabelle's brother Arthur Hubbard and his wife visited from Dayton, Ohio, in October 1947. The Lathams took a three-week trip to Florida in April 1948.

After Arthur's death, Mabelle moved to Auburn. She worked at the Lewis Drug Store. Mabelle married Edward A. Beacham (1886–1964)—a retired employee of the Smith and Pearson Hardware Co. In Auburn, Mabelle was an active member of the Immanuel Baptist Church, where she served as a deacon, sang in the choir, and was a member of the music committee. Mr. Beacham had three children from a previous marriage. Mabelle continued to work as a pharmacist well into her 80s.

Lawrence, Donald & Elizabeth

North Poplar Street. 1940 monthly rent: $16.
Donald J. Lawrence (1912–1981), 28, head of household, store clerk and buyer, 52 weeks, $1,500.
Mary Elizabeth Tellier Lawrence (1910–2001), 30, wife, homemaker, substitute teacher, 4 weeks, $80. (Elizabeth's maiden name was pronounced "tuh-LEAR.")

DONALD AND ELIZABETH WERE BOTH natives of North Rose, and were both valedictorians of their NRCS class (1930 and 1926, respectively). Donald was a clerk and buyer in his family's hardware store, North Rose Supply Company, which his father, Henry Lawrence (1884–1967), started in the 1920s. (See "Lawrence, Henry & Grace.") Elizabeth's father had been a state assemblyman and president of North Rose National Bank. (See "Tellier, Harry & Maude.")

Donald studied piano with Estella Roney, but the trombone was his favorite musical instrument. He was a diligent member of the Boy Scouts. Donald was the leader of the junior choir of the Rose Baptist Church. In October 1939 Donald received the Republican caucus's nomination for Town Clerk. That same month, Donald and Elizabeth toured the World's Fair in New York City. Harry Partrick defeated Donald in the November general election. In August 1941 Donald and Elizabeth went camping along the St. Lawrence River with Hollis and Thelma Todd. In September 1942 the Lawrences moved to the Yancey House on Huron Street. Donald enlisted in the Army in April 1943. He injured his knee during basic training and received a discharge from the armed services. Most years, Donald and Elizabeth attended a hardware convention in either Rochester or Syracuse. Donald and Elizabeth enjoyed camping and fishing on the St. Lawrence with Jane Gilmore.

After graduating from Keuka College, Elizabeth taught history at Williamson's junior high school. Elizabeth was a member of the Mission Circle of the Rose Baptist Church. She filled in for Mildred Hetzke when the NRCS teacher was ill in January 1936. Elizabeth was a member of the North Rose Literary Club and played an active part in the Health Committee's work. When the Rose Health Committee created a medical equipment loan chest, Elizabeth stored the items at her home on Wolcott Road. Elizabeth had a close relationship with her extended family—often exchanging visits with Tellier relatives, including her parents in East Palmyra. Elizabeth taught social studies at the Alfred–Almond High School at the start of the fall 1945 semester as an interim teacher. She was the matron of honor at the July 1947 wedding of her sister Ellen Tellier of East Palmyra and Lt. Newell Whitcomb (1924–2013) of Syracuse. The bride and groom left for Colorado Springs, where Lt. Whitcomb underwent officer training in mountain warfare. In October 1947 Donald and Elizabeth visited Newell and Ellen after they had settled in Cazenovia (Madison County). In 1940 Ellen was a lodger in Donald's parents' home. (See "Lawrence, Henry & Grace.")

In January 1952 Donald and Elizabeth had a daughter, Margaret G. "Maggi" Lawrence. After living in Knoxville, Tennessee; Norfolk, Virginia; and Yonkers (Westchester County), Maggi returned to her family home in North Rose. She won election to the board of directors of the Town of Rose Historical Society.

Lawrence, Henry & Grace

Estimated 1940 value: $2,500.
Henry Lawrence (1884–1967), 55, head of household, proprietor of hardware store.
Grace Lawrence (1888–1957), 52, wife, homemaker.
Ellen Tellier (1921–), 19, lodger, student.

BORN IN HITCHIN, HERTFORDSHIRE, ENGLAND, Henry Lawrence departed with his family from Liverpool, England, for New York at age 3. The Lawrences settled in Williamson. Henry grew up working on his father's farm; he was the eldest of six children born to John Lawrence (1863–1935) and Elizabeth Lawrence (1863–1947). Henry married Anna Grace Crane (1888–1957) about 1908 and they had one son, Donald (1912–1981). (See "Lawrence, Donald & Elizabeth.") Henry and Grace first lived together in Marion, where he farmed into the 1920s. He was a director of the Marion Cooperative Canning Crops Association, Inc. By 1924 Henry and Grace lived in North Rose, and by 1926 Henry had opened North Rose Supply Company.

Grace Lawrence was in the hospital 1951. She died at 69 in Clifton Springs Sanitarium after a six-year illness. After Grace's death, Henry married Estella Peck (1897–1979), the widow of a Williamson farmer who had two sons, Elwood and Dean.

Living with Henry and Grace in 1940 was Ellen Tellier, their daughter-in-law's sister. Ellen married Newell "Newt" Whitcomb in 1947 (1924–2013). After serving in the Philippines and Okinawa during World War II, Newt graduated from RPI with a degree in metallurgical engineering and settled in northern Delaware. Newt and Ellen had four sons: Jim, Tim, Chip, and Jon.

James N. Whitcomb (1951–) was a self-described long-haired hippie surfer working as a plumber in Hawaii in the 1970s when he founded a solar hot water company based in Maui. His wife, Beth (1958–2001), was vice president of the company when she died at 42 of smoke inhalation trying to put out a house fire. Jim and their two children, Matthew and Lynn, all worked at Haleakala Solar.

Newell "Chip" Whitcomb (ca. 1956–1991) died at 35 of leukemia. He had worked as a mechanical engineer based at the Philadelphia Naval Shipyard.

Timothy H. Whitcomb (1954–) went to the University of Delaware. Jonathan P. Whitcomb (1962–2019) got a business degree from West Chester University. They both worked for North Star Enterprises, a pipe distribution company their father founded after he retired.

Ellen made it past her 103rd birthday.

Leaird, Charles & Etta

Estimated 1940 value: $1,600.
Charles Moses Leaird (1871–1948), 69, head of household, night engineer at the Cold Storage, 36 weeks at $1,008.
Etta Thompson Leaird (1878–1969), 62, wife, homemaker.

CHARLES AND ETTA MARRIED IN 1897 and they first made their home in Wolcott. Charles changed professions multiple times: In 1900 he was a butcher; in 1910 he was a carpenter; in 1920 he was a farmer in Huron; in 1930 he was a chemical engineer at the Cold Storage.

Charles and Etta had two sons, Charles (1900–1972) and George (1909–1939). In 1920 both their sons were living with them in Huron, along with Charles's new wife, Anna Campbell. The younger Charles was a truck driver. In 1940 he was living with Anna and their four children—Stanley, Doris, Ruby, and Esther—in his mother-in-law's house in Wolcott.

Charles and Etta's younger son, George, died the year before the 1940 census. George's wife and children lived in North Rose. (See "Leaird, Dorothy.")

Leaird, Dorothy

North Poplar Street. 1940 monthly rent: $10.
Dorothy Louise Shaver Leaird (1915–2000), 24, mother, homemaker, self-employed.
Betty Jean Leaird (1932–2023), 7, daughter, student.
George William "Bill" Leaird (1933–1982), 6, son, student.
Shirley Mae Leaird (ca. 1935–), 4, daughter.
Nancy Anne Leaird (1936–2014), 3, daughter.

DOROTHY LOUISE SHAVER LEAIRD, a youthful widow, and her four children rented a home on North Poplar Street. Her late husband, George John Leaird (1909–1939), a truck driver, died of pneumonia. They wed in Charlton (Oswego County) in July 1931. Dorothy was born in Oswego County. By 1920 her parents, William H. Shaver (1884–1973) and Mary Elizabeth Knapp Shaver (1893–1975), had moved to Shaddock Road in Huron. William was a general farmer. His father had been born in Germany.

In April 1939, after George's death, Dorothy and her family returned from a stay with the Shavers to their home on North Poplar Street. Dorothy hosted a Halloween party for the younger members of the North Rose Presbyterian Church in 1940. In 1947 the Dorothy Leaird family and her parents-in-law, Charles and Etta (see "Leaird, Charles & Etta"), moved into the Knapp house on Maple Avenue in North Rose. Charles and Etta had purchased the property from Frank Fink. In 1950 Dorothy and her children lived in Lyons; Dorothy was working in a hospital as a nurse. In 1953 she lived in Newark. In May 1964 Dorothy married Henry Palmer (1924–2017) in Newark.

William Leaird, NRCS Class of 1951

Dorothy's son, Bill, won an NRCS basketball letter in 1948. He moved to Rochester and worked as a cook. He married Jean Peters in 1959. They had three daughters: Lorie, Sandy, and Pamela.

After her father's death, Betty sometimes lived with her grandparents, Charles and Etta. She married James Oliver Washburn of Savannah, and they settled in Clyde, where she owned and ran a store, Fabrics Plus. Betty and James had six children: Carol, Linda, Donna, Jeffery, Kathleen, and Patricia. Later, after their children were grown, Betty and James lived in North Rose.

In May 1943 Shirley and Nancy entertained 10 friends in honor of their birthdays. Shirley and Nancy were both regularly listed on the honor roll at the North Rose Central School. Shirley Leaird was the treasurer of her freshman class at NRCS in 1949, but her family moved to Lyons before she could finish her school year. In June 1953 Shirley graduated from Newark High School. She married Peter Laurette (1934–2005), who was also from Newark. The Navy cited Peter in March 1952 for rescuing a man from a burning seaplane that hurtled into Guantanamo Bay, Cuba. Their daughter, Kimberlee A. Laurette, graduated from SUNY Alfred with a degree in accounting in June 1986. By that time, Shirley and Peter had separated, and Peter moved to Clermont, Florida; Shirley lived in Newark.

Nancy married Donald Frederick Facer (1932–2001) of Lyons in January 1954, her senior year of high school. They lived in Williamson and had two daughters, Daisy and Debby.

Lewis, Lloyd

1940 monthly rent: $7.
Lloyd Lewis (1873–1947), 66, head of household, retired.

We were unable to obtain more than the cursory information provided by the census for this household. If you have information about the Lewises, see page 32.

Little, Ray & Iona

North Poplar Street. 1940 monthly rent: $10.
Willis "Ray" Little (1913–1983), 27, head of household, truck driver, 32 weeks at $480.
Iona Mae Van Amburg Little (1918–1991), 21, wife, housekeeper, 16 weeks at $80.

RAY GREW UP IN HIS GRANDMOTHER'S house in North Rose. When he was a young boy, his father, Fletcher Little (1885–1917), died of appendicitis. So his mother, Inez Carpenter Little (1882–1969), and her three young children went to live with her mother, Hannah Carpenter (1852–1932), on South Poplar Street. Inez married again in the early 1920s, to Earl Hilts (1889–1991), and Earl moved into Hannah's house as well. (See "Hilts, Earl & Inez.") Ray was still living there in 1930, working in a coalyard.

Ray married Iona Mae Van Amburg in 1936; they were renting a house on North Poplar Street in 1940. Their son, Charles, was born around 1944. In July 1947 Ray got a job working as a mechanic for Wolcott's newest auto dealer, Wilmoth Motors—a Hudson car and Mack truck dealer. Charles was in the Wolcott Cub Scouts.

Ray worked for 10 years for the state highway department before retiring. Ray and Iona moved back to North Rose and lived on Elm Street. Charles and his wife, Gaye, lived in Conesus (Livingston County) when Iona died in 1991.

Looke, Charles & Maud

1940 monthly rent: $9.
Charles Looke (1881–1961), 58, head of household, farm laborer, 15 weeks at $210.
Maud Looke (1883–1968), 56, wife, trimmer at the Canning Factory, 5 weeks at $65.

We were unable to obtain more than the cursory information provided by the census for this household. If you have information about the Lookes, see page 32.

Lord, Emma

Estimated 1940 value: $2,000.
Emma Drury Lord (ca. 1877–1956), 63, head of household, trimmer, apple dryhouse, 26 weeks at $260.
Frank Drury (1879–1962), 61, brother, laborer at the Cold Storage, 30 weeks at $425.
Richard Drury (1920–2011), 20, nephew, student.

Emma Lord and Frank Drury were the brother and sister of Albert Drury. (See "Drury, Bert & Theresa.") Richard was a nephew to all three of them; he was the son of their brother Benjamin Drury (1882–1948) and Clara Bell Grinnals (1885–1932).

We were unable to obtain much more than the cursory information provided by the census for this household. If you have information about the Drurys, see page 32.

Lundergun, Jim & Kittie

13 Maple Avenue, now 10403 Maple—Built in 1903. Estimated 1940 value: $2,500.
James Lundergun (1877–1957), 61, head of household, not employed.
Catherine "Kittie" M. Grady Lundergun (1885–1965), 54, wife, postmaster, 52 weeks for $33 a week.

Frances "Fannie" Louisa Clark Grady (1862–1943), 77, mother-in-law.

MARRIED IN 1915, Jim and Kittie Lundergun shared their home with Kittie's widowed mother, Fannie Grady. Kittie served as the postmaster at the North Rose post office from February 1936 to March 1950. In 1940 Jim was not employed outside the home. Jim had completed tenth grade, Kittie the eighth, and Frances the sixth.

The Lunderguns both had Irish ancestors. Jim's parents were both Irish immigrants. His mother, Bridget Dunn (ca. 1851–), may have been a servant in Galen in 1870 at the age of 19. She married Michael Lundergun (ca. 1848–). In 1892 the couple was living in the Town of Rose with three children: James, Theresa, and William. All three lived in North Rose in 1940. (See "Lundergun, Will & Dora" and "Drury, Bert & Theresa.) (In "Lundergun," we use the final vowel of "u" although both "a" and "o" spellings of the name were widely used in newspapers and other sources. "Lundergun" is how it appears most often—and it's what appears on the family gravestone in the Rose Cemetery.)

Kittie's father, Thomas J. Grady (1862–1932), was the child of Irish immigrants but was born in Canada and immigrated to the U.S. at the age of 2. Kittie's mother, Frances Louisa Clark (1863–1943), was born in the U.S. Thomas and Frances married in 1882 and lived at Sodus Point for 50 years—until Thomas passed away following an operation at Sodus's Northern Wayne Hospital in November 1932. At the time of her death in February 1943, Fannie had been living with her daughter and son-in-law for several years.

In 1905 Jim was elected vice president of a new North Rose young men's club with meeting rooms above Benjamin Johnson's meat market. By 1908 Jim was running his own apple-drying business and often traveled. In 1915 the Lunderguns lived on Maple Avenue; Jim worked for William Marshall as a laborer and teamster, and Kittie was a homemaker. In 1924 Jim fell and broke several of his ribs. By that time, he was a general laborer, a job he continued at least until 1930. Jim bought new Hudson automobiles in 1925 and December of 1931. In February 1935, when Mr. and Mrs. Harry Quereau took an auto vacation to Florida, Jim substituted at their store for Harry.

Jim received the Rose Democratic caucus nomination for assessor in 1929. He ran unopposed and therefore won the election. He was also an early trustee of the North Rose Fire Department. Among the numerous friends with whom the Lunderguns enjoyed socializing were Dr. B.R. Stone of Rochester and his wife, Frank and Ann Oliver of Weedsport, and Henry and Hattie Gage of North Rose. In July 1930 the Lunderguns vacationed at Fourth Lake in the Adirondacks with their frequent traveling companions, Harry and Laura Harris Payne. In August 1941 the couple—along with Bert and Theresa Drury, and Miss Mary Drury—were among the 25 attendees at the Lundergun family picnic at Panther Lake (north of Oneida Lake).

As a child, Kittie lived with her extended family—including her parents—in her grandparents' home in Sodus. As an adult, she was active in the Home Missionary Society of the North Rose Methodist Church and was a member of Kappa Phi and the Thursday Club. An enthusiastic Democrat, she was given the position of postmaster as a reward for her 14 years of service on the Town of Rose Democratic Committee. In June 1945, Kittie, Mary Drury, Eva Firra, Carol Davis, and Margaret McCall traveled together to Gananoque, Ontario, Canada, and the nearby Thousand Islands.

Lundergun, Will & Dora

93 South Main Street, now 4936 South Main—Built in 1910. Estimated 1940 value: $2,000.

William "Will" Lundergun (1882–1948), 57, head of household, school bus driver, 40 weeks at $15 a week.

Dora Elizabeth Satterlee Lundergun (1881–1968), 58, wife, homemaker/trimmer, 12 weeks at $13 a week.

Benjamin H. Satterlee (1857–1941), 83, father-in-law.

WILLIAM AND DORA LUNDERGUN WERE married in 1906. They both had attended school for eight years and were sharing their home with

Dora's father, Benjamin. Will grew up in Rose and was employed as a farm laborer in 1900, a miller for George W. Marshall and Son feed mill in 1918, a truck driver for Kulp Express in 1930, and a school bus driver for NRCS in 1940. That year Dora was a homemaker and also worked seasonally as a trimmer at the Canning Factory. Benjamin was a retired farmer and had received six years of education.

Will's brother, Jim, and his sister, Theresa Drury, both lived in North Rose. (See "Lundergun, Jim & Kittie" for information about Will's parents—and a note about the spelling of "Lundergun.")

An active Democrat, Will ran in the Town of Rose for a position as a town constable in 1929 and received the Democratic Party nomination for the two-year Town Assessor post, but he lost the general election 418 to 149. In October 1947, when the North Rose Board of Education purchased a new Mack bus, they assigned it to Will.

Dora was active in the missionary society of the Methodist Episcopal Church, was a member of the Women's Society of Christian Service associated with the North Rose Methodist Church, was initiated into the Order of the Eastern Star in December 1938, and in 1943 was a part of Kappa Phi.

Dora's mother, Luranda Satterlee (1858–1934), of Big Indian (Ulster County) spent the winter of 1933 with the Lunderguns. At the August 1938 Lundergun family reunion, held in Pultneyville, Dora was elected president of the family organization.

The Lunderguns took in a schoolteacher as a lodger in 1920 and were avid bridge players. Twenty-five of their friends held a surprise 25th-anniversary party for them in December 1931. In July 1936 the couple bought a new Plymouth. They spent a September Sunday in 1939 with Jim and Kittie Lundergun in Hot Bottom, Pennsylvania.

Benjamin had spent most of his life in Ulster County—most recently in Big Indian in the Town of Shandaken, but he was raised about 20 miles east in Woodstock. His father was a farmer, and at the age of 22 Benjamin was a servant in the Vanalkenburgh household. He married Luranda E. Smith in 1880, and by 1900 they had three children at home: daughters Dora and Katherine "Katie," and a nephew Benjamin (whom he later adopted). Benjamin farmed, as he did for the remainder of his working life. He was very ill in June 1937 and died in August 1941.

Marshall, Ella   *Ella Marshall*

Estimated 1940 value: $2,800.
Ellinor "Ella" Fidelia Redman Marshall (1872–1961), 68, head of household, homemaker.

THE DAUGHTER OF Lafayette Redman (1840–1906) and Sarah "Fidelia" Redman (1843–1928), Ella was born in Nebraska and spent part of her childhood there. Her father was a farmer who was born in Camillus (Onondaga County) but moved to Pembroke (Genesee County) as a young boy. Ella's two eldest siblings were born in Pembroke—Celia and Ossian—but in the 1860s Lafayette decided to try his luck out west. Ella's older brother David was born in Illinois; Ella and her younger brother George were born in Nebraska in the 1870s. But by the time Ella was 8, the family was back in Pembroke, where she did most of her growing up.

Ella married George William Marshall (1869–1938) in April 1892; their first son, Lloyd Marion Marshall (1893–1970), was born the following year in Rochester. George grew up in Newstead (Erie County), just east of Buffalo, where his father was a farmer. His parents were Marion T. Marshall (1850–1891) and Rachel Juliana Beidick (1849–1916).

In the last decade of the 19th century, after his father's death, George and his mother, brother, and sister all moved to Wayne County. George's brother, William, became a farmer in the Town of Rose. (See "Marshall, Harold & Leona" for more about William; Harold was a son of William's who lived in North Rose in 1940.)

In 1900 George was 30 and the head of a household in Galen that included his wife, Ella, 28; his son, Lloyd, 7; his sister, Gertrude, 14; and his mother, Rachel Fisher, 50. Over the course of the previous decade, Rachel's husband died, she got married again in 1893, to Rose farmer William Fisher (1818–1896), and was widowed again.

George was working as a foundryman. Clyde had several foundries during the 19th century. Probably George worked in one that produced metal castings: Rodwell's Foundry, Humphrey & Dolph Foundry, or S.W. Wood and Son Machine Shop and Foundry. Some of these metal casting businesses survived into the 20th century.

In 1905 George was still the head of a multigenerational household, but the extended family had moved to North Rose. George was working as a coal dealer. With George's mother doing housework, Ella was able to work as a bookkeeper. George's sister, Gertrude, was a milliner. George and Ella had two children in school: Lloyd and Olive Gertrude Marshall (1900–1994).

In 1906 George's sister, Gertrude, died of typhoid fever at 21. In 1910 George was still a coal dealer, but he also sold automobiles and wagons. In 1913 Lloyd got married; the newlyweds settled in North Rose. (See "Marshall, Lloyd & Ruth.)

George and Ella's youngest child, George "Clifford" (1914–1996) arrived two years before George's mother died. Rachel Beidick Marshall Fisher was 66. In 1920 Ella's mother, Sarah, had joined the household.

Olive married William "Clark" Wilson (1895–1963) in 1921. He was a farmer and cider mill operator in the Town of Rose. He and Olive had two boys: William Clark Wilson Jr. (1924–2004), who worked with his father in their orchards, and Richard Marshall Wilson (1925–1976), who lived in Antwerp, Belgium, at the time of Clark's death.

In 1922 George W. Marshall and his son, Lloyd Marshall, agreed to form a new company, building a colossal cold storage warehouse to preserve the fruits and vegetables picked from the area's orchards and mucklands. Area farmers desperately needed this cold storage building. The new business was so successful that the Marshalls built an addition within two years of the enterprise's commencement. The whole facility was called the General Storage and Ice Company. The original building had a storage capacity of 180,000 bushels of apples. The second building increased the capacity by 90,000 bushels. George was president and general manager of the Cold Storage until his death at 68 in 1938.

Ella, a 60-year member of the North Rose Methodist Church, died at 89 on LeRoy Island, at Olive and Clark's summer home.

Marshall, Harold & Leona

Estimated value in 1940: $2,500.
Harold J. Marshall (1899–1974), 41, head of household, self-employed, farmer (Muskland Farm).
Leona Marshall (1908–2005), 31, wife, homemaker.
Lawrence Marshall (1927–2000), 13, son, student.
Shirley Marshall (1928–2011), 11, daughter, student.
Glenn Marshall (1932–), 7, son, student.

Larry Marshall, NRCS Class of 1945

Shirley Marshall, NRCS Class of 1946

HAROLD J. MARSHALL WAS THE SECOND of six children born to William Marion Marshall (1874–1955) and Susan Mary Fisher Marshall (1877–1965). At the turn of the century, before becoming a longtime farmer in the Town of Rose, William was the Clyde–North Rose stage driver. William's brother, George, lived in North Rose at the time of the 1940 census, as did William's nephew, Lloyd. (See "Marshall, Ella" and "Marshall, Lloyd & Ruth" for more information about the Marshall family.

We were unable to obtain much more than the cursory information provided by the census for this household. If you have more information, see page 32.

Marshall, Lloyd & Ruth

22 South Main Street, now 4952 South Main. Estimated 1940 value: $6,500. Telephone 3641. Office Telephone 5301.
Lloyd Marion Marshall (1893–1970), 47, head of household, manager of the Cold Storage, 52 weeks for $4,526.
Ruth Moore Webers Hotchkiss Marshall (1892–1985), 48, wife, homemaker.
Yvonne Carolyn Marshall Bates (1913–2005), 27, daughter, homemaker.

Arnold Lloyd "Arnie" Bates (1934–2018), 6, grandson.
Jack Elliott Bates (1937–1996), 2, grandson.

LLOYD AND RUTH MARSHALL OCCUPIED a spacious house on Main Street. Lloyd was the manager of the General Storage and Ice Co. (the Cold Storage). Ruth was a homemaker. Both were high school graduates. She was from Clyde. Her father, Julius Webers (ca. 1854–1919), was born in Germany. He was a tobacconist with a cigar store on the Graham block of Glasgow Street, the main street in Clyde. Ruth's mother was Martha "Mattie" Jones Webers (1865–1948). Julius and Mattie married in 1885 in the Town of Rose.

In 1903, during a special term of the state Supreme Court held in Lyons, a divorce petition from Julius Webers was considered. The Clyde Times reported, "Mrs. Webers has lived apart from her husband for the past year or two, making her home in New York City most of the time." The suit was apparently brought on the basis of faulty information. "The innocence of Mrs. Webers in the matter was clearly shown and Mr. Webers had good reason to feel imposed upon by the information that was furnished and on which he began his suit. When Justice Dunwell rendered his decision, Mrs. Webers was somewhat overcome, for the moment, but did not collapse as has been reported."

In 1909 Mattie spent several days in Rome (Oneida County) for Ruth's graduation from the Academy of Holy Names, an all-girls Catholic school. A talented pianist, Ruth graduated with honors in the music department, which was affiliated with the Grand Conservatory of Music of the University of the State of New York.

In 1911 Ruth married Calvin Hotchkiss in June and buried him in December. Calvin died of his injuries after a barge canal accident in Lyons. The *Democrat and Chronicle* reported, "It is now thought that Mr. Hotchkiss went to oil some gears on the front part of the dredge and in some way fell into the gearing." A year and a half later, the young widow married Lloyd Marshall in Syracuse and the couple settled in North Rose.

Lloyd and Ruth's married daughter, Yvonne Carolyn Bates, and her two children, Arnold and Jack Eliot, lived with the Marshalls. Yvonne helped around the house; she had three years of high school.

In 1900 Lloyd lived with his parents in Clyde. His parents had married in April 1892. Lloyd's mother, Ella (1872–1961), was a homemaker. (See "Marshall, Ella.") His father, George William Marshall (1869–1938), was a foundryman. Lloyd's paternal grandmother and an aunt also lived in this multi-generation household. By 1910 the family had moved to North Rose. Lloyd graduated from Leavenworth High School in Wolcott in 1911. (Until the completion of North Rose's new high school, North Rose's school had limited high-school staff and facilities.) Lloyd then went on to study at the Rochester Business Institute.

In 1922 George W. Marshall and his son, Lloyd Marshall, agreed to form a new company, building a colossal cold storage warehouse to preserve the fruits and vegetables picked from the area's orchards and mucklands. Area farmers desperately needed this cold storage building. The new business was so successful that the Marshalls built an addition within two years of the enterprise's commencement. The whole facility was called the General Storage and Ice Company. The original building had a storage capacity of 180,000 bushels of apples. The second building increased the capacity by 90,000 bushels. Following the death of his father in 1938, Lloyd took over the management of the corporation.

Lloyd and Ruth's only child, Yvonne, was born in 1913. In 1915 the Marshalls had a 16-year-old live-in servant, Myrtle Roberts, to aid with the housework. In April 1920 Lloyd obtained a large Curtis airplane in Buffalo for $2,800. Lloyd and Ruth hosted a party for 20 friends in January 1921 to announce Lloyd's sister Olive's engagement to Clark Wilson of Rose. The table was decorated with favors consisting of tulips filled with candy hearts. At Olive's place at the table, the tulip contained a diamond engagement ring.

Lloyd smashed his new airplane into a tree while racing an Essex car from Rose to Clyde. Neither Lloyd nor Ruth, his passenger, received injuries. Lloyd was an automobile salesman in the first part of 1930. In April of that year, Hayes and Frances Catchpole accompanied Lloyd and Ruth on a trip to Texas. The next month, Lloyd took a job at the American Rio Grande Land Company and moved to Mercedes, Texas. Lloyd sold his farm on South Main Street to Albert Drury. The Marshall family—Lloyd, along with his parents and siblings—owned a substantial cottage on LeRoy Island which the Marshalls collectively kept and shared. Elsie Crocker helped maintain it. The Marshalls' move to Texas occasioned farewell parties held by the friends of both Lloyd and Ruth. In August 1930 they started for their new home in Texas. Malcolm Jacques accompanied them. In September 1932 Lloyd and Ruth drove to North Rose to call on friends and relatives and to pick up Yvonne, who was visiting Lloyd's parents. Lloyd and Ruth hosted a sizable gathering of friends at the Marshall cottage on LeRoy Island.

By March 1934, the Marshalls had moved back to North Rose from Texas. They settled into the Garlic house on Main Street, which was just being vacated by A. Gray Skutt, his wife, Jane, and his brother, Watson Skutt. In 1936 Lloyd was a dealer of Plymouth automobiles. About 30 friends helped celebrate Lloyd and Ruth's silver wedding anniversary at a dinner at Hotel Wayne in Lyons in January 1938. In July 1938 the General Storage and Ice Company, which Lloyd was now running after his father's death, erected a new building on Railroad Avenue for washing celery. Lloyd and Ruth entertained Oscar and Alice Weed, Harry and Josephine Partrick, George and Doris Catchpole, and Traver and Ruth Garlic at their LeRoy Island cottage in June 1939.

In June 1940 Lloyd piloted himself and Don Welch from North Rose to New York and returned after a three-day visit to the World's Fair. This trip was Lloyd's longest flight to date. At the 1941 Democratic town caucus, Lloyd received the Democratic nomination for Town of Rose Supervisor. In May 1942 Lloyd bought a grand cabin cruiser—one of the biggest boats on Sodus Bay. Lloyd, Ruth, George Catchpole, Harry Quereau, and Don Welch motored the craft from Rochester to Sodus Point. Lloyd was one of several North Rose businesspeople who took part in the August 1942 apple shippers' convention in Buffalo. Also attending were A. Gray Skutt, Traver Garlic,

George Catchpole, Hayes Catchpole, and Oscar Weed.

 Lloyd attended the International Cold Storage Convention in Chicago in February 1943. In March 1948 the General Storage & Ice Co. of North Rose purchased the North Rose Cold Storage Co. The North Rose Cold Storage became a subsidiary company. Officials of the subsidiary company were: president, Lloyd Marshall; vice president, G. Clifford Marshall; and secretary, Hayes Catchpole. Lloyd and Ruth divorced. In late 1951, Lloyd married Lila S. Tod Smith (1898–1993), daughter of Edwin L. Smith (1854–1943) and Lila Stafford Smith (1864–1922). Lila had earlier married John W. Walsh of Clyde. The Walshes had at least three children. Lloyd flew to California in June 1954 with Lee Barnes. In 1970, friends found Lloyd dead of a probable heart attack after he spent a night alone on his boat.

 In September 1938 the PTA organized North Rose's first flower show. Ruth had one of the outstanding floral exhibits in the school auditorium: a Mexican-themed display. In 1940, over a hundred members of the Library Study Club thronged the Clyde Central School for an antique glass exhibit. Ruth addressed the club about her collection of blue glass. During World War II, Ruth was active in the Red Cross. By August 1950, Ruth had moved to Clyde after she and Lloyd divorced. A year later, Ruth moved to Smyrna Beach, Florida. She spent Christmas of 1951 with her daughter Yvonne and her family in Clyde. Before returning to Florida, she was the guest of Susie Graham. Ruth died in Flagler Beach, Florida, in July 1985.

 Yvonne Marshall attended Starkey Seminary in Lakemont (Yates County) at the same time as Henrietta Quereau. In the summer of 1932, after her family had moved to Mercedes, Texas, Yvonne paid a lengthy visit to her grandparents, George and Ella Marshall, back in Wayne County. She had graduated from high school. Yvonne married Jack Bates of Mercedes in March 1933. They became the parents of two sons, Arnold and Jack. In June 1936 Jack and Yvonne and their two children moved to San Benito, Texas. Jack worked as a draftsman for the International Boundary Commission.

 In 1937, film star Clark Gable was asked by an interviewer what more he could want after a string of professional successes. Without hesitating, he said he sought Jack Bates to express his gratitude for saving his life. Jack and Clark Gable were both in Butte, Montana, in 1927. Jack noticed Gable's emaciated condition and bought him a solid meal. In his pre-Hollywood days, Clark was roaming the country as a hobo. Clark accompanied Jack to Portland, Oregon. On their parting, Jack gave Clark a five-dollar bill. Later Gable often recalled the gift as necessary for his survival. Leon Salter, a friend of Jack's from North Rose, wrote Clark and advised him where he could locate his rescuer.

Jack Bates helped out Clark Gable (above, in an early publicity still) before his stardom.

In December 1939 Yvonne and her two sons, Arnie and Jack, visited her parents from her new home in Little Rock, Arkansas. By 1940 Yvonne had separated from Jack and was living with her parents. Yvonne and her sons enjoyed spending time at the Marshall cottage on LeRoy Island. Yvonne was a friend of Mary Drury. By 1951 Yvonne married Floyd Groat (1908–1977), son of William J. Groat (1872–1953) and Maude Milliman Groat (1880–1964) of Monroe County. In 1940 Floyd was one of the North Rose census enumerators. William and Maude later moved to North Rose. Floyd died in September 1977 in the Veterans Hospital in Canandaigua. Yvonne moved to Florida. Yvonne and Ruth were both living in Flagler Beach, Florida, in 1985 when Ruth died at the age of 93.

In March 1948 Arnie Bates was a member of North Rose's new model airplane club and a piano student of Estella Roney. In 1951 Arnie constructed six electric steel guitars. Arnold and his mother were living in Clyde and Arnold attended Clyde Central School. The next summer, Arnold was a swimming instructor for the American Red Cross. Arnold enlisted in the Marines and was a PFC by July 1954. In 1961 Arnold Bates lived in Macedon Center.

Arnie married three times and had three children: Steven, Scott, and Shawn. As an adult, Arnie continued to build things: a trimaran, a houseboat, dobro guitars. He was an avid musician, and played with a bluegrass band, Willow Creek. He lived in Shelby, Ohio, the last 30 years of his life, and had owned and operated a lawn care company there before his death at 84.

In 1954 Jack Bates was on the NRCS tennis team. Jack married Clara Doris Byron (1940–2024) in November 1959. Clara was the daughter of Edward Frank Byron (1893–1979) and Elizabeth C. Weber Byron (1910–1993) of Marion. The newlyweds lived in North Rose. Before they divorced, Jack and Clara had two children: Dawn Lorraine Bates and Jack Marshall Bates, both of whom moved to Mesa, Arizona, where Clara lived until her death at 83 in 2024. Jack had another daughter, Tiffany Yvonne Bates, from a subsequent marriage. She lived in Virginia Beach, Virginia, at the time of Jack's death at 59 in 1996.

Jack Bates, NRCS Class of 1955

May, Charles & Fran

Eastern North Rose house. 1940 monthly rent: $11.
Charles Cook May (1915–1980), 24, head of household, proprietor, 48 weeks.
Renee Francine "Fran" Mitchell May (1918–1990), 21, wife, homemaker.
Joan May (1938–2018), 2, daughter.
Norma May (ca. 1938–2009), 1, daughter.
Earl Raymond Cook (1923–1972), 16, nephew, student.
Howard M. Harris (1918–2003), 21, lodger, truck driver, 48 weeks at $17 a week.

CHARLES AND FRAN MAY LIVED with their two daughters, Joan and Norma; their nephew Earl Cook; and a lodger, Howard Harris. Charles was the proprietor of a long-distance trucking company; Fran was a homemaker; Earl attended high school; and lodger Howard Harris was a truck driver—presumably for May's company. Later on, Charles and Fran had two more children: Geraldine and Kathleen. Charles completed nine years of school; Fran, 11; and Howard, 10.

Charles Cook May had two sets of parents. He was born Charles Cook to Charles George Cook (1873–1926) and Bessie E. Wilber Cook (1884–1936) in Seneca Falls (Seneca County), who were married in 1902. Charles had two older brothers—Raymond Earl Cook (1904–1937) and Walter Hugh Cook (1905–1987)—and a younger brother, Kenneth Cook (1919–). By 1920, Bessie was institutionalized at Willard State Hospital in Ovid (Seneca County) and Walter was institutionalized at the Rome State School. It's unclear whether Bessie ever left Willard, but she died there in 1936. Walter was still at the Rome State School at 24, in 1930. In 1940, at 35, he was an unpaid servant in the household of 77-year-old Charles Ball in Butler. Charles was the brother of George Ball Sr. and the uncle of George Ball Jr. (see "Ball, George & Maude") and Myrta Salter (see "Salter, Edward & Myrta"). Walter lived at the Newark State School in 1950. He spent decades at the Syracuse Developmental Center before dying there in 1987.

In 1920, with his mother at Willard, Charles was a 4-year-old who had been taken in by Porter and Mary May. Porter May (1871–1927) was a farmer in Savannah. Mary Evans May (1867–1960) was the daughter of the Hon. David H. Evans (1837–1920), who was a state senator and state assemblyman from Seneca County; he lived his whole life on the family farm in Tyre. After graduating from Brockport Normal School, Mary taught school in New York City for more than 20 years, returning to Savannah each summer. She was 40 when she married Porter and moved permanently to Savannah; they had no children of their own. By the time Charles was 9, Porter and May had adopted him. He went by Charles Cook May the rest of his life.

It's unclear where Charles's infant brother Kenneth lived after their mother went to Willard, but in 1925 two Cook households were living next to each other in Tyre. Kenneth, 6, was living with their father, Charles G. Cook, 52. Next door, their brother Raymond was living with his wife, Esther (whose maiden name was also Cook), and their 1-year-old son, Earl. (Raymond and Esther married in 1922, when he was 18 and she was 16.) Both Raymond and his father were farmers.

Charles G. Cook died the next year in Auburn, and Kenneth joined his brother Raymond's household. Raymond and Esther had a second son, Charles Frederick Cook (1928–1997), who went by Fred. In 1930, at 6, Earl lived in a different house in Tyre with his parents, his brother, and his uncle Kenneth. Two years later Earl's mother died at 24. His father remarried in August 1934, to Ina Ripley (1913–2003), and they had a daughter, Alice "Marie" Cook, in 1936. Raymond died in 1937, leaving Earl and Fred orphans at 13 and 9. Kenneth was 18 when Raymond died, and no further information could be found about him. Ina and Marie went to live with Ina's parents in Conquest (Cayuga County). Ina remarried a U.S. Army veteran after the war. Marie took the last name of her mother's new husband, Charles Jenks (1911–1968). Earl ended up with Charles and Fran. Fred went to live with his mother's sister, Ethel Reed, and her family in Butler.

Fred married Shirley Sanderson (1932–2003) in July 1948 and they settled in Auburn. Two years later he worked at a rope factory and their daughter Georgiana was born, with many sons to follow. In 1970 they lived in Seneca Falls.

In 1950 Earl lived in Louisville, Kentucky, with a cousin, Agnes Spencer. He was divorced and worked as a furnace-man at a foundry. He later married Agnes Jeanette "Jennie" Hawkes Watkins (1906–1987), who was also divorced. Earl died at 49 on New Year's Eve 1972, succumbing to the burns covering most of his body after an arc furnace explosion at the Corhart Refractories Company 19 days earlier.

Charles Cook May's adoptive father died when he was 11; he lived with his adoptive mother in Savannah. After one year of high school, Charles enrolled in an aviation school in Valley Stream, Long Island. Soon he was back in Wayne County and "piloting" trucks. He and Fran married in the late 1930s. He began advertising that he sold chickens, horses, and registered German shepherd puppies in 1945. He served as a trustee of the Savannah school district. In February 1951 he was elected vice president of the Wayne Dairymen's League.

Fran was born in France. In 1935 she lived on a farm in Moravia (Cayuga County). In May 1942 she was hospitalized, and Frank and Addie Thompson helped care for the May children. When the Mays moved to Savannah in the mid-1940s, Fran was active in the Home Bureau—instructing fellow Home Bureau members in sewing. She solicited for the Red Cross in March 1948 and canvassed for the

Heart Fund in February 1964 and February 1966. She bred German shepherds and ran a boarding kennel in Savannah.

The Mays' eldest daughter, Joan was named to the Savannah honor roll in seventh grade in 1948. The Mays' four daughters were frequently on the honor roll in the Savannah schools.

Norma attended Ithaca College starting in 1955. She enrolled in the School of Health and Physical Education and was elected president of Phi Delta Pi—a physical education sorority. Norma got engaged to Ithaca College classmate Carl Wambold in the fall of 1958. The couple raised two children in Ovid (Seneca County): Carla and Michael. Norma was an English teacher. The Wambolds retired to Fort Myers, Florida.

Geraldine (ca. 1941–) married Donald Van Duyne in 1960. The couple first made their home in Syracuse before moving to South Butler, where they raised their three children: Gregory, Glenn, and Lynne Anne. Both Donald and Glenn worked at Over and Under, a pipeline construction company in Auburn (Cayuga County). Glenn died of cancer at age 60 in 2024.

Kathleen (ca. 1942–) won the local DAR essay contest in December 1958. She matriculated at Brockport College. In 1961 she transferred to Northeastern University in Boston, where she majored in English. Kathleen married Robert Whittier and taught in Durham, North Carolina. In March 1970 the Whittiers moved to Kenya for two years. Robert did research for Duke University and Kathleen worked toward her PhD.

The Mays' lodger, Howard Harris, was born in Maine. He lived in the Town of Conquest (Cayuga County) as a child and on a farm in Wayne County in 1935. In 1942 he enlisted in the Army Air Corps and married Jeanette Ruth Burley in February of that year. His wife accompanied him to several domestic bases, and he soon rose to the rank of lieutenant.

Harris became one of the most acclaimed Wayne County heroes of World War II. On September 3, 1943, the plane on which he was a bombardier was shot down in a raid on the Nazi-controlled Renault factory near Paris. Sustaining leg wounds while parachuting from the burning plane, he still managed to elude the Germans. With the help of the French underground, he returned to England, where he rejoined his unit in December 1943. By the end of the war, he had attained the rank of first lieutenant. Upon his return to the United States, Howard graduated from a Class A pilots' training class. Gregory H. Harris, Howard's son, was born in June 1947. The Harrises moved to Wolcott. During the Korean War, Howard was called up again and assigned to the 5th Air Force. After the truce, he resumed his trucking career—until his retirement from Maislin Transport in 1983. Howard died in Clifton Springs (Ontario County).

McOmber, Donald & Doris

Estimated 1940 value: $1,200.
Donald Hiram McOmber (1908–1986), 31, head of household, refrigeration engineer at Cold Storage, 52 weeks at $2
Dorothy Mae "Doris" Marriott McOmber (1908–1982), 31, wife, bookkeeper at the Canning Factory, 23 weeks at $350.
Joan Lucille McOmber (1934–1998), 6, daughter, student.

Joan McOmber, NRCS Class of 1952

DONALD AND DORIS MCOMBER married in April 1930. Donald's 16-year-old brother Paul was best man. Paul also lived in North Rose in 1940; Donald's wife, Doris, and Paul's wife, Margaret, were sisters. (For more information about the McOmber and Marriott families, see "McOmber, Paul & Helen.") Both Donald and Doris were high school graduates.

Donald and Doris's daughter, Joan, graduated from the Rochester Business Institute and married Robert Fromholzer (1931–2010) of Webster (Monroe County) in January 1956. They had three daughters: Cheryl, Debra, and Susan.

We were unable to obtain much more than the cursory information provided by the census for this household. If you have more information, see page 32.

McOmber, Paul & Helen

17 Caroline Avenue. 1940 monthly rent: $10.
Paul Ross McOmber (1913–2006), 26, head of household, farm laborer, 51 weeks for $750.
Helen Margaret Marriott McOmber (1913–1991), 27, wife, homemaker and part-time trimmer at the Canning Factory, 16 weeks for $240.

PAUL MCOMBER WAS A HIGH SCHOOL graduate; Helen completed three years of high school.

Paul McOmber

Paul was a native of the Town of Rose. His parents were Ross H. McOmber (1881–1932) and Harriett "Hattie" A. Harris McOmber (1885–1976). Ross was a fruit farmer. He moved from his home in Albion (Orleans County) to North Rose in 1911. Ross became a member of the North Rose Fire Company. He died while Paul was in high school.

In August 1922 a playmate shot Paul, then 9 years old, over the ear with a pistol loaded with a blank. At such proximity to his face, the blank charge injured Paul. Dr. Roney performed minor surgery to remove powder driven into Paul's skin.

In April 1930 Paul was best man at his brother Donald's wedding to Doris Marriott. At NRCS Paul was a star athlete on the hardwood and the diamond. He was captain and high scorer for the 1932 North Rose cagers, who went 13–1 in the regular season. They gained the postseason championship, coming from behind to beat Hammondsport in a game played at the University of Rochester Palestra. (In ancient Greek, the word "palæstria" meant a rectangular enclosure connected to a gymnasium where athletes competed before an audience. The Rochester basketball arena took its name from the storied Palestra in Philadelphia on the University of Pennsylvania campus. That facility is perhaps the most famous arena in college basketball.)

Anna Baldridge and Paul McOmber got the nod as queen and king from North Rose in the May 1932 Sodus Cherry Blossom Festival. In January 1934 Paul became an uncle when Donald and Doris

McOmber had a daughter, Joan Lucille. (See "McOmber, Donald & Doris.") Paul, Charlotte Marshall, and Helen Marriott visited Old Forge (Herkimer County) in August 1935. Later that month, Paul and Helen married. Paul and his brother Donald married sisters. Therefore, the two wives shared parents. Their parents were William H. Marriott (1888–1977) and Fannie R. Marshall Marriott (1890–1987). William was a laborer on a dairy farm.

The newlyweds honeymooned in Niagara Falls and settled in North Rose. Paul and Helen socialized with Paul and Charlotte Marshall. Charlotte was Paul McOmber's sister. In November 1935 Paul went hunting at Wanakena (St. Lawrence County) with his brother Donald, Melvin Marshall, and Dell Ormsby.

Paul's car was stolen in April 1943. The thieves got only as far as Geneva, where the state police intercepted them. Sherman Goodrich confessed to the crime. He declared that he and his mother were driving to Hancock, Maryland. Paul departed North Rose for the Army in July 1943. Paul and Charlotte Marshall marked his departure by hosting a dinner to which they invited many of his friends. He served in the U.S. Army Signal Corps and was assigned to Harding Field in Baton Rouge, Louisiana. He advanced to the rank of sergeant. Shortly after Paul entered the Army, Helen's parents, then living in Rochester, visited Helen, Donald, and Doris. In March 1945 the military sent Paul back to the U.S. from England for treatment at the Walter Reed Hospital in Washington. Helen joined Paul in Washington. In August, Paul had recovered so he could join his wife, then living in Pawling (Dutchess County).

Paul was a member of the Mullen Flow Hunting Club. He was a 74-year member of the North Rose Fire Department; at one time he was fire chief. In September 1947 the North Rose Fire Company celebrated its 32nd anniversary with a parade. Paul, as fire chief, led the parade—viewed by a crowd of 5,000—driving a Packard convertible containing five charter members of the company. Paul McOmber and Paul Marshall bagged deer on a hunting trip with friends in November 1947. In 1950 Paul was making ladders at the Seelye Ladder Company (see "Seelye Ladders," page 290). In both 1954 and 1955,

Helen led the North Rose March of Dimes campaign. Paul McOmber vacationed with Paul and Charlotte Marshall at Goose Lake (Hamilton County) in August 1956.

Paul and Helen's son, Gary Paul McOmber (ca. 1947–), was a versatile athlete at NRCS, lettering in baseball his freshman year (1961) and in soccer, basketball, and track his sophomore year (1961–1962). In March 1963 he snapped a 60–60 tie in the final moments of the North Rose–Wolcott game with two foul shots to seal the victory. Gary was the sixth-highest scorer in the Wayne County A-B-C-D Basketball League his senior year. He was vice president of his junior class (1962–1963).

Gary married Janet Ruth Stark, daughter of Garry Austin Stark and Doris A. Old Stark of Lockport (Niagara County). The couple honeymooned in New York City and Bermuda. Gary graduated from SUNY Oswego. Janet was a graduate of SUNY Potsdam and Universite de Poitiers in Tours, France. Gary and Janet lived in Rochester and in Pittsford.

Mills, Elery & Leona

5047 North Poplar Street. 1940 monthly rent: $12.
Elery Sterling Mills (1904–1985), 35, head of household, truck operator, 52 weeks, self-employed.
Leona Irene Failey Mills (1908–1969), 31, wife, homemaker.
Bruce Mills (ca. 1932–), 7, son, student.
Donald Lynn Mills (1933–1999), 6, son.

ELERY WAS AN INDEPENDENT truck operator. He had finished three years of high school. Leona had completed eight years of school.

The Millses married in 1925. Elery was born in North Rose. Leona was born in Clarendon (Monroe County). Her family had relocated to Huron by 1920, where her father, William Failey (1881–1973), was a farm laborer. Her mother was Florence E. Daniels Failey (1885–1982). The Faileys returned to Monroe County in the 1920s.

In 1925 Elery lived with his parents on North Main Street in North

Rose. (See "Mills, Robert & Lena.") At that time, he worked as an inspector of auto accessories.

Early in their married life, ca. 1928, Leona spent 13 months in the Iola Sanitarium for tuberculosis treatment in Rochester. In 1930 Elery and Leona rented a home at 60 Locust Street in Rochester for $35 a month and Elery worked as a laundry company truck driver. Later in the 1930s, Elery and Leona moved back to North Rose.

In November 1940 Elery joined his brother Glenn Mills (see "Mills, Glenn & Laura"), Fremont Powers, Dr. Ray Kenan, Reg Catchpole, Roy Davenport, Oscar Weed, Clark Wilson, and Gray Skutt, all from North Rose, and Rodney Powers of Palmyra, for a weekend of hunting at Limekiln Lake (Hamilton County).

In August 1940 Elery and Leona became parents of a third child, Sandra (1940–). Elery's parents, Robert and Lena Mills hosted granddaughter Sandra's first birthday party in 1941. In July 1942 Bruce and Donald spent four days at Grassy Point at the cottage of their uncle and aunt, Harris and Julia Failey. Julia was Harris's first wife; they divorced in the mid-1940s. His second wife was Ida.

Sandie celebrated her 2nd birthday with a visit to her maternal grandparents in Rochester, William and Florence Failey, in August 1942. That evening they came back to North Rose for cake and ice cream with her paternal grandparents.

In December 1944 Elery won election as first assistant fire chief of the North Rose Fire Department.

In February 1945, Elery, Leona, and their children and Glenn Mills (Elery's brother) and Laura Mills (Glenn's wife) hosted a birthday dinner for their parents, in honor of Lena Mills's 80th birthday. In February 1949 Elery achieved an appointment as an elder in the North Rose Presbyterian Church.

Harold and Alta Wilcox (Leona's sister) and children Richard, Larry, and Diane of Rochester were particularly frequent guests of Elery and Leona.

Harold and Alta Wilcox. Alta was Leona Mills's sister.

Leona took part in the Women's Missionary Society of the North Rose Presbyterian Church.

Bruce Mills, NRCS Class of 1951

Young Bruce Mills severely burned his foot by walking through a bed of hot coals in October 1938. Despite that, in 1949 he played junior varsity basketball and varsity tennis in 1950. In May 1951 Bruce won a basketball award from NRCS. That fall Bruce settled in Rochester, and as did his maternal grandfather, worked for Eastman Kodak. He joined the Army in December 1952. In June 1953, Bruce married Onnalee Van Steen, daughter of Jacob and Lottie Van Steen of Resort.

In March 1954, while he was in the service during the Korean War, PFC Bruce Mills arranged a pleasant visit with Pvt. Roy Betts, likewise of North Rose, in Pusan, Korea. When Bruce left the Army, he and Onnalee lived in Rochester. Later, they moved to Williamson, where they became parents of a son, Bradley Harris, in February 1959.

Donald Mills fractured his skull in a fall at school in November 1950. His 1953 marriage to Joyce Marie Vandewinckel (1935–2024) of Wolcott ended in divorce. A subsequent marriage produced a daughter, Jacqueline. Donald served in the U.S. Army and was a member of the Wolcott Elks Club.

Sandie Mills was the flower girl at her cousin Glenn A. Mills Jr.'s wedding to Geraldine Williams of Wolcott in 1946. Sandie had a record of perfect attendance in second grade (1947–1948) and fourth grade (1949–1950). She was a regular honoree on the NRCS honor roll in her elementary school years. She served as one of two student council representatives for the Class of 1958 in her senior year. Sandie was the maid of honor at the July 1959 wedding of Maxine Clingerman and Robert Rawden.

Sandie married Harold "Bill" Bean (1941–2021), who served in the U.S. Marine Corps from 1960 to 1969; they had two boys, Derek and Thomas, before divorcing. In 1991 she married Lynford W. Hunt (1934–1997). He died a year after retiring as chief engineer at Mercury Aircraft in Hammondsport (Steuben County). Sandie moved to Wolcott after his death.

Mills, Glenn & Laura

THURSDAY, NOVEMBER 21, 1946
Cut Wedding Cake After Rite

Glenn Mills Jr. married Geraldine Williams of Wolcott.

Estimated 1940 value: $1,800.
Glenn Arthur Mills (1898–1970), 42, head of household, sales manager, wholesale feeds, 52 weeks at $4,200.
Laura J. Chappell Mills (1900–1984), 39, wife, homemaker.
Glenn Arthur Mills Jr. (1925–1990), 14, son, student.
Robert Francis Mills (1928–1986), 12, son, student.
Patricia Ann Mills (1934–), 6, daughter.

GLENN ARTHUR MILLS WAS the older brother of Elery Mills (see "Mills, Elery & Leona") and the son of Robert Mills (see "Mills, Robert & Lena").

We were unable to obtain much more than the cursory information provided by the census for this household. If you have information about the Millses, see page 32.

Mills, Robert & Lena

Estimated 1940 value: $1,100.
Robert James Mills (1869–1952), 70, head of household, laborer at the Canning Factory, 24 weeks at $230.
Mary Magdalena "Lena" Moyer Mills (1865–1949), 75, wife, homemaker.

ROBERT AND LENA WERE BOTH BORN in Ontario, Canada. Their two surviving children both lived in North Rose in 1940. (See "Mills, Elery & Leona" and "Mills, Glenn & Laura.") Two children born between Glenn and Elery died in infancy—Ethel (1900–1901) and Russell (1902–1903)—and Robert and Lena's youngest, Franklin (1906–1926), died at 19 of scarlet fever at Fort Ontario (Oswego County).

We were unable to obtain much more than the cursory information provided by the census for this household. If you have information about the Millses, see page 32.

Miner, J. Odell & Belle
Estimated 1940 value: $2,500.
J. Odell Miner (1881–1969), 59, head of household, field superintendent, manufacturing inlet goods, 20 weeks for $600.
Belle Miner (1886–1973), 53, wife, postal clerk, 52 weeks for $780.
Ruth Miner (1922–2011), 17, daughter, student.
Dorothea Miner (1925–2014), 15, daughter, student, bookkeeper for the Cold Storage, 14 weeks for $126.

We were unable to obtain more than the cursory information provided by the census for this household. If you have information about the Miners, see page 32.

Mitchell, George & Josephine*
Wilson Road, Huron. Estimated 1940 value: $25,000.
George Johnson Mitchell (1887–1959), 52, head of household, farm operator, 52 weeks.
Josephine Mitchell (ca. 1893–), 47, wife, homemaker.
Jean Mitchell (1925–1991), 15, daughter, student.
Allan Dickerman Mitchell (1927–), 13, son student.
Bernice Mitchell (1929–2017), 10, daughter, student.

THE MITCHELL FAMILY IS INCLUDED HERE because Allan Mitchell contributed to this book as a fact-checker. Allan was the son of George Johnson Mitchell (1887–1959), a Huron fruit farmer, and Berenice Dickerman Mitchell (1888–1936). George, who had graduated from Cornell in 1912, owned a farm east of Canandaigua, where he mostly grew cabbages. He traded that farm for a 100-acre fruit farm where

Allan grew up on Wilson Road in Huron. Berenice was from Philadelphia; her father was in the then-profitable ice business.

In the 1920s and '30s, Allan's father bought other farms. He purchased a 65-acre farm near Clyde and went into partnership with his nephew Elwood to operate the farm. Next, George purchased the 54-acre Winchell farm on Fifth Road. George's grandson and namesake George II, known as Duke, lives there now. Finally, George bought yet another farm north of North Rose—partly orchard and partly pasture. George traded grazing rights to a neighbor, Charles O. Oaks, in exchange for the Mitchell household's milk needs. George sold that farm to Charles Fornier.

The Mitchells lost their first two children to terrible accidents. George Jr. (a different individual than George II; George Jr. was the uncle of George II) died in a car accident at 19 (Allan was then 7). Mary, the next child, died at the age of 2 when her clothes caught fire from a lit jack-o'-lantern. The children's mother, Berenice, died of pneumonia when Allan was just 9. The three surviving children were Jean, Allan, and Bernice. Soon after Berenice's death, with three young children in the house, George remarried. In the 1950s, George and Josephine moved to Henderson Harbor (Jefferson County).

Allan played on the NRCS team that beat Genesee–Orleans in the 1943 section V, class C high school basketball championship 37–34. North Rose got a 24–16 lead at the halfway mark. They held on for the win, never letting their lead fall to fewer than three points. The game took place in a nearly full river campus gymnasium at the University of Rochester. Outstanding scorers for North Rose were Dick Williams and Allan Mitchell, each tallying 14 points.

After attending Cornell for one semester, Allan enlisted in the Navy around his 18th birthday, February 2, 1945. In May he was at Sampson Naval Base in the Finger Lakes region awaiting assignment. He was allowed home on leave in August 1945. After receiving an honorable discharge from the Navy, he returned to Cornell University, where he was a member of the fraternity Sigma Phi Epsilon. Allan played soccer on the Cornell team in 1947.

Allan married Ann Early (1930–1957) before he graduated from

Cornell at the end of the fall 1949 semester with a BS in agriculture. Ann was the daughter of Robert Rainey Early (1895–1958) and Constance Rendell Early (1894–1984) from Hawthorne, Florida. Allan and Ann became parents of George II ("Duke") and Robert.

In January 1957 Allan was elected local committeeman for the Grange League Federation, a cooperative farmers' supply store. The revenue of the store in Wolcott was about $1 million per year. (The GLF eventually evolved into Agway.) After being widowed, Allan married his second wife, Roxie Ann Wood (1931–2010), in Williamson in February 1959. She was the daughter of Joseph Wood (1903–1997) and Martha Pratt (1903–1997). Roxie was a graduate of the Crane School of Music at Potsdam State Teachers College. After her graduation, she taught music in the Sodus school system.

Allan followed in his father's footsteps as a fruit farmer. In August 1950 Allan had to advertise in the *Lake Shore News* for apple pickers. Allan's classified ad announced the job as starting on September 15.

In the late 1950s Allan served on the New York Marketing Order's advisory committee, which advises the state on advertising and promoting sour cherries. New York State ranked third among states in sour cherry production.

In January 1959 and 1960 Allan was elected junior warden of the Rose Masonic Lodge. Allan lived on Glenmark Road slightly west of the census boundary of North Rose. He married Susan "Sue" Bruner in December 1969. With that marriage, Allan gained two stepdaughters and one stepson. Allan's granddaughter, Heather Mitchell, married Enrique Oviedo. They had a daughter, Stella Elizabeth Oviedo. Stella was the granddaughter of Duke and Becky Mitchell and thus was the great-granddaughter of Allan and Sue.

Duke set the NRCS record for the mile run at 4:50.2 in a county league meet where North Rose and Wolcott beat Wayne on May 8, 1969. Duke won the 2.5-mile cross-country and set a course record as he led the North Rose harriers to victory in a three-team cross-country meet. North Rose defeated Red Creek and Williamson.

Allan was chosen by the superintendent of schools and ratified by the board of education as an official volunteer in the North Rose–

Wolcott Central School District. Sue was an active member of both the Huron and Wolcott Presbyterian Churches.

Mitchell, Jessie

Estimated 1940 value: $3,000.
Jessie E. Mitchell (1863–1950), 76, head of household, retired.

We were unable to obtain more than the cursory information provided by the census for this household. If you have information about Jessie Mitchell, see page 32.

Moore, Joseph & Nettie

Estimated 1940 value: $4,000.
Joseph Moore (1881–1963), 57, head of household, self-employed, wholesale feed proprietor.
Nettie Moore (1884–1951), 55, wife, homemaker.
Lloyd Merton Richardson (1921–2014), 21, grandson-in-law, laborer, Canning Factory, 31 weeks at $455.
Doris H. Chalupa Richardson (1924–2018), 18, granddaughter, unemployed.

We were unable to obtain more than the cursory information provided by the census for this household. If you have information about the Moores, see page 32.

Moore, Robert & Lucy

1940 monthly rent: $10.
Robert Moore (1889–1962), 50, head of household, carpenter, 30 weeks at $900.
Lucy Moore (1889–1968), 50, wife, bean picker, 40 weeks at $350.
Helen Moore (1927–2008), 13, daughter, student.

We were unable to obtain more than the cursory information provided by the census for this household. If you have information about the Moores, see page 32.

Munson, Helen

12 Maple Avenue, now 10406 Maple—Built in 1910. Estimated 1940 value: $1,500.
Helen Ana Munson (1858–1945), 81, head of household, homemaker.

Helen Munson was a widow, lived alone, and had completed the eighth grade.

Helen married Warren A. Munson (1848–1926) in 1895. He was a farmer and lived in the Town of Sodus. Warren outlived his first wife, Sarah A. Cartman (1853–1884), and both of their children, Artemus Miles (1878–1882) and Daisy Florence (1880–1897).

Both of Helen's parents were English immigrants, as was Warren's mother. In 1900 the Munsons farmed next to Warren's father, Abner Munson, who was still listed on the census as a farmer when he was 88, and reportedly still plowed at the age of 90. In 1902 a quantity of canned fruit was burgled from Helen and Warren's cellar.

Helen moved to North Rose after her husband's death. During the winter of 1930–1931, she lived with Mrs. E.W. Watson of Fair Haven. Helen and Miss Neva Monroe visited Niagara Falls over the Columbus Day weekend in October 1931. In 1935 Helen visited Mrs. Lillian Fleming in Williamson for two weeks. In June 1939 she took a lengthy trip to Cleveland to visit Mr. and Mrs. A.W. Jones. Helen spent the winter of 1939–1940 with Mrs. Georgia Jeffers, and died of a stroke in July 1945.

Noyes, Frank & Louise

15 Maple Avenue, now 10409 Maple—Built in 1900. Estimated 1940 value: $2,500.
Frank M. Noyes (1895–1991), 45, head of household, retailer, 50 weeks, self-employed.
Louise B. Lander Noyes (1902–1978), 38, wife, homemaker.
Richard "Dick" Walter Noyes (1937–2018), 3, son.

Frank and Louise Noyes married in August 1935. Their son, Richard, was born two years later. Frank was a high school graduate and the proprietor of a retail coal and feed business. Louise was a homemaker, but prior to her marriage she had worked at the telephone company and as a servant in a home in rural Wayne County. Louise had completed the ninth grade.

As a youth, Frank lived with his parents, six brothers, and two sisters in Scriba (Oswego County). His father was a carpenter, and most of his siblings continued to live in Oswego County as they became adults. Both parents were immigrants from England via Canada, and Frank often visited them after he moved out.

In World War I Frank served in the Armed Forces. He worked as a laborer in a bakery in 1920. By 1930 he had moved to North Rose and had established a coal yard. He boarded with the Nelson Abbott family at that time.

Frank was active in Odd Fellows Lodge 606. In January 1935 he was elected vice president of the North Rose Fire Department. In October 1941 he was elected to the Rose Republican Town Committee. He was also a member of the Masons and commander of the Rose American Legion Post. During World War II he was co-chairman of the blood donor committee of the local American Red Cross. In 1946 he was elected a trustee of the North Rose School District.

Frank was involved in several different business ventures. In 1944 and for several successive years, he bought large quantities of cider apples. Then, in February 1946, he purchased the agricultural spray material business formerly conducted by Traver Garlic and sold the sprays out of the Weed, Garlic, and Wilson warehouse. Later the sprays were advertised as being available from the Frank M. Noyes Warehouse. In December 1949 Frank advertised for the acquisition of 25,000 bushels of canning apples: "Baldwins, Greenings, Starks, Romes, Etc. A few Bens." He also offered "Reading" coal for sale by delivery in North Rose and Wolcott.

Frank lived to be 96 and was still a resident of North Rose at the time of his death in 1991.

Louise, like Frank, was quite active in the community. She was a member of the Kappa Phi organization, the Ladies' Aid Society, and the Women's Society for Christian Service, all affiliated with the North Rose Methodist Church. Additionally, she was an adult leader in the Girl Scouts and a founding member of the North Rose Home Bureau.

In August 1943 Louise gave birth to Eileen (1943–). At the age of 20 months, Eileen fell into a shallow pond on Traver Garlic's property. Fortunately George Powell, working in a nearby yard, rescued her. At NRCS, Eileen was regularly named to the honor roll and was a member of the spelling team. In August 1951 Eileen and her family took a road trip to Michigan, Illinois, and Tennessee.

Eileen Noyes, NRCS Class of 1961

In the fall of 1959, Eileen played on the girl's field hockey team—tying the Newark freshman girls' team for the Wayne County championship. At the 1961 annual school banquet, Eileen was awarded the first citizenship award as well as an athletic letter. She attended Rochester Business Institute and gained employment at Kodak. In December 1965, she married Richard Clark of Rochester and moved with him to Hilton (Monroe County), where she had their first child, Byron Keith Clark, in February 1967.

Richard Noyes, NRCS Class of 1955

Eileen's older brother, Dick, was a model airplane enthusiast as a child and a regular member of the honor roll at NRCS. In high school he was the star of the successful North Rose High tennis team. In the 1953 season he achieved four wins with two losses and also had good seasons in 1954 and 1955 when the North Rose tennis squad enjoyed a 13-game winning streak. Dick also played varsity basketball and was treasurer of his senior class.

In May 1957 Dick married Barbara Mae Griswold. Barbara's mother lived in Wolcott and her father lived in Yucaipa, California. The newlyweds first lived at the Richardson farm on Salter Road, then moved into the Maple Avenue house vacated by Harold Burns. Their son, Donald Frank Noyes, was born in December 1958. They later divorced and Barbara remarried in 1965.

Dick worked with his father in the coal and feed business, which was renamed Noyes and Son. In January 1960 Dick was elected chief of the North Rose Fire Department. In the 1950s and '60s Dick was an outstanding bowler. In December 1967 Dick married Mrs. Diane Summer Bramer (née Curran) of Wolcott. She had two daughters from a previous marriage: Stacey and Monica. Diane and Dick had a daughter together, Andrea. Dick's last job before retiring was as maintenance supervisor for North Rose–Wolcott schools.

In his later years, Dick was still involved in North Rose affairs. He won the 1995 Ted Woods Award as an outstanding supporter of student-athletes at North Rose–Wolcott School. He was a ham radio enthusiast. He and Diane were both active in the North Rose Methodist Church.

Oaks, Seth & Hazel

Estimated 1940 value: $2,500.

Seth Oaks, in a picture of the school board in the 1957 NRCS yearbook

Seth Oaks (1893–1983), 46, head of household, self-employed, proprietor of retail lumber.
Hazel Oaks (1893–1992), 46, wife, homemaker.
Miriam Ellen Oaks (1922–2019), 17, daughter, student.
Marilla Gene Oaks (1923–2014), 16, daughter, student.

We were unable to obtain more than the cursory information provided by the census for this household. If you have information about the Oakses, see page 32.

Osgood, Ray & Aora

Estimated 1940 value: $2,000.
Ray Osgood (1884–1962), 55, head of household, self-employed, proprietor of retail hardware, 52 weeks for $2,700.
Aora Osgood (1890–1990), 50, wife, homemaker.

Dorothy Osgood (1918–1988), 21, daughter, unemployed.
Ruth Osgood (1922–2023), 17, daughter, student.

We were unable to obtain more than the cursory information provided by the census for this household. If you have information about the Osgoods, see page 32.

Painter, Benjamin & Ida

1940 monthly rent: $10.
Benjamin Painter (1867–1953), 72, head of household, retired.
Ida Painter (1875–1951), 65, wife, retired.

We were unable to obtain more than the cursory information provided by the census for this household. If you have information about the Painters, see page 32.

Palmer, George

1940 monthly rent: $3.
George Washington Palmer (1880–1962), 60, head of household, retired.

We were unable to obtain more than the cursory information provided by the census for this household. If you have information about the Palmers, see page 32.

Pardwin, John & Myrtle

Estimated 1940 value: $1,000.
John F. Pardwin (1863–1949), 77, head of household, retired.
Myrtle Pardwin (1869–1940), 70, wife, retired.
Maria Weber (ca. 1865–), 75, sister-in-law, retired.

We were unable to obtain more than the cursory information provided by the census for this household. If you have information about the Pardwins, see page 32.

Partrick, Harry & Grace

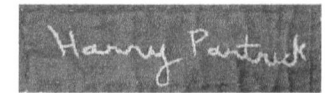

52 South Main Street, now 4874 South Main—Built in 1915. Estimated 1940 value: $2,500.
Harry E. Partrick (1890–1975), 49, head of household, railroad station agent, 52 weeks at $35 a week.
Grace E. Burns Partrick (1892–1970), 48, wife, homemaker.
Eleanor J. Stevenson (1922–1990), 17, servant, 4 weeks at $12.50 a week.

According to the census, Harry and Grace Partrick had a live-in "domestic," Eleanor Stevenson, who had 11 years of school. Harry and Grace Partrick got married in January 1911. Harry was a high-school graduate and had been the railroad station agent in North Rose since at least 1915. Grace had attended school for nine years and was a homemaker.

Harry was brought up in Volney and Fulton (Oswego County). In 1914 Harry was elected president of the new Hook and Ladder Company, which soon merged with the North Rose Chemical Company due to war conditions. In 1936 Harry and several friends attended World Series games in New York City. That year the Yankees beat the Giants in six games during a Subway Series (meaning all of the games were accessible via the subway). Harry was selected to serve on a committee to organize North Rose adult education. Harry was the Democratic nominee for Town of Rose Clerk in 1937, 1939, and 1941. He won the last two elections, then was nominated by both major parties in 1943 and 1945. In 1947 and 1949 he ran unopposed.

Grace was the proprietor of an ice cream parlor in 1920 but had gotten out of that business by 1925. She gave piano lessons to local children, was a Girl Scout leader, and belonged to both the Catholic Daughters of America and the Luncheon Club. In October 1929 she went to Montreal and Ottawa with three friends for a week. She was hospitalized in Lyons in April 1932 with an acute illness. She attended the New York State Convention of the Democratic Party in October 1936. In March 1937, Grace, her mother Cora Burns, and Earl and Lillian Langley Barnes took a three-week trip to Florida. While they were in Georgia, Grace had to be hospitalized for the flu. At the wedding of Henrietta Quereau to Claude Collier in January 1938, Grace supplied the musical accompaniment. She was also head of the sewing committee for Red Cross volunteers during World War II.

The Partricks organized and often led the Catholic Study Club. In November 1929 the North Rose Literary Club's first meeting was held in the couple's home. In 1930 their household included a "servant," Bessy Gould, as well as a schoolteacher who was boarding with them. When Bessy, who lived with the Partricks for several years, married Malette Jacques in June 1931, Harry gave away the bride and Malette's father performed the ceremony. The Partricks often visited relatives in Fulton. They spent a few days in Detroit in January 1936, vacationed in California in February 1938, and went to Florida in March 1940.

Grace and Harry each lost a parent in 1948. Grace's father, William C. Burns, died in March and her mother, Cora, came to live with the family a few weeks later. Harry lost his 98-year-old mother, Nora Partrick, in June.

Eleanor, the "domestic," was more than an employee. She considered the Partricks' home her home and continued to visit after she moved away. And she helped celebrate the 54th wedding anniversary of Grace's parents; the majority of the attendees were from North Rose. Eleanor accepted a position with a hotel in Ontario Center in July 1941. She was living in Newark in March 1942 and was employed by the Newark State School that December. In May 1943 Eleanor and Grace visited New York City together. In July 1945 Eleanor secured a position at the Holl's Inn at Inlet—in Hamilton County in the Adirondacks—for the remainder of the season. By October 1946 she had moved to Rochester.

Payne, Harry & Laura
Estimated 1940 value: $2,000.
Harry Payne (1888–1958), 51, head of household, self-employed, proprietor of retail coal and feed.

Laura Payne (1892–1979), 48, wife, homemaker.
Leland DeKing (1919–2005), 22, stepson, student, unknown occupation, 8 weeks for $140.

We were unable to obtain more than the cursory information provided by the census for this household. If you have information about the Paynes, see page 32.

Peck, Martha
24 North Huron Street, now 5058 North Huron—Built in 1916. Estimated 1940 value: $2,500.
Martha Jane Salter Peck (1886–1977), 53, head of household, bookkeeper at the Canning Factory, 25 weeks for $550.

We were unable to obtain more than the cursory information provided by the census for this household. If you have information about the Pecks, see page 32.

Penner, Gary & Minnie
1940 monthly rent: $10.
Garrison "Gary" Penner (1858–1942), 82, head of household, retired, self-employed.
Minnie Willis Penner (1862–1945), 79, wife, homemaker.
Lena B. Penner (1892–1972), 47, daughter, homemaker and trimmer, 15 weeks for $150.

GARY COMPLETED FOUR YEARS of school and by 1940 had retired from a colorful career as a chicken rustler. Minnie completed three years of school and was a homemaker. Their daughter Lena resided with them. Lena completed eight years of school, shared homemaking duties with her mother, and worked part of the year as a trimmer at the Canning Factory.

Gary's parents, farm laborer Joseph Yates Penner (1822–1864) and his Maryette "Mary" Fisher Penner (1828–1906), wed in 1844 in Clyde. In 1860 Gary was the youngest of five children living with their parents in the Town of Sangerfield (Oneida County). At 14, Gary's eldest brother lived with a local lawyer. The last of Joseph and Mary's children was born later that year.

In 1862 Joseph enlisted to fight in the Civil War. He died, most likely of scurvy and diarrhea, as a prisoner of war in Andersonville, Sumter County, Georgia.

After being widowed, Mary wed Ezra S. Beebe. In 1870 Gary lived with his mother and stepfather, three other Penner children, and Ezra and Mary's 2-year-old son, Frank Beebe, in Sangerfield. Ezra died the following year. By 1880 Mary was living in Savannah and her son Frank had taken the last name "Penner."

In his book *The Loomis Gang*, author George Walter asserts that Gary was a member of the most notorious 19th-century rustling, robbing, and general-purpose outlaw gang in Central New York. His gang name was "Gary Gossin." "Gary was a member of the gang at least as early as May 1, 1878, and a frequent guest at the Waterville [Oneida County] lock-up for his habit of stealing chickens. He made his home with [Amos] 'Plumb' [Loomis] when he was at 'liberty.'" The author of this book was surprised to learn that some people in upstate New York made their living by rustling chickens.

After 14 years as an alleged criminal, by 1892 Gary worked more conventionally as a laborer in the Town of Butler. He lived with his wife, Minnie, their daughter Nina B. Penner (1885–1938), and their son Jay G. Penner (1886–1970). Gary and Minnie's third child, Lena, was born later that year. In 1900 Gary was a farmer in the Town of Butler. In his household were his wife, three children, and a niece, Hazel Penner (1893–1968). Whether or not Gary and Minnie later adopted Hazel is unclear, but Lena and Hazel, born less than a year apart, considered each other sisters, and Gary and Minnie are recorded as Hazel's parents on her marriage license.

In 1907 Hazel married Cornelius Wilkinson.

Nina Penner married Fred Adams (1872–1930) of Ontario in 1908. They made their home first in Clifton Springs (Ontario County) and then in the Town of Rose.

Jay Penner married Mabel Miles (1886–1968) in 1910. They lived with Gary and Minnie at first, but eventually moved to Huron and had five children: Jay Penner Jr., Miles E., Robert P., Willis K., and Ross D. Penner. In March 1943 Jay purchased the Boughton house on Gray Street. Jay Penner died in Phoenix, Arizona, in 1970.

In 1910 Gary was a farmer in Bristol (Ontario County). He and Minnie lived with their newlywed son Jay and daughter-in-law Mabel, as well as Cornelius Wilkinson (who is listed as a servant in that year's census). It's unclear where Hazel was living in 1910; Cornelius and Hazel's daughter, Marie Pauline Wilkinson (1910–1976), was born later that spring in Canandaigua (Ontario County). Hazel divorced soon after, perhaps because the young Cornelius had similar outlaw tendencies as Gary. As reported in *The Savannah Times* on February 14, 1913, under the headline "Swift Justice for Thieves": "It was a piece of fine detective work, engineered by Police Justice Harvie and Superintendent [of Highways Fred] Taylor [the victim of the theft], and aided by that fearless officer, Chief of Police, George W. Ingersoll, that apprehended the self-confessed criminals and placed them behind bars. Locating the goods, officer Ingersoll, armed with a warrant, and Mr. Taylor took the 9:16 p.m. trolley car for Syracuse, and two hours later the intrepid Ingersoll had the hand-cuffs on Cornelius Wilkinson and Sam Ingraham. Mr. Taylor was on hand to identify his goods, which except the meat, were found in Wilkinson's room. Indeed, Cornelius Wilkinson and Sam Ingraham were found quietly sleeping under Fred Taylor's horse blanket and wolf-robe, not dreaming that the brave policeman from Savannah was to lay the heavy hand of the law upon them. Mr. Taylor wrapped up his belongings, and a little after midnight had the prisoners safely lodged in the Savannah lock-up." The next morning Cornelius "received six months in the Monroe County Penitentiary, and a fine of $50 additional."

In 1912 Lena gave birth to a daughter, Helen Marie Penner (1912–1986). (It's unclear who Helen's father was. Lena never married, and Helen's marriage license lists her father as "Garry Penner.")

In 1920 Gary and Minnie lived in the Town of Rose with their daughter Lena and two granddaughters: Lena's daughter Helen Penner and Hazel's daughter Marie Wilkinson. Later that year, Gary and

Minnie mourned the death of their grandson, infant son of Nina and Fred, Charles Adams (1919–1920).

Marie Wilkinson married Charles Riggs in 1927; they eventually settled in Weedsport (Cayuga County) and had 10 children. Hazel worked as a cook in Rochester most of her adult life but moved in with her daughter Marie in Weedsport a decade before she died at 76.

In 1928, at 16, Helen married Leonard Hoskins (1903–1979) and moved to Canandaigua, where Leonard was a mail carrier. Lena exchanged visits with Helen and Leonard Hoskins and their growing family regularly.

Gary and Minnie lived with their daughter Lena in the Town of Rose in 1930. Gary worked as a farm laborer. Their daughter Nina also lived in the Town of Rose with her husband Fred, also a farm laborer) and their two surviving sons, Harry James Adams (1914–1978) and James Henry Adams (1922–1982). Fred died later that year, and Nina died in 1938; their two boys stayed in the house. In 1940, Harry, head of the household at 25, worked 25 weeks at the Salter Canning Company for $400. James Henry, 17, attended his first year of high school. On Christmas Day that year, Harry married Marguerite Shove, a widow with two sons. He and James Henry moved to Rochester, and both served in World War II. Harry divorced and remarried, to Eleanor Redman. He was survived by Eleanor and a son, Charles, when he died at 63. After the war, James Henry married Teresa DiSanto (1917–2010). They made their home in Rochester and had two daughters, Helen and Betty.

In December 1938 Gary fell while uptown and fractured his hip. Lena cared for her ailing infant grandson Kenneth before he died at 17 months old in 1939. Gary rustled his last chicken in September 1942. In April 1943 James Henry Adams called on his grandmother, Minnie. Minnie fell at home and broke her arm in July 1943. In April 1944 the North Rose Fire Department was called to Minnie's house after an oil stove exploded when she was trying to light it. She survived, with burns, but died in March 1945.

The following month, Lena moved in with the Hoskins family in Canandaigua. By 1950 Helen and Leonard had eight surviving children and had separated. Lena lived in Helen's household with Margaret, 16; Barbara, 15; Kathleen, 9; Doris, 5; and Robert, 3. Leonard lived with Nancy, 20, and her husband, Gordon Murphy; Eugene, 13; and Allen, 12. Lena and Helen both worked as hospital attendants. In 1952 tragedy struck the Hoskins family. Two days after Christmas, Nancy and Barbara were passengers in an automobile that collided with a tractor trailer when a snow squall caused a sudden whiteout. Barbara, 18, who had married Joseph Guino in May, died at the scene. Nancy, 21, succumbed 12 days later, leaving her husband, Gordon Murphy, and their infant son Larry.

Peters, John & Grace
South Poplar Street. 1940 monthly rent: $9.
John Peters (1889–1959), 51, head of household, roofer, 15 weeks, self-employed.
Grace Peters (1901–1980), 38, wife, trimmer, 16 weeks for $12 a week.
Wesley C. Peters (1921–1970), 18, son, student.

JOHN AND GRACE PETERS LIVED with their son, Wesley, who was attending high school. In August 1936 the Peters moved to North Rose from Conquest in Cayuga County—just east of Wayne County. In Conquest, John worked as a barber. In North Rose, he was working as a self-employed roofer but was seeking other work. Grace was also looking for a job but had worked part of 1939 as a trimmer at the Canning Factory. John had completed the sixth grade, and Grace was a high school graduate.

Wesley performed in a high school production of the musical comedy *Way Out West* while he attended NRCS. He was working as a roofer in October 1942 when he enlisted in the armed services. In the fall of 1943 he married Zoie A. Camp of Rochester. In May 1948 Wesley went on a fishing trip with friends to the Thousand Islands. In November 1955 Wesley and Zoie purchased a Chris Craft 27-foot cruiser and owned the former Wignal cottage on the south shore of

Sodus Bay. That same year, they lived in Rochester with their daughter Nancy.

Phelps, Edward & Bertha

1940 monthly rent: $11.
Edward F. Phelps (1890–1974), 50, head of household, salesman, food distribution products, 50 weeks for $2,330.
Bertha Phelps (1888–1980), 52, wife, homemaker.
Edward Phelps (1928–2011), 12, son, student.
Ella Phelps (1858–1943), 81, mother, retired.
Anna Curtis (1871–1943), 68, lodger, retired.

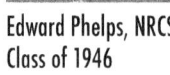

Edward Phelps, NRCS Class of 1946

We were unable to obtain more than the cursory information provided by the census for this household. If you have information about the Phelpses, see page 32.

Phillips, Ella

16 Elm Street, now 4956 Elm—Built in 1910. Estimated 1940 value: $3,000.
Ella Gardner Phillips (1882–1972), 58, head of household, bookkeeper, 52 weeks.
Marion Phillips (1909–1970), 30, son, unemployed.

A modern photo of Ella Phillips's Elm Street home

ELLA PHILLIPS AND HER SON Marion were sharing the home. Ella worked year-round as a bookkeeper for the Canning Factory. Marion was not employed in 1940. Ella completed one year of college. Marion graduated high school and had been treasurer of his junior class.

Ella played bridge and was a member of the Literary Club. Her mother was from Ireland and her father was a farmer in the Town of Rose. Ella's husband, Elmer Phillips (1873–1932), died of a heart attack while building a henhouse with Gilbert Hill in November 1932.

In 1931 Ella, Marion, Frances R. Laird Winchell, and a group of high school students went on a whirlwind Easter-week bus trip to Washington, D.C. They visited New York City, Scranton, Philadelphia, Baltimore, Norfolk, Harrisburg, Wilmington, Watkins Glen, Washington, Arlington, Annapolis, Alexandria, Mt. Vernon, Gettysburg, Delaware Water Gap, Old Point Comfort, Trenton, Yorktown, Hampton Roads, Jamestown, Newport News, and Williamsburg!

In March 1939 Ella and Marion took a trip south. During the 1940s the two took many road trips together, visiting Virginia, Kentucky, Canada, Lake George, and Boston. In July 1940 Ella and Marion attended a Gardner family picnic at Sodus Point with 40 of their relatives. In May 1950 Ella bought a new Chevrolet. Marion Phillips and his friends Richard Drury and Leslie Thompson enjoyed attending Rochester Red Wings baseball games. In 1944 Marion moved to Rochester, where he was employed for the remainder of the decade.

Ella also had a daughter, (Lina) Marguerite Phillips (1905–1959), who was an enthusiastic pianist and taught school in 1925. After she married Ralph M. Leadley (1902–1959), the couple lived in Geneva and Seneca Castle (where Marguerite was appointed postmistress). Marguerite and her family frequently spent Thanksgiving and other major holidays with Ella and Marion, and the families often visited one another. The Leadleys had three children: Morgan, (Allen) Douglas, and Martha.

Morgan served in the U.S. Navy during World War II. In December 1949 he married Helen Palmer in Rochester. When Helen gave birth to Phillip Duane Leadley in 1950, Ella became a great-grandmother. In February 1946 Douglas suffered a three-month-long illness and died. He was only 15.

Poole, Wade & Catherine

North Poplar Street. 1940 monthly rent: $10.
Wade Grant Poole (1917–1988), 22, head of household, job unknown, 52 weeks, $900.
Catherine E. Lapp Poole (1919–1994), 20, wife, laborer, 20 weeks, $300.

WADE WORKED FULL-TIME. Catherine worked part-time as a laborer on a muck farm. She was looking for a new job. Each of them had completed eight years of school. Wade was born in Maryland. He lived in Hancock, Maryland, in 1935. His parents were Oscar H. Poole (1892–1956) and Clara Shipley Poole (1895–1918), who married in January 1916. After losing his mother, from a very young age Wade lived with his grandfather William Poole (1872–1959) of Mann Township, Pennsylvania. Oscar worked away from home as a Baltimore & Ohio Railroad repairman and later at a tinplate mill. Oscar lived in Cumberland, Maryland.

Catherine, a native of the Town of Rose, was the daughter of Mathias Lapp (1873–1951) and Bertha Harrington Lapp (1901–1990).

At the time of the 1940 census count—the census came on April 3, 1940, for the Pooles—they did not yet have any children but later that month their first child, Wade L. "Mike" (1940–2006), was born. Wade (father) attended the January 1941 fruit show in Rochester with George Aldrich and Walter Reed. In September 1941, Wade, Catherine, and Mike moved from the Aldrich tenant house to the Allie Brown house on Maple Avenue. The Pooles moved to Lyons in November 1941.

In slightly more than a year, the family returned to North Rose. Wade was employed by George Aldrich. On furlough from his armed services posting in California, Catherine's brother, Cpl. Albert Lapp, visited Catherine and their parents. For a substantial time, Wade was an assembly operator at Sylvania in Seneca Falls (Seneca County) while commuting from North Rose.

Mike Poole married Priscilla "Pat" Ann Reynolds (1939–1984). Then, after Priscilla's death, he married Elaine VandenBout. He had seven children or stepchildren. Mike was the proprietor of Alpha and Omega Transportation, a trucking company.

Wade and Catherine Poole also had three daughters: Nancy Ann (1942–2023), born in Clyde; Joyce (1945–1984), born in North Rose; and Cheryl Lee (1955–2024), born in Lyons.

Nancy Poole married Roger E. Blondale (1937–2022) of North Rose. Roger was the son of Katherine Blondale (1917–1972) of Alton. Nancy and Roger had two sons, Ronald A. and Barry Lynn.

Joyce Poole married William "Bill" VerStraete (1944–2005) and lived in Newark. She worked as a nurse at Newark–Wayne Hospital for 40 years. She was the Marbletown Fire Department's first female firefighter.

Cheryl Poole married Thomas Bailey (1953–) and lived in Baldwinsville (Onondaga County). They had two sons, Tim Bailey (1974–2012) and Chris Bailey. Cheryl worked as a hairdresser and owned a cleaning business.

Porter, George & Eva

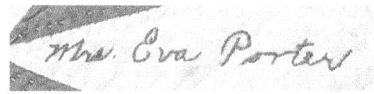

22 South Maple Avenue, now 10384 South Maple—Built in 1900. Estimated 1940 value: $2,000

George Spencer Porter (1871–1948), 68, head of household, farmer, 52 weeks, income unrecorded.
Evelyn "Eva" Mae Andrus Porter (1874–1941), 65, wife.
Pauline Porter (1900–1985), 39, daughter, teacher, 40 weeks for $35 a week.
Maria Vanhout (1878–1965), 62, housekeeper/trimmer, 30 weeks for $17 a week.

GEORGE AND EVELYN PORTER WERE LIVING with Pauline, an adult daughter, and their housekeeper, Maria Vanhout. George was a farmer, Evelyn was a homemaker, and Pauline was a beloved first grade schoolteacher. In addition to working as a housekeeper, Maria worked occasionally as a trimmer in the Canning Factory.

Pauline attended two years of college. The other members of the household had each completed the sixth grade.

In 1910 the Porters and their two daughters, Pauline and Mildred C.B. (1902–1955), lived in rural Rose with Evelyn's parents, Andrew (ca. 1849–1928) and Cynthia Andrus (1844–1915). On the census, George listed his occupation as "laborer—odd jobs." By 1920 George had moved his family in to North Rose and was an apple barrel manufacturer. In 1930 Mildred had moved away from North Rose, George was farming, and Pauline was a schoolteacher.

Mildred C.B. Porter graduated from Elmira College and did graduate work at Mount Holyoke, Cornell, and Columbia. She taught one semester at Elmira College. She was associated with the Peabody Museum of Natural History at Yale University in New Haven, Connecticut, beginning around 1930 and became its librarian. In April 1941 Mildred married 28-year-old Preston E. Cloud Jr. in White Plains, Missouri. Cloud was a faculty member of the School of Mines at the Rollo branch of the University of Missouri (now known as the Missouri University of Science and Technology). Preston returned with her to New Haven to work at the Peabody Museum, but the marriage was not long lasting. It was the first of three nuptials for Cloud.

At the age of 80, totally deaf and blind in one eye, Evelyn's father, Andrew Andrus, was struck and killed by a New York Central locomotive on March 6, 1928. In October 1929 Evelyn was active in the North Rose Methodist Episcopal Missionary Society. George and Evelyn hosted a meeting of the Literary Club in March 1930. The next month Evelyn entertained 26 of her friends at a Saturday luncheon and card party. In March 1932, Earl Gilfilian and his family moved from Huron to the Porter farm. Romain Cole and family, of Rochester and later of Newark, were frequent visitors at the Porters' home. Evelyn passed away in early spring 1941. Maude Barnes of Clyde spent some time with her brother George in July 1946. He died in May 1948.

Pauline Porter graduated from the Geneseo Normal School in 1926. Shortly before graduation, Pauline was hired to replace Lela Rose, the first-ever first grade teacher at the consolidated North Rose school. Lela had held the position for 35 years and was retiring that year. Pauline, like her predecessor, held the position for her entire career.

Pauline Porter with her first grade class in 1949

Shortly after she retired, Pauline departed on a long-anticipated trip around the world. An example of Pauline's kindness and generosity was that she returned to the United States with a selection of foreign coins as a gift for the author.

In December 1929 Pauline was elected an officer of the Methodist Episcopal Church Sunday school. In the summer of 1930 Pauline attended classes at Buffalo Normal School. She was also a member of the Kappa Phi class associated with the North Rose Methodist Episcopal Church. She spent Memorial Day at the Thousand Islands with Grace Bowell, Jennie Alessi, and Mildred Hetzke. In July 1935, Pauline, Marian Metcalfe, and three friends from New York City took a 30-day motor trip to California. In March 1936 Pauline purchased a Chevrolet. In December 1936 Pauline hosted the Teachers' Sewing Club. In the summer of 1937 Pauline returned to Buffalo Normal School for additional classes. Pauline was an active member of the Women's Society of Christian Service and often played the piano or organ at weddings. She spent Christmas Day 1948 with Mr. and Mrs. Harry Payne and Genevieve Valentine.

The Porters' housekeeper, Maria Gaffield Vanhout (1878–1965), was from the Town of Rose. In 1910 she lived in Huron and was married to Daniel Vanhout (1869–1932). Daniel was nine years her senior and both his parents were born in The Netherlands. Maria and Daniel's son, Clayton G. Vanhout (1909–1979), married Hulda E. Legg in Wolcott in February 1929. He had left his parents' home by 1930. The couple had a daughter and two sons. Hulda spent the winter of 1939–1940 with the Porters.

Powell, George & Lulu
6 South Huron Street, now 4982 South Huron—Built in 1910. Estimated 1940 value: $3,000.
George Henry Powell (1896–1952), 44, head of household, foreman, 51 weeks for $35 a week.
Lula "Lulu" E. Messinger Powell (1896–1983), 43, wife, homemaker.

GEORGE AND LULU POWELL HAD been married since 1914 and were the only two residents of the household. The Powells' son, Gerald, was already an adult. George earned $1,785 a year, working long hours as a foreman at the Cold Storage, while Lulu was a homemaker. Both Powells had completed the eighth grade.

George was born in Huron and died in Wolcott. In 1905 he was living with eight siblings in the Town of Rose. By 1910 he and his family lived on a different farm in the Town of Wolcott. In 1917 George was working for George Marshall as a farm laborer. By 1930 he owned a home on Huron Street and was a foreman at the Cold Storage.

George was a member of the Bay Shore Lodge No. 606 of the Odd Fellows and the North Rose Fire Department. In 1942 he recovered nicely from surgery at Barber Hospital in Lyons. In April 1945 he pulled 20-month-old Eileen Noyes from a shallow pond in Traver Garlic's yard and successfully administered first aid.

George's wife, Lulu, lived in Butler and the Town of Rose as a girl. Her father was a farmer. As an adult, she was active in the American Legion Auxiliary, the Rebekah Lodge, and the Home Bureau. In 1938 she had a serious operation at the Barber Hospital in Lyons. In

1940 the Powells attended the New York World's Fair.

George and Lulu's son, Gerald, married Alice Waldorf in 1936. They purchased a home on South Poplar Street. (See "Powell, Gerald & Alice.")

George and Lulu were divorced in February 1947. By October, Lula had moved to Rochester. Charles Williams, Frances Sisson Williams, and their son moved into the Powell house.

In 1950 George was living with Bertha Harper Howell (1910–1995) and her 18-year-old daughter in Butler. Bertha and her husband were separated; they also had three older daughters who had married and moved out. Bertha's husband, Kermit Howell, lived with his parents in Clyde. He died at 47 in an automobile accident in July 1950.

George and Bertha married in 1952. Gerald Powell, George and Lulu's only child, died the next year at 35.

Powell, Gerald & Alice

9 South Poplar Street, now 4971 South Poplar—Built in 1900. Estimated 1940 value: $1,800.

Gerald E. Powell (1916–1953), 23, head of household, laborer, 52 weeks at $23 a week.

Alice Theresa Waldorf Powell (1915–2015), 24, wife, apple trimmer, 32 weeks at $10 a week.

GERALD AND ALICE POWELL were married in January 1936. Gerald worked long hours as a laborer at the Cold Storage. Alice had worked as an apple trimmer at an apple drying house, but she was seeking new employment. The Powells had both completed the 11th grade.

Gerald's parents were North Rose residents George Henry Powell and Lulu Messinger Powell (see "Powell, George & Lulu"). As a youth, Gerald was an active participant in Seth Oaks's Boy Scout troop. As an adult, Gerald enjoyed hunting with the Guthries, the Marshalls, and other friends.

Alice's parents were Guy Dillow Waldorf (1877–1957) and Lillian Richardson Waldorf (1878–1917). Alice was just a toddler when her mother passed away in June 1917. Elsie Glanzel, an 18-year-old housekeeper, lived in the Waldorf household in 1920. Alice's father married Elsie in 1924.

Gerald and Alice were members of the Starlight Club and the Young Married Couples Anniversary Club. They often socialized with Mr. and Mrs. Edward Powell of North Wolcott and often spent holidays with Gerald's parents. The Powells enjoyed traveling with Freda and Graydon Guthrie, as well as Russell and Eunice Thompson. In April 1940 the Powells entertained at a farewell party in honor of the Thompsons, who were moving to Rochester.

Gerald joined the Navy during World War II. In September 1943 he was promoted to Seaman 2/C. In March 1944 he was stationed in Gulfport, Mississippi, when he received 11 days' leave to visit his wife and parents, but at the end of that month he was hospitalized with a collapsed lung. In June he was again granted leave to visit his family. He was stationed with the Seabees in Oahu, Hawaii, a few months later but was subsequently sent to California for medical care—then to the WWII Naval Hospital at Sampson, on the eastern shore of Seneca Lake in Romulus (Seneca County). He received an honorable medical discharge in February 1945.

Sadly, Gerald was only 35 when he died in the Veterans Hospital in Buffalo in May 1952. After Gerald's death, Alice married Maurice Richardson, sold the house on South Poplar Street to John Maust and Mabel Lucille Clark, and moved to Wolcott. Maurice's spouse had also died in 1952, of a cerebral hemorrhage, at 36.

Gerald and Alice had a son, John Carl Powell (1948–2018), in March 1948. John was a self-described "bay rat," growing up on LeRoy Island in Sodus Bay. He became the historian for the Town of Huron and wrote a few books on the local history. He married and had three daughters.

Quereau, Florence

17 South Polar Street, now 4963 South Poplar—Built in 1890. 1940 monthly rent: $9.

Florence Boyd Quereau (1887–1969), 48, head of household, bookkeeper, 52 weeks at $20 a week.

Florence Quereau was a high school graduate and worked year-round as a bookkeeper at the Cold Storage plant. She was divorced and had an adult son, James "William" Quereau (1915–1979), who no longer lived at home.

Florence grew up in Huron and Wolcott. Her father, James Boyd (see "Boyd, Jim & Gertie"), was born in Ireland and worked as a blacksmith. Her mother, Dalinda, was a homemaker. She died in 1903.

Florence married Ross W. Quereau (1886–1950) in August 1912. In 1921 Florence was active in the Literary Club. She taught Sunday school at the Methodist Church and, in 1929, was active in the Arbor Vitae Chapter of the Order of the Eastern Star. She went on an auto trip to Bath and Hammondsport with William and Dora Lundergun, as well as Nettie Julia Gardner Meone and Joseph Moore. In 1930 she was working as a secretary at the ice company when she slipped on some ice and badly cut her head.

Florence often exchanged visits with her sister, Effie E. Foote, and Effie's husband, George N. Foote, and their children in Rochester and later in Geneva. In 1933 Florence moved into the "Little" house on South Poplar Street. She was elected treasurer of the American Legion Auxiliary in October 1935. In September 1936 Florence was a passenger in a car that her son was driving when the brakes malfunctioned. The car rolled over just south of Rose, and Florence suffered several broken ribs and went into shock.

Florence was chosen to be the teacher of the North Rose Methodist church's Sunday School class, Kappa Phi, in 1943. In September 1945 she moved into the "Donlon" house on Gray Street. Florence was treasurer of the Red Cross Fund in 1955 and 1956.

Florence's ex-husband, Ross, and his cousin Harry Quereau operated a general store in North Rose. (See "Quereau, Harry & Lena.")

In 1926 Ross was living in Detroit but returned to North Rose in June to visit relatives. His new Hudson automobile had been recently stolen. Ross Quereau died in Rogers, Arkansas, in June 1950.

Florence and Ross's son, William, went on a western trip with his father in September 1936. In December 1938 William was in another bad accident. He totaled his car, breaking a telephone pole into several pieces. He lived in Fort Niagara and San Francisco in 1941. In December 1942, when he married Mary Ellen Hill of Rochester, he moved there. They had a son, James William Quereau Jr. (1943–2003), and a daughter, Kathleen Hill Quereau (1946–). William and his family spent the summer of 1946 with his mother in North Rose.

Quereau, Harry & Lena

Mrs. H. Quereau

Estimated 1940 value: $2,500.
Henry "Harry" Newton Quereau (1877–1959), 61, head of household, self-employed, proprietor of retail dry goods store.
Lena Gordon Quereau (1877–1963), 61, wife, homemaker.
Virginia Quereau Fish (1902–1980), 37, daughter, welfare investigator for the county, 52 weeks for $1,200.

FOR MORE THAN HALF A CENTURY, Harry Quereau ran the general store that doubled as a social center for the hamlet of North Rose. He started the store with his father, George Henry Quereau (1846–1918), sometime around the turn of the century. Harry and Lena married in 1899 and moved in with Harry's father and mother, Henrietta M. Bean Quereau (1845–1930), in the Town of Rose. Harry and Lena's first daughter, Virginia, was born in 1902, and the three of them were still living with George and Henrietta in 1905.

In December 1907 Harry won three chickens and a lamp at the fair given by the ladies of the Methodist Episcopal church. In September 1908 Harry took a number of railroad officials in his automobile to view several large orchards to determine how many cars would be needed to transport that fall's apple crop. By 1910 Harry, Lena, and Virginia had moved into their own home, and the following year their second daughter, Henrietta (1911–1997), was born.

In 1915 Harry bought a new Haines automobile. Lena was active in the Methodist church. In November 1918 Lena fell down the cellar stairs at the Quereau & Quereau general store and broke her wrist. Lena Quereau and Olive Welch entertained the North Rose Literary Club in December. In September 1922 Harry and Lena hosted a surprise double anniversary party for Frank and Flora Hill and Frank and Nellie Quereau, who'd had a double wedding 25 years earlier.

Harry and Lena had each completed three years of high school; Virginia had graduated from Wells College. Virginia Quereau married William Cornelius Fish (1902–1931) of Alton in July 1925. After a trip to Quebec and the Adirondacks, the couple settled in Alton and then moved to North Rose. William died at 28 after a brief illness. Virginia moved back home with her parents after being widowed. She and William had no children and Virginia never married again.

Henrietta Quereau married Claude Clayton Collier (1906–1963) of Rochester in 1938. (Claude's sister married George Aldrich; see "Aldrich, George & Millie." A photograph of all four of them, plus another Collier sister, is on page 43.) In 1940 Claude had his own business as an ice dealer in Rochester. Claude and Henrietta's first child, William H. Collier (1939–), was born when they were living in the Rochester area, but in the early 1940s they moved to North Rose. Their two daughters were born in Wayne County: Catherine B. in 1942 and Virginia in 1949. Claude Collier joined Harry Quereau in the retail business and they changed the name to Quereau & Collier Department Store. The author remembers Claude Collier wrapping packages in brown paper and tying them up with red string.

Claude Collier was very active in the community. He was a longtime councilman on the Rose Town Board, served as chairman of the board for the North Rose Methodist Church and sang in the choir, was treasurer of the North Rose Fire Department, served multiple terms as chairman of the board for the Chamber of Commerce, was a scoutmaster, and was a secretary and master of the Rose Masonic Lodge 590.

Harry Quereau died in the summer of 1959 of a heart attack

at age 82. He and Lena had celebrated their 60th anniversary that spring. Claude Collier sold the store in the spring of 1963 and died in December of that year, at age 57.

When Henrietta Quereau Collier died in 1997, all three of her children—William Collier, Catherine Bowler, and Virginia Robinson—lived in North Rose.

From left: Henrietta Quereau, Lillian Hill (daughter of Frank and Flora Hill), and Virginia Quereau. That's most likely Harry Quereau at far left.

Reed, Walter & Viola

39 North Poplar Street, now 5097 North Poplar—Built in 1915. 1940 monthly rent: $10.
Walter David Reed Jr. (1900–1990), 39, head of household, farm laborer, 30 weeks for $600.
Viola F. Alford Reed (1904–1992), 36, wife, homemaker.
William "Bill" A. Reed (1925–2020), 14, son, student.
Lucille Esther Reed (1929–1997), 10, daughter, student.
Shirley Jane Reed (1936–2006), 4, daughter.

WALTER AND VIOLA REED RENTED a home in the rear of the Carrie Fisher property near the east side of the North Poplar Street spur north of Aldrich Avenue. Walter was a farm laborer, on the Fisher (Aldrich) farm. He had completed eight years of school. Viola had completed seven years of school. The Reeds married in June 1922.

Walter was born in Wolcott. His parents were Walter Waywood Reed (1868–1937) and Iva A. Baldwin Reed (1879–1965). In 1910 his family lived on a farm in Sterling (Cayuga County). By 1915 the Reeds had moved to the Town of Wolcott. In 1920 Walter worked on the family farm on West Road in Wolcott. Ten years later Walter worked as a laborer on a poultry farm. He lived in the Town of Ledyard (Cayuga County) with his wife, Viola, and their three young children: Bill, Paul, and Lucille.

As a young child, Viola lived in the Town of Rose. Her parents were George Alford (1864–1913) and Esther "Etta" E. Johnson Alford (1878–1952). George and Etta married when Etta was only 14. Viola had a twin sister named Leola. George was a farmer. By 1920 her family had moved to a farm in the Town of Wolcott. Viola's father worked his farm while her three older brothers "worked out" at other farms.

In October 1932 Walter and Viola's son Paul died of appendicitis at the age of 5. In 1935 Walter and Viola lived in Butler. Their youngest child, Shirley Jane, was born in 1936. In March 1940 the Reeds moved to the tenant home on the Fisher/Aldrich farm in North Rose. Walter attended the Syracuse Fruit Show with George Aldrich and Wade Poole in January 1941. In June 1944 the Reeds moved to Alton.

In October 1943 Bill won election as vice president of the NRCS Future Farmers of America. Bill was on the NRCS 1944 baseball team. Upon his graduation in June 1944, Bill won the Outstanding School Citizenship Prize. Bill joined the Armed Forces, and in July 1945, the Army posted him to Las Vegas after completing training as a tail gunner. He served in France and the occupation of Germany. Bill married Patricia Joan McDorman (1930–2020) of Wolcott in July 1949. He worked at Featherly's garage in Alton for 19 years, then at Xerox for 30. Bill and Patricia had four children: Paul, Daniel, Joanne, and Robert.

Lucille transferred to a new school for her freshman year of high school. She moved from North Rose to Wolcott. She graduated from Leavenworth High School in June 1948 and married Edward Isadore

Zaborowski (1925–2005) in September. The groom had spent nearly four years in the Navy. Edward's parents, Stanley Zaborowski (1900–1986) and Jadwiga ("Hattie") Urbanik Zaborowski (1907–2000), were immigrants from Poland.

Shirley was in a serious auto accident in August 1951. She and Mildred Sigel were passengers in a car driven by Robert Capron, 19, of Red Creek. The driver lost control of his vehicle when it hit a patch of rough road in the Town of Victory (Cayuga County) and struck a tree. Shirley flew into the air and bounced off the hood of the car. Both women were hospitalized in Wolcott in fair condition. The driver received treatment at the hospital and then made his way home. Shirley married Donald Edward O'Dell (1928–2018), an Army veteran and the son of Claude W. O'Dell (1900–1969) and Grace Irene Stevens O'Dell (1908–1993) of Wolcott. Shirley and Donald moved to Red Creek. Later they lived in Cains Corners, near Hannibal (Oswego County). They had a son, Russell, and two daughters, Cindy and Tracy.

Rhodes, Charles & Gertrude

25 Elm Street, now 4935 Elm—Built in 1915. 1940 monthly rent: $20.
Charles G. Rhodes (1871–1965), 68, head of household, engineer, 52 weeks for $46 a week.
Gertrude Savage Rhodes (1881–1965), 58, wife, homemaker/worker, 12 weeks for $9 a week.
Sadie Savage Pahl (1888–1957), 50, sister-in-law, laborer in the Canning Factory, 24 weeks for $12 a week.
Reginald Pahl (1909–1955), 29, nephew, self-employed truck driver, 36 weeks.

CHARLES AND GERTRUDE RHODES shared their Elm Street home with Gertrude's sister Sadie and Sadie's adult son Reginald. The combined annual income of this extended family exceeded $3,000 in 1940. Charles was an engineer at the Cold Storage, worked long hours and earned a large salary for the time, $2,400. Gertrude was a homemaker but also worked outside the home for three months. Sadie worked as a weigher in the Canning Factory in 1939 but was seeking other work in 1940. All four residents of this home were high school graduates.

Charles's parents were born in Germany. Gertrude and Sadie's parents were born in England. Both families often visited relatives in Lockport (Niagara County)—the hometown of Gertrude, Sadie, and their sister Jeanette "Jane" Savage of North Rose. Eventually Charles and Gertrude moved to Lockport.

In September 1913 Charles was hired for a responsible position at the Cold Storage. In 1915 Charles and Gertrude lived on Poplar Street. By 1930 Charles was a foreman at the Cold Storage and the Rhodeses had moved to Elm Street, where they were paying $16 a month in rent.

In August 1948, Charles, Gertrude, and Gertrude's sister Jane were seriously injured in an auto accident on their way to Brockport (Monroe County) when a car attempting to pass them caught their bumper, throwing their car into a tree. Gertrude had an injured left eye and cuts to her forehead; Jane suffered a fractured hip. Both women were hospitalized until February 1949. While the sisters were recuperating, Charles spent time in Lockport.

Sadie Pahl, Gertrude's sister, lived separately from her husband almost from the start of their marriage. In 1910 she lived with her sister Jane's family in Lockport. In 1930, as well as in 1940, she was living with Gertrude.

In 1930 Sadie's son, Reginald, was working as an electrician and living in Lockport with another uncle and aunt, John and Ruth Stauch. By 1940 he had moved to North Rose and was living with his mother in the Rhodeses' home. In August of that year he married Ruth Vincent, originally from Butler, and they honeymooned in Cleveland. Their daughter, Mary Louise Pahl, was born in 1941. Mary was a Girl Scout Brownie and often appeared on the honor roll at NRCS. During the early 1940s, Reginald and Ruth lived in several North Rose homes:

Mary Pahl, NRCS
Class of 1955

the Jeffers house on South Main Street; the Knapp house, also on South Main; the Graham house on Elm Street; and the Ote Gray house on North Main. Reginald died in 1955.

Roney, Estella

7 Gray Street, now 5029 Gray. Estimated 1940 value: $3,000.
Mary "Estella" Merrill Roney (1887–1968), 53, head of household, self-employed piano teacher.
Frank F. Roney Jr. (1916–1952), 24, son, laborer in the Canning Factory, 10 weeks for $150.
Henry J. Merrill (1859–1941), 80, father, retired.
Mary Eliza Kidder Merrill (1860–1946), 79, mother, homemaker.
Gilbert "Gib" Flood (1915–1967), 23, lodger, bookkeeper for wholesale bean dealer, 50 weeks for $1,170.

ESTELLA COMPLETED TWO YEARS of college and was an independent music teacher. Scores of now-grown North Rose children remember Mrs. Roney—with respect and affection—as a kind and skillful piano instructor. In an era when many families had a piano in the home, Estella's lessons, at only $1 or less per visit, were a luxury that many families could afford for their child.

Why the Piano?

Why did Estella Roney teach piano playing to so many North Rose children? Through the 19th century, the piano was the principal way that music came into middle- and upper-class American homes. Today, if you want to hear a song, you stream it from the Internet using Spotify, SoundCloud, YouTube, or any of a myriad other sources. In the last three-quarters of the 20th century, you would buy a phonograph record or listen to the radio and hope it would play the song that you wanted to hear. For 125 years before that, you would buy sheet music, and a good pianist in the family would play the song and the other interested people in the family would crowd around the piano to read the lyrics and sing along.

A modern upright piano was a substantial instrument. It had a massive cast-iron frame to keep the instrument from buckling under the tension of the tightly stretched wire "strings" that felt hammers struck as the pianist pushed down the keys. The manufacturer hid the works behind a handsome wooden cover. The piano served as an attractive piece of furniture and a musical instrument. There were many manufacturers and retailers. And most of them offered time-payment plans.

The piano lacked portability, but it had many good qualities. For someone with a moderate amount of musical talent, it was easy to play. It had a great range of over seven octaves. If the instrument was kept in tune, each key sounded clear and clean when you pressed it. The loudness of the piano depended on how hard you struck the keys. The sustain pedal allowed skillful players to start the melody while a lower chord was still sounding. Besides its utilitarian function of bringing music into the home, a piano in the house was a sign of refinement. The presence of the piano silently announced that the children in that house were being given every advantage.

As for the younger people in the family, it was fun to gather around the piano and sing along with favorite songs. And parents considered it respectable for a young man and a young woman to play four-handed piano, even though it was likely that the musicians' arms would get entangled at some point!

A player piano was an upright piano with an amazing bonus: It could be played by someone with absolutely no musical talent! Its songs were stored on punched paper rolls. The "player" pumped the pedals on the piano with his or her feet. The pedals powered bellows that created a partial vacuum. Air could enter holes in the player only where they were aligned with the holes in the moving punched paper roll. By way of an ingenious mechanism, the flowing air was channeled to push the correct keys to play a song. The keys went down appropriately for each note that was sounded. It looked like an invisible person was playing the piano!

Piano playing retained its popularity longer in North Rose than in metropolitan areas of the country. North Rose wasn't always on the cutting edge of cultural change. Janet Clingerman tells of an old joke about the area: The Town of Rose is so far out in the wilderness that the only culture we had was in the buttermilk! A large factor in the sustained interest in piano playing in North Rose was because of the personality of Mrs. Roney, as her students universally called her. She was a very likable and kind woman and a serious instructor.

The phonograph and the radio spelled the end of the piano's universal popularity. These devices brought music into the home effortlessly. Piano sales peaked in 1909, then plummeted for one hundred years, with annual sales falling by 90 percent by 2009. Most of the sales that remain are of digital instruments. The classic upright piano is no longer manufactured in the United States.

Electric, digital, and acoustic pianos still are very important instruments in popular music. And the grand piano is a fixture on the classical musical stage. However, the piano has lost its prominent spot in today's middle-class homes.

Estella's son Frank Roney, a graduate of Hartwick College, resided in his mother's home. He was the second oldest of her three sons and did graduate work at the University of Rochester. Estella's parents also shared the house. Her father, Henry, had one year of high school; her mother, Mary, finished the eight years of grammar school. Gilbert Flood, the youngest brother of Jane Skutt, lived in the Roney house as a lodger. Gilbert was a high school graduate who served as a bookkeeper for his brother-in-law, A. Gray Skutt, at the Bean House, O. A. Skutt Company.

Estella was the widow of Dr. Frank Fiero Roney (1876–1932), a medical doctor. Frank was the son of Adelbert Roney (1849–1923) and Josephine Turk Roney (1848–1899) of Milo (Yates County). Adelbert was a laborer. Frank was a graduate of Genesee Wesleyan Seminary at Lima (Yates County). In September 1897 Frank enrolled in a teacher training class at Penn Yan Academy. That year he was working in Dresden (Yates County). In 1900 Frank was a hardware salesman in Penn Yan (Yates County).

Frank and Estella married at Estella's home in Kendall (Orleans County) in June 1912. At the time of his marriage to Estella, he was studying at the University of Buffalo to earn an MD degree. Estella had attended Syracuse University for two years. In June 1914 the Rev. J.W. Searles and his family, Dr. and Estella Roney, and Flora Russell spent a day playing tennis at H.E. Wellman's home in Kendall. By 1915 Dr. Roney was practicing medicine in North Rose. Dr. Roney served in an Army hospital late in World War I. Adelbert, Frank's father, died in Rochester in June 1923. Calling hours were at his sister Mary Yost's home, in Himrod (Yates County). Dr. Frank Roney was with his father at the time of his father's death.

In May 1927, Dr. Roney, Charles Betts and Fred Shepard of Lyons, and Elias and Bertha Croucher of Newark embarked—most likely from New York City or Philadelphia—on the *S.S. Mohawk* of the Clyde Steamship Company to Jacksonville, Florida. Thomas Clyde, the marine engineer who designed the first screw-drive steamship in America, founded the steamship company in 1884. It bore no connection with Clyde, New York. In August 1930 Dr. Roney was driving his car when it collided with a motorcycle ridden by Orlie Miles. The 17-year-old from Flint (Ontario County) perished. Two passengers who Miles was carrying sustained injuries. For reasons not related to the accident, Dr. Roney died in a New York City hospital in March 1932. He had served as North Rose's physician for 17 years.

In March 1951 Frank married Nancy Cynthia Russell (1926–1999) of Brookline, Massachusetts, at the Old South Church in Boston. Nancy graduated from Smith College. Frank and Nancy made their home in Cambridge, Massachusetts. In October 1952 Frank died in a car accident in Paramus, New Jersey, where he'd recently started a new job as a chemist, leaving his wife and infant daughter, Cynthia Roney. Nancy then married a Canadian, George Yetman (1923–1977), and Cynthia grew up in Grand Falls, Newfoundland and Labrador. Like her mother, Cynthia graduated from Smith College. She also got master's degrees from Columbia and the Yale School of Management. She has worked at Bankers Trust and the Bank of America and served as chairman of the board of the International Grenfell Association, a nonprofit that aims to keep the spirit of service alive in Newfoundland and Labrador. She married Robert Goldstein, a graduate of Vassar College and the New York University School of Law, in 1986. The couple made their home in New York City.

Estella, Martha Peck, Belle Fox, and Florence Quereau visited Watkins Glen in February 1956. In April 1957 Estella and her cousin Flora Roney held a 10th-anniversary dinner at Palmyra's Garlock House in honor of her son Merrill and his wife, Marie. Guests were Frank and Louise Noyes, Ernest and Carrie Favreau, Ernest Jr., and Charles and Doris Castor.

Estella Roney's eldest son, Gordon Heyd Roney (1914–1969), was in a group of Boy Scouts who traveled in May 1930 to see the Oakfield (Genesee County) gypsum mines. Gordon married Rose Ellen Conway (1918–1988); they had 12 children (in no particular order): John, Gordon, Jimmy, Donald, Jean Ellen, Rebecca, Beth, Charles, Robert, Frank, Kathleen, and Rick. Gordon worked as an engineer for GE in Bridgeport, Connecticut, and Louisville, Kentucky.

Estella's youngest son, Judson Merrill Roney (1920–2009), settled in Palmyra with his wife, Marie Hunter Roney (1925–2016), and their three children: Lee Albert, Lincoln Merrill, and Diane Marie. Judson worked as a lab assistant at Eastman Kodak in Rochester in 1941.

He served for nearly three years in the Army Signal Corps in Eritrea, East Africa, during World War II. Marie taught French for almost three decades in the Palmyra–Macedon school district.

In the late 1950s, Estella moved in with Judson and his family in Palmyra and offered piano lessons from a music studio in his house. The headline in the *Democrat and Chronicle* when she died at 81 in 1968 read: "Piano Teacher to 1,500 Passes."

Salter, Edward & Myrta*

Estimated 1940 value: $6,000.
Edward Adrian Salter (1880–1948), 59, head of household, proprietor, self-employed, 52 weeks for $4,200.
Myrta Ball Salter (1880–1956), 59, wife, officer of corporation, $1,600.

THE CANNING FACTORY OWNER, followed by his son Leon, headed what was probably North Rose's most prosperous family. In 1881, at the age of 1, Edward A. Salter moved with his family to North Rose from Sodus. His father was a foreman on the railroad. Edward graduated from North Rose Grammar School and then finished high school in Wolcott. He started his business career working with Orrin A. Skutt drying apples in Hop Bottom, Pennsylvania. The next year Edward dried apples in Ohio and Michigan. In 1907 he traded his village home for Nelson Graham's farm just east of North Rose. He also worked as a carpenter and as a warehouse laborer. That same year Edward bought the first car in use in North Rose, a Cadillac. In 1910 Edward began canning apples in Lyons. Two years later, he had built a canning factory in North Rose, which he operated for many years, canning many different fruits and vegetables. He passed the day-to-day business of the Canning Factory on to his son upon Leon's graduation from Dartmouth in 1924. (See "Salter, Leon & Thelma.")

Meanwhile, both Salters earned the ire of North Rose homemakers. When the Canning Factory produced canned fruits and vegetables, cooking was part of the canning process. A quantity of dark black soot accompanied the smoke out of the Canning Factory chimney. In the days before homes had clothes dryers, the homemaker often hung the laundry out to dry, pinned onto clotheslines. Depending on the wind's direction, the homemaker had to scramble to bring the still-damp wash inside before it was "decorated" with small black spots. If the homemaker was not fast enough to gather in the wash before the black soot landed on the clothes, the conscientious homemaker had to start the labor-intensive wash-day process all over again.

For information on Myrta's family, see the entry for her adopted brother: "Ball, George & Maude."

Salter, Leon & Thelma*
Estimated 1940 value: $10,000.
Leon Jay Salter (1903–1979), 36, officer of corporation, 52 weeks for $5,000.
Thelma B. Salter (1904–1962), 36, wife, homemaker.

EDWARD'S SON LEON WAS A MAN of many interests. In addition to operating the Canning Factory, he was an excellent amateur painter; he had a beautifully displayed and documented collection of Native American artifacts. Leon also was a collector of fine art. Marilyn Skutt's late husband, John M. Roberts, was surprised to see a monumental sculpture by Henry Moore in Leon's garden. Many art critics consider Moore to be the best sculptor of the 20th century. Some critics have called him the best artist of any sort of that era. In recent years, sculptures by Moore sold at auction in the seven figures.

Leon studied literature at Dartmouth. He married Thelma Brede of Schenectady (Schenectady County) in 1924, also an artist.

In May 1941 both Leon and Thelma were awarded prizes at the New York State Exhibition of Oils and Water Colors in Syracuse, the first of its kind. Sixteen of the 169 artists represented from across the state won $250 for oil or $150 for watercolor, with the best in class receiving an additional $50. From the *Syracuse Herald-American*: "The paintings shown are from 'unknowns,' mostly self-taught and painting on New York State farms and in villages in various sections of the State." Thomas Watson, president of International Business Machines and honorary chairman of the exhibition committee, spoke at a dinner at the Century Club before the opening at the Syracuse Museum of Fine Arts. Another prize winner that year: "81-year-old Anna Mary Moses of Eagle Bridge, who took up painting only three years ago and whose work, show directors say, merits serious consideration of the judges," according to *The New York Times*.

The Salters were back at the newly renovated Syracuse Museum of Fine Arts in October 1944, sitting at the head table for an "Autumn Supper" with guest of honor Grandma Moses, who was completing a solo exhibition there. Leon was a longtime friend and mentor to the famous folk artist. Leon painted under the pseudonym Zouté, said to be a play on his last name: "zoute" is Dutch for "salty." Zouté had one-man shows at the Whitney Museum in New York City and the Mortimer Levitt Gallery.

At the 1946–1947 State University of Iowa International Show, Zouté exhibited alongside such artists as Picasso, Klee, and Braque. It's reported that he painted only from 1940 to 1954, when Thelma became ill. She died in 1962 and Leon never painted again.

Satterlee, Gene & Mae

42 North Huron Street, now 5098 North Huron—Built in 1910. Estimated 1940 value: $2,000.
Eugene Satterlee (1879–1942), 61, head of household, laborer in the Canning Factory, 25 weeks for $350.
Mae Elizabeth Thomas Satterlee (1895–1981), 44, wife, homemaker and bean picker (sorter) at the bean elevator, 24 weeks for $250.
Edwin D. Thomas (1860–1945), 79, father-in-law, retired.
Mary Elizabeth Hess Thomas (1858–1944), 81, mother-in-law, retired.

GENE HAD COMPLETED FIVE YEARS of school and worked as a laborer for the Salter Canning Company. He grew up in Big Indian (Ulster

County). Mae completed two years of high school and worked as a bean picker (in the O. A. Skutt Co. Bean House). She was from Huron. Mae's parents lived with Gene and their daughter.

Edwin and Mary Thomas had each completed five years of school. Edwin was the son of Philip Thomas Sr. (1825–1904), a veteran of the Civil War, and Charlotte Morey (1823–1907). Edwin worked on E.B. Dowd's farm that year. Edwin and Mary wed in December 1883. Around 1910 Edwin led the singing at a temperance meeting held in North Huron. In December 1911 the North Rose Methodist Church chose Mae to be the organist at Sunday school. She attended the Epworth League Convention in Waterloo in May 1912. Edwin and Mary moved to Wolcott in 1943.

Before he married, Eugene was a bit of a wanderer. He spent the winters of 1913 and 1914 in Florida. In the summer of 1914 Eugene lived in Clinton County near Lake Champlain. Gene and Mae married in July 1915. The groom's parents were Uriah Satterlee (1837–1917) and Delia Wright Satterlee (1845–1905). During their first wedded month, Gene and Mae, along with Will and Dora Lundergun, visited the B.H. Satterlee family in Oliverea (Ulster County). (Dora was Gene's cousin.) The next month, Gene, Mae, and the Lunderguns took an automobile trip to the Adirondacks. Gene and Mae soon had two sons: Harold (1916–1970) and Russell (1917–1996). In November 1917 the Satterlees moved to Fulton. In the winter of 1920 Mae lived with her relatives by marriage: Gene's cousins Dora Satterlee Lundergun and Katherine "Katie" Satterlee Proseus. In August 1924 Gene purchased the George house on Huron Street in North Rose.

In March 1926 Mae achieved selection as secretary of the Ladies Aid Society. In May 1941 Gene and Mae visited Roy and Nancy Du Bois in Johnson City (Broome County). Their favorite traveling companions remained Will and Dora Lundergun, who accompanied them on this trip. Gene died in July 1942. Two years after Gene's death, Mae married a widower, Jesse Terry Briggs (1875–1955). (See "Briggs, Jesse & Eunice.") Jesse was a tailor working in Wolcott and North Rose. For several years he was employed by Eastman Kodak.

His parents were Birney Briggs (1842–1927) and Anna Terry-Briggs (1845–1922) of North Rose.

Gene and Mae's son Harold moved to Clyde. He married Mary Johnson at Street John's Catholic Church in Clyde. Harold was in the produce business. Harold and Mary had children named Mary Jean, Harold Jr., and Samuel. In World War II, Harold fought in the South Pacific. Mary's 20-year-old brother died in action in France in August 1944. In 1954 Harold founded an American Legion Post in North Rose. In 1967 he was the commander of the Brown-DiSanto Post 226 of the Veterans of Foreign Wars.

Mary Jean, a social studies teacher, married James Munger, a science teacher and an alumnus of Cornell University. Mary Jean attended Auburn Community College and the State University College in Oswego. She became a history teacher at Mexico Academy and Central School (Oswego County). Her husband also taught at Mexico Academy and Central School. They had a son and a daughter.

Gleason Corporation, a machine tool and gear manufacturer in Rochester, employed Harold Jr. (Gleason was said to have the most handsome factory building in Rochester. The neoclassical building was constructed in 1910.) In July 1971 Harold Jr. married Dorothy Baker, an employee at the North Rose Pharmacy. They lived in Rose.

Harold's brother Russell joined the Army in 1939. He qualified as a cook, and by 1942 he was a staff sergeant. By 1948 Russell married, had a daughter, Gladys Jean, and lived in Wichita, Kansas. In the early spring of 1950, Jesse and Mae paid a multi-week visit to Russell's family in Wichita. They repeated the holiday trip in 1953 and 1954. In 1957 another daughter joined Russell's family. At the time of the new addition, Gladys was 12 years old.

Seager, Candace

9 Elm Street, now 4965 Elm—Built in 1938. Estimated 1940 value: $1,000.

Candace O. Bumpus Seager (1860–1944), 79, head of household, homemaker.

Alta C. Seager Vernoy (1893–1979), 47, daughter, home worker, 10 weeks for $5 a week.
Bertha Seager (1894–1941), 45, daughter, home worker, 8 weeks for $5 a week.

CANDACE SEAGER, A WIDOW, and her two daughters—Alta Vernoy, also a widow, and Bertha, who was single—were living together. Candace was a homemaker. Alta and Bertha had been home workers for a private family, but both were unemployed in April 1940. Candace finished the seventh grade, Bertha completed the ninth, and Alta was a high school graduate.

Candace was born in the rural Town of Richland (Oswego County). When she was 20, she moved from Richland to the nearby village of Pulaski to live with her uncle and grandmother. In 1890 Candace married one of the three George Seagers living in the region at the time. Candace's George Seager was born in 1852 and died in 1938. A second George Seager was living in Alton. The third lived in Rose, was a Civil War veteran, and was about 10 years older than Candace's husband.

In 1900 the family included Candace and George Seager, the Seagers' two young daughters, and Earl A.W. Seager (1880–1980)—George's son from his previous marriage to Emma Mariah Sprong. George had two other children from his first marriage. His daughter Maude (1872–1946) had left the household after marrying Arthur Tryon (1871–) in 1899. They made their home in Aurelius (Cayuga County) and had two daughters, Ruth and Grace. The Tryons moved to North Tonawanda after 1910, where Arthur worked as a carpenter. George's son Ernest (1877–1941) lived in a boarding house in Rome (Oneida County) in 1900. A few years later he married Catherine "Kitty" Cronk (1877–1935). They raised four children in Rome: Wayne, Wesley, Winifred, and Kenneth.

In 1900 George and Earl were employed as farm laborers. In 1910 the Seagers lived on a farm that George worked in a rural area of the Town of Rose; Earl had married his first cousin Ada and left the household. (See "Seager, Earl & Ada.") In 1920 George was employed as a state road patrolman. He was also a member of the Masonic Lodge. Mr. and Mrs. William Kennedy of Lyons were frequent guests at the Seagers' home.

In November 1934, after George was diagnosed with cancer, Earl and his wife drove his parents to Buffalo so his father could enter the Gratwick Institute for treatment. (The institute began as an experimental laboratory funded by the Gratwick family and operated by Dr. Roswell Park.) Unfortunately the Seagers' car was in an accident in Buffalo, and Candace suffered a broken arm and injured shoulder. George survived for another four years—dying in June 1938.

Candace spent a few days in Rochester with her sister Mattie Bumpus Sprague in May of 1941 and died in 1944.

The Seagers' daughters, Bertha and Alta, both joined the Methodist Church in their youth. In the fall of 1921 Bertha fell and broke several ribs while working in the Canning Factory. None of the three Seager ladies were employed in 1930. Bertha died in 1941.

A graduate of Wolcott's Leavenworth High School, Alta was a member of the Class of 1913. In 1917 she married Hugh Vernoy (1896–1930) in Wolcott. The couple established a home on Covell Road in the western portion of the Town of Rose and had two children: Leon Seager Vernoy (1918–2005) and Olive Ruth Vernoy (1920–2012). In the late spring of 1924, the Vernoys were living in Skaneateles Junction in the Town of Elbridge (Onondaga County), when Alta's sister, Bertha, paid them a six-week visit. In 1925 Hugh Vernoy was a laborer for an ice company. The Vernoys owned a $3,000 home in Auburn when Hugh died in Wolcott in 1930. Hugh had been self-employed as a trucker and owned his own truck.

By 1940 Alta's children were grown and she had moved into her mother's home in North Rose. In 1954 she was living in Willard (Seneca County). She died at the Willard Psychiatric Center in 1979.

Seager, Earl & Ada

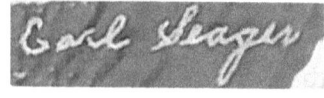

9 Maple Avenue, now 10393 Maple—Built in 1910. Estimated 1940 value: $1,000.

Earl Asher Washington Seager (1880–1980), 59, head of household, laborer, 35 weeks for $15 a week.
Ada Seager (1881–1972), 58, wife, trimmer, 23 weeks for $12 a week.

FIRST COUSINS EARL SEAGER AND Ada Seager were married in March 1909. Earl had six years of education. In 1940 he was unable to work but had worked 35 weeks as a laborer in a fruit-packing house during 1939. Ada completed the eighth grade, was a homemaker, and also worked part-time as a trimmer at the Canning Factory.

In 1900 Earl was living with his parents in the Town of Rose. He was a farm laborer, as was his father. At that time Ada was living with her parents and working as a milliner's apprentice. Soon after they were married, the Seagers fostered a 1-year-old: Eleanor F. Elmhurst. She soon returned to her birth family and went on to graduate from Geneseo Normal School. During the First World War, Earl worked at a Rochester munitions plant, Symington Machine Corporation.

Belle Kitchen, Ada's half-sister, was living with the Seagers and working as a clerk in the post office in 1920. She married a widower, James Odell Miner, in February 1921 and had two daughters, Ruth and Dorthea. Belle was still working at the post office in 1940.

Earl was a member of the North Rose Methodist Church, a former director of the North Rose Cold Storage, and, in time, a 60-year member of the Rose Masonic Lodge No. 590. In October 1931 Earl entered the Clifton Springs Sanitarium for treatment. In 1932 he served as tax collector for the NRCS in the towns of Huron and Rose. Earl filled in as a mail carrier during Chelsea Harper's vacation in June 1940. He lived to the age of 100.

Seelye, Frank & Alda

8 Gray Street, now 5032 Gray—Built in 1850. 1940 monthly rent: $10.
Frank Ernest Seelye (1891–1968), 49, head of household, proprietor, ladder manufacturer.
Alda Chloe Luffman Seelye (1892–1988), 48, wife, homemaker.

FRANK AND ALDA HAD BOTH graduated from high school. Frank owned a shop that manufactured ladders. Its specialty was ladders for fruit picking. Alda was a homemaker. Frank was born in Okobojo, South Dakota, and Alda was born in Calumet, Wisconsin. Frank was the son of Ernest Osgood Seelye (1858–1937) and Edith Gertrude Chaddock Seelye (1862–1940). Both of Frank's parents were born in New York State.

Alda was the daughter of George Leroy Luffman (1840–1926) and Ada Marie Merrill Luffman (1862–1953). George Luffman previously married Mary McIntyre in 1863, but that marriage ended in divorce in the 1870s. George was a native of Wolcott, who had moved to Chilton, Wisconsin. There he met Ada Merrill. George and Ada married in 1887. By 1905 George and Ada had moved to Wayne County. George farmed in Butler. Years later, after George's death, Ada moved to Wolcott.

Ernest, Edith, and their son Frank lived in South Dakota for several years. Then the family returned to New York State about 1893. Ernest farmed in the Town of Rose in 1900. Frank, his father, and Judson Sheffield fished together on Sodus Bay in September 1911. Frank and Alda married in 1912. Before marrying Frank, Alda taught school in Resort. Frank and Alda spent the early years of their marriage in Butler, where Frank farmed. (His mother was named Ada Seelye and his wife was named Alda Seelye!) Frank purchased Mary Atkinson's home in February 1920 and lived there while he worked his father's farm. In November 1920 Frank hunted in the North Woods.

Frank and Alda had two sons: Carson Luffman Seelye (1913–2000) and Dorr Frank Seelye (1914–2001). In August 1923 Frank and Alda lived in Wolcott. By 1930 the four Seelyes had moved to the Town of Rose. Frank was still farming. After a brief stay in Oswego, Frank and his family moved into the North Rose Inn in March 1935. He had planned to move into the house formerly occupied by Ed Laird, but that plan didn't come together. Frank owned and operated Seelye Apartments across from NRCS for many years. Each unit was partially furnished and was suited for one or two persons. Because of their proximity to the school, they were popular with teachers.

Frank was an avid collector of Native American artifacts. He was a member of the Archaeological Society of Central New York. His other memberships included the North Rose Volunteer Fire Company and the Wolcott Baptist Church. In 1965 Frank won the election for the first vice president of the North Rose Lions Club.

Carson married Nedra Lucille Armstrong (1913–1990) in April 1934. In September 1934 the newlyweds lived in Weedsport. They entertained Frank, Alda, Dorr, and Dorr's future wife, Beatrice Briggs, at Thanksgiving dinner in 1934. Carson and Nedra soon moved to Clyde, and Carson worked as a grocery clerk. In February 1935 Carson and Nedra held a large birthday dinner for Frank. In April 1935 Carson and Nedra moved into the Farrow house on Main Street in North Rose. Just the next month, Nedra's 18-year-old sister Virginia Armstrong of Rose perished in a one-car auto accident at 3 a.m. after a dance held near Wolcott. Kenneth Fowler, the driver, who had attended the party with his wife, also died. The accident occurred on the Wolcott–Red Creek highway. In October 1935 Carson and Nedra moved to the Winters Block in Clyde. Carson was working for his brother-in-law LaVerne Terbush. Frank began manufacturing ladders around that time.

In September 1936 Carson and Nedra took a trip to Callender, Ontario, Canada, with William Rice and they saw the Dionne quintuplets. The quintuplets, born in Ontario, Canada, in 1934, were the first known quintuplets to have survived infancy. When the five sisters were four months old, the Ontario government ruled their parents unfit and took control of the baby girls. Ontario began to see their value as a tourist attraction. The provincial authorities constructed a nursery complex where visitors could watch the quintuplets playing on a playground. They designed the nursery so that visitors could see the sisters, but the girls could not see the viewers. Almost 3 million people walked through the gallery from 1936 to 1943. Their mother ran a nearby souvenir store and concession stand. The two midwives who assisted a doctor in the babies' births also opened a shop. The Dionne sisters led regimented lives, and nurses raised them. They endorsed many products. "Quintland" during this period was Canada's most popular tourist attraction, surpassing Niagara Falls. The family won control of the girls in 1943. In 1998 the surviving sisters reached a $2.8 million settlement with the Ontario government as compensation for their exploitation. The Seelyes and William Rice saw the girls when they were 2. On Christmas Day in 1937, Carson and Nedra hosted Nedra's parents, Merton and Elsie Armstrong, Lellavene Armstrong, and LaVerne and Hazel Terbush (a sister of Nedra), and the Terbushes' son, Dick.

Frank and Alda took a trip to Pulaski (Oswego County) and Camden (Oneida County) in August 1941. They ate a picnic dinner on the dry rocks along the Salmon River, which flows west to Lake Ontario. Alda read and dipped her feet in the water. Frank explored along the riverbed. Suddenly, the flow of water in the river intensified. Alda left her shoes and stockings to the torrent and clambered to safety. Frank was standing on the opposite bank of a river now too deep to cross. Unbeknownst to the Seelyes, authorities had opened a dam upstream, and it discharged a great deal of water. Frank walked until he reached a bridge. He crossed the river and returned to Alda and their automobile.

In January 1958 Frank and Alda traveled to Florida for a few weeks with Henry and Hattie Gage.

In 1939 a daughter, Carol Linda, was born to Carson and Nedra. Carol matriculated in the autumn of 1957 at SUNY Cobleskill in a two-year program of nursery education. In October 1959 Carol married Olan W. Shipley (1937–2015), the son of Warren (1906–1993) and Thelma Edith Poole Shipley (1910–2000) of North Rose.

Nedra took a job as a cashier at the Clyde Cash Market in June 1948. She had earlier worked in the Red and White grocery assisting her brother-in-law LaVerne Terbush, who managed the enterprise. Carson and Dorr began working with their father at Seelye Ladders.

Thirty-five business owners established the Town of Rose Chamber of Commerce in April 1956. Carson was a Chamber officer for many years, including in the role of president in 1957. A crowd of 50 enjoyed a bullhead dinner preceding a business meeting at Lotus Lodge. Carson was a leader of the North Rose Lions Club at its founding in 1958. The Wolcott Lions Club sponsored the fledgling North Rose organization.

Dorr was the salutatorian when he graduated from NRCS in June 1933. In February 1935, Dorr, Frank, and Alda lived in Oswego. Carson and Dorr ran Seelye Ladders in the 1950s. They had added metal ladders and "related equipment," such as backyard playgrounds, to their repertoire. The company was a distributor and a manufacturer, so it is unclear whether the North Rose plant produced the metal ladders. Their newspaper advertisements proclaimed that Seelye Ladders had been in business "since 1935."

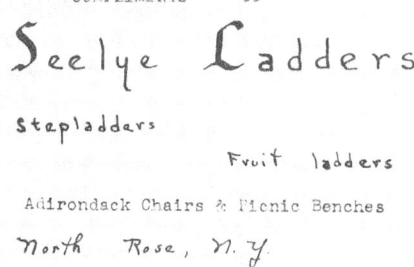

This advertisement for Seelye Ladders appeared in the 1946 NRCS yearbook.

Dorr married Beatrice "Bessie" Belva Briggs (1912–1994) in June 1936. They honeymooned at Niagara Falls. The couple's first home was on a farm north of North Rose. In 1941, Dorr, Beatrice, and their daughter, Ellen, moved to the Mitchell farm near North Rose. Dorr and Beatrice lived in Clyde in 1940. They had two children, Ellen Ann and James D. In the 1950s Dorr and Fred Durbin attended the layman's conference of the Central New York Council of the Methodist Church at Casowasco on a September 1953 weekend. Dorr was the leader of the Laymen's Sundays, in which the members of the congregation took over the responsibilities of the minister for the week, at the North Rose Methodist church in October 1954, October 1957, and October 1958.

In November 1949 Dorr went on an eventful hunting trip with several friends from the area around North Rose. A spark from the campfire set two large tents ablaze. The hunters were outside the shelters, as were their guns, but the fire destroyed lots of camping equipment, and the intrepid hunters—who included Dorr, Claude Collier, Vincent Galloway, and Paul McOmber—went home. The most sensational moment of this escapade was when the boxed ammo began exploding!

Carson bought control of the Seelye Ladder Company from Dorr in June 1961 and became a grandfather in March 1962, when Carol and Olan became the parents of Sonia Michele Shipley. In a lengthy jury trial in January 1964 in Albion (Orleans County), 12 jurors found the Carson Seelye Ladder Company bore no responsibility for a ladder-related accident that occurred in the Duffy-Mott plant in Holley (Orleans County).

Seelye Ladders
A remembrance from Allan Mitchell:

My dad used Seelye ladders on our fruit farm for as long as Frank and the boys made them, and when I took over the farm I used them. I remember as a young boy when Frank made a ladder he put the top end on a bench and the bottom end on the floor. He would then walk up on the rungs and if the ladder didn't break it was ready for sale. They always used basswood for the sides and ash for the rungs. This made a light ladder. They had a sawmill on the premises and sawed their material. They then stacked it to carefully dry it.

They also repaired broken ladders. They would take them apart and replace any broken parts.

I knew both Carson and Dorr and did business with them for years. Carson sold the business to a man (don't know his name) from Syracuse. The last owner was Bub Seager, who had the business at the corner of Brick Schoolhouse Road and Route 104. Bub quit building ladders because of the liability. The regulations that government put on the owner was too much.

One other thing—they made the best ladder available.

Carson Seelye won the election as treasurer of the North Rose Chamber of Commerce in May 1974. Carson lived in Manatee County, Florida, from 1978 until his death in 2000. After Dorr sold controlling interest in the Seelye Ladder Company to Carson, Dorr secured a job at Sidney B. Ruby industrial auto supplies in Rochester.

Ellen graduated from NRCS in 1958; she earned a degree in music education from SUNY Potsdam in 1962. In August of that year her parents announced Ellen's engagement to Eugene Schwarz of Fair Haven. Both Ellen and Eugene worked in Virginia. Eugene had served four years in the Navy.

Ellen Seelye, NRCS Class of 1958

James was a member of Scout Troop No. 109. In August 1956 the troop spent a week at Camp Babcock-Hovey in Ovid on the east side of Seneca Lake. In August 1956 James received his first-class Boy Scout designation. In July 1957 James attended the Methodist camp at Loyalsock, Pennsylvania. In October 1960 James garnered election to a post in the Intermediate Methodist Youth Fellowship. James graduated from NRCS in 1961. He suffered a rib injury in May 1963 when his car overturned while proceeding north on Route 14. In 1994 he lived in Trout Run, Pennsylvania, with his wife Virginia.

Shear, Steven & Margaret
1940 monthly rent: $18.
Steven Shear (1864–1940), 76, retired.
Margaret Shear (1869–1947), 70, retired.

We were unable to obtain more than the cursory information provided by the census for this household. If you have information about the Shears, see page 32.

Sidler, Harry & Lena
Estimated 1940 value: $1,800.
Harry Sidler (1886–1955), 53, head of household, laborer (private road builder), 32 weeks at $650.
Lena Sidler (1889–1975), 50, wife, homemaker.
Albert Sidler (1917–1993), 23, son, salesman for correspondence school, 30 weeks at $450.

Lawrence Sidler (1918–ca. 2013), 21, son, magazine subscription salesman, 20 weeks at $300.
Nina Sidler (1927–2016), 12, daughter, student.
Lois Barnes (1918–2013), 21, lodger, comptometer operator at the Canning Factory, 15 weeks at $150.

We were unable to obtain more than the cursory information provided by the census for this household. If you have information about the Sidlers, see page 32.

Skinner, Bud & Virginia
Eastern North Rose home—rent unknown.
(Marion) Boyce "Bud" Skinner (1914–1983), 25, head of household, laborer, 25 weeks for $16 a week.
Virginia M. Conrow Skinner (1919–2008), 20, wife, bean picker (sorter), 30 weeks for $8 a week.
(Francis) Mark Skinner (1913–2002), 27, brother, mechanic, 52 weeks at $12 a week.

By March 1939 Virginia and Bud Skinner were married and sharing a rental home with Bud's older brother Mark. Bud and Mark had been living in the house since at least 1935—before the couple was married and while Virginia was still living in Clyde. Bud was a laborer at the Cold Storage, Virginia was a sorter at the Bean House, and Mark was a mechanic at a retail hardware store. Bud completed the ninth grade. Virginia and Mark were high school graduates.

Bud and Mark were born in Baltimore, Maryland, and moved to Clyde with their parents, Francis M. "Pete" Skinner (1882–1948) and Margaret May Mark Skinner (1895–1924). Pete remarried after Margaret May died; he opened a barbershop in North Rose and moved there with Ethel and his children. (See "Skinner, Pete & Ethel.")

Bud and Virginia vacationed in Florida in March 1939. In July 1940 they bought the Kellogg Farm, halfway between Rose and North Rose. In the 1940s they moved to various spots in Cayuga, Onondaga, and Wayne Counties, finally settling in Jordan (Onondaga County), where Bud owned and operated the Jordan Liquor Store and was a school bus driver for 11 years. He retired in 1976.

Virginia was active in the Rebekah Lodge in both North Rose and Clyde. She and Bud moved in 1981 to Weedsport (Cayuga County). Virginia worked at GTE and OCM BOCES (Onondaga Cortland Madison Board of Cooperative Extension). She died in 2008.

Bud and Virginia had two sons: Ronald "Ronnie" Boyce Skinner (1946–2005) and Robert "Bob" A. Skinner (1952–2008). Born in Syracuse, Ronnie lived in Jordan (Onondaga County) and was employed as a custodian and substitute bus driver by the Jordan-Elbridge School District until 1972. Then he moved to California and became a truck driver. He had three children, Ronald Jr., Christine, and Neil. The first two lived in California; and Neil in Baldwinsville (Onondaga County). Ronnie died at his home in Pleasant Grove, California, in September 2005.

Ronnie's brother, Bob, was also born in Syracuse. He lived in Camillus (Onondaga County) and Weedsport (Cayuga County), and was a 1971 graduate of Jordan-Elbridge High School. An avid motorcyclist, Bob was the owner of Skinner's Custom Cycles in Elbridge. His wife, Chyrl, died in 1996, and he died in September 2008. Bob was survived by his daughter, Tammy M. Skinner of Jordan, and two stepdaughters, Rachel Connor and Jennifer Smith, of Vermont.

Mark Skinner and Leona Burns on their wedding day in May 1942. Leona's mother, Addie Burns, is watching from the porch.

In April 1941 Mark Skinner was working at Sargent and Greenleaf (a precision lock and safe manufacturer) in Rochester. In May 1942 Mark married Leona Burns, a nurse at Highland Hospital in Rochester, and Bud was his best man. The couple had two sons, Dale and Dean. In July 1949 Mark and Leona visited Mr. and Mrs. Russell Satterlee in Wichita, Kansas. Both Mark's and Boyce's families often visited Elery Mills and Leona Irene Faily Mills in North Rose. Mark lived in Rochester and then Henrietta (Monroe County) until he died at the age of 89.

Skinner, Pete & Ethel

Estimated 1940 value: $3,000.
Francis Marion "Pete" Skinner (1882–1948), 57, head of household, self-employed, proprietor of barbershop.
Ethel May Harris Hill Skinner (1895–1970), 44, wife, bean picker, 2 weeks for $20.
Paul Edward Baker (1922–1976), 18, stepson-in-law, student.
Margery Elizabeth Hill Baker (1922–2015), 18, stepdaughter, occupation omitted, 10 weeks for $105.

PETE SKINNER AND ETHEL HILL MARRIED in 1927; it was a third marriage for Pete and a second for Ethel. Pete's first marriage, in 1903 to Maude Ethel Conklin of Newark, ended in divorce in 1907. Pete grew up in Clyde and Galen, the son of a farm laborer, Francis Marion Skinner Sr. (1847–1912). Pete married Margaret May Mark, and the first three of their four children were born in Baltimore, Maryland: Francis "Mark" Skinner (1913–2002), Marion Boyce "Bud" Skinner (1914–1983), and Adella May "Della" Skinner (1916–2005). The Skinner family moved back to Clyde soon after Della's birth.

In 1920 the Skinner household in Galen was multigenerational, with Pete and Margaret and their three children; Margaret's grandmother, Emma Mark (1852–1927); Pete's mother, Delphine (1856–1923); and Pete's 17-year-old nephew Leroy Cole (1903–1961), the son of his late sister Adella Skinner Cole (1881–1911), who Pete and Margaret's daughter was named after. Pete worked as a barber.

In 1923 Pete's mother died and Pete and Margaret's youngest son, Wayne, was born. Margaret died in 1924. Wayne died in 1925.

After the death of his wife and son, Pete married Ethel Harris Hill, the widow of Roy J. Hill (1887–1923), in 1927. Roy and Ethel had a daughter, Margery Elizabeth Hill (1922–2015), who joined the Skinner household. (Roy was the brother of Frank Hill; see "Hill, Frank & Flora.") In September 1929 Pete opened a barbershop in the Odd Fellows building in North Rose.

In 1930 the Skinner household was comprised of Pete and Ethel, Pete's three surviving children, and Ethel's daughter. By 1935 Pete's sons would move to their own home in North Rose. (See "Skinner, Bud & Virginia.")

Pete's daughter Della appeared in the 1930 census in two places: in North Rose, as the daughter of Pete, in the Skinner household; and in Sparta, New Jersey, as the niece of the Rev. Frederick Mudge and his wife, Jennie Owens Mudge. Frederick Mudge was a Presbyterian minister in Clyde in the mid-1920s before taking his final post in Sparta. It seems Della was sent to live with them in 1930. She graduated from Wilson College in Chambersburg, Pennsylvania, and married Lieutenant Roy Kenneth Nattress (1915–1998) in the Sparta, New Jersey, Presbyterian Church in April 1940. Della's father and her brother Mark attended the wedding. She appeared as the daughter of the Mudges in the 1940 census.

Because Roy Nattress was an Army man, the Nattresses lived in a number of places, including Washington, where their son Roy Kenneth Jr. was born; Massachusetts, where their daughter Jane was born; North Carolina; Colorado; California; Alaska; and Michigan. They retired to Lake Havasu City, Arizona.

In March 1941 Ethel convalesced from a hospital stay at the home of her sister Laura. (See "Payne, Harry & Laura.")

After Pete's death, Ethel sold her home in North Rose to Richard and Dorthea Ball. (See "Ball, George & Maude.") She married her third husband, Roger S. Ewing of Sodus, in July 1950.

Paul Baker's sister and wife had the same name but spelled differently. He grew up in North Rose with his sister, Marjorie (see "Baker, William & Millicent"), and then married Margery Hill.

Paul took part in the senior class play "Look Who's Here" at NRCS in December 1939. Later that month, on the day after Christmas, he and Margery married. In April 1940 the first of their four daughters was born.

Gloria Jean Baker (1940–) married Robert Young in 1960; both were graduates of RIT. They lived in Clearwater, Florida, and Riverton, Utah.

Sharon Baker (1946–1966) died at 20 at Strong Memorial Hospital in Rochester.

Pauletta Baker (1951–) married David Leewood in 1977 and raised a family in Crystal Lake, Illinois, a suburb of Chicago.

Becky Baker (ca. 1953–) married Michael "Sammy" Connelly and had three children: Paul (ca. 1979–2023), Scott, and Kate. They lived in Holley (Orleans County), and Becky taught school at Byron-Bergen Central Schools. Becky divorced Sammy and then married Scott Empey (1955–2014), a beloved hockey coach who led Brockport High School (Monroe County) to a state championship.

In 1942 Paul Baker worked at the Gleason Works in Rochester. In 1950 he was an assistant superintendent at the Canning Factory. Paul died in 1976.

Margery moved from North Rose in 2001 to live with her daughter Pauletta and her family in Crystal Lake, Illinois. She died there at 93 and was buried in the Rose Cemetery.

Skutt, Gray & Jane

67 North Main Street, now 5091 North Main—Built in 1912. Estimated 1940 value: $3,200.

Alexander Gray Skutt (1903–1955), 37, head of household, proprietor, O. A. Skutt Company, self-employed.

Marie Jane Flood Skutt (1909–1968), 31, wife, homemaker.

Joan Marilyn Skutt (1936–2023), 3, daughter.

As was tradition in the Skutt family, Alexander Gray Skutt used his middle name as his personal identifier. He was the son of Orin Alexander Skutt (1878–1933) and Arloa "Loa" Shaver Skutt (1880–1929). Orin was a wholesale commodities dealer, who founded O. A. Skutt Company. Gray and his brother, Orin Watson Skutt (1908–1991), were the fifth generation of Skutts to live in the North Rose area—Jonathan Skutt (1790–1864), who was born in Livingston (Columbia County), was the first to arrive; one of his seven sons was born in Wolcott in 1820 and one of his three daughters was born in Rose in 1825. Jonathan's son Orrin (1811–1892), the second generation of Skutts to live in the North Rose area, married Almira Lamb (1814–1886), a daughter of Isaac Lamb, the first settler of what would become North Rose. (For more about Isaac Lamb, see "Aldrich Land" in "Aldrich, George & Millie.")

Gray grew up in North Rose with his parents and his brother on land carved out of the Aldrich holdings at the intersection of Aldrich Avenue and North Main Street. Gray's best friend and neighbor was George Aldrich.

After he graduated from high school, Gray matriculated at Cornell University, majoring in economics. His brother, who was an enthusiastic trapper, stayed in touch with almost daily letters and he greatly enjoyed opportunities to spend the night with his big brother on campus. Gray finished his required classes in three and a half years,

Gray Skutt (left) and George Aldrich, best friends and next-door neighbors, were both born in 1903.

but his father encouraged him to complete four years of college by taking courses that interested him.

Gray then gained employment in New York City, working on Wall Street selling stocks. Unfortunately this was when the stock market crashed and the North Rose bank failed. It was the Great Depression.

A. Gray Skutt (far right) poses with friends at Cornell University, ca. 1923.

Gray returned to North Rose to help save his father's O. A. Skutt Co. enterprise. He performed this task with great imagination and decided to concentrate on one commodity instead of many. That commodity was red kidney beans. Sadly his mother died shortly after his return to North Rose in 1929 and his father died four years later. At this point Gray became president of the family's principal business, O. A. Skutt Co., with his brother Watson as vice president. They opened bean warehouses throughout Wayne County wherever there was good railroad service. Through their efforts, the business was saved. It ran until the 1970s and helped supply the U.S. forces in World War II with red kidney beans.

Watson married Ruth Lee Town (1908–2004) in October 1936. Ruth was worldly by North Rose standards. For instance, she went to China as a member of a dance troupe in her early years before her marriage. She invited a friend from China to visit her in Rose, which he did to the surprise of some of their neighbors. Ruth would organize plays in which children in the neighborhood would take roles. She collected and repaired dolls. Watson had a good sense of humor. He also had a cabin cruiser that he moored at Henderson Harbor in Jefferson County. He loved boating, fishing, and playing golf at the Sodus Country Club. His brother Gray shared these interests. Ruth and Watson adopted two young girls who were sisters, Judith Ruth "Judy" Skutt (1946–2018) and Doris Lee Skutt (1942–).

Alexander Gray Skutt and Marie Jane Flood on their wedding day, March 30, 1933, in Jane's hometown of Canandaigua

In 1933 Gray married Marie Jane Flood of Canandaigua (Ontario County). Jane also went by her middle name, although this wasn't as strong a tradition in her family. Jane's parents were John Flood (1872–1959) and Clara Engert (1882–1942). Jane had one sister, Elizabeth "Bet" Flood (1903–1992), and three brothers, Arthur "Art" Flood (1905–1959), John "Jack" Flood (1911–1981), and Gilbert "Gib" Flood (1915–1967).

One of Jane's formative experiences was working in a state-funded puppet troupe in high school, traveling the countryside and performing for small audiences in state parks. Her encore performance was a comic routine called the "Crooked Mouth Family" that always brought down the house. Before marrying Gray and moving to North Rose, Jane worked in Rochester at the General Signal Corporation and then for *The Newark Courier* as a society reporter.

In 1936 Gray and Jane had their first child, Joan Marilyn Skutt. Marilyn had a great relationship with her father. When she was old enough, Gray would take his daughter to the movies at least one night a week in Clyde or Wolcott, since there was no longer a movie theater in North Rose at the time.

After a 12-year gap between children, Gray and Jane had Alexander G. Skutt, your author, in 1948. His early childhood was idyllic. One of the best features was the backstop and baseball diamond that Gray had built for him. It was a major attraction for all the kids in the neighborhood.

The Palace was the name of the movie house in North Rose. George Deady built it in 1917 and operated it until selling to Harry Partrick. The business was not sustainable, and the building was demolished in 1932.

Marilyn had the highest GPA of any student in Wayne County her senior year. She got into Cornell, like her father, and moved to Ithaca to begin studying history and political science and, later, education.

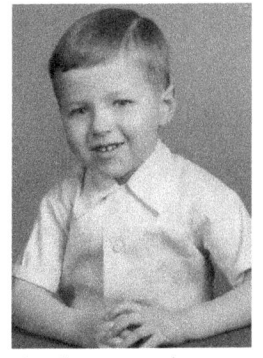

Alex Skutt, your author, in the early 1950s

Both Gray and Jane were very active in community organizations. Gray was the chairperson of the Wayne County Democratic Committee and led the party to more than its share of victories despite the large majority of people registered as Republicans. He attended a presidential nominating convention, where he was an alternate delegate. Among his community services, he was a trustee of the North Rose Methodist Church, a director of the First National Bank of Wolcott, and he served several terms on the North Rose school board. He was a member of a host of local organizations, including Masonic Lodge 590, the North Rose Firemen, the Rose Grange, and the Boy Scout Committee.

Jane was a volunteer for the Aircraft Warning Service during and after World War II. She sometimes took her children to a small building above North Rose's school. They had plastic cards that they held at arm's length to measure the size of airplanes. The code they used when relaying information was "Papa Papa Zero Zero Black" which established that a legitimate report was being made. With her daughter, Marilyn, they headed up the "Cradle Roll" project of the North Rose Methodist Church. This involved sending birthday cards to all the North Rose children on their special day on behalf of the church.

Tragically, in 1955, Gray died of a stroke following kidney surgery. Marilyn was in her freshman year at Cornell, and Alex was only 6 years old. Upon Gray's death, the bean business went to Watson, but the apple farm was left to Alex and Marilyn. Jane, without pay, kept the accounting books and negotiated the deals for the sales of the apples. In 1957 Jane moved the family to Ithaca (Tompkins County) to support Marilyn, who was upset over her father's death. The family continued to visit North Rose on the weekends and spent much of their summers in their cottage on LeRoy Island in Sodus Bay.

Marilyn graduated from Cornell University in 1959. She began her career teaching elementary school at the Belle Sherman School in Ithaca, while still living with Jane and Alex. It was during that time she met John M. "Jack" Roberts (1916–1990), their next-door neighbor, who was an anthropologist at Cornell. Jack was the widower of Marie Louise Kotouc (1917–1957) with two teenage daughters, Tania Marie Roberts (1943–) and Andrea L. Roberts (1946–). Marilyn and Jack married in October 1961, and Marilyn moved in with Jack and his daughters. In 1962 they had their first child, James "Jim" Roberts (1962–). Two years later, they had their second child, John M. Roberts Jr. (1964–).

Marilyn Skutt as a young woman

On August 1, 1968, Jane, Marilyn, and her two sons were in a terrible car accident. Jane was killed, and Marilyn and the boys suffered moderate injuries. The loss was devastating

Marilyn's sons, Jim (left) and John Roberts

for the family. Soon after Jane's death, Alex and Marilyn sold the apple farm because neither of them wanted to pursue farming as a vocation. Shortly after the accident, Marilyn, Jack, and the boys moved to Newport, Rhode Island, for a year while Jack taught at the Naval War College. After returning to Ithaca for another year, they moved to Pittsburgh, where they settled permanently.

Alex had begun attending Cornell University in 1966, studying engineering physics. He was interested in achieving peace, and decided not to accept an aerospace fellowship and instead devoted his attention to combating the war in Southeast Asia with his now longtime friend Steph Cassella. He became co-chair of Movement for a New Congress, an organization that trained students in upstate New York to become political activists. Their efforts helped deliver John Dow of the Hudson Valley back to Congress in the critical midterm election of 1970. Dow was one of only four people in the House who had voted against the passage of the Tonkin Gulf Resolution, which gave President Lyndon B. Johnson permission to conduct the war in Vietnam. In 1972 Alex was active in the McGovern for President efforts in the Southern Finger Lakes area.

The year after McGovern's terrible defeat, Alex decided to open a bookstore with two friends, and so began a lifelong career in the world of books. McBooks Bookstore, named in honor of George McGovern, opened in July 1973. Located at the bottom of Ithaca's east and south hills, convenient for students from both Cornell and Ithaca College, McBooks featured trade paperbacks. A few years later, Alex opened a second store called Quest's End, which specialized in science fiction, mysteries, and games. It was also during this time that Alex began his own publishing house, McBooks Press.

In 1980 Alex moved to Evanston, Illinois, with his girlfriend Katharyn Machan, who was returning to graduate school for a PhD in interpretation at Northwestern University. While in Evanston, Alex analyzed the competition and opened Notoriety, a bookstore that also specialized in cards, gifts, games, toys, and *Dr. Who* memorabilia. At the completion of Katharyn's program, Alex sold the store and the couple returned to Ithaca. While in Illinois, Alex had observed the success of new video-rental businesses, and upon his return added a video-rental section to Quest's End. This addition proved so popular so rapidly that Alex and his business partner Richie Berg decided to sell the bookstores and open a stand-alone video rental store. Alex met his future wife, real estate agent Carol Bushberg, when she was negotiating the sale of the bookstores. They were married in 1990 and had their one child, Ethan B. Skutt, in 1997.

Alex and Richie named their new venture Video Ithaca. In quick succession, they opened a second store in East Hill Plaza, a third in the Cayuga Mall, and then moved the flagship store from the corner of State and Corn streets to a larger retail space at the corner of Route 13 and Cascadilla Street. Their video business became very successful. Alex and Richie sold Video Ithaca in 1996, and Alex turned his attention back to McBooks Press, publishing books for the rest of his career. He specialized in photo books of the Finger Lakes region and nautical fiction. Despite being hampered by Parkinson's disease and blindness in his later years, Alex was still writing and editing and spending time with family and friends in 2025.

Jim Roberts went on to earn both an MBA and a law degree. He worked first in banking, and then as a lawyer in Pittsburgh. John followed in his father's footsteps, getting a doctorate in sociology. He married Aki Takeuchi (1972–) and taught first at the University of New Mexico and then at the University of Wisconsin, Milwaukee.

Ethan earned a BS in mechanical engineering from Northeastern University in Boston. In 2022 he moved back to his hometown of Ithaca with his partner Rebecca Hellman. They enjoyed hearing Alex's stories of the "old days" in North Rose.

The Michigan Lands

The sizable clans of Jonathan Skutt (1790–1864) and his brother Daniel Skutt (1779–1850) heard tales of the inexpensive black farmland in southern Michigan and headed west. After Orrin (one of Jonathan's sons) decided that he preferred New York State to Michigan Territory, he and his wife, Almira Lamb, returned to North Rose. In general, Orrin and Almira's children remained in Wayne County without even giving Michigan a look. Most of the other Skutts settled in Michigan. (Jonathan Skutt was one of the author's great-grandfathers, as was Isaac Lamb.)

An intriguing academic paper by Paul Frymer, "A Rush and a Push and the Land Is Ours: Territorial Expansion, Land Policy, and U.S. State Formation" in *Perspectives on Politics*, volume 12, number 1 (March 2014), argues that the country would benefit in more ways than merely food production from this migration. The two-county-wide band of the southern border of the new Michigan territory would be defended by these settlers, many of whom came armed with rifles. They would alert the U.S. military if the "Indians" returned looking for battle. In fact, the farmers could probably slow any advance by Indian tribes looking to refight the war between the British Army and their Indian Allies known as the Western Confederacy.

After the decisive victory of the U.S. in the Battle of Fallen Timbers in 1794, the British finally evacuated in 1796 and the new United States took over Michigan. Although there was a steady flow of immigrants into Wayne County from the Hudson and Mohawk Valleys and New England, the number of emigrants from Wayne County to Michigan nearly offset the expected population increase. In 70 years, from 1850 to 1920, Wayne County's population increased only 16%, from 44,953 to 48,927.

Although many homesteaders abandoned their home state of New York, nostalgia caused them to repeat some city, town, and village names when they had to make up names for such places in Michigan. Some examples: Rose City, Elmira, Fulton, Geneva, Hudson, Ithaca, Lockport, and Rochester.

Smith, Herbert & Sabra

Main Street. Estimated 1940 value: $1,800.
Herbert Watson Smith (1866–1954), 73, head of household, self-employed, painter/contractor.
Sabra Anna Quereau Smith (1873–1982), 67, wife, trimmer at the Canning Factory, 16 weeks for $191.

SABRA ANNA QUEREAU GREW UP on a farm in Huron. At 16 she worked at a resort in the Catskills owned by her uncle. She remembers serving food to the widow of Gen. George Custer in 1889.

In January 1897 Sabra played the wedding march at the double wedding of Flora Sidler to Frank Hill and Nellie Smart to Frank Quereau (Sabra's cousin).

The October 8, 1897, edition of the *Oswego Daily Times* reported that "Miss Sabra Quereau has returned from the Adirondacks, where she has spent the summer." What they neglected to mention was that she came back as Mrs. Herbert Watson Smith, having married in Hunter (Greene County) on October 3. The couple's first son, George Arthur Smith (1898–1995), was born the following April.

Both Herbert and Sabra completed eight years of school. At the time of the 1900 census they lived with 2-year-old Arthur at the home of Alfred Dowd (1835–1908), a cousin of Sabra's mother's, in Huron. Herbert was a laborer for Alfred on his farm. Alfred's wife had died that February; his only son had died at 8 of diphtheria, and his only daughter was a schoolteacher in Queens.

Herbert and Sabra moved to their own home in Rose before the birth of their younger son, William Howard (1903–1974). Both of Herbert and Sabra's children went by their middle name.

In 1910 and 1920 Herbert had his own cooper shop. Herbert was made a Mason in 1911. He served two terms as Master of Rose Lodge No. 590 and acted as marshall for many years. Sabra was a member of the North Rose United Methodist Church and The Order of the Eastern Star. In 1920 both of their sons were still living with Herbert and Sabra. Arthur was 21 and worked as a clerk for the railroad. Howard was still in school.

Three hundred guests assembled at St. John's Episcopal Church in September 1924 for the wedding of Arthur Smith to Cathleen C. Martin (1903–1925) in her hometown of Sodus. Arthur's brother Howard was best man and Gray Skutt was an usher. Cathleen died 10 months later, perhaps in childbirth. Arthur married again in 1928, to Helen Gallery (1909–1981) of Rochester. Arthur served in the Marines. In 1940 he was a postal clerk in Sodus. In 1950 he was office manager for a processed foods company. Helen was a librarian. Arthur was survived by six children: Clark, Sally, James, Charles, Lizbeth, and Wallace.

Howard Smith left Sodus for New Jersey, where he lived most of his adult life. He worked for 25 years in the savings bond division of the U.S. Treasury Department. His wife, Elizabeth (1906–1995), was a librarian for the Library of Congress in Washington, D.C., for many years. They had two sons, Frederic and Gerald.

After Herbert's death in 1954, Sabra moved to Sodus. In July 1957 Sabra spent a week with Ella Marshall at the Marshalls' cottage on LeRoy Island.

At 98, Sabra took her first plane ride to New Jersey to visit her son Howard. At 101, Sabra was living with her son Arthur in Sodus when she fell and broke her hip. She moved into Blossom View Nursing Home. An article in the *Syracuse Post-Standard* about her 102nd birthday described her volunteer duties as mailman at the nursing home: "She dons a special mail hat, and rolls her wheelchair around from room to room, delivering the mail, sunshine and goodies to all of the patients." She died in her sleep at Blossom View at 109.

Sabra Anna Quereau Smith was one of many Quereaus who settled in North Rose or other towns in Wayne County. Her brother Ross Quereau was a partner in the Quereau general store for many years. (See "Quereau, Florence"; she was Ross's ex-wife.) Harry Quereau, who ran the store for most of his adult life, was her first cousin. (See "Quereau, Harry & Lena."

The first Quereau to come to America was Josue Quereau (1692–1764), who arrived from France sometime before 1722, when his only son, Elias Quereau (1722–1822), was born in New York City. Three generations later, John Quereau (1786–1871) was born in Fredericton, New Brunswick, Canada, where his father, a physician, had moved for about a decade with his family from Yorktown (Westchester County). After returning to Yorktown, John, at about 23, married Phoebe Ryder, who was six or seven years his junior. The couple had 14 children (though the last three did not live to adulthood). John was a farmer. He moved from Yorktown to Standford (Dutchess County) and then in the late 1820s to Sterling (Cayuga County).

Sabra's paternal grandparents were William Quereau (1819–1860) and Sabra A. Myers Quereau (1821–1865). William, a son of John Quereau's, was born in Standford but had moved with his family to Sterling by the age of 10. William and Sabra had eight children—seven boys and a girl—though, like William's parents, John and Phoebe, the last three of their children did not live past the age of 10.

By 1850 William was a farmer living in Wolcott. Six of William's 10 surviving siblings lived in Wayne County at the time: Elias Quereau, Henry Quereau, Margaret Church, and Fanny Mitchell in Wolcott; Joshua Quereau and Ann Swart in Red Creek.

William had a son who was also named William Quereau (1847–1927). The younger William Quereau grew up in Wolcott, married Mary Dowd (1852–1931) in late 1868 or early 1869, and settled in Huron. He was a farmer, like his father, and had four children: Sabra Anna Quereau, Elliott R. Quereau (1875–1949), Ross Watson Quereau (1886–1950), and Dewitt Raymond Quereau (1890–).

Sabra was also descended from Henry Doude, who came over from England in 1639 and settled in Guilford, Connecticut.

Spade, Frank & Mary

10 South Huron Street, now 4990 South Huron—Built in 1900. Estimated 1940 value: $2,000.
Frank Benjamin Spade (1893–1943), 46, head of household, laborer at a sawmill, 32 weeks for $16 a week.
Mary Ethel Brown Spade (1902–1988), 38, wife, homemaker, Canning Factory worker, 12 weeks for $21 a week.

Marion Harry Spade (1924–1995), 16, son, laborer at a sawmill, 16 weeks for $10 a week.
Leo S. Spade (1924–1991), 15, son, student.
LaRue Aileen Spade (1927–1954), 13, daughter, student.

FRANK AND MARY SPADE WERE LIVING with three of their four children: Harry, Leo, and LaRue. The couple's eldest son, Fred Levi Spade (1921–1974), had joined the Army and left home. Frank was a laborer at a sawmill, and Mary was a homemaker who also worked part of the year as a trimmer in the Canning Factory. Their 16-year-old son, Harry, had left school after the ninth grade (three more years of school than either of his parents had attained) and was working alongside his father as a laborer. The two youngest children were students. The boys were all born in Pennsylvania, but LaRue was born in New York State.

Frank was originally from West Virginia but lived in Fulton County, Pennsylvania, as a young man. He was an Army private in World War I. Though he was a resident of North Rose in 1941, his wife and daughter were living in Rochester. In July 1942 Frank lost control of his car, and it overturned in a ditch. Although badly injured, he was taken home by ambulance. Later, he had to be taken to the Barber Hospital in Lyons. He died in 1943.

Mary was born in West Virginia. Her mother, Elizabeth Emery Brown Hendershot (1877–1945), was born in England. Mary underwent serious surgery at Strong Memorial in Rochester in 1934. She married Sidney J. Rupert after Frank died.

Fred served in the Army from January 1940 to August 1945. Assigned to Hawaii, he witnessed the Japanese attack on Pearl Harbor. Later he was injured and was hospitalized at Camp Butler, North Carolina. He was promoted to sergeant. In 1949 Fred married Pearl Lilhan Parks (1911–1997). After the war, he lived in Rochester and worked as a bus driver.

Harry and Leo were both Boy Scouts. Harry was drafted in May 1944. In October, while on leave from the Army, he married Leah Mock of Bradford, Pennsylvania, at his mother's home in Rochester.

Shortly thereafter he was sent to Germany. After being injured in Germany, he was hospitalized in England. Upon his return to the United States, he and Leah moved to North Rose and had three children: Martha Jane, Robert H., and Judy. In March 1950 the family moved into a new home on Caroline Street. Harry was active in the Miner-Young Post 582 of the American Legion, worked as a mason, trucked water, and plowed snow.

In August 1934, when he was about 10, Leo fell from the roof of a building that was under construction. He was knocked unconscious and badly injured. During World War II he became a POW and wasn't liberated until the end of April 1945. After being honorably discharged from the Army, he moved in with his grandfather, Raymond Hendershot. In April 1946 Leo married Violet Younker, in Rose, and the couple had a son, Leo A. Spade.

Leo Sr. was only in his mid-20s when he survived a heart attack in 1949. He worked at the Newark Developmental Center until he retired. He died in Fairport (Monroe County) in May 1991.

LaRue had 26 guests at her 13th birthday party and was selected for the team to represent the second school supervisory district in the Wayne County Spelling Bee. She worked for Todd Forte Telegraph Company of Rochester and then for General Electric in Clyde. She married Graydon D. Lauster (1906–1982) of Clyde and had three daughters, Marie, Marsha, and Maureen. After LaRue's untimely death—she was only in her mid-20s—Graydon Lauster remarried, gaining five stepchildren in the process.

Stone, Homer

14 North Huron Street, now 5040 North Huron—Built in 1875. Estimated 1940 value: $1,000.

Homer Stone (1870–1951), 70, apple sorter at the Cold Storage, 25 weeks for $500.

HOMER DID NOT ATTEND SCHOOL. He worked as a part-time apple sorter at the Cold Storage.

Homer was the son of Warren J. Stone (1825–1890) and Elvira Lovejoy Stone (1825–1870). At 10, Homer lived in the Town of Rose with the family of his aunt, Sophronia Chaddock. Homer was a widower. He married Isabel "Belle" M. Stone (1871–1936) of Iowa in 1891. They had a son, Lyle N. (1893–1915), and a daughter, Verna E. (1896–1991). In 1905 the Stones lived in East Rose. In December 1906 Homer won the election as an officer of the North Rose Camp of the Modern Woodsmen of America. (The Modern Woodsmen is a fraternal and financial service organization.) Belle died at her daughter's home in Milton (Ulster County) in June 1936.

Lyle participated in the Young Men and Boys Bible Study Class of the Presbyterian Church. In October 1911 three tramps attacked Lyle, then 17 years old. They bound him with a rope, beat him, and left him unconscious on the railroad tracks. He suffered nervous trauma from the attack and, for some time, became frenzied when he heard a train whistle. Apparently, he overcame his fear of train sounds, because Lyle took a job as a freight helper on the railroad called the mysteriously named "Hojack" line.

The "Hojack Line"

There are many theories, but no agreement, on the origin of the word "Hojack." One typical story is that an early engineer was more familiar with driving horses or mules than locomotives. When he slowed to a stop at a station, he would call out "Whoa, Jack" as the train came to a halt. This railroad—rather than emulating the Erie Canal and running east and west—hugged the southern shore of Lake Ontario before curving northward towards the St. Lawrence River. This was the path that trains followed through North Rose. The main tracks of the New York Central passed eight miles south through Clyde.

The northern branch that passed through North Rose was the Rome, Watertown, and Ogdensburg railroad. Like many American railroads, it had a disparaging nickname based on its initials. The RW&O Railroad received the informal title "Rotten Wood & Old Rusty Rails." In 1878 the railroad merged into the Delaware, Lackawanna & Western, nicknamed the "Delay, Linger & Wait."

After service extended from Rochester to Sackets Harbor (Jefferson County), it first operated as an autonomous entity; then, in 1891, it became part of the New York Central system. In 1913 the RW&O merged into the New York Central Railroad. Then the N.Y. Central added passenger service on what it called the "water level" route from New York City—to and from the St. Lawrence River. Passenger service ended in 1961 and freight service in 1964.

As a girl in North Rose, Homer's daughter Verna was a member of the Bluebirds. (The Bluebirds were a division of the Camp Fire Girls for younger children.) Verna was an active member of the North Rose Presbyterian Church. In April 1911 she began work at the local bakery. The young woman lost the end of one of her fingers while grinding coffee for the firemen battling the January 1917 conflagration that devastated the center of the North Rose business district.

Verna's class of 1917 was just the second class to graduate from North Rose High School. She was vice president of the seven-member class. Verna moved to Rochester and in July 1918 married George Henry Barnes (1893–1955) at Camp Dix, New Jersey. Verna and George lived in North Rose in the 1920s. They had a daughter, Lila Esther (1921–2004). In the 1930s and 1940s, George, Verna, and Lila lived in Milton (Ulster County). The Barnes family went on an automobile trip to Niagara Falls and northern New York with Charles and Hazel Bertilina in July 1931. In 1940 George was a cold storage engineer, Verna was a sewing machine operator, and Lila was a college student who worked as a waitress in the summer.

In July 1942 Lila visited Betty Lou Dillingham in North Rose. Lila enlisted in the WAVES (Women Accepted for Volunteer Emergency Service; 1942–1948) in 1943. She married Edwin F. Guth Jr. in 1941.

They divorced in 1975.

Gordon and Betty Lou Acker visited the Barneses in Milton in March 1947. Then the four friends traveled to Patterson, New Jersey. In May 1947 Verna and George returned to North Rose and lived with Homer Stone. They resided in Clyde in April 1950.

Stubley, Perry & Ethel

1940 monthly rent: $10.
Perry Stubley (1902–1981), 38, head of household, laborer, road building, 36 weeks for $720.
Ethel Van Sicklen Stubley (1901–1992), 38, wife, bean picker, 4 weeks at $50.
Elizabeth Stubley (1924–2008), 15, daughter, student.
Arlene Stubley (1927–), 13, daughter, student.
Rodney Stubley (1928–2000), 11, son, student.

Arlene Stubley, NRCS Class of 1945

Rodney Stubley, NRCS Class of 1947

We were unable to obtain more than the cursory information provided by the census for this household. If you have information about the Stubleys, see page 32.

Tellier, Harry & Maude

Estimated 1940 value: $4,000.
Harry Adrian Tellier (1883–1944), 56, head of household, warehouse manager, O. A. Skutt Company, 52 weeks for $1,300.
Maude Almyra Muhl Tellier (1886–1978), 53, wife, homemaker.
Anne Wood Fennell (1916–2006), 23, lodger, schoolteacher, 12 weeks at $300.
Marjorie Hookway (1915–2009), 24, lodger, schoolteacher, 12 weeks at $300.

HARRY ADRIAN TELLIER (pronounced "tuh-LEER") from Iowa was a cashier at the North Rose National Bank, then became the bank's president. He served as secretary-treasurer of the Wayne National Farm Loan Association. From 1926 to 1931 Harry represented Wayne County in the New York State Assembly. For the last 10 years of his life, he directed O. A. Skutt Company activities in Palmyra.

Maude was born in Pultneyville. Her father, Philip Muhl (1860–1929), was the son of immigrants—his father, a cooper, was born in France and his mother in Bavaria. Philip grew up in Sodus and worked as a blacksmith and a farmer. Maude and Harry married in June 1907 in Williamson.

Harry and Maude had four children: Mary Elizabeth (1910–2001; see "Lawrence, Donald & Elizabeth"), Harry Jr. (1912–1991), Eugene (1915–2010; see "Winchell, Marvin & Fanny"—he married their daughter Jane), and Ellen (1921–; see "Lawrence, Henry & Grace"—she was a lodger with her sister's in-laws in 1940).

Harry Jr. married Mildred Vanderwall (1916–2012) in 1937. The couple moved to East Palymra, where they raised two daughters, Ann and Martha. Harry Jr. took over his father's duties for O. A. Skutt. In 1950 he was foreman for all operations, purchasing and selling beans for the O. A. Skutt Bean House.

Anne Fennell graduated from Central High School in Syracuse, where she lettered in tennis, and Elmira College. She married George Roland Maloy (1916–1999) in October 1940. Anne became a freelance journalist and George an insurance salesman. The couple lived in Clyde and had two daughters, Susanne and Nancy. Anne served on the board of directors for the Clyde-Savannah Public Library and was the Clyde town historian.

Marjorie Hookway married Edward Byerly (1911–1991) in New Jersey in 1942. Their son Richard was born in Michigan and their son Bruce was born in New Jersey before they settled in Milford, Connecticut. Edward was a music professor and Marjorie became a much-loved music teacher. Once a year she took caravans of yellow school buses full of students from Bassick High School in Bridgeport to dress rehearsals of the Metropolitan Opera: *Turandot, Carmen, The Flying Dutchman*. The couple retired to Venice, Florida.

Thomas, Elsie

19 South Poplar Street, now 4947 South Poplar—Built in 1920. Estimated 1940 value: $1,200.

Elsie J. Thomas (1864–1952), 75, head of household, laborer at Canning Factory, 24 weeks for $12 a week.

Elsie Thomas, a widow, lived alone and was employed part-time as a laborer in the Canning Factory. She was also seeking work—despite her age and despite the fact that she had been working in the same factory for nearly 30 years. She had completed eight years of school.

Elsie's first marriage, in 1882, was to Daniel Robinson (ca. 1852–1932). Elsie and Daniel had six children: Archer, Leslie, Lottie, Samuel, Benjamin, and Frederick. In 1906 Elsie married a farmer, George E. Thomas (1848–1929), who also had six children from a previous marriage. After the wedding, George and Elsie were living in Huron. Lottie was the only one of the couple's children that was living with them.

In 1920 the Thomases had moved to North Rose. George was working as an engineer in the Canning Factory. Lottie was living at the Newark State School (a mental hospital). Elsie was a member of the Utopia Rebekah Lodge. By 1930 George had passed away and Elsie's daughter Leslie was living with her.

Elsie attended the Lake family picnic in Pultneyville with her son Frederick and his family. Her coworkers gave her a blanket as a gift in honor of her 80th birthday and her 32 years of employment at the Salter Canning Company. In the 1940s Elsie sometimes wintered with her son Samuel and his wife in Interlaken (Seneca County). Elsie died in December 1952 and her home was sold to Mrs. Elizabeth Warden in January 1953.

George Thomas married his first wife, Sarah E. Little (1849–1909), in 1870. They had six children who lived past infancy: Jerome E., Frankie, Della, Sarah A., Vinnie L., and Eva. By 1900 all of George and Sarah's children had moved away from their parents' home. In September 1901 George was badly hurt when the straw carrier of his threshing machine fell on him, causing multiple injuries—including breaking some of his ribs.

George's son Jerome married Miss Frankie Payne of Sodus Point. The couple had one son. Jerome's wife and mother both worked in C.E. McQueen's dry house. In October 1902, while he was on an evening row with a friend, Jerome was pitched out of a rowboat and into Sodus Bay, where he drowned. Though he was only 31, it was speculated that he had suffered a heart attack.

George's daughter Vinnie married William M. Green of Wolcott, in 1892. In about 1900 George's daughter Eva married an E. Dolan. The couple moved to Buffalo, then Pittsburgh. In September 1902, after the death of their infant son, Eva separated from her husband and moved back to New York. For the next couple of years, she worked in both a Rochester box factory and at an apple evaporator in Huron. In January 1905 she married Lester Cody, who later became the Huron tax collector.

Della married and moved to Clyde. Her husband, George R. Lamb, died in a rail yard accident in Clyde the same month that her brother Jerome drowned. The couple had no children, and Della moved back in with her parents.

One night in 1905, Della survived a terrifying incident with a man who had been courting her. Masked and armed with a revolver, Ben Drury entered Della's bedroom (in her parents' North Rose home) and aimed a pistol at her. Drury was arrested and charged with assault. The issue of Ben Drury's sanity became the subject of extended legal proceedings conducted by a judge-appointed referee, Joel Fanning. Eva, Sarah, and Della all took the stand and testified that Ben had threatened to kill Della and himself. Two physicians also certified that Ben was insane. One of them was Dr. Gay A. Jones of Huron. Jones operated the local telephone company out of his home and was Della's part-time employer. In addition to the revolver incident, Ben had broken the glass in a door of Jones's home when he was refused admittance to speak to Della while she was at work there.

Judge S. Nelson Sawyer received the referee's report in the sanity hearing and pronounced Ben Drury sane. The report stated that Ben was only subject to periodical spells of mild insanity caused by being deeply in love with Della Lamb, so Justice Sheldon of Huron resumed Ben's hearing on the assault charge. Extensive testimony caused him to believe that Ben had not actually planned to commit a crime when he entered Della's bedroom. Justice Sheldon also commented that Della herself testified that she and Ben were on friendly terms before the alleged assault. In consideration of these facts, the justice dropped the criminal charges against Ben and released him as a free man.

Thompson, Ernie & Ida
8 South Poplar Street, now 4970 South Poplar—Built in 1920. 1940 monthly rent: $20.
Ernest "Ernie" Thompson (1883–1961), 56, head of household, self-employed, proprietor of an inn.
Ida Anna Thompson (1885–1947), 54, wife, apple grader at the Cold Storage, 20 weeks for $200.
Eunice Thompson (1916–2007), 24, daughter-in-law, clerk, retail grocery, 5 weeks for $75.
Russell Thompson (1909–1988), 30, son, laborer at Optical Works, 25 weeks for $300.

IDA THOMPSON'S RESTAURANT AND ROOMS at some point burned down. Apartments were built on its location on North Main Street just north of the bank that was on the northeast corner of Railroad.

We were unable to obtain more than the cursory information provided by the census for this household. If you have information about the Thompsons, see page 32.

Thompson, Frank & Addie
16 South Main Street, now 4970 South Main—Built in 1870. Estimated 1940 value: $2,000.
Frank Thompson (1870–1962), 70, head of household, self-employed.
Addie Mae Thompson (1877–1959), 62, wife, homemaker.

Addie M. Cahoon Thompson (1877–1959), 62, wife, homemaker.
Leslie Edwin Thompson (1919–1975), 20, son, student and laborer, 5 weeks at $15 a week.

FRANK AND ADDIE THOMPSON SHARED their home with their son Leslie, who was a student. Leslie spent the previous summer as a laborer in the Canning Factory. Orin, Leslie's older brother, had died before Leslie was born. Addie was a homemaker and Frank had been a painter but was not employed in 1940. Frank and Addie had both completed the eighth grade, while Leslie had two years of high school.

Frank was a member of the Masonic Lodge and an officer of the Bay Shore Lodge, No. 606, Odd Fellows. After 52 years in the Odd Fellows—and as the only charter member still living—Frank was guest of honor at the North Rose Lodge dinner in April 1943.

Addie lost her mother, Calista Cahoon, in June 1939. Addie was a Rebekah, active in the Home Bureau, and a member of the North Rose Presbyterian Church's Mission Society and Sigma Society. Many friends and neighbors of the Thompsons eagerly anticipated the yearly blossoming of Addie's night-blooming cereus, which simultaneously sported seven fragrant white flowers and five buds in August 1944. Addie joined the American Legion Auxiliary of Rose in October 1945. In January 1946 the American Red Cross Auxiliary honored Addie for donating 500 hours of service. In February 1948 Addie hosted the Sigma Sewing Circle of the Presbyterian Church. In May 1950 the Utopia Rebekah Lodge held a banquet at the Hotel Wayne in honor of Addie, their only living charter member.

The Thompsons visited Fulton, Oswego, the Thousand Islands, and Niagara Falls in August 1929. About 60 of the couple's friends gave them a surprise party in November 1930. Miss Arlene Hamm of Newark was often a weekend guest in the Thompsons' home. The couple hosted a Fresh Air child in the summer of 1940 and through that organization developed an ongoing friendship with Mildred Grasiosa, who visited the Thompsons several times in the summer as well as during some Christmas vacations in the early 1940s.

In September 1940 the Thompsons attended the Cahoon family

picnic at Chelsea Harper's cottage on LeRoy Island. For their 50th anniversary, the Thompsons received 109 guests at their open house.

Leslie enlisted in the Army in February 1942 and was stationed in Kentucky by April. He married Harriet Cecelia Aldrich (1918–2002) in May 1949 in West Bloomfield (Ontario County) and the couple moved in with her parents there. The couple operated a gift shop in Lima (Livingston County). In 1953 the couple had a daughter, Elaine. The family moved to Honeoye Falls (Ontario County). In March 1967 Leslie was working as a real estate salesman for Youngs & Linfoot, Inc.

Leslie and Cecelia's daughter Elaine married John Vollmer and raised a family in Avon (Livingston County).

Frank and Addie's son Orin Albert Thompson (1897–1918) joined the Fulton Naval Militia (a branch of the Naval Reserve) in July 1917—during World War I—and was almost immediately called to active duty. He was in training in New York City when he died at the naval hospital on March 30, 1918.

The 1918 flu pandemic had reached Queens, New York, by March 11. Oren was young, healthy, and a soldier in the wrong place at the wrong time. Due to wartime censorship these deaths weren't publicized at the time, but it doesn't seem too much of a stretch to speculate that the flu may have killed him. His death certificate states the cause of death as lobar pneumonia.

> THOMPSON, ORIN ALBERT, seaman, second class, United States Navy.
> Enlisted: Fulton, N. Y., July 12, 1917.
> Died: Naval hospital, New York, N. Y., March 30, 1918.
> Cause: Pneumonia, lobar.
> Next of kin: Mother, Mrs. Addie M. Thompson, North Rose, N. Y.

Towne, Lottie

Estimated 1940 value: $1,600.
Lottie Towne (ca. 1880–), 60, head of household, retired.
Eugene Towne (1908–1946), 32, son, laborer, Canning Factory, 26 weeks for $700.

We were unable to obtain more than the cursory information provided by the census for this household. If you have information about the Townes, see page 32.

Valentine, Jackson & Genevieve
Estimated 1940 value: $3,000.
Jackson Wade Valentine (1902–1962), 37, head of household, insurance agent (owned his own agency), 51 weeks at $1,500.
Genevieve Lanola Shear Valentine (1897–1967), 42, wife, schoolteacher, 40 weeks at $1,400.

We were unable to obtain more than the cursory information provided by the census for this household. If you have information about the Valentines, see page 32.

Van Hoff, Charles & Julia
2 or 4 South Huron Street, now 4968 or 4976 South Huron—Built in 1908 (2) and 1900 (4). Estimated 1940 value: $2,000.
Charles L. Van Hoff (1869–1947), 70, head of household, retired railroad foreman.
Julia U. Van Hoff (1871–1952), 69, wife, homemaker.

CHARLES AND JULIA VAN HOFF were married in 1889. They owned two adjacent homes, now numbered 4968 and 4976 South Huron Street. Presumably, they lived in one and rented out the other. Charles was a retiree and Julia was a homemaker. The Van Hoffs had both completed the sixth grade.

Charles was born in Holland; his family immigrated to the United States in 1874. He was an employee of the New York Central Railroad for 54 years and section foreman on the railroad from approximately 1910 to 1930. Julia's parents were both from Sweden, but she was born in the United States. In November 1934 she was fined $200 and given a six-month suspended sentence by Justice Marvin Winchell for selling beer without a license in the Town of Rose, a "dry" community where beer sales were not permitted.

The Van Hoffs had one son, Corwin (1901–1951). Corwin married Laura T. Leblanc. The couple had two children and moved into a house a couple of doors down from Charles and Julia. (See "Van Hoff, Corwin & Laura.")

Van Hoff, Corwin & Laura

8 South Huron Street, now 4986 South Huron—Built in 1920. 1940 monthly rent: $8. Owned by Charles Van Hoff.
Corwin Charles Van Hoff (1901–1951), 38, head of household, laborer, 30 weeks for $23 a week.
Laura T. LeBlanc Van Hoff (1897–1972), 42, wife, homemaker and worker at the Canning Factory, 30 weeks for $12 a week.
Carl C. Van Hoff (1924–1995), 15, son, student.
Lorraine Arlene Van Hoff (1926–1996), 14, daughter, student.

CORWIN AND LAURA VAN HOFF RENTED the home that they lived in from Corwin's parents. (See "Van Hoff, Charles & Julia.") Corwin was a laborer on the railroad, and Laura was a homemaker and a trimmer at the fruit cannery. They married when Corwin was 17 and Laura was 21. Their children, Carl and Lorraine, were a year apart, but both attended the eighth grade in 1940.

In 1907, when she was about 9, Laura emigrated from Quebec to Oswego (Oswego County) with her parents, (Joseph) Isadore Leblanc and (Marie) Desneige Larocque Leblanc, and six brothers and sisters. Three more siblings were born in Oswego. Corwin completed the ninth grade; Laura had finished the fifth.

In 1920 the Van Hoffs lived in Rochester and were both working at the Kodak factory. They rented a room from Louis and Irene Wera, Italian immigrants who had two daughters who also worked at the Kodak factory.

By 1930 they had returned to Corwin's hometown of North Rose. Corwin was an inspector at a machine shop, and Laura worked at the Canning Factory. In the early 1940s the Van Hoffs moved first to Maple Avenue and then, in March 1944, to Buffalo—where they had spent the previous summer. Lorraine stayed behind temporarily, in South Huron, to finish her senior year of high school. Mr. and Mrs. Nelson Showers from North Wolcott began renting the family's former home.

Carl enlisted in the Navy in November 1942 and was transferred to Virginia for training as a gunner's mate in 1943. Honorably discharged in February 1946, he reenlisted until 1951. He married and lived in such diverse places as Pittsford, Buffalo, and Washington, D.C., as well as in Henderson, Nevada—where he died.

Lorraine was a Girl Scout and a varsity cheerleader at NRCS and was elected secretary of her senior class. In August 1942 she traveled to Cleveland to visit relatives. After graduation, in September of 1944, Lorraine moved to Buffalo and got a job at an aircraft factory. That October, Lorraine was maid of honor at her friend Katherine Foster Barnes's wedding in South Huron.

Lorraine later married Allan Daniel Boone (1924–2009) of Lancaster (Erie County, just east of Buffalo). They had a son and four daughters: Allan D. Jr., Desneige Alayne (Desneige was Lorraine's maternal grandmother's name), Sharon Alice, Robin, and Allison. The couple eventually lived in the Baltimore area and then in Ormond Beach and Sun City Center, Florida. Lorraine died in Sun City Center, Allan in The Villages.

Laura remarried in 1965, more than a decade after Corwin's death, to John Billingsley.

Van Hout, Lloyd & Elsie

Gray Street home—1940 monthly rent: $8.
Lloyd J. Van Hout (1913–1964), 27, head of household, laborer, bean elevator, 37 weeks for $450.
Elsie Vanderlyke Van Hout (1913–1978), 26, wife, homemaker.
Jean Ann Van Hout (ca. 1935–2008), 4, daughter.
Sandra Kay Van Hout (1937–), 2, daughter.
Herbert L. Van Hout (1938–2014), 1, son.

LLOYD COMPLETED TWO YEARS of high school and worked as a laborer at the O. A. Skutt Co. Bean House. Elsie completed eight years of school. In 1940 Lloyd and Elsie and their three young children moved into a home on Gray Street. Lloyd and Elsie had five more children after their move. In August 1943 the Van Houts became parents of a daughter, Donna Fay (1945–). Four months later the Van Hout family moved to Auburn (Cayuga County), then to Throopsville (Onondaga County). The Van Hout family (pronounced "van-HOWT") visited Lloyd's parents, Dr. Jacob Van Hout (1876–1958), and Florence Ina Van Hout (1882–1967), in North Rose in January 1945. Jacob earned the use of the honorific "doctor" because of his work as a veterinarian. "Van Hout" was sometimes spelled "Van Houte." Lloyd and Elsie continued to pay regular visits to Lloyd's parents. At least once, Lloyd's sister's family accompanied them. The sister was Wreatha E. Van Hout (1903–1982) of Wallington, a hamlet in Sodus. Wreatha and John Vanderzille (1900–1992) had a double wedding in June 1923 with their friends Ethel Van Sicklen and Perry Stubley.

Lloyd's father, Jacob Van Hout, was from Holland and was a doctor of veterinary medicine in North Rose. Lloyd's mother, Florence, was a homemaker. Her parents were both native-born. (Florence's two younger brothers lived in North Rose; see "Borden, Albert & Hattie" and "Borden, Raymond & Viola" for more about Florence's family.)

John and Wreatha Vanderzille's children were Richard Lloyd (1928–2009), who married Marie Beck (1928–2007); and Doris (1930–2011), who married Cyril Mills (1920–).

Elsie Vanderlyke was born in Walworth and lived in Palmyra before she moved to North Rose. Her father and mother, Herbert Vanderlyke (1874–1951) and Elizabeth Pieternella Fremouw Vanderlyke (1884–1953), were born in The Netherlands. Herbert was a farmer. Herbert and Elizabeth married shortly after their arrival as immigrants to America. In Holland Herbert's family's surname was "Van der Lijcke."

Lloyd died in a bulldozer accident in February 1964. Lloyd was employed by Bradley and Williams Company of Syracuse. While clearing the way for power lines three miles south of Cardiff (Onondaga County), the bulldozer he was operating slipped from its path. Lloyd attempted to leap free from the tumbling machine, but the heavy vehicle crushed him.

At the time of Lloyd's death, his eight children (with spouses included, where known) were: Jean Ann Van Hout (ca. 1935–2008) and Charles A. Franklin Jr. (1938–) of Auburn; Sandra Kay Van Hout

(1937–) and Anthony J. Guidone (1934–2019) of Port Byron (Cayuga County); Herbert L. Van Hout (1938–2014) and Gloria Behm (1941–) of Port Byron; Inez E. Van Hout (ca. 1941–) and Thomas Lynch of Auburn; Donna F. Van Hout (1945–) and Jack S. Mead; Wreathea Van Hout (1945–2024) and William O'Hara of Port Byron; Bonnie Lou Van Hout (1948–2014); Jeffrey Lloyd "Bud" Van Hout (1951–2004) and Linda Horning of Auburn.

Vernoy, Leon & Thelma

North Poplar Street. 1940 monthly rent: $7.
Leon Seager Vernoy (1918–2005), 21, head of household, clerk at a soda fountain.
Thelma Mabel Claus Vernoy (1915–1996), 24, wife, telephone operator.

LEON AND THELMA WERE BOTH high school graduates. Leon was a soda jerk; Thelma was a telephone operator. Leon and Thelma wed in June 1939.

Leon's parents were Hugh Houston Vernoy (1895–1930) and Alta Candace Seager Vernoy (1893–1979). Hugh's father was from Wisconsin. Hugh was a farmer who lived in Huron, then in the Town of Rose. (For further information about the Hugh and Alta Vernoy family, please turn to the Candace Seager section of this book.)

Thelma's parents were George Earl Claus (1885–1953) and Mabel E. Baxter Claus (1888–1983). ("Claus" rhymes with "house.") In 1925 George was a carpenter, and the Clauses lived in the Town of Wolcott. In 1930 George was a farmer, and the Clauses had moved to Huron.

In July 1941 Thelma won election as secretary-treasurer of the NRCS Alumni Association. By 1943, Leon and Thelma had a daughter named Bonnie. Leon often said of North Rose, "I will be mayor of this burg." Alas, it was not to be. North Rose was a hamlet with no mayor, and the Vernoys moved to Lyons, where they lived from around 1943 to 1956.

After the family moved to Wayne County's county seat, Bonnie often returned to North Rose and Rose to visit friends and to take part in church activities. In August 1949 she spent a week in her hometown with her aunt and uncle, Ella and Ray Converse. Bonnie repeated these summer family visits over the next decade. Bonnie joined the North Rose Methodist Church in May 1954. In April 1955 Bonnie spent three nights in Elmira with other Methodist church youth at the spring convocation of the Methodist Youth Fellowship. In August 1955, and again in 1956, Bonnie attended the Casowasco Methodist summer camp. In January 1957 Bonnie joined other members of the Methodist Church Forum Class on a chilly weekend at Casowasco. By 1958 she was a member of the North Rose Methodist Church's Chancel Choir.

Casowasco

For decades, Casowasco has been a significant place for many North Rose Methodists. It is a beautiful 200-acre campground on Owasco Lake, one of the eastern Finger Lakes. Methodist children remember it as a favorite summer camp. It was also the site of many church meetings and retreats. Casowasco was formerly the home of the Case family—hence the name. (Casa is Spanish for a house, and it is also a variation of the original owner's family name: Case.) Gertrude Case sold the property to the Methodist Church in 1946 for a fraction of its market value. One prominent member of the Case family was Gertrude's husband, Theodore "Teddy" Case, who invented the most successful system for adding sound to motion pictures. Now Casowasco serves as a gathering place for both secular and Methodist events.

In the 1950s Leon and Thelma worshiped at the Rose Baptist Church. Around 1958 the Vernoys moved to Olean (Cattaraugus County). Leon and Thelma joined Olean's First Methodist Church Couples Club, and Leon became a lay leader of the church. Bonnie graduated from Olean High School in 1959. Leon held a job for 37 years organizing home sales of beauty supplies for Stanley Home Products. In May 1961 Thelma's photograph appeared in a good-sized advertisement for Sunbeam Bread in the *Olean Times Herald*.

Later the Vernoys settled in Montoursville, Pennsylvania, just outside Williamsport, the home of the Little League World Series. In 1968 Thelma and her sister Dorothy Mierke (1923–2000) threw an 80th birthday party for their mother, Mrs. Mabel Day, at the Methodist Church in North Rose. Bonnie, who had married and settled in Olean, brought her four children: Pamela, Dawn (1961–2003), Douglas (1964–2019), and Mark Lindauer.

In 2006 Bonnie married Fredrick Spiller (1941–2021), her high school sweetheart who'd been widowed, and moved to his home in Buchanan Dam, Texas.

Vincent, Fred & Ethel

Northeastern North Rose. 1940 monthly rent: $10.
Fred Alexander Vincent (1893–1948), 46, head of household, laborer in the Cold Storage.
Ethel J. Curtis Vincent (1898–1968), 42, wife, homemaker.
Albert LeRoy Vincent (1918–2000), 21, son, laborer at a cider mill.
Frederick Vincent (1921–1993), 18, son, laborer in the Canning Factory.
David Kenneth Vincent (1926–1966), 13, son, student.
Donald Vincent (1928–1950), 11, son, student.
Faith Vincent (1932–2004), 7, daughter, student.
Dale E. Vincent (1938–1941), 1, son.

Fred completed six years of school and worked at the Cold Storage as a laborer. Ethel completed eight years of school and worked as a homemaker. Fred Vincent was the son of Alexander Vincent (1867–1901) and Lucy Groves Vincent (1874–1948). Alexander was from Michigan, and Lucy was from Kidderminster, Worcestershire, England, by way of Pennsylvania. After Alexander's death, Lucy married Milton R. Green Jr. Ethel was the daughter of Fred James Curtis (1867–1937) and Nellie Elizabeth Curtis (1872–1949) of Wolcott.

In June 1922 Fred Vincent tried his hand at auto sales. He offered used Fords for sale—$90 and up. "Leave word with Fred Curtis, Auburn Street [Wolcott]," read the advertisements. Fred and Ethel lost a seven-month-old baby boy, Claude R. Vincent, in October 1924. Fred bought A.J. Week's home in Glenmark in January 1925. In 1930 the Vincent family resided in Rochester.

In August 1938 Fred suffered a fractured collarbone and an injured pelvis when a two-ton tractor that he was driving plunged over an eight-foot embankment while he was proceeding along the side of the road in Kitchens Corners—two miles east of North Rose. He crawled out from beneath the machine, and the driver of a passing bakery truck stopped and assisted him. Fred went to the Barber Hospital in Lyons in critical condition. Fortunately he recovered. Fred and Ethel moved to Wolcott in the early 1940s. They lived on Parce Avenue. Fred's next move was to Fairport (Monroe County). He was a member of the Fairport Volunteer Fire Department. They found him dead in his home in March 1948—a victim of suicide.

In August 1939, while living in Newfane (Niagara County), Ethel accidentally struck and killed a pedestrian with her car. Stanley Chase, a kennel operator, was walking along Lockport-Olcott Road about a mile north of Lockport when he was hit by Ethel's car. Ethel received no legal sanction for the incident.

Six children lived with Fred and Ethel in 1940. The Vincents' eldest son, Curtis E. (1916–1943), and their eldest daughter, Vivian Edith (1919–1986), had already left their parents' home. Albert completed one year of high school and worked at a cider mill as a laborer. Frederick finished one year of high school and worked as a laborer in the Salter Canning Factory.

Curtis enlisted in the Army. Private Curtis Vincent died in Italy on November 13, 1943, as the Allies advanced up the Italian boot during World War II. That day was the birthday of two of his siblings—Albert and Vivian. Curtis had served as an ambulance driver in the Army Medical Corps. The original 1864 Geneva Convention—when the representatives of nearly every country met in Geneva, Switzerland—protected vehicles and shelters that displayed the International Red Cross or Red Crescent emblem, indicating the presence of wounded or ill soldiers. One hundred sixty-eight nations have signed this treaty. An intentional attack on Curtis's ambulance would have been a war crime. That first Geneva Convention also established the principle that wounded should be cared for without regard to which army they belong.

Vivian married George O'Neil Wolf (1916–1980) and lived in Rochester. George and Vivian had three children: Edith (who married Bruce W. Hopkins and lived in Binghamton in Broome County), Dorothy (who married Charles Mitchell and lived in Hamlet, North Carolina), and George B. Vincent (who lived in Springfield, Missouri).

In the 1940s Al Vincent moved to Macedon Center. After he married Mary Steves (1915–1980) of Rochester, they lived on Ridge Road in Webster (Monroe County). Mary was the daughter of Nelson R. Steves and Mary R. Shaughnessy Steves of Syracuse. She was a member of the West Webster Fireman's Auxiliary. Al was Sergeant at Arms of the Webster Area Volunteer Exempt Firemen's Club.

The Exempt Firemen's Club

The Exempt Firemen's Club was a social club with the stated purpose of supporting firefighters. Like many other social clubs, one of the principal attractions of the Exempt Firemen's Club was the bar that it provided for its members. Exempt firefighters were those with seven or more years of service, as well as good attendance records at fires. The term "exempt" was used because after seven years of active duty, volunteer firefighters became exempt from some other civic responsibilities, such as jury duty and paying some specific state or local taxes.

Al's family regularly visited the Robert Hornsby family in Macedon Center. Al and Mary's daughter Carol Ann Vincent received the Marian Award—the Catholic religious award in Girl Scouting. The award was presented by Bishop Lawrence B. Casey of Rochester. In 1970 the Vincents' daughter Marie was attending Rochester Business Institute, majoring in data processing. Marie moved west in 1973 when she took a job with the judicial department of the State of Colorado as a computer programming consultant. Al and Mary had two other daughters, Virginia and Rita. Al worked for Eastman Kodak.

Frederick and Donald both moved to Fairport (Monroe County). Following in his older brother Curtis's patriotic footsteps, Frederick served in the Army in World War II. He was stationed in England as a member of the Quartermaster Corps. When Frederick was in the Army, he often wrote letters to the editor of his local newspaper, *The Fairport Herald-Mail*.

Frederick returned to the United States in October 1945—disembarking in Newport News, Virginia. He married Rose Divincenzo (1931–1995) and moved to Webster (Monroe County). Rose was the daughter of Daniel Divincenzo and Carmella Giovine Divincenzo of East Rochester. Frederick and Rose had a son named James J., who joined the Coast Guard in October 1965. YN3 James Vincent married Gail A. Johns of West Webster in August 1968.

Donald, born in Wolcott, joined the Armed Services in Rochester in July 1948. After basic training, they assigned him to Seattle, Washington. Donald then spent over one year with the occupation troops in Japan. He was slain in action in Korea in July 1950. His mother, Ethel, received notification in August that Donald had been missing in action since July, two days after his 22nd birthday.

Kenneth suffered a broken arm in a fall on the NRCS steps in September 1934. In the 1940s he moved to Pittsford (Monroe County), where he gained employment with Rochester Products, a division of General Motors that manufactured carburetors and other auto components. In the early 1940s Rochester Products was doing war work in anticipation of the U.S.'s entry into World War II. The company won the Army-Navy "E" for Excellence Award on February 8, 1943. During the war it manufactured 75 types of aircraft generators, 60 types of airplane starter motors, and numerous models of relays, controls, and other tank and plane parts for the war effort.

Kenneth entered the Navy in May 1944, underwent basic training at Sampson, and then traveled by sea to Hawaii, where he worked at a naval ammunition dump. In May 1946 Kenneth received his honorable discharge. In September 1947 he married Esther Zornow Woods, daughter of Harry and Pauline Woods of Pittsford (Monroe County). Harry was born in Canada and became a naturalized citizen of the United States. Kenneth and Esther lived in Pittsford and subsequently in West Bloomfield and Rochester. He was an early volunteer at the West Bloomfield Fire Department in 1952. Kenneth and Esther had five children: Kathleen, David, Leslie, Harry, and Richard.

Faith married Gerald Michael Sherman (1927–1992) of Fairport in 1949. The wedding was at Ethel's home in Perinton (Monroe County). Gerald was the son of Leon A. Sherman (1886–1951) and Rose M. Bushey Sherman (1888–1948). Faith and Gerald became parents of Gary, Ronald, Rebecca, Gail, Lori, Mark, and Glen. Later, Faith married John P. Kendrot (1926–1999), lived in Webster, and became the stepmother of Jim, Jack, and Diane Kendrot.

In May 1941 Dale Vincent died at age 3 in the family car while in Wolcott. Fred and Ethel, who were living in Marion, left him in the auto while they were shopping. Ethel reported that Dale had been in chronically bad health since birth.

Wadsworth, Grace

Estimated 1940 value: $1,800.
Grace Wadsworth (1867–1951), 73, head of household, retired.

We were unable to obtain more than the cursory information provided by the census for this household. If you have information about the Wadsworths, see page 32.

Washburn, Katherine

1940 monthly rent: $20.
Katherine Washburn (1919–1999), 21, head of household, operating agent, telephone company, 52 weeks for $660.

Beatrice Washburn (1920–1989), 19, sister, telephone operator, 50 weeks for $250.
Clinton Washburn (1929–2005), 11, brother, student.
James Betts (1930–1989), 9, lodger, student.

We were unable to obtain more than the cursory information provided by the census for this household. If you have information about the Washburns, see page 32.

Weeks, Russell & Hazel

5 Elm Street, now 4973 Elm—Built in 1915. Estimated 1940 value: $2,000.
Russell O. Weeks (1893–1975), 47, head of household, deputy sheriff, 20 weeks for $40 a week.
Hazel Boyle Weeks (1897–1985), 42, wife, retailer, 52 weeks, self-employed.
Earle R. Weeks (1923–1998), 17, son, student.

RUSSELL AND HAZEL WEEKS LIVED with their son, Earle, who was a high school student. The couple married in 1920. Russell worked as a Wayne County deputy sheriff, and Hazel was the proprietor of a dry goods and dress shop. Russell and Hazel had both completed the 11th grade.

Russell was a member of the Armed Forces during World War I. In 1920 he and Hazel lived in the Town of Lockport (Niagara County) while he worked as an inspector at a radiator works. In October 1924 they moved to North Rose. By 1930 Russell had opened a grocery store there. Hazel, an accomplished pianist, worked in the store as a clerk. Russell's parents, Edward A. and Harriet "Hattie" E. Weeks, lived in Rose.

Russell and Charles Bond of Alton attended a Red and White grocery meeting in Buffalo in May 1930. In May 1932, Russell opened a dry-goods store in the Masonic block on Main Street. Active in the Salter Hose and Chemical (Fire) Company, Russell was elected president in February 1933. Upon his retirement—after a one-year term—he was presented with a gold watch by his fellow firefighters. Russell also raised funds from fellow businesspeople to pay band director Glen Waldorf to conduct the NRCS band and give open-air concerts during the summer.

In December 1942 Russell was elected president of the North Rose Fire Department (an amalgamation of Salter Hose and Chemical [Fire] Company and another regional fire department, North Rose Chemical Company No. 1). A few months later, the family relocated to Rochester, where Russell's mother spent the winter of 1943–1944 with them.

Their son, Earle, found work with the Hedges Undertaking Company in Rochester. In 1945 Russell and Earle were still living in Rochester, but Hazel had returned to North Rose. They rejoined Hazel, and then Russell's mother, Hattie, moved back in with the family for the winter of 1946–1947. In June 1948 Russell was honored at a dinner for his 25 years of service to the North Rose fire departments. Russell and Hazel moved to Lyons with their son later that year. They divorced some years after that.

Earle Weeks graduated from NRCS and enlisted in the Armed Forces in February 1943. After his discharge, he attended Simmons School of Embalming in Syracuse. In the summer of 1948 he moved to Lyons to open a funeral chapel. In June 1952 he married Thora Marie Reynolds (1926–2013), the proprietor of Canary Beauty Salon in Lyons. Together the couple ran the Weeks Funeral Home for 45 years. Earle and Thora had three daughters: Barbara, Sharon, and Dawn. From about 1953 to 1956, Earle was president of the Lyons Rotary Club.

In 1956 Russell married Agnes Robinson (1901–1975), the proprietor of Robinson's Beauty Shop in Lyons. Agnes was widowed in 1954 and had two daughters, Margaret and Doris. When Russell died in March 1975, he was the last surviving charter member of the Rose Fire Department. Agnes died later that year.

Weiland, Albert & Ella

18 North Poplar Street, now 5046 North Poplar—Built in 1910. Estimated 1940 value: $1,800.
Albert D. Weiland (1869–1952), 70, head of household, retired, self-employed.
Louella "Ella" Ditton Godkin Weiland (1861–1945), 79, wife, homemaker.

Ella Weiland's first husband was Samuel Godkin. Samuel's parents—Thomas Henry Godkin Jr. (1829–1864) and Mary Ann French Godkin (1826–1906)—married in 1844 in Morristown (St. Lawrence County), directly across the St. Lawrence River from Brockville, Ontario, Canada, where Mary Ann French was born. Thomas Godkin had emigrated from Ireland to Canada. Thomas and Mary's first child, a son, was born in 1845 and died in 1846. The next few of Thomas and Mary's children were born in Canada but by 1850 they were living in Sodus, where Thomas was a cooper. Samuel Godkin was born in Sodus in 1851.

In 1862 Thomas enlisted to fight in the Civil War with the 160th NY Infantry. He died in 1864 in a Baton Rouge hospital after being wounded in a skirmish with Confederate guerrillas, leaving behind his wife and eight children. Samuel (1851–1903) was about 13.

Ella grew up in South Butler. Her father, John Ditton (1818–1880), was born in England. Her mother, Mary A. Ditton (1822–1928), was born in New York State. The Dittons had married in 1838. Ella, one of nine children, completed six years of school. By 1880 Samuel and Ella had married, had their first child, Myrna (1879–1962), and settled in Butler, where Samuel worked as a cooper.

Samuel's cooper shop and barn in South Butler burned to the ground in March 1885. In July 1890 Myrna and Fred—Ella and Samuel's eldest son—graduated from grammar school in Williamson. By 1900 Myrna and Elizabeth (1884–1954) had left their parents' household. That year Samuel and Ella lived in Buffalo with the other five of their seven surviving children: Fred (1882–1931), Inez Mae (1889–1974), Samuel Jr. (1891–1965), Ethel (1896–1961), and Ward

(1897–1917). (One of Samuel and Ella's eight children did not survive infancy.)

Samuel Godkin died in 1903, leaving Ella with four children under 15. Inez went to live with her sister Myrna; Ethel went to live with Ella's sister in Auburn (Cayuga County). By 1905 Ella had remarried, to Albert Weiland, who also worked as a cooper in Buffalo; her two youngest children, Samuel Jr. and Ward, were part of the Weiland household. Albert completed five years of school.

Albert Weiland was born in Chicago; his parents had been born in Germany. In July 1906 Albert, Ella, and Ella's son Ward decided that they would like to move to North Rose. As a youngster, Albert lived in Sodus, so he was familiar with Wayne County. The three stayed with Ella's brother John Ditton while they shopped for a new home. They found one: Mrs. William Dickinson's house. They rented their new home and moved from Buffalo.

Myrna Godkin married William C. Becker Sr. (1877–1941), an engineer. They lived in Buffalo and had six children: Harold Roy (1899–1980), Lester (1900–1918), William Charles (1904–1995), Ruth (1906–1943), Earl (1908–1973), and Arthur (1910–1979).

Fred Godkin married Jeanette Sarsnett around 1901 and settled in Buffalo. The couple had one child who did not survive. In 1910 Fred worked as a shipping clerk for a bottle company. Jeanette belonged to the Jolly Twelve Pedro Club, one of many pedro clubs in Buffalo, and she was one of three winners in the card game on March 25, 1913. In 1917 Fred found work accepting classified ads for the *Buffalo Evening News*. In 1920 he ran a candy shop. In 1925 Fred and Jeanette were landlords, sharing the home they owned with lodgers—a single man and a young couple with a 10-year-old son—but were not otherwise employed. In 1930 their renters were in a separate unit in their home. Fred died in 1931.

Elizabeth Godkin married Alfred W. Horn in October 1907. They had five children: Milton V. (1902–1945), Wesley E. (1905–1967), Vera E. (1908–1935), Helen I. (1909–1994), and Robert F. (1911–1982). Later Elizabeth married Louis B. Kelley.

Inez Godkin was about 14 when her father died; she went to live with her sister Myrna Becker and her family. Inez married Clarence Ivan Lanich, owner of a shoe store. The Laniches lived in Buffalo and had a daughter, Dorothy (1911–1971), and a son, Clarence L. (1919–2007).

About 1911 Samuel Godkin Jr. married Ruth I. Porter. Samuel was a fruit farmer and soon would fight in the First World War. Samuel and Ruth lived in Huron and had five children: Harold W. (1911–1985), Clarence G. (1915–1981), Robert (1916–1971), Milton (1923–1986), and Donald (1923–2012). In 1940 Samuel Jr.'s 2-year-old niece Carol Riggle (ca. 1938–1968) had joined the household.

Ethel Godkin, who was about 7 when her father died, was sent to live with her aunt and uncle in Auburn. Elizabeth Ditton Stokes (1852–1921) was Ella's sister; Charles Stokes (1851–1923) was a hotel keeper; they had no children of their own.

In June 1917 Ethel volunteered to work at an Army recruiting tent in Auburn. In December 1918 Ethel married William Elias Chambers (1892–1962) at the Fifth Avenue Presbyterian Church in New York City. After a honeymoon to New Orleans and Beaumont, Texas, they lived briefly in Buffalo, where William worked as a furnace man for a steel company. In 1920 they shared a home with William's parents in Forward, Pennsylvania, outside Pittsburgh. The couple had four children: Elizabeth Luella (1919–1992), William Elias Jr. (1921–1994), Charles Newton (1925–2015), who was awarded a Purple Heart in World War II after being a prisoner of war in Germany, and Dorothy Margaret (1928–2011).

In 1914 Ward Godkin married Elizabeth Van Pelt (1896–1964), a Wayne County native who'd been adopted by a couple in Buffalo. Elizabeth Van Pelt and several of her siblings had been put out for adoption at the behest of their new stepfather—years earlier—when Elizabeth was very young. She didn't know her birth name, her birth mother's name, nor the town where she had originally lived. When she was 16, she discovered her adoption papers in her adoptive father's office and learned she was born Laural Valentine, daughter of Frank Valentine (1853–1901) and Ida May Abbott (1869–1924). She set out on a successful quest to North Rose to find her mother, who was then

Mrs. Frank Turbush. They had a happy reunion. Elizabeth obtained a job at the same North Rose hotel where her mother worked. (For more about the Abbott family, see "Abbott, Foster & Edith"; Foster was Ida's brother.)

Ward and Elizabeth had a son, Valentine "Bus" Grove Godkin (1916–1963). Ward died from diphtheria at 20, before Valentine was a year old. His young widow and their infant son moved in with Albert and Ella Weiland. (Elizabeth was Ella's daughter-in-law and Valentine was her grandson.) The pair stayed at the Weilands' home until Elizabeth married prominent North Rose insurance agent Clinton D. Dillingham in January 1926. (For more about Elizabeth, See "Dillingham, Clinton & Elizabeth.")

In 1939 Valentine married Mary Ammerman in Clyde. They had a daughter, Claire (1942–2018), but the marriage did not last. In 1940 Valentine was working and living at the Newark State School. He enlisted in the Air Force in 1942. While stationed in Texas at the San Antonio Cadet Aviation Center, Valentine made national news in August 1943 when he was flown to Chicago by the Red Cross and the Army Emergency Relief organizations to give a blood transfusion to 19-year-old Marie Barker, who was suffering from staphylococcus septicemia. Valentine had given 14 such transfusions since recovering from the usually fatal disease himself in 1938. Nineteen transfusions from several survivors of the disease failed to save her life.

Valentine married twice more: to Bernadine Burse in 1944, with whom he had four children—Jan Kurt, who served in the Navy; Katheryn Lynn; Richard Creig; and Stephen (1948–2018), who served in the Air Force in Vietnam—and to Pauline Gaver in 1959. Like his stepfather, Valentine went into the insurance business. He died of a heart attack at 46 at his home in Wolcott.

In 1928 Albert Weiland received an eight-tube Crosley radio as a Christmas gift. In October 1949, four years after Ella's death, Albert married Edith Pitcher of Rose. Both of Ella's husbands and her first father-in-law were coopers. Coopers (barrel makers) had plenty of work to keep them busy in North Rose in the late-nineteenth and early-twentieth centuries.

Apples by the Barrel

Shipping apples in barrels was a common way to transport apples from orchards to city markets. Apple barrels were large, but they were relatively easy to make, because they didn't have to be watertight. Incidentally, when apples were packed in barrels, first a layer of the largest and best-looking apples were placed in the upside-down barrel. Then the barrel was filled with apples that were not necessarily picture-perfect. When the barrel was full, the bottom was affixed, and two men flipped over the barrel into the right-side-up position. A barrel will hold about 130 pounds of apples, or a bit over three bushels. That's why it takes two strong men to load barrels of apples onto a wagon or railroad car.

Some farmers and farm laborers could make apple barrels, which did not have to be perfectly crafted. However, for the much more challenging task of constructing barrels that were built to hold liquids, a highly skilled professional was needed. The staves had to be carefully shaped by bending them after heating and softening them with boiling water or steam. Their edges had to be carved flawlessly so that the pressure generated by forcing on the barrel hoops locked the wooden barrel together so firmly that fluids could neither enter nor escape.

Welch, Olive

Estimated 1940 value: $3,500.
Olive Welch (1871–1965), 69, head of household, retired.
J. Donald Welch (1897–1947), 42, son, manager at the Cold Storage, 52 weeks for $2,500.
Mary J. Welch (ca. 1923–), 17, granddaughter, student.

Olive Mary Briggs was about 20 when she married Thomas B. Welch in 1891. Harold J. Welch was born the next year, followed by Russell Thomas Welch in 1896 and Joseph Donald Welch in 1897. Widowed in 1920, Olive would also outlive all three of her children.

We were unable to obtain much more than the cursory information provided by the census for this household. If you have information about the Welches, see page 32.

Wilson, Benjamin & Lu

1940 monthly rent: $10.
Benjamin Harrison Wilson (1888–1957), 51, head of household, self-employed, farmer.
Luna Lee Hayes Wilson (1892–1995), 47, wife, homemaker.
Charles H. Wilson (1921–2007), 18, son, student, farm laborer, 8 weeks for $150.
Marjorie Wilson (1922–2015), 16, daughter, student.
James LaVerne Harrington (1924–1986), 15, ward, student.
Stanley Eugene Stevenson (1928–2012), 11, ward, student.
James Charles Frazier (1929–1950), 11, ward, student.

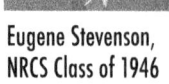
Eugene Stevenson, NRCS Class of 1946

James Frazier enlisted in the Army in 1949 and served in the Korean War. He was killed in action at 21.

We were unable to obtain more than the cursory information provided by the census for this household. If you have information about the Wilsons, see page 32.

Wilson, William

1940 monthly rent: $2.
William Wilson (ca 1872–), 68, head of household, self-employed, barber.

We were unable to obtain more than the cursory information provided by the census for this household. If you have information about the Wilsons, see page 32.

Winchell, Marvin & Fanny

22 North Main Street, now 5032 Main. Estimated 1940 value: $1,800.
Marvin Webster Winchell Sr. (1883–1955), 56, head of household, butcher, self-employed.
Frances "Fanny" Rebecca Laird Winchell (1883–1968), 56, wife, homemaker.
Virginia Rae Winchell (1913–1990), 27, daughter, bill collector and reporter, self-employed.

MARVIN OWNED WINCHELL'S MEAT MARKET in North Rose. He had concluded two years of high school. Fanny was a homemaker; she had attended two years of college. Their daughter Virginia, who lived with her parents, was a high school graduate. She worked at home as a newspaper columnist. She also operated a utility payment office. Virginia Winchell entered the General Hospital in Rochester in July 1919. Probably this was when she experienced a devastating attack of polio, which impaired her mobility for the rest of her life.

Marvin was born near Lyons. His father was William R. Winchell (1858–1933), a butcher who lived in the Town of Galen. Later his son and grandson made the same career choice. Marvin's mother, Elizabeth "Libby" M. Keller Winchell (1859–1935), was from Michigan. Marvin's parents moved, first from Rose to Lyons, then to Penn Yan. By 1900 Marvin had moved to Huron and lived with his paternal grandparents, John Winchell (1827–1908) and Caroline M. Winchell (1833–1905).

Marvin and Fanny married in 1908. Fanny was born in Michigan. Her family had moved to Rochester. Fanny's father, John Ellis Laird (1856–1918), was from Canada and worked as a foreman. Her mother, Eliza Jane Snell Laird (1855–1930), was from St. Ewe, Cornwall, England. John and Eliza married in 1878 and immigrated to the United States in 1891. Marvin worked for a while as a farm laborer in Huron. As a young woman, Fanny worked as a shoemaker. The Census Bureau counted Fanny twice in 1910: she was tallied with her parents in Rochester and with her husband and their young son in Huron. In November and December 1929, Fanny spent more time than usual in Rochester with her ailing mother, Eliza Laird, who died in February 1930.

Fannie's niece Flossie E. Briggs spent two weeks with her in August 1930. (Fanny's sister, Adelia May "Ada" Briggs, was Flossie's mother). Fanny was a chaperone on the NRCS Class of 1931 trip to Washington, D.C. In May 1933 Fanny won election as president of the Sigma Society of the North Rose Presbyterian Church. She was also a member of the Missionary Society. Marian S. Winchell of Rose, a Syracuse University graduate, and Fanny spent July and August 1940 at their cottage at Lake Bluff. Marian and Fanny were probably distant cousins by marriage. Marian's father, Dr. George Winchell, was an elderly physician who served as the Town of Rose coroner. In October 1944 Fanny's nephew Sgt. Fred Lynch of Rochester was killed in action in World War II.

Marvin and Fanny's three children were Marvin W. Jr. (1909–1970), Virginia, and Elizabeth Jane (1917–2017), who went by Jane. By 1915 the Winchell family had moved from Huron to Maple Avenue in North Rose. In 1920 the Winchells rented a home on North Main Street and Marvin Sr. was operating his meat market. Marvin Winchell, Gilbert Hill, and Lyle Brown went on a hunting trip in the Adirondacks in November 1921. In September 1929 the Town of Rose Republican Caucus nominated Marvin for the office of assessor.

In April 1930 the three Winchell children still lived at home. Marvin Jr. had a job as a clerk in an A&P Grocery Store (perhaps in Wolcott). In August 1930, Marvin Sr., Fanny, Virginia, and Jane attended the Harper family picnic at Fair Haven (Cayuga County). Marvin drove to Buffalo with other members of the Rose Town Board—including George Catchpole, George Valentine, Wells Dodds, Ray Osgood, Bert Valentine, and Harry Payne—to buy a new steam shovel for the town.

In 1930 Marvin Winchell Jr. moved to Rochester, where he lodged with the Vielle family at 237 Garson Avenue and worked in a grocery store. By June 1930 Marvin Jr. had moved to Hornell (Steuben County). He was back in Rochester, working as an insurance agent, when he married Leone Myra Bush (1905–1999), a schoolteacher from Pittsford, in May 1934. They became the parents of Richard "Dick" Marvin Winchell in January 1935. Marvin Jr. worked as a meat cutter.

In May 1932 Marvin's car struck Robert Butler's garbage truck that was backing into the street. The Winchell car was a ruin, but Marvin escaped with bruises. In July 1932 the Winchell family took an automobile trip to Bellville, Ontario, Canada. Jane Winchell was the valedictorian of the NRCS class of 1934.

In November 1935, Marvin Jr., Leone, and Dick, Victor and Gladys Winchell, and Dora Winchell (all residents of Rochester) visited the Winchell family of North Rose. Victor and Dora were Marvin Sr.'s siblings. Leone was substitute teaching in the West High School in Rochester.

In June 1942 Marvin Jr. and Myra had a daughter, Hazel Jane Winchell. Marvin Jr. spent April 1945 in North Rose working in the meat market while his father was ill. In about 1947 Leone and her two children moved to San Antonio, Texas. In 1950 she was back in Rochester, living on Oxford Street with their two children and 10 lodgers. Marvin Jr. was back in North Rose with his second wife, Marjorie B. Westfall Fuller (1913–1990). Marjorie had two sons and a daughter from her first marriage, which ended in divorce: Thomas, Gary, and Sharon Fuller. In June 1950 Marvin Jr. resigned from the Star Market, where he managed the meat department, and went to work with his father.

Jane Winchell married Eugene Hugh Tellier (1915–2010) in 1939. Eugene's parents lived in North Rose (see "Tellier, Harry & Maude"). Jane had starred with Eugene in the school play when she was a junior and he a was a senior at NRCS, and they became high school sweethearts. Eugene graduated from Hartwick College in 1937 and Jane from the University of Rochester in 1938.

In October 1939 the Town of Rose Republican Party Caucus nominated Marvin Sr. for another term as Town Justice. Marvin was victorious on Election Day and maintained his position as Rose Justice of the Peace, which he held for the whole decade. Seven months later, Marvin and Fanny visited Fanny's sister Mrs. Agnes Mae Lauder Briggs, who was recovering nicely from an auto accident. Marvin, Fanny, and Virginia were dinner guests of Jane and Eugene Tellier of Palmyra in November 1940.

In May 1942 Louise Yost of New York City visited the North Rose Winchells. Louise had been a foster daughter of the Winchells. She married Herbert Busch in New York City in July 1945. They made a short wedding trip to North Rose and then returned to live in New York City. In the summer of 1947, Louise Busch and her son, Glenn, visited the Winchells for a month. Hebert Busch drove them to North Rose and lingered a week.

In August 1942 Virginia organized the knitting of turtleneck sweaters for servicemen. Virginia sought out news—particularly social items—for the weekly North Rose columns she penned for the *Lake Shore News* published in Wolcott and the *Lyons Republican*. Virginia was also the regional correspondent for the *Rochester Democrat and Chronicle* and the *Rochester Times-Union*. She had a steady set of informants that she phoned for news tips on the same day and at the same time each week. Virginia also operated a payment office for taxes and utility bills. In addition, she operated North Rose's Western Union Agency from her North Main Street home. In February 1959, at the 107th annual convention of the New York Press Association, Virginia won the first-place award as Champion Country Correspondent.

Eugene Tellier ran Winchell's Market while Marvin and Fanny were on vacation in August 1945.

In August 1948 about 55 guests attended a 40th wedding anniversary open house in honor of Marvin and Fanny hosted by their daughter Jane. In 1950 Jane and Eugene Tellier lived in Palmyra with their four children: John "Jack" Marvin (ca. 1942–), Eugene H. "Toby" Jr. (ca. 1945–), Susan Katherine (ca. 1947–), and David W. (ca. 1949–). Eugene managed the Palmyra and Marion plants of the O. A. Skutt Company. Gene and Jane often socialized with Donald and Elizabeth Lawrence; Elizabeth was Gene's older sister (see "Lawrence, Donald

& Elizabeth"), and they often visited Marvin and Fanny.

In the early 1950s Eugene resigned from the O. A. Skutt Company and moved to Rushville (on the border of Ontario and Yates Counties, between Canandaigua and Penn Yan) to work at the Rushville branch of the Security Trust Company of Rochester. In 1953 he was promoted to branch manager.

Eugene and Jane's fifth child, Stephen R. "Tex" Tellier (1953–2016), was born in Rochester.

Marvin Winchell Jr. entered Hermann Biggs Sanatorium in Ithaca in August 1954 suffering from tuberculosis.

Marvin Winchell Sr. retired in 1954 and died on Thanksgiving Day 1955.

Stephen Tellier visited with his grandmother in July 1956 when the rest of the Tellier family went on a two-week camping trip to Algonquin Provincial Park in Ontario, Canada. In September 1956 Eugene Tellier attended a Methodist layman's retreat at Camp Casowasco.

The Telliers moved to Chelmsford, Massachusetts, in the early 1960s and then to Orleans, Massachusetts, in 1964, when Eugene was named president of the First National Bank of Cape Cod. Jane and Eugene's youngest son, Stephen, was born with Down syndrome, and Jane was instrumental in getting special education services in Orleans for five local children with special needs. In 1968 she founded the Nauset Workshop, which provided a place for people with disabilities to work and enrich their lives. The program evolved into Cape Abilities, a nonprofit organization with the same mission.

Fanny Winchell died in 1968. (The author's mother, Jane F. Skutt, a longtime North Rose resident, died in an automobile accident while returning home to Ithaca after attending Fanny's funeral.)

Jane Winchell Tellier lived to be 100 and lost a husband, son, and grandson in her last decade. Eugene died at 95 in 2010; Stephen died at 63 in 2016; and her grandson Zachary Tellier died at 31 in 2007. A 1998 graduate of American University, Zach enlisted in the Army in 2005 and became a decorated sergeant, with two Bronze Stars and two Purple Hearts. He deployed to Afghanistan as a paratrooper in January 2007 and died there in September.

Wise, Sammy & Esther

26 Salter Road, now 10410 Salter. Estimated 1940 value: $2,100.
Samuel Wise (1905–1985), 34, head of household, retail grocer, self-employed.
Esther Phillips Wise (1905–1991), 34, wife, homemaker.
Robert "Bruce" Wise (1934–1981), 6, son.
Philip "Gordon" Wise (1940–2012), 0, son.
Rena Phillips (1878–1953), 62, mother-in-law, retired.

Gordon Wise, NRCS Class of 1958

SAMMY SERVED AS SUPERVISOR of the Town of Rose. Sammy's parents, Francis S. Wise (1866–1953) and Marion Wise (1867–1931), were born in Berkeley Springs, West Virginia. Esther was born in Rose to parents Clayton I. Phillips (1872–1928), born in Wolcott (Wayne County), and Rena Jones Phillips (1878–1953). Esther was active in the Women's Society of Christian Service of the North Rose Methodist Church. She and Sammy operated the Market Basket Store in North Rose for over 30 years. Bruce married Beverly Duga (1934–). Beverly was from Hamilton (Hamilton County), and they moved there. Bruce was a longtime accounting professor at SUNY Morrisville and there is a scholarship in his name at the university. Bruce and Beverly had two daughters and a son. From Esther's obituary: Demaris A. "Dee" Wise of Florida; Kathelyn A. (Kachie) Wise of Florida; Robert B. "Robbie" Wise of Hamilton.

In 1959 Gordon began apprenticing at Young Funeral Home in Williamson, about 20 miles west of North Rose, and never left. Gordon bought the business from the Young family on January 1, 1973, and continued as owner and manager of the funeral home until his death on December 14, 2012. He was awarded the Rochester-Genesee Valley Lifetime Achievement Award from the Funeral Directors of America in 2009.

Wolf, George & Vivian

1940 monthly rent: $8.
George Wolf (1915–1986), 25, head of household, farm laborer, 15 weeks at $135.
Vivian Wolf (1919–1986), 20, wife, homemaker.
Edith Wolf (1938–2020), 1, daughter.
Dorothy Wolf (1939–), 11 months, daughter.

We were unable to obtain more than the cursory information provided by the census for this household. If you have information about the Wolfs, see page 32.

Wolven, Ernest & Edna

17 Gray Street, now 5051 Gray—Built in 1900. Estimated 1940 value: $1,500.
Ernest Thomas Wolven (1896–1983), 43, head of household, farm laborer, 45 weeks for $500.
Chloe Edna Elwood Wolven (1889–1979), 40, wife, bean picker (sorter), 32 weeks for $200.
Jeanette Ernestine Wolven (1924–2005), 15, daughter, student.
Joyce Edna Wolven (1927–1991), 12, daughter, student.

Ernest Wolven was a farm laborer who finished one year of high school. Edna completed eight years of school. She was a bean sorter at the Bean House of O. A. Skutt Company. The Wolvens had two daughters attending school: Jeanette and Joyce.

Ernest's parents were Elisha Sheridan Wolven (1867–1942) and Sarah Millie Mayo Wolven (1870–1954). Elisha was a carpenter from Butler. Sarah was born in North Adams, Michigan. Her father, Thomas Mayo, was born in Over Norton, Oxford, England. At 21, Ernest worked on George Colvin's farm in Butler. Ernest enlisted in the Marines in July 1918 during World War I. His "Abstract of Military Service" noted "Character Excellent." In August 1919 Ernest married Edna Elwood, and he lived with and performed farm work for his mother-in-law, Alzadah E. Elwood, on Wolcott Street in North

Rose. In the spring of 1927 Ernest played shortstop for the Wolcott town baseball team. Later that year the family briefly moved to the Town of Lincoln (Madison County). In 1930 Ernest, Edna, and their daughters Jeanette and Joyce lived in Butler, and Ernest worked as a farm laborer. By November 1938 the Wolvens had relocated to Sodus. Ernest was a member of the Wolcott American Legion in 1942. Ernest later worked as a field inspector for the Salter Canning Company and an equipment operator for the New York State Department of Transportation.

Edna was a volunteer in the Red Cross Fund collection for several years in the 1950s and '60s. She was an enthusiastic member of the American Legion Auxiliary.

Jeanette graduated from NRCS and the Rochester School of Nursing. She had been employed at the Barber Hospital in Lyons for three years at the time of her marriage to Wayne Clingerman (1922–1990) of North Rose. The wedding took place at the Lyons Methodist Church in May 1949. Joyce was the maid of honor. Wayne was the son of Millard H. Clingerman (1902–1966) and Clara Ida Leasure Clingerman (1903–1982). Millard and Clara were part of the group of "immigrants" to North Rose from Bedford and Fulton Counties in southern Pennsylvania and adjacent areas in Maryland and West Virginia. (Janet Clingerman wrote an excellent article on this migration called "Moving North to Rose" in the Winter 2014 issue of the Rose Historical Society Newsletter).

Millard was a farm manager. Wayne was a decorated veteran who had served three years in the 101st Airborne Division. At the time of his wedding, he worked at Smith Farms in Sodus. Jeanette and Wayne began married life at 2 Broad Street in Lyons. They had a daughter, Audrey Jean Clingerman (1952–). When she became an adult, Audrey married James Barber of Lyons. James was the son of Howard L. Barber (1920–1997) and Dorothy Wood Barber (1923–2015) of the Town of Rose. Audrey was a volunteer for the Home Meal Service in Lyons. Wayne and Jeanette's son, Neil Wayne Clingerman (1961–), was born nine years after his sister. In 1977 Jeanette was working at the Newark Developmental Center.

In July 1942 Joyce attended the weeklong Young People's Institute at Keuka College. This was a Methodist youth program. Joyce graduated from NRCS. She was the maid of honor in June 1947 when Jeanette Pierson wed Robert Caves. In the fall of 1947 Joyce lived in Lyons. By the fall of 1948 she was back in North Rose. Joyce and her friends Caroline Wallace, Alice Nickolette, Joyce Buhlmann, Phyllis Smith, and Patricia Heifer spent a week at the Legacy cottage at Sodus Point during July 1949. In February 1952 Joyce again lived in Lyons.

Joyce Wolven, NRCS Class of 1947

In July 1953 Joyce married Albert Louis DeJohn (1929–2016), son of James DeJohn and Mary V. DeJohn. Louis's parents were both born in Italy, and James ran a neighborhood grocery store in East Newark for 35 years. After Louis secured his discharge from the Army, he worked as a carpenter. Joyce had been working at Sarah Coventry Jewelry, the largest direct seller of costume jewelry in the world, in the 1960s and '70s. They employed "home parties" to sell their jewelry.

Louis and Joyce DeJohn settled in Newark. Their daughter, Pamela (1953–), worked at Seneca Foods in Marion. Their son, Gerard Ernest (1961–), enlisted in the Air Force and spent his career there. Joyce and Louis divorced, and Louis later remarried. In 1978, Louis, who had been serving in the Newark Police Department, was designated Newark's first full-time youth officer.

Yancey, Ben & Eva

36 North Huron Street, now 5098 North Huron—Built 1910. Estimated 1940 value: $3,500

Benjamin Alvin Yancey (1898–1992), 41, self-employed, proprietor of auto repair shop.
Eva Briggs Yancey (1899–1993), 40, wife, homemaker.
Phyllis Yancey (1923–2019), 16, daughter, student.
Donald B. Yancey (1924–1991), 14, son, student.
Boyce Robert Yancey (1927–1999), 12, son, student.
Paula Yancey (1930–2010), 9, daughter, student.

Boyce Yancey

Ben Yancey ran an auto repair garage and appliance store on North Main Street. All four of Ben's grandparents, as well as his mother, emigrated from Europe. Some family members reported that they were from France in one census and from Germany in another. That's because most were from Alsace-Lorraine, a long-contested region that belonged to France from the 1600s but became German territory in 1871 following the Franco-Prussian War. France would not get it back until after World War I in 1919. "Yancey" was originally spelled "Jantzi" or "Yantzi."

Ben and Eva Yancey with their four children (eldest to youngest), Phyllis, Donald, Boyce, and Paula, circa 1935.

Ben's father, Daniel Yancey (1860–1940), was born and raised in Croghan (Lewis County). Daniel, like his father, Peter Yancey (1822–1904), was a farmer. In 1833, at about 11 years old, Peter emigrated from Lorraine, France, with some of his siblings and his widowed mother. He lived in Lewis County the rest of his life.

Ben's mother, Lena Reyn (1866–1937), arrived from Europe at 18 in the summer of 1885, pregnant by a German soldier. Her first son, Edward, was born that October. In French, Lena's surname was "Rienie"; in German, "Rienia." Lena's brother Theodore had come to America the year before. Lena traveled across the Atlantic with Theodore's wife and three children. (The couple would have five more children after reuniting in America.) Family lore has it that Lena and Theodore's father died in the old country, after falling off a load of hay while working on a Sunday. The Reyns made their home in various villages in the neighboring towns of Croghan and Lowille (Lewis County), where their uncle, William Reyn (1833–1911), was a groceryman. William was responsible for the Anglicization of the family name, after arriving in 1851. He fought in the Civil War.

Daniel Yancey and Lena Reyn married in 1887. Daniel continued farming; they had six more children, with Ben the second-to-youngest. (Edward, Lena's first-born, took the Yancey name.) Ben went to school for eight years, then began working as a farm laborer. In the winter of 1918 he worked as a logger in neighboring Herkimer County. Later that year, Daniel and Lena left Lewis County for Wayne County, moving next door to Lena's brother, Theodore Reyn, who'd made the move from Lewis County in the early 1890s. Daniel purchased a grist mill on Slaght Road in what is sometimes listed as North Huron and other times as Wolcott. Daniel and Ben's younger brother Nelson eventually turned the grist mill into Wayne County's only water-powered cider mill. Nelson became known as the Cider King before his death in 1971.

Ben worked at a number of places from 1918 to 1920: at his father's farm in Wolcott, at an automobile factory in Rochester, Ben and in the auto repair garage of J.J. Colling in North Rose. In January 1920 Ben's older brother Theodore married Lena Briggs, the daughter of a farmer in Huron. In June of that year, Ben married Lena's younger sister, Eva Briggs, in the Huron Presbyterian Church.

Mary Drury remembers attending first grade in Ben Yancey's home in the early 1920s, as there were too many students for the old school. It was a two-story house next to the fire hall, which was also serving as a temporary school at the time.

In 1927 Ben went into business on his own. B.A. Yancey's Garage Automobile Repair, Appliance and Gas Sales started on Huron Street, then moved to North Main Street. His storefront was a fixture there for the next 54 years.

Ben Yancey's auto repair shop and appliance store on Main Street in North Rose in the early 1980s, after Ben had retired and the building had been cleared out.

In 1957 Ben won a GE sales contest. The prize was a trip for him and Eva to Miami with other prize winners. Ill health forced Ben to close the business in 1982 at the age of 84. Ben was a member of the North Rose Fire Department for more than 60 years and was a longtime member of the IOOF lodge. He died in July 1992, about two weeks after his 72nd wedding anniversary. Eva died the following year.

Phyllis Yancey graduated from NRCS in 1940. That year she was the queen of the Firemen's Festival. In August 1948 Phyllis married Victor William Koney (1917–2002) in Scotia (Schenectady County), where the couple eventually settled. Victor served in World War II. In 1950 Victor was a salesman and Phyllis worked as a

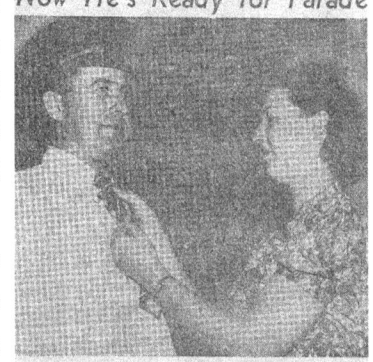

Ben Yancey was a longtime member of the North Rose Fire Department.

stenographer. Their two children, Vickie and Brent, were born in the 1950s. Phyllis was a longtime secretary at the East Glenville Community Church.

Donald Yancey graduated from NRCS in the class of 1942, then moved to Rochester, where he worked at Bausch and Lomb, grinding lenses for Navy rangefinders. He enlisted in the U.S. Marine Corps and in April 1943 left for Parris Island, South Carolina. He was promoted to corporal from private first class in October 1943 and served in the Philippines.

In December 1946 Donald married Anna Lavada Mundy (1928–2024) at the North Rose Methodist Church, before what Donald claimed was the largest congregation the church had ever witnessed. In 1948 Donald served as master of ceremonies for the Rosebud Ball in North Rose, where Betty Facer was selected and coronated as queen of the ball, and lady-in-waiting Jane Mertz was named runner-up.

In 1950 Donald was living in Rose, working as an auto mechanic, presumably for his father. He and Lavada also had a lodger in their household, a 36-year-old truck driver.

Donald returned to the armed services. In September 1956 the *Lake Shore News* reported: "Sgt. and Mrs. Donald Yancey and daughter Donna have returned to Cherry Point, N.C., after spending a leave with his parents, Mr. and Mrs. Ben Yancey."

The couple eventually moved back to North Rose, where they raised their four daughters: Donna, Debbie, Dawn, and Delene.

Donald made a career at General Electric, working for the company in both Clyde and Auburn. He was a member of the Wolcott Elks Club, the North Rose Fire Department, and the Rose Baptist Church. He served on the Rose Planning Board. He was a longtime member and one of the founders of the Goose Pond Fish and Game Club, still in existence, in Harrisville (Lewis County). Donald and Lavada's camp at Goose Pond in the Adirondacks was their home away from home. Lavada returned to enjoy time on her screened-in porch there for many years after Donald died of cancer at 66.

Lavada worked as a bookkeeper and office manager at Sodus Cold Storage in North Rose for more than 20 years. She died at 96 on New

Year's Eve.

Boyce Yancey married Anne Gilkey (1920–2009) in the early 1960s. Anne was born in Lyons but grew up in Clyde and the couple settled there after their marriage. Anne's first marriage, to Frank Finch, ended in divorce. Their son Keith was born in 1959. By the time of his death in 1991 at the age of 71, Boyce had had a leg removed due to diabetes and suffered a stroke.

Paula Yancey sang at numerous weddings in her late teens: among them the Allen/Moore wedding in 1945, the Clingerman/McQueen wedding in 1947, and the Wilson/Wagner wedding, in which she also served as a bridesmaid. In June 1946 she was named queen of the Moonlight and Roses Ball in Newark. She won honors at NRCS and was awarded a $200 scholarship to the Rochester Business Institute, where she graduated. She married Richard Carter Burch (1929–1985) in December 1950 and moved with him to California, where he was stationed in the Navy. Their daughter Maxine was born in 1953.

Paula's first marriage ended in divorce, as did her second one. Her third marriage, to widower Leonard James Baker (1927–1990), lasted until his death. They made their home in Wolcott, where Paula lived for 20 more years. She died of a heart attack the day after her 80th birthday.

In April 1955 Ben and Eva hosted all four of their children for Easter: Paula Burch and daughter Maxine of Syracuse; and Phyllis and Victor Koney and daughter Vickie of Schenectady; Donald and Lavanda Yancey and daughters Donna and Debbie; and Boyce, who was living at home.

Ziegler, Henry & Mabel

29 South Poplar Street, now 4931 South Poplar—Built in 1923. Estimated 1940 value: $1,200.

Henry Van Allen "Van" Ziegler (1898–1963), 41, head of household, office clerk, 52 weeks at $22 a week.

Mabel Clista Brown Ziegler (1899–1976), 40, wife, bean picker (sorter), 46 weeks at $10 a week.

Louise Lucille Ziegler (1920–2006), 19, daughter, not yet employed.

HENRY AND MABEL ZIEGLER WERE married in 1919. Henry was a native of the area, and a clerk in the railroad office. Mabel was a fulltime bean picker (sorter) in the Bean House. Living with them was their daughter, Louise, who was looking for a job. Louise was a high school graduate; her parents had each completed the eighth grade.

(Note: The author often found spelling variations in family names. Even government documents and gravestones do not necessarily sport consistent spellings of surnames. Newspapers and census forms are even less consistent. The "Ziegler" family name was very often spelled "Zeigler" and was occasionally spelled "Zigler.")

Henry's middle name, Van Allen, was his maternal grandmother's maiden name. In 1918 he was working as a laborer on his father's farm in Huron. In 1920 he and Mabel were living in the North Rose home of Mabel's stepfather and mother: William and Rose Lyman (previously Rose Brown). Louise was born that November, and Henry was working as a laborer on the state roads at the time. The Ziegler family next moved into the South Poplar Street home formerly occupied by the Petersons. Henry was a freight agent for the railroad by 1925. The Zieglers enjoyed camping at Sodus Point and had a cottage on LeRoy Island. In August 1940 they attended the World's Fair in New York.

Henry's father became ill and stayed with Henry and his family in March 1930. In January 1936 Henry was elected assistant chief of the Salter Hose and Chemical Fire Company. He and his friends attended games of the 1936 World Series in New York. In 1945 he was chosen to be one of two representatives of the North Rose–Huron Fire District to the Wayne County Firemen's Association.

Mabel was active in the Rebekah Lodge and in Kappa Phi. She rose to the office of deputy district director of the Rebekahs. Her father's name was Robert Brown.

Louise was a music student of Grace Partrick. (See "Partrick, Harry & Grace.") She graduated from NRCS and went on the senior class trip to Washington, D.C., in 1939. After graduation, she attended Rochester's Culver Beauty Academy to become a hairdresser. She worked for the New York Telephone Company in 1940 and was living in Lyons in 1942. Louise was friends with Jean Boughton (her cousin), Mary Drury, and Marian Edwards. Marian and Kate Boughton Louise's aunt and Henry Ziegler's sister; see "Boughton, Raymond & Kate") each threw Louise a bridal shower shortly before her 1947 marriage to Howard Henry Burns (1914–1993) of Huron. Louise and Howard had a son, David Howard Burns (1949–), and two daughters, Diane and Denise, and made their home on Main Street in Wolcott.

David Burns graduated from Husson College in Bangor, Maine, and married Jacqueline Steele in 1975. They started their married life in Rochester, where David worked as a salesman for Burke Steel, but almost half a century later David and Jacqueline Burns were living in Henry and Mabel Ziegler's former house in North Rose.

Henry died at home of a heart attack at 64.

Epilogue
North Rose 2025

RAILROAD TRACKS STILL RUN THROUGH NORTH ROSE. Passenger service ended on the Hojack line in 1961 and freight service in 1964. The railroad, so central to North Rose's history—indeed, its reason for being—was gone. It was the end of an era, to be sure. But, just as surely, not the end of the North Rose story.

Much endures. Lake Ontario continues to moderate the temperature, and Wayne County continues to be one of the nation's largest apple-producing counties. The Cold Storage, now Sodus Cold Storage, still stores apples in its warehouse beside the tracks. Fleischmann's Vinegar, part of the Irish food group Kerry, makes apple cider vinegar just south of town. From 1940 to 1960, there was little change in life in North Rose. But as the 1950s came to an end, technology began to impact agriculture. The average size of fruit farms in North Rose was growing larger; fruit pickers were primarily migrant workers of color, then later, Spanish speakers; loading required 20-bushel bins, each weighing 800 to 1,000 net pounds, as opposed to a one-bushel crate. Pesticides were outlawed. Apples today are grown on wire mesh, allowing farmers to more easily modify their crop mixture, changing to new varieties of fruit every three or four years. Orchards no longer resemble the orchards of the past, but instead look like vineyards.

Much of the hamlet (2020 population: 664) has visibly changed little, neat homes still line the streets of North Rose. The North Rose Central School is now the North Rose-Wolcott Elementary School, still housed in its 1928 building. North Rose remains overwhelmingly white and overwhelmingly Republican. More wars came and men from North Rose went to fight them; the 2020 census shows 16 Vietnam War veterans and 29 Gulf War veterans living in the village. The village's retailing, however, has been hollowed out compared with earlier decades: By the 1970s, more shopping was done at chain stores rather than individually owned village stores. Today fewer businesses remain, among them a diner, a gas station, a convenience store (selling beer—Rose is no longer dry), and a lumberyard.

Religious and social organizations are still present but smaller in number and in active participation. Two church buildings had dominated the North Rose landscape in the 1940s and '50s. The Presbyterian Church closed in 1970, one of the many church closures by mainline Protestant denominations in the postwar period—national Presbyterian church membership declined from 3.2 million in 1960 to 1.4 million in 2022. The old church is now the Town of Rose town hall. The Methodist Church remains open: average attendance in 2022 is 101 per week. The website lists a youth group and a women's group, but it is unclear how active they are. *North Rose 1940* makes clear the enormous role that churches and church groups had in the life of the village in the past, a chapter that is now largely closed. In *Bowling Alone*, Robert Putnam chronicled the erosion in recent years of the very rich associational life of mid-twentieth-century America. The Odd Fellows seem to have almost disappeared from Central New York. The Masons have seen their national membership shrink from 4,000,000 in the 1950s to 800,000 today. In 2010 the North Rose Masons merged with the Wolcott Masons, and the North Rose Lodge closed.

Like many former Masonic lodges around the country, the North Rose Lodge has been repurposed. Built originally for the short-lived Bank of North Rose, it is now home to the Farnsworth Museum and Rose Historical Society. The museum is named after Bernard Farnsworth, the local funeral director who donated his collection of historical materials. The Town of Rose Historical Society was founded in 1972 as a bicentennial product of the Lions Club and moved to its present location in 2007. One early donation was Ote Gray's collection of hand woodworking tools. It also holds a large collection of historic photos (including many featured in this book), old parade banners, the wooden sign from the Knotty Pine restaurant, furniture from office buildings, and other items representing the history of North Rose.

As you look through the 1940 manuscript census for North Rose, the occupation "bean picker" appears time and again. Along with the railroad and the Cold Storage, the Bean House was a mainstay of the village economy. The O. A. Skutt Company was founded in the early twentieth century, and the wholesale company came to specialize in red kidney beans. The Bean House was their sorting and storage facility. Kidney beans are no longer a major New York farm product, and the Skutt Company closed in the 1960s. But the Bean House building still stands beside the railroad tracks and is not empty. Since 2004 this massive building has been transformed from a kidney bean factory into a model railroad empire—the North Rose Railroad Company, founded by Gary Poole, owner and curator. The highly detailed and animated scenery includes wind farms, city and suburban scenes, construction sites, amusement parks with working roller coasters, bridges, trestles, fast food restaurants, and much much more.

My ardor for North Rose was strengthened upon my first visit to the North Rose Railroad Company, where I saw the work that Gary had undertaken. As the town of my birth and childhood, North Rose will always hold a special place in my heart.

About the Author
A short autobiography of Alexander G. Skutt

I WAS BORN IN 1948 in North Rose, New York. When I was very young, my parents constructed a baseball diamond for me on the far side of the barn, complete with a backstop behind home plate and heavy chickenwire in front of the barn windows. Those windows remained intact throughout my childhood.

Alex at 11, when the family home in North Rose was sold

After my father died in 1955, when I was 6 years old, my mother and I moved to an apartment in Ithaca (Tompkins County), where my sister, Marilyn, was attending Cornell University. For the next four years, until the family home was sold, we returned to North Rose every summer and for many weekends. I had three groups of playmates: the children I met in the North Rose neighborhood; the children of the migrant workers who worked for the Aldrich family picking apples and sour cherries; and my schoolmates in Ithaca.

Alex in high school

I always did well in school, majoring in applied physics at Cornell University. I was offered a generous stipend to study aerospace engineering but declined due to my antiwar sentiments. I spent several years involved in the peace movement, working in the Finger Lakes region for George McGovern's presidential campaign.

I next turned to retailing with two women whom I had met during the McGovern campaign: Diane Bruns and Vivian Singer. We opened McBooks, a bookstore on North Aurora Street in Ithaca which focused on paperbacks, then opened Quest's End, which specialized in science fiction, mysteries, and games. During the two years I lived in Evanston, Illinois, I opened Notoriety,

Alex posing for the cover of a catalog for a publishing house in the 1970s

featuring books, cards, gifts, and games. During my stay in Evanston, I became interested in video recorders (VCRs); after I sold Notoriety and returned to Ithaca, my good friend Richie Berg and I opened a video rental store, Video Ithaca. One store soon became three.

My next business venture was McBooks Press, also named in honor of George McGovern. I developed McBooks Press into a respected home for important authors of nautical fiction, including Alexander Kent, Julian Stockwin, and Dudley Pope. McBooks published about 200 books of historical nautical fiction as well as lavish photography books of my beloved Finger Lakes and books on boxing. I co-authored five editions of *The Boxing Register* with my nephew Jim Roberts.

Over the years, my fond memories of North Rose persisted, and over a decade ago I decided to write a book about this small town. I retired in 2019 after selling McBooks Press to Rowman & Littlefield, which continues to bring nautical fiction titles to market. My retirement enabled me to focus my attention on *North Rose 1940*.

Alex with his former wife, Carol Bushberg; son, Ethan Skutt; and Ethan's partner, Rebecca Hellman

Acknowledgments

FEW BOOKS ARE THE WORK of one individual. Authors depend upon the writings of previous authors, fact-checkers, editors, proofreaders, and stylists in writing books and other publications, and this book is no exception. The first four people I'd like to thank grew up in or near North Rose in the 1940s: Frank Dennis, Janet Clingerman, Sandie Hunt, and Allan Mitchell. Though Frank, Janet and Allan's families did not live in North Rose proper during the 1940 census, they are included (with asterisks) in the Families section of this book. Some additional biographical information can be found here.

FRANK GEORGE DENNIS JR. PLAYED A PIVOTAL ROLE as the co-author and copy editor of this book.

Frank grew up on his parents' fruit farm in Huron. The challenges faced by their farm, particularly its unsuitable conditions for fruit production, led Frank Jr. to gain experience elsewhere. He assisted in managing the Sodus Fruit Farm and worked for a peach and apple grower in Niagara County. Subsequently, Frank and his wife, Katharine, returned to Cornell for graduate studies, with Katharine earning her MS in 1959 and Frank completing his PhD in 1961.

A year in France followed, where Frank utilized an NSF post-doctoral fellowship to delve into plant hormone identification within apple seeds. When the Dennises return to the U.S., Frank worked at the Geneva Agricultural Experiment Station, focusing on diverse research projects, including those initiated in France. However, he preferred interacting with students rather than entirely doing research.

In 1968 Frank embraced a teaching position at Michigan State University, marking the beginning of a dedicated 22-year period researching the chemical thinning of apples, strategies to prevent freeze injury in apples and peaches, and the role of naturally occurring hormones in fruit trees' seeds and buds. He taught fruit growing at Michigan State University until 1996.

His research interests especially included the dormancy in cherry trees and the damaging effects of frost on those trees. He also worked in parthenocarpy (the development of seedless fruit.) His research projects centered on gibberellins, which were naturally occurring compounds in the fruit that inhibit flowering, thus reducing the fruit set, so berries are farther apart and become larger.

Following his retirement, Frank remained active in his field, editing a horticultural journal and chronicling the history of the horticulture department at Michigan State University, the nation's first land-grant college.

Frank's passion for his community was evident through his involvement with the Rose Historical Society. He edited the quarterly newsletter and contributed significantly to a project aimed at photographing every tombstone in the township. Additionally, he maintained meticulous computer records, documenting local burials and the service records of men and women veterans spanning the Spanish-American to the Vietnam War period. Frank Dennis Jr.'s unwavering dedication to both his profession and community has left an indelible mark on the fields of horticulture and local historical preservation. For more about Frank and his family, see "Dennis, Frank & Corinne."

AT THE SPRY AGE OF 86, **JANET HARPER CLINGERMAN** was a major contributor to *North Rose 1940* in her role as one of the fact-checkers. Fact-checkers for this project were people who lived in North Rose at the time of the 1940 census and who confirmed the accuracy of the information in the book.

Janet was a key figure in the creation and development of the family business, Clingerman Taxidermy, in the 1970s. In the 1990s Janet met the daughter of Shi Wen-long, a wealthy Taiwanese businessman whose ambition it was to create a natural history museum surpassing the Smithsonian and the American Museum of Natural History in New York. Janet subsequently accompanied her husband, Larry, on numerous trips to Africa to collect the animals for what became the Chimei Museum in Taiwan.

In a second semi-retirement, Janet remains active in the Town of Rose Historical Society. For more about Janet and her family, see "Harper, Roscoe & Louise."

Sandie Mills Hunt served as a fact-checker on this book. After spending much of her life in the Town of Rose, she relocated south in the mid-1990s to the Finger Lakes region. Upon her return several years later, Sandie joined the Rose Historical Society and is now curator of the Farnsworth Museum. Sandie generously recalls some of her experiences in contributing to *North Rose 1940:* "It has been my privilege and an honor to proofread the chapters in the book. I looked forward to receiving each packet and learning so much about North Rose and its residents, including my family." For more about Sandie and her family, see "Mills, Elery & Leona."

Allan Dickerman Mitchell served as a fact-checker on this book. Allan followed in his father's footsteps as a fruit farmer in the Town of Rose and has expanded the family farm and the production of apples and tart (formerly called sour) and sweet cherries, as methods have changed over time. Apples were produced on seedling rootstocks in the 1930s, and ladders up to 28 feet long were used to harvest the fruit. Today dwarfing rootstocks allow the fruit to be picked with stepladders or from the ground. Many apple orchards are trellised. Handheld spray guns were used with one person on the sprayer, and another driving the tractor; today only the driver is needed and the spray is delivered by fans. Apples were picked by hand and transferred to one-bushel crates or baskets; today they are still manually picked but placed in 20-bushel bins and handled by tractors with forklifts. Similar changes have occurred in cherry production. Dwarfing rootstocks may soon be available for sweet cherries; tart cherries are mechanically harvested. Trees were planted by hand, with augurs used to dig the holes; today tree planters dig trenches—labor is used only to place the tree in the furrow.

Allan was a member for 20 years of the board of directors of Pro Fac Cooperative, a national processor of fruits and vegetables that was later sold to Birdseye Foods. For more about Allan and his family, see "Mitchell, George & Josephine."

I began this project to make sure the stories of North Rose—the stories of my childhood hometown—were never forgotten. Despite facing significant health challenges in these past 10 years—including Parkinson's disease and later blindness—I have been able to finish this project with the help of a team of assistants and editors. I am deeply grateful to them and all those who've helped bring *North Rose 1940* to life.

Kenan Baldrich, who was a great help in keeping track of the comings and goings of the Baldrich family in North Rose

Rebecca Barry, for being an early editor of the book

Carol Bushberg, for support and for business advice

Terry Catchpole, an experienced editor, for providing invaluable information on the Catchpole family, fact-checking, and contributing a blurb to the back cover

Lucinda Collier, for being an enthusiastic supporter of the project and for contributing a blurb to the back cover

Tommy Dunne, for being the book and cover designer and multi-skilled editor

Rose Fritzky-Randolph, for being an early editor of the book

Leigh Keeley, for general assistance

Ginny Collier Robinson, for providing digital images and textual information

Hannah Stedman, for researching and being the primary indexer

Richard Stott, for being the co-author of certain sections of the book and copyediting

Carolyn Tomaino, for being an overall advisor and computer whiz

Ethan Skutt, for all the ways in which you've helped and supported me and the book project

Bibliography

Websites

ancestry.com

genealogy.com

wikipedia.org

zillow.com

findagrave.com

web.co.wayne.ny.us/hist-search

wayne.nygenweb.net

familysearch.org

Sites that include archives of individual newspapers:

newspapers.com

nyshistoricnewspapers.org

newspaperarchive.com

fultonhistory.com (by Tom Tryniski)

Newspapers & Periodicals

Albany Knickerbocker News

Albany Times Union

Attica New York News

Auburn Citizen Advertiser

Baldwinsville Gazette Farmer's Journal

Bridgeport Post

Buffalo Courier

The Cato Citizen

The Cayuga Chief (Weedsport)

Chronicle-Express (Penn Yan)

The Clyde Herald

The Clyde Independent and the Rose Times

The Clyde Times

Cold Spring Reporter

Commercial Advertiser (Potsdam Junction)

Cortland Standard

Cumberland Times (Cumberland, Maryland)

The Daily Messenger (Canandaigua)

Daily Sentinel (Rome)

Elmira Star-Gazette

The Fairport Herald

Gazette & Farmers' Journal (Baldwinsville)

The Geneva Times

Hardware magazine

The Herald (Jasper, Indiana)

The Herald-Mail (Fairport)

Hilton Record

Interlaken Review

Kingston Daily Freeman

Lake Shore News (Wolcott)

The Lyons Republican

The Lyons Republican & Clyde Times

Madison County Leader and Observer

The Marion Enterprise

The Messenger (Oswego)

Mexico Independent

Middletown Times Herald

Monroe County Mail (Fairport)

The Newark Courier

The Newark Union

Newark Union-Gazette, The Marion Enterprise

Oneonta Star

Orleans Republican (Albion)

Oswego (alumni magazine)

Oswego Valley News

Palladium-Times (Oswego)

Port Byron Chronicle

The Record (Sodus)

The Record Gazette (San Gorgonio Pass, California)

Red Creek Herald

Rochester Democrat and Chronicle

Rochester Union & Advertiser

Schenectady Gazette

Sodus Record

The St. Augustine Record

Syracuse Post-Standard

Wayne County Alliance (Sodus)

Wellsville Daily Reporter

Wesley Dispatch (North Rose Methodist Church)

Books

Countryman, Jon E., *Wolcott, New York: Strolling Down Main Street*, compiled by Norma Pearson (Wolcott, N.Y.: The Jacobs Press, Inc., 2011)

Countryman, Jon E., *Wolcott, New York: Strolling Down the Side Streets*, compiled by Norma Pearson (Wolcott, N.Y.: The Jacobs Press, Inc., 2010)

Craig, John, *An Apple Orchard Survey of Wayne County, New York* (Safwan Press, 2015)

Eisenstadt, Peter, *The Encyclopedia of New York State* (Syracuse, N.Y., Syracuse University Press, 2005)

Jacobs, Stephen W., *Wayne County: The Aesthetic Heritage of a Rural Area* (New York, Center of Cultural Resources, 1979)

Kerr, James P., *The Fruit Industry in Wayne County, New York 1823–1984* (Lyons, N.Y., Wayne County Historical Society, 1985)

Lehmann, Joyce W., *Migrant Farmworkers of Wayne County, New York: A Collection of Oral Histories From the Back Roads* (Lyons, N.Y.: Wayne County Historical Society, 1990)

Linson, Amber (editor), *Voices of Wayne County: A Bicentennial Commemorative Book* (Wayne County, New York, Wayne Historical Society, 2022)

McKelvey, Blake, *Rochester, An Emerging Metropolis 1925–1961* (Rochester, N.Y., Christopher Press, 1961)

McKelvey, Blake, *Rochester, the Flower City 1855–1890* (Philadelphia, Pa., J.M. Jordan, 1905)

McKelvey, Blake, *Rochester, the Quest for Quality 1890–1925* (Cambridge, Mass., Harvard University Press, 1956)

McKelvey, Blake, *Rochester, The Water-Power City, 1812–1854*, (Cambridge, Harvard University Press, 1945)

Pierce, Frederick Clifton, *Forbes and Forbush Genealogy* (Legare Street Press, 2022)

Proceedings of the Board of Supervisors of the County of Wayne

Rambler (North Rose Central High School yearbook), 1950–1963

Roe, Alfred S., *Rose Neighborhood Sketches, Wayne County, New York* (Worcester, Mass.: self-published, 1893)

Shultz, Duane *Into the Fire: Ploesti, the Most Fateful Mission of World War II* (Westholme Publishing, 2008)

Sortheron (North Rose Central High School yearbook), 1946 and 1947

Towne, Edwin Eugene, *The Descendants of William Towne* (Newtonville, Mass.: self-published, 1901)

Thanks to:

Elizabeth Young, Penfield Library Special Collections, SUNY Oswego

Family History Library, Salt Lake City, Utah

Index

Abbazia, Albert J.: 60
Abbazia, Ruth Whalen: see "Whalen, Ruth"
Abbott, Edward: 33
Abbott, Ella Goss: see "Goss, Ella"
Abbott, Foster Henry: 33, 34, 336
Abbott, Francis Edith Garlick Riggs: see "Garlick, Francis Edith"
Abbott, Ida May: 123, 335, 336
Abbott, Jennie McLaury: see "McLaury, Jennie"
Abbott, Maude Torrey: see "Torrey, Maude"
Abbott, Nelson: 33, 34, 248
Acker, Betty Lou Dillingham: see "Dillingham, Elizabeth Lucille"
Acker, Clinton Gordon: 36, 171
Acker, Darlene: 36
Acker, Edna: 35, 36
Acker, Herbert J.: 34
Acker, Jane Johnson: see "Johnson, Jane"
Acker, Kate Satterlee: see "Satterlee, Kate"
Acker, Lorel Francis: 36
Acker, William Gordon: 14, 34, 35, 36, 37, 313
Acker, William Henry: 34, 35, 36
Adams, (Clark) Everett: 119, 120, 121, 129
Adams, Ann Marie: 121
Adams, Betty: 257
Adams, Charles (father: Fred): 37, 257
Adams, Charles (father: Harry): 257
Adams, Earl Herbert: 191
Adams, Elizabeth LeVal: see "LeVal, Elizabeth"
Adams, Etta Armstrong: see "Armstrong, Etta"
Adams, Fred: 37, 255, 257
Adams, Gladys Little: see "Little, Gladys"
Adams, Harry James: 37, 257
Adams, Helen: 257
Adams, Henry: 14
Adams, Herbert "Bert": 121
Adams, Herbert Clark: 14, 119, 121
Adams, James Henry: 37, 257
Adams, Janet: 120, 122
Adams, Jennie Dickinson: see "Dickinson, Jennie"
Adams, John "Jay": 119, 121
Adams, Luella Brown: see "Brown, Luella"
Adams, Mary Belle "Mae": 80, 122
Adams, Nina Penner: see "Penner, Nina"
Adams, Norma Jean: 121
Adams, Ralph Everett: 120, 122
Adams, Robert K.: 120, 122
Adams, Suzette Lenihan: see "Lenihan, Suzette"
Adams, William F.: 190
Adams, William H.: 191
Aderhold, Helen Louna: 95, 195, 196
Agnew, Carol Dennis: see "Dennis, Carol"
Agnew, Walter: 119

Albright, Eleanore: 190
Aldrich, (John) Clarence: 39, 40, 41
Aldrich, Amos: 38, 39, 40
Aldrich, Benjamin: 40
Aldrich, Carol Price: see "Price, Carol"
Aldrich, Carrie Dillingham: see "Dillingham, Carrie"
Aldrich, Ellen Carrier: see "Carrier, Ellen"
Aldrich, George Delos: 36, 37, 38, 39, 40, 41, 42, 43, 44, 270, 299
Aldrich, George W.: 39, 40
Aldrich, Harriet Cecelia: 319
Aldrich, Hilda Anna McMullen: see "McMullen, Hilda Anna"
Aldrich, John Clarence (b. 1944): 36, 39, 44, 45
Aldrich, Linda Jane: 36, 39, 44, 45
Aldrich, Mildred Collier: see "Collier, Mildred"
Aldrich, Susan: 45
Alessi, Jennie: 264
Alford, Esther "Etta" Johnson: see "Johnson, Esther"
Alford, George: 272
Alford, Leola: 272
Alford, Viola: 271, 272
Allen, Mattie: 188
American Legion: 27, 28, 37, 54, 70, 119, 144, 163, 177, 191, 192, 197, 248, 265, 268, 284, 310, 318, 346
American Legion Auxiliary: 54, 70, 144, 163, 197, 265, 268, 318, 346
American Legion NY Post 582 (North Rose): 27, 28, 284
American Legion NY Post 881 (Wolcott): 27, 28, 37, 177, 192, 346
Ammerman, Mary: 36, 336
Anderson, (Elsie) Grace: 193, 194
Anderson, Lincoln C.: 193, 194
Anderson, Rea N.: 193
Anderson, Sarah Annabel "Anne": 193, 194
Andrus, Andrew: 263
Andrus, Cynthia: 263
Andrus, Evelyn "Eva" Mae: 262, 263
Anniversary Club: 2, 31, 129, 132, 176, 267
Anthony, Alan: 44
Anthony, Edward William: 84, 136
Anthony, Lois Edwards: see "Edwards, Lois"
Armitage, Sarah Elizabeth "Sadie": 123
Armstrong, Edgar: 45, 46
Armstrong, Elizabeth Head: see "Head, Elizabeth"
Armstrong, Elsie: 290
Armstrong, Etta: 121
Armstrong, Hazel: 290
Armstrong, James: 46
Armstrong, Lellavene: 45, 46, 47
Armstrong, Mary Eliza Sweet: see "Sweet, Mary Eliza"

Armstrong, Merton: 290
Armstrong, Nedra Lucille: 47, 289, 290
Armstrong, Virgil Sweet: 45
Armstrong, Virginia: 289
Atkins, Betty Galloway: see "Galloway, Betty Jean"
Atkins, Cheryl Lynne: 159
Atkins, Robert L.: 159
Atkinson, Mary: 288
Atwater, Olive L.: 50
Austin, Andrea: 78
Austin, James: 78
Austin, Shirley Bullock: see "Bullock, Shirley"
Austin, William G.: 14
B.A. Yancey (auto repair and GE appliances): 23, 74, 348, 349
Bacon, Dan: 126
Bacon, Matt: 126
Bagshaw, Ruth: 136
Bailey, Cheryl Poole: see "Poole, Cheryl"
Bailey, Chris: 262
Bailey, Gertrude: 30, 64, 65, 66, 67, 169, 170, 209
Bailey, Sophronia: 65
Bailey, Thomas: 262
Bailey, Tim: 262
Bailey, William Jr.: 67
Bailey, William Sr.: 65
Baker, Barry Lee: 192
Baker, Becky: 298
Baker, Carlton: 14
Baker, Dorothy: 284
Baker, Gloria Jean: 48, 297
Baker, Leonard James: 352
Baker, Marcus M.: 148
Baker, Margery Elizabeth Hill: see "Hill, Margery Elizabeth"
Baker, Marjorie Elizabeth: 47, 48, 297
Baker, Mary Genung: see "Genung, Mary"
Baker, Maude: 148, 157
Baker, Millicent Sarah Strong: see "Strong, Millicent"
Baker, Paul Edward: 48, 296, 297, 298
Baker, Paula Yancey Burch: see "Yancey, Paula"
Baker, Pauletta: 298
Baker, Sharon: 297
Baker, William: 47, 48, 174
Balch, Hazel Dean: see "Dean, Hazel"
Balch, Helen Reilly: see "Reilly, Helen"
Balch, Leslie Raymond: 110, 111, 112
Baldridge, Alta: 50
Baldridge, Anna Irene: 20, 49, 50, 51, 63, 237
Baldridge, Anna Waldron: see "Waldron, Anna"
Baldridge, Earl L.: 49
Baldridge, Edward: 49, 50
Baldridge, Herbert Simpson: 49, 50, 51
Baldridge, Kenan Stone: 52, 53, 156
Baldridge, Mark Steen: 52, 156

Baldridge, Meda Moore: see "Moore, Meda"
Baldridge, Virginia Stone: see "Stone, Virginia"
Baldridge, Warren E.: 49, 50, 51, 52, 53, 155
Baldridge, Warren Scott: 51, 156
Baldridge, William E.: 49, 50
Baldwin, Iva: 272
Ball, (George) Milton: 14, 53, 54, 55
Ball, Alan: 55
Ball, Brenda: 55
Ball, Charles: 233
Ball, Dorothy Milton: see "Milton, Dorothy"
Ball, Dorothy Morey: see "Morey, Dorothy"
Ball, Dorthea Miner: see "Miner, Dorthea"
Ball, Douglas: 26, 55
Ball, George H. Jr.: 19, 20, 53, 54, 97, 167, 172, 176, 197, 233
Ball, George H. Sr.: 20, 54, 233
Ball, Maude Garton: see "Garton, Maude"
Ball, Myrta Sarah: 30, 54, 66, 97, 233, 280, 281
Ball, Richard: 53, 54, 55, 174, 197, 297
Ball, Sarah Seager: see "Seager, Sarah"
Bancroft, Esther Ann: 61
Baptist Missionary Society: 24, 163
Barber, Audrey Clingerman: see "Clingerman, Audrey"
Barber, Dorothy Wood: see "Wood, Dorothy"
Barber, Howard L.: 346
Barber, James: 346
Bargy, Etta: 147
Bargy, Mary Elizabeth Rowe: see "Rowe, Mary Elizabeth"
Bargy, Peter: 147
Barker, Marie: 336
Barnes, Arthur (d. 1892): 55
Barnes, Arthur L. (d. 1984): 186
Barnes, Barbara Black: see "Black, Barbara"
Barnes, Benjamin Samuel: 55, 95, 96
Barnes, Clara Ferguson: see "Ferguson, Clara"
Barnes, Earl Nelson: 55, 56, 96, 166, 211, 252
Barnes, Frank: 55
Barnes, George Henry: 312, 313
Barnes, Gladys: 55
Barnes, Harvey Linwood: 56
Barnes, Helen Dagle: see "Dagle, Helen"
Barnes, Irving: 56
Barnes, Isabel Coon: see "Coon, Isabel"
Barnes, Kathryn Foster: 186, 322
Barnes, Lee: 230
Barnes, Lila Esther: 312
Barnes, Lillian Langley: see "Langley, Lillian"
Barnes, Linwood Walter: 55, 56, 96
Barnes, Lois: 294
Barnes, Lucy: 55
Barnes, Maude Porter: see "Porter, Maude"
Barnes, Nelson T.: 55
Barnes, Ola Dagle: see "Dagle, Ola"

Barnes, Verna Stone: see "Stone, Verna"
Barrett, Anna Brace: see "Brace, Anna"
Barrett, Margaret Mae: 66, 133, 135, 136
Barrett, Peter L.: 135
Bartley, Frances Dapolito Edwards: see "Dapolito, Frances"
Bartley, William C.: 133
Barton, Doris Jane: 109, 110, 111
Barton, Mary Ruth: 109, 110, 111
Barton, Nettie Seager: see "Seager, Fanette"
Barton, Peter Raymond: 76, 80, 110, 111, 145, 157
Barton, Ruth Dean: see "Dean, Ruth"
Bastian, Mary E.: 57
Bastian, Roy G.: 57
Bastian, Ruth M.: 57
Bastian, Wesley: 14
Bates, Arnold Lloyd: 227, 228, 230, 231
Bates, Clara Byron: see "Byron, Clara"
Bates, Dawn Lorraine: 232
Bates, Jack Elliott: 227, 228, 230, 231, 232
Bates, Jack Marshall: 232
Bates, Jack: 230, 231
Bates, Scott: 231
Bates, Shawn: 231
Bates, Steven: 231
Bates, Tiffany Yvonne: 232
Bates, Yvonne Marshall: see "Marshall, Yvonne"
Baxter, George: 162
Baxter, James Dean: 162
Baxter, James Jr.: 162
Baxter, Jane Gilmore: see "Gilmore, Jane"
Baxter, Jeanne Alice: 162
Baxter, Julianna Mikeltish: see "Mikeltish, Julianna"
Baxter, Mabel: 91, 92, 93, 324, 326
Baxter, Mary Ruffino Otto: see "Otto, Mary"
Baxter, Orselah Williba: 92
Bay Shore Lodge No. 606 of the IOOF: 29, 37, 43, 47, 123, 191, 248, 265, 318
Baylard, Leon: 178
Beacham, Edward A.: 213
Beacham, Mabelle Hubbard Latham: see "Hubbard, Mabel"
Beam, Caroline Isabelle "Carrie": 99
Bean, Derek: 241
Bean, Harold "Bill": 241
Bean, Henrietta: 269
Bean, Sandra Mills: see "Mills, Sandra"
Bean, Thomas: 241
Bean House: see "O.A. Skutt Company"
Beck, David W.: 57
Beck, Edith Weeks: see "Weeks, Edith"
Beck, Marie: 323
Beck, Mary E.: 57
Beck, Walter Adam: 57
Becker, Arthur: 334

Becker, Earl: 334
Becker, Harold Roy: 334
Becker, Lester: 334
Becker, Myrna Godkin: see "Godkin, Myrna"
Becker, Ruth: 334
Becker, William C. Sr.: 334
Becker, William Charles: 334
Beckett, Charlotte Rebecca: 171
Beebe, Ezra: 255
Beebe, Frank: 255
Beebe, Maryette Fisher Penner: see "Fisher, Maryette"
Beehive Apartments: 34, 93, 102
Behm, Gloria: 324
Benedict, Grace Mable: 136
Benjamin, David L.: 107
Benjamin, James E.: 107
Benton, Mary: 78, 79
Berg, Richie: 304
Bertilina, Charles: 312
Bertilina, Hazel: 312
Betts, Cecille Guthrie: see "Guthrie, Cecille Mary"
Betts, Charles "Ivan": 57, 58, 145, 278
Betts, Donald Elvin: 58
Betts, Edith Chase: see "Chase, Edith"
Betts, Eva Fink: see "Fink, Eva"
Betts, George Elvin: 57, 58
Betts, Iva: 20, 58, 143, 145, 146
Betts, James William: 58, 331
Betts, Roy L.: 58, 241
Betts, James: 57, 58, 145
Biedick, Rachel Juliana: 224, 225
Billingsley, John: 322
Billingsley, Laura LeBlanc Van Hoff: see "LeBlanc, Laura"
Bishop, William: 22
Black, Barbara Ann: 56
Blake, Brent: 128
Blake, June Kepner: see "Kepner, (Ida) June"
Blake, Lee R.: 128
Blake, Lois Engel: see "Engel, Lois"
Blake, Robert James: 128
Blanchard, Dorothy: 176
Blanchard, Edwin: 176
Blauvelt, Kenneth R.: 14
Blauvelt, Walter: 14
Blondale, Barry Lynn: 262
Blondale, Katherine: 262
Blondale, Nancy Poole: see "Poole, Nancy"
Blondale, Roger: 262
Blondale, Ronald A.: 262
Bly, Charles: 60
Bly, Gertrude Gladys: 59, 60
Bly, John W.: 58, 59, 60, 61
Bly, Lida May Pierse: see "Pierse, Lida May"
Bohrer, Esther Virginia: 91

Bohrer, Virginia Albert: 91
Bohrer, Walter: 91
Boll, Anna: 69
Bond, Charles: 331
Bond, Myrtle Susan: 155
Bonney, Charles: 89, 90
Bonney, Eva Sommer: see "Sommer, Eva"
Bonney, Evelyn: 90
Bonney, Kathryn Elizabeth: 88, 89, 90
Boone, Allan D. Jr.: 322
Boone, Allan Daniel: 322
Boone, Allison: 322
Boone, Desneige Alayne: 322
Boone, Lorraine Van Hoff: see "Van Hoff, Lorraine"
Boone, Robin: 322
Boone, Sharon Alice: 322
Borden, Albert Hiram: 61, 62
Borden, Celia Lovejoy: see "Lovejoy, Celia"
Borden, Florence Ida: 62, 323
Borden, Harriett McOmber: see "Harris, Harriett "Hattie""
Borden, Ina Davenport: see "Davenport, Ina"
Borden, Jennie Hamm: see "Hamm, Jennie"
Borden, John H.: 61
Borden, Raymond: 62
Borden, Velma: 61
Borden, Viola Correll: see "Correll, Viola"
Borys, Katie: 73, 74
Boughton, Alanson: 64
Boughton, Emily Jane: 64
Boughton, Ida Garton: see "Garton, Ida"
Boughton, Jean K.: 20, 63, 64, 353
Boughton, Katherine Ziegler: see "Ziegler, Katherine"
Boughton, Margaret Kellicutt: see "Kellicutt, Margaret"
Boughton, Raymond W.: 62, 63, 64
Boughton, Wallace: 64
Bowell, Grace: 161, 264
Bowen, Mary: 207
Bowler, Catherine Collier: see "Collier, Catherine"
Boyd, Clayton: 65
Boyd, Dalinda: 65, 268
Boyd, Effie E.: 65, 268
Boyd, Florence: 65, 68, 268, 269, 279
Boyd, Gertrude "Gertie" Bailey: see "Bailey, Gertrude"
Boyd, James Jr.: 64, 65, 66, 67, 68, 75, 169, 209
Boyd, James Sr.: 65, 268
Boyd, Jay Wilgar: 65, 67
Boyd, Leslie: 65, 67, 68, 200
Boyd, Marion: 65, 67, 68
Boyd, Mary Ellen: 67, 68
Boyd, Minnie: 65
Boyer, Steve: 26
Boyle, Hazel: 331, 332
Brace, Anna: 135
Bramer, Diane Curran: see "Curran, Diane"

Bramer, Monica: 250
Bramer, Stacey: 250
Brandes, Charles A.: 14
Braun, Florence Anna: 69
Brecht, Belle: 141
Brecht, Caroline: 141, 142
Brede, Thelma: 281, 282
Brewster, James D.: 14
Brewster, Keith C.: 14
Briggs, Adelia "Ada" Laird: see "Laird, Adelia"
Briggs, Agnes Mae Lauder: see "Lauder, Agnes"
Briggs, Anna Terry: see "Terry, Anna"
Briggs, Ardella Correll: see "Correll, Ardella"
Briggs, Barbara Farrow: see "Farrow, Barbara"
Briggs, Beatrice Belva: 72, 289, 291
Briggs, Bernard: 68, 69, 73
Briggs, Bernice Marie: 68, 70, 73
Briggs, Bessie B.: 72
Briggs, Beulah B.: 72
Briggs, Birney: 71, 120, 121, 284
Briggs, Bruce: 68, 70
Briggs, Cleon Laverne: 68, 69, 70, 72, 73
Briggs, Constance: 69, 70
Briggs, Eddie: 14
Briggs, Emeline Delia "Emma": 119, 120, 121
Briggs, Ernest Cleon: 68, 69, 70, 73, 126
Briggs, Ernest E.: 68, 72
Briggs, Eunice Mitchell: see "Mitchell, Eunice"
Briggs, Eva Belle: 72, 74, 347, 348, 349, 350, 352
Briggs, Flossie: 340
Briggs, Grace: 56
Briggs, Harry: 72
Briggs, Helen Doremus: see "Doremus, Helen"
Briggs, Ila Seager: see "Seager, Ila"
Briggs, Irene Elizabeth: 72, 133, 134
Briggs, Jesse Terry: 70, 71, 121, 283, 284
Briggs, John: 92
Briggs, Jonathan: 40
Briggs, Judy: 70
Briggs, Keith: 68
Briggs, Lyman (d. 1923): 72
Briggs, Lyman Laverne: 68, 69, 70, 72, 73
Briggs, M.L.: 37
Briggs, Mae Thomas Satterlee: see "Thomas, Mae"
Briggs, Magdalene Elizabeth "Lena": 71, 72, 73, 74, 349
Briggs, Magdalene Yancey: see "Yancey, Magdalene"
Briggs, Mariam Dowd: see "Dowd, Mariam"
Briggs, Mary Stoutenger: see "Stoutenger, Mary"
Briggs, Maynard: 37
Briggs, Michael: 69
Briggs, Mildred Farnam: see "Farnam, Mildred"
Briggs, Olive Mary: 26, 270, 337, 338
Briggs, Richard: 69
Briggs, Roy Eugene: 72, 73, 133

Briggs, Ruth: 60
Briggs, Stephen: 71
Briggs, Terry: 69
Briggs, Verda: 92
Brisbin, Margaret: 55
Brockhuisen, John: 15, 118
Brockhuisen, William: 15, 118
Broekhuizen, Adrian "Dutch": 118
Broekhuizen, Anthony: 118
Broekhuizen, Maria DeKreij: see "DeKreij, Maria"
Broekhuizen, Mary Jane: 118, 119
Broekhuizen, Teunis: 118
Broekhuizen, Willem: 118, 119
Brown, Addie A.: 210, 211
Brown, Allie: 261
Brown, Ann Miles: see "Miles, Ann"
Brown, Claude Erwin: 75, 76, 77, 110, 143, 144, 145
Brown, Elizabeth June "Bess": 185, 186
Brown, G. Isabel: 75, 76, 77, 143, 145
Brown, George: 15
Brown, Greta Fink: see "Fink, Greta"
Brown, Jean: 134
Brown, Jessie: 101, 197
Brown, John David: 75
Brown, Luella V.: 121
Brown, Lyle: 340
Brown, Mabel Clista: 352, 353, 354
Brown, Mary Ethel: 308, 309
Brown, Myrtle Josephine: 84, 137, 140
Brown, Robert: 353
Brown, Rose: 353
Bruner, Susan: 245, 246
Brush, Adeline E.: 77
Brush, Elizabeth: 62, 72
Brush, Emily McQueen: see "McQueen, Emily"
Brush, Eunice Rounds: see "Rounds, Eunice"
Brush, Grace B.: 77
Brush, James N.: 77
Brush, James S.: 77
Brush, Knowles Sears: 77
Brush, Laverne Jerome: 77
Brush, Neta Mary: 77
Buerman, Charles H.: 84
Buhlmann, Joyce: 347
Buhlmann, Ruth: 144
Buhlmann, Ward: 144
Bullock, Betty Willey: see "Willey, Betty"
Bullock, Brenda: 78
Bullock, Doris M.: 77, 78
Bullock, Edwin Herbert: 15, 77, 78
Bullock, Emma Belle: 148
Bullock, Ethel Ferguson: see "Ferguson, Ethel"
Bullock, Herbert Rowe: 77, 78
Bullock, Lewis Clark: 77, 78
Bullock, Mary Ann Chadwick: see "Chadwick, Mary Ann"
Bullock, Michael: 78
Bullock, Robert: 78
Bullock, Shirley Ann: 77, 78
Bullock, Stephen: 78
Bulson, Josephine: 98
Bumpus, Candace O.: 284, 285, 286
Bumpus, Mattie: 286
Burch, Charles: 35
Burch, Ellen: 138
Burch, George: 138
Burch, Jane ("Jennie") Acker Johnson: see "Johnson, Jane"
Burch, Maxine: 352
Burch, Paula Yancey: see "Yancey, Paula"
Burch, Richard Carter: 352
Burley, Jeanette Ruth: 235
Burnett, Ada "Addie" Mae: 78, 79, 80, 81
Burnett, Bertha Stickles: see "Stickles, Bertha"
Burnett, Eleanor: 119
Burnett, Franklin H.: 78, 79
Burnett, George Theodore: 78, 79
Burnett, Mary Benton: see "Benton, Mary"
Burnette, George: 188
Burns, Addie Burnett: see "Burnett, Ada"
Burns, Cora: 252, 253
Burns, David Howard: 80, 354
Burns, Denise Rebecca: 80, 354
Burns, Diane Roberta: 80, 354
Burns, Grace: 63, 68, 167, 252, 253, 353
Burns, Harold Joseph "Bing": 79, 80, 86, 122, 142, 249
Burns, Howard Henry: 79, 80, 354
Burns, Jacqueline Steele: see "Steele, Jacqueline"
Burns, Joseph John: 79, 80, 81
Burns, Leona Mae: 79, 80, 81, 295
Burns, Louella Nesbitt: see "Nesbitt, Louella"
Burns, Louise Ziegler: see "Ziegler, Louise"
Burns, Margaret Byrne: see "Byrne, Margaret"
Burns, Margaret F.: 79
Burns, Mortimer: 79
Burns, William C.: 253
Burse, Bernadine: 336
Busch, Glenn: 342
Busch, Herbert: 342
Busch, Louise Yost: see "Yost, Louise"
Bush, Gertrude: 46
Bush, Leone Myra: 341
Bushberg, Carol: 304
Bushey, Rose: 330
Butler, Robert: 341
Buttaccio, Anna C.: 174
Button, Thorne: 157
Byerly, Bruce: 314
Byerly, Edward: 314

Byerly, Marjorie Hookway: see "Hookway, Marjorie"
Byerly, Richard: 314
Byrne, Margaret: 79
Byron, Clara Doris: 232
Byron, Edward Frank: 232
Byron, Elizabeth Weber: see "Weber, Elizabeth"
Cahill, Wende L.: 134
Cahoon, Addie Mae: 234, 317, 318
Cahoon, Calista: 318
Cahoon, Mary Bethania: 177
Caldwell, Elizabeth Carnell: see "Carnell, Elizabeth"
Caldwell, Homer E.: 186
Caldwell, Lee Jackson: 186
Caldwell, Sarah: 186
Calkins Barber Shop: 9
Camp, Edgar G.: 15
Camp, Zoie: 258
Campbell, Anna: 105, 217
Campbell, Barbara: 99
Campbell, Florence: 168
Campbell, Isaac George: 167
Campbell, James: 99
Campbell, Josephine Minot: see "Minot, Josephine"
Campbell, Mabel M.: 66, 167, 168, 169
Canning Factory: see "Salter Canning Company"
Canty, Alta Baldridge Parkhurst: see "Baldridge, Alta"
Canty, Earle W.: 50
Capron, Robert: 273
Carnell, Catherine Blanche: 186
Carnell, Dora Eva: 185, 186
Carnell, Elizabeth "Lizzie": 186
Carnell, Elmira Smith: see "Smith, Elmira"
Carnell, Leonard H.: 186
Caroline Moore's Beauty Shop: 21
Carpenter, Anna Walhizer: see "Walhizer, Anna"
Carpenter, Frederick Troop: 82, 83
Carpenter, Hannah Hewson: see "Hewson, Hannah"
Carpenter, Inez: 82, 190, 191, 192, 219
Carpenter, John: 82
Carpenter, Mary Phillips: see "Phillips, Mary"
Carpenter, Nancy: 82
Carpenter, Reuben Eliphant: 82
Carrier, Ellen: 40
Cartman, Sarah: 247
Case, Fred A.: 15
Case, Gertrude: 325
Case, Theodore "Teddy": 325
Casey, Lawrence B.: 329
Cashady, Aminda Cook: see "Cook, Aminda"
Cashady, Chester: 85
Cashady, Esther: 85
Cashady, Frances: 85
Cashady, Guy: 83
Cashady, Mabel Johnson: see "Johnson, Mabel"
Cashady, Marian Koch: see "Koch, Marian"

Cashady, Olive Streitle Preston: see "Streitle, Olive"
Cashady, Thomas: 84, 85
Cashady, Ward Charles: 83, 84, 85
Cassella, Steph: 303
Castor, Charles: 15, 279
Castor, Doris: 279
Castor, Howard: 15
Catchpole, (Ruth) Shirley Hartman: see "Hartman, (Ruth) Shirley"
Catchpole, Alice Rich: see "Rich, Alice"
Catchpole, Amy: 88
Catchpole, Belinda: 88
Catchpole, Catherine: 87
Catchpole, Charles "Chuck": 88, 89, 90, 91
Catchpole, Doris: 90, 91, 229
Catchpole, Edwin W. (d. 1951): 66, 85, 89
Catchpole, Edwin Watson (d. 1963): 88, 89, 91
Catchpole, Elizabeth Caldwell "Betsy": 89
Catchpole, Erminie: 90
Catchpole, Esther Bohrer: see "Bohrer, Esther"
Catchpole, Frances Green: see "Green, Frances"
Catchpole, George: 85, 91, 160, 229, 230, 340
Catchpole, J.Terry: 80, 86, 87, 91
Catchpole, James: 59
Catchpole, Joseph: 80, 89
Catchpole, Kathryn Bonney "Kay": see "Bonney, Kathryn"
Catchpole, Lynda: 43, 85, 86, 87, 90, 91, 130
Catchpole, Nancy (father: George): 91
Catchpole, Nancy Alyssa "Alice": 88, 89, 90
Catchpole, Olga: 89, 90, 91, 165
Catchpole, R. Hayes: 89, 160, 228, 230
Catchpole, Reginald Caldwell "Reg": 43, 80, 85, 86, 89, 91, 194, 240
Catchpole, Robert "Bobby": 88
Catchpole, Victor Caldwell: 88, 89, 90, 91
Catchpole, Yvonne: 88
Caves, Jeanette Pierson: see "Pierson, Jeanette"
Caves, Robert: 347
Chaddock, Edith Gertrude: 288
Chaddock, Florence: 81
Chaddock, Norris: 81
Chaddock, Sophronia: 311
Chadwick, Mary Ann: 78
Chalupa, Doris Helen: 144, 246
Chalupa, Frank: 129
Chambers, Charles Newton: 335
Chambers, Dorothy Margaret: 335
Chambers, Elizabeth Luella: 335
Chambers, Ethel Godkin: see "Godkin, Ethel"
Chambers, William Elias Jr.: 335
Chambers, William Elias Sr.: 335
Chandler, Marion Edwards: see "Edwards, Marion Ruth"
Chandler, Sidney: 136

Chapin, Dora: 30
Chappell, Laura J.: 240, 242
Chase, Edith L.: 57, 58, 145
Chase, Ever: 108
Chase, Ralph: 104
Chase, Stanley: 327
Church, Charlotte Prince: see "Prince, Charlotte"
Church, Frances Jane: 156
Church, Margaret Quereau: see "Quereau, Margaret"
Clark, Byron Keith: 249
Clark, Eileen Noyes: see "Noyes, Eileen"
Clark, Frances Louisa "Fannie": 221
Clark, Mabel Lucille: 267
Clark, Richard: 249
Claus, Clara Davenport: see "Davenport, Clara"
Claus, Daniel: 92
Claus, Dorothy: 92, 93, 326
Claus, George Earl: 91, 92, 93, 324
Claus, Mabel Baxter: see "Baxter, Mabel"
Claus, Thelma Mabel: 92, 324, 325, 326
Clingerman, Agnes Virginia: 93, 94
Clingerman, Alice Elizabeth "Betty": 196
Clingerman, Audrey Jean: 346
Clingerman, Brenda: 180, 181
Clingerman, Bruce: 180, 182
Clingerman, Clara Leasure: see "Leasure, Clara"
Clingerman, Clarence E.: 179
Clingerman, Emma Pleasant Virginia: 94
Clingerman, Emma Smith: see "Smith, Emma"
Clingerman, Frances "Effie" Foreback: see "Foreback, Frances"
Clingerman, Helen Aderhold: see "Aderhold, Helen"
Clingerman, Helen: 94
Clingerman, Jacob "Jack": 15, 94
Clingerman, Janet Harper: see "Harper, Janet"
Clingerman, Jeanette Wolven: see "Wolven, Jeanette"
Clingerman, Jonnie Kay: see "Taylor, Jonnie Kay"
Clingerman, Kathryn Taylor: see "Taylor, Kathryn"
Clingerman, Larry Bruce: 179, 180, 181, 182
Clingerman, Lenard Carlton: see "Foisia, Lenard Carlton"
Clingerman, Madeline Foisia: see "Foisia, Madeline"
Clingerman, Maggie Ellen: 94
Clingerman, Marion: 95, 196
Clingerman, Maxine: 241
Clingerman, Millard Harrison: 94, 346
Clingerman, Neil Wayne: 346
Clingerman, Pamela: 196
Clingerman, Ralph W. I.: 93, 94, 95
Clingerman, Renee: 180
Clingerman, Robert Jr.: 196
Clingerman, Robert: 196
Clingerman, Rosa May: 94
Clingerman, Roy Cecil: 94
Clingerman, Shelia Seager: see "Seager, Shelia"

Clingerman, Thomas: 93, 94
Clingerman, Walter: 15
Clingerman, Wayne: 15, 346
Clinton D. Dillingham Insurance: 20, 123
Closs, Edward: 141
Closs, Ellen: 26
Closs, Mary: 26
Cloud, Mildred Porter: see "Porter, Mildred"
Cloud, Preston E. Jr.: 263
Clum, Glenn: 15
Cody, Eva Thomas Dolan: see "Thomas, Eva"
Cody, Lester: 316
Coffee Shoppe: 84
Cohoon, Everett: 15
Colburn, Irving: 21
Colburn, James A.: 15
Cold Storage: 2, 8, 21, 22, 57, 68, 71, 79, 93, 128, 133, 145, 148, 165, 175, 182, 187, 190, 216, 217, 220, 225, 226, 227, 228, 229, 230, 236, 243, 265, 266, 268, 273, 274, 294, 310, 317, 326, 337, 355, 356
Cole, Adella Skinner: see "Skinner, Adella (d. 1911)"
Cole, Alice Clingerman: see "Clingerman, Alice"
Cole, Frank Benton: 58
Cole, Leroy: 296
Cole, Raymond: 196
Cole, Romaine: 66, 263
Cole, Sandra Lee: 196
Cole, Terry: 196
Cole, Thomas Benton: 45, 58
Collier, Catherine B.: 270, 271
Collier, Claude: 26, 43, 44, 253, 270, 271, 291
Collier, Ethel Morey: see "Morey, Ethel"
Collier, Henrietta Quereau: see "Quereau, Henrietta"
Collier, Henry R.: 42
Collier, John: 44
Collier, Katie: 26
Collier, Leora A.: 42
Collier, Lucinda Hance: 6, 10
Collier, Mildred Cornelia "Millie": 36, 37, 38, 39, 42, 43, 44, 270
Collier, Phoebe Jane: 43
Collier, Virginia: 26, 270, 271
Collier, William H.: 270, 271
Colling, J.J.: 74, 349
Colvin, George: 131, 345
Comella, Anthony Rossario: 103
Comella, Dorothy Davis Kelley: see "Davis, Dorothy"
Comella, Joseph J.: 103
Comella, Maria: 103
Comella, Phillip John: 103
Comella, Phillip: 103
Compson, Mervin M.: 41
Conklin, Maude Ethel: 296
Connelly, Becky Baker: see "Baker, Becky"

Connelly, Kate: 298
Connelly, Michael "Sammy": 298
Connelly, Paul: 298
Connelly, Scott: 298
Connor, Rachel: 295
Conrow, Virginia: 81, 294, 295
Contract Bridge Club: 2, 30, 44, 90, 161, 167, 169, 207
Converse, Caroline Marie: 211
Converse, Charles E.: 15
Converse, Ella: 325
Converse, Ernest E.: 15
Converse, John E.: 15
Converse, Ray: 325
Converse, Seth: 15
Converse Hotel: 6
Conway, Rose Ellen: 279
Cook, Agnes "Jennie" Hawkes Watkins: see "Hawkes, Agnes "Jennie""
Cook, Alice Marie: 234
Cook, Aminda: 83
Cook, Bessie Wilber: see "Wilber, Bessie"
Cook, Charles (d. 1980): see "May, Charles Cook"
Cook, Charles Frederick "Fred": 233, 234
Cook, Charles George: 232, 233
Cook, Earl Raymond: 232, 233, 234
Cook, Esther M.: 233
Cook, Georgiana: 234
Cook, Ina Ripley: see "Ripley, Ina"
Cook, Kenneth: 233, 234
Cook, Raymond Earl: 233, 234
Cook, Shirley Sanderson: see "Sanderson, Shirley"
Cook, Walter Hugh: 233
Coon, Isabel May: 55
Coonrod, Dennis: 15
Corey, Sedate E.: 108
Correll, Ardella Elizabeth: 72
Correll, Daniel: 62, 72
Correll, Elizabeth Brush: see "Brush, Elizabeth"
Correll, John: 107
Correll, Viola: 62
Costello, James: 48
Cottage Hotel: 8
Cotton, Richard: 136
Cotton, Robert M.: 15
Cotton, Thomas: 136
Cottrell, Anna W. "Annie": 115, 116
Cottrell, Bertha Mae: 115, 116
Cottrell, Libanus H.: 115, 116
Cottrell, Marna Wemelsfelder: see "Wemelsfelder, Marna"
Countryman, Elizabeth Mae: 158
Countryman, Eunice Stickles: see "Stickles, Eunice"
Countryman, Ralph "Obee": 158
Crane, (Anna) Grace: 215, 216
Crawford, Elizabeth R.: 123

Crocker, Elsie: 229
Cromback, Sheila: 91
Cronk, Catherine: 285
Croucher, Bertha: 278
Croucher, Elias: 278
Cunningham, Joseph O.: 46
Cunningham, Mary: 46
Curran, Diane Summer: 250
Curtis, Anna: 259
Curtis, Ethel: 326, 327, 329, 330
Curtis, Fred James: 327
Curtis, Nellie Elizabeth: 327
Curtis, Ruth: 102
Cutting, Minnie: 149
Dagle, Addison: 96, 97, 108, 197
Dagle, Albert: 55, 66, 95, 96
Dagle, Alfred: 178
Dagle, Charles: 96
Dagle, Cora Lamb: see "Lamb, Cora"
Dagle, Esther Seager Wagner: see "Seager, Esther"
Dagle, Grace Briggs: see "Briggs, Grace"
Dagle, Harriet DeNeef: see "DeNeef, Harriet"
Dagle, Harvey: 56
Dagle, Helen Adelia: 55, 56, 196
Dagle, Mervin Lewis: 96, 97, 98
Dagle, Minnie Lamb: see "Lamb, Minnie"
Dagle, Ola: 95
Dagle, Virginia: 97, 98
Daniels, Florence: 239, 240
Dapolito, Antonia Desentoli: see "Santoli, Antonia"
Dapolito, Frances Marian: 132, 133
Dapolito, Mary Santola: see "Santola, Mary"
Dapolito, Phillip Antonio: 133
Darling, Arthur W.: 98
Darling, Grace Washburn: see "Washburn, Grace"
Darling, Mildred Riesdorph: see "Riesdorph, Mildred"
Darling, Theresa Mildred: 98, 99
Darling, William: 98
Davenport, Clara: 92
Davenport, Fred: 149
Davenport, Ina: 61, 62
Davenport, Leroy "Roy": 80, 100, 240
Davenport, Pearl Knox Seager: see "Knox, Pearl"
Davis, Caleb U.: 156
Davis, Carol: 222
Davis, Clifford Lewis: 54, 100, 101
Davis, Dorothy Jean: 102, 103
Davis, Elizabeth "Betty Jane": 100, 101
Davis, Frances Church: see "Church, Frances"
Davis, Hattie: 156, 157, 222, 290
Davis, Jessie Shortsleeve: see "Shortsleeve, Jessie"
Davis, John Heck: 102, 103
Davis, Lena Garton: see "Garton, Lena"
Davis, Lewis Hiram: 102
Davis, Margaret Heck: see "Heck, Margaret"

Davis, William "Billy": 100, 101
Dawson, Margaret M.: 155
Day, Albert Henry: 93, 103, 104, 105
Day, Deleon: 15
Day, James: 103, 104
Day, Katherine Maude: 104, 105
Day, Lucretia Pettit: see "Pettit, Lucretia"
Day, Lucy: 102
Day, Lydia Lapp: see "Lapp, Lydia"
Day, Mabel Claus: see "Baxter, Mabel"
Day, Martin: 105
Day, Maude Lapp: see "Lapp, Maude"
Deady, Alice: 108
Deady, Caroline "Carrie" Swift: see "Swift, Caroline"
Deady, Charles Swift: 106, 107, 108
Deady, Eva: 108
Deady, George: 301
Deady, Ida Lansing-Phillipson: see "Lansing, Ida"
Deady, James W.: 106
Deady, Phoebe Lake: see "Lake, Phoebe"
Deady, Theresa: 107
Deady, William: 107
Dean, Anna Dickinson: see "Dickinson, Anna"
Dean, Anna Priebe: see "Priebe, Anna"
Dean, Charles "Charlie" Edwin: 109, 110, 111, 112, 113, 120
Dean, Edgar W.: 109
Dean, Ella Parslow: see "Parslow, Ella"
Dean, Hazel Maude: 110, 111, 112
Dean, James Nelson: 109, 110, 113
Dean, Leslie: 15
Dean, Marian: 109, 110, 111, 112
Dean, Robert E. Jr.: 113
Dean, Robert Edgar "Eddie": 69, 109, 110, 111, 112, 113
Dean, Ruth Irene: 76, 109, 110, 111, 145
Dean's Service Station: 20, 109
DeBack, Inez Vanderzell: see "Vanderzell, Irene"
DeBack, Jennie DeCook: see "DeCook, Jennie"
DeBack, Lawrence Harold: 113, 114, 115
DeBack, Molly Rita: 113, 114, 115
DeBack, Paul: 113
Decker, J.M.: 107
DeCook, Jennie: 113
DeJohn, (Albert) Louis: 347
DeJohn, Gerard Ernest: 347
DeJohn, James: 347
DeJohn, Joyce Wolven: see "Wolven, Joyce"
DeJohn, Mabel Brown: see "Brown, Mabel"
DeJohn, Mary V.: 347
DeJohn, Pamela: 347
DeJong, Adriana: 118, 119
DeKing, Leland: 15, 254
DeKreij, Maria: 118
DeLeys, Karolyn: 173

DeLisio, Elena Marie: 119
DeLisio, John P.: 119
DeLisio, Joseph: 119
DeLisio, Lauralea Paula: 119
DeLisio, Lorena Jean: 119
DeLisio, Mary DiSanto: see "DiSanto, Mary"
DeLisio, Mary Jane Broekhuizen: see "Broekhuizen, Mary Jane"
DeLisio, Randolph James: 119
Demaris, Sylvia: 140
DeNeef, Anna Cottrell: see "Cottrell, Anna"
DeNeef, Bertha: see "Cottrell, Bertha"
DeNeef, Harriet Katherine: 97
DeNeef, John: 115, 116
Dennis, Carol A.: 116, 117
Dennis, Corinne Smith: see "Smith, Corinne"
Dennis, Frank George Jr.: 116, 117, 118
Dennis, Frank George: 116
Dennis, Jean A.: 116
Dennis, Katharine Merrell: see "Merrell, Katharine"
DeRuischer, Adriana DeJong: see "DeJong, Adriana"
DeRuischer, Audrey: 119
DeRuischer, Eleanor Burnett: see "Burnett, Eleanor"
DeRuischer, Ida J.: 118, 119
DeRuischer, Isaac "Jim": 119
DeRuischer, Isaac Jr. "Ike": 118, 119
DeRuischer, Isaac: 118, 119
DeRuischer, Jan Michael: 119
DeRuischer, Kathleen J.: 118, 119
DeSanto, Teresa Mary Jane: 37, 257
Desmond, Charles: 168
Desmond, Florence Campbell: see "Campbell, Florence"
DeVall, Donald: 15
DeVay, Dale: 131
DeVay, Gilbert: 130
DeVay, Lucille Drury: see "Drury, Lucille"
DeVay, Richard: 78
DeVay, Susan: 131
DeVol, Harold: 138, 139
DeVol, Maude: 138, 139
Dickerman, Berenice: 243, 244
Dickinson, Anna: 109, 110, 111, 112, 113, 120, 121
Dickinson, Emeline Briggs: see "Briggs, Emeline"
Dickinson, Jay: 120
Dickinson, Jennie V.: 119, 120, 121, 129
Dickinson, Robert D.: 72, 113, 119, 120, 121
Dillingham, Carrie: 30, 36, 39, 40, 41, 42, 66, 271
Dillingham, Clinton Delos: 20, 36, 40, 123, 203, 336
Dillingham, Delos Waldorf: 40, 123
Dillingham, Elizabeth Lucille ("Betty Lou"): 36, 123, 312, 313
Dillingham, Elizabeth Stanton: see "Stanton, Elizabeth"
Dillingham, Elizabeth Van Pelt Godkin: see "Van Pelt,

Elizabeth"
Dillingham, Hilda Jane: 123
Dillingham, Sarah Armitage: see "Armitage, Sarah"
Dimon, Donald: 208
Dimon, Patricia Kenan: see "Kenan, Patricia"
DiSanto, Mary: 119
Ditton, Elizabeth: 335
Ditton, John Jr.: 334
Ditton, John: 333
Ditton, Louella "Ella": 333, 334, 336
Ditton, Mary A.: 333
Ditton, Mary Eileen Burns: see "Burns, Mary Eileen"
Divelbliss, Charles E.: 186
Divelbliss, Sarah Caldwell: see "Caldwell, Sarah"
Divincenzo, Carmella Giovine: see "Giovine, Carmella"
Divincenzo, Daniel: 329
Divincenzo, Rose: 329
Dobbin, Myrtle: 151, 154, 155
Dodds, Brian John: 126
Dodds, Christopher Zane: 126
Dodds, Donald Gilbert: 124, 126, 127
Dodds, Eric Martin: 126
Dodds, Fred J.: 124
Dodds, Frederick D.: 188
Dodds, Grace Scalzo: see "Scalzo, Grace"
Dodds, Harriett Seager: see "Seager, Harriett"
Dodds, Jacqueline Ann: 126
Dodds, John "Jack": 69, 124, 125, 126, 188
Dodds, Kathleen: 127
Dodds, Margaret Langford: see "Langford, Margaret"
Dodds, Martin John: 126
Dodds, Norma Weed: see "Weed, Norma"
Dodds, Pearl Hoppel: see "Hoppel, Pearl"
Dodds, Phillip Brian: 126
Dodds, Tracey: 127
Dodds, Wells Munson: 22, 124, 125, 188, 340
Dolan, E.: 316
Dolan, Eva Thomas: see "Thomas, Eva"
Doremus, Helen: 72
Doremus, Jeanette: 84
Doremus, Lydia: 189
Doude, Henry: 308
Dow, John: 303
Dowd, Alfred: 306
Dowd, Cassie: 72
Dowd, E.B.: 283
Dowd, George W.: 72
Dowd, Lee H.: 72
Dowd, Mariam Irene: 68, 71, 72, 74
Dowd, Mary (d. 1931): 308
Dowd, Mary E.: 72
Downing, Carole Arlene: 35, 36
Downing, Edna Acker: see "Acker, Edna"
Downing, Raymond Francis: 35, 36
Doyle, Earl James: 60

Doyle, Kathleen Whalen: see "Whalen, Kathleen"
Driscoll, Eleanor: 58
Drury, (Alyce) Harriett: 128
Drury, Albert "Bert" Lewis: 20, 129, 130, 131, 220, 222, 229
Drury, Benjamin (d. 1948): 220, 316, 317
Drury, Benjamin F.: 128
Drury, Bessie Grinnels: see "Grinnels, Bessie"
Drury, Clara Grinnals: see "Grinnals, Clara"
Drury, Claude: 131
Drury, Emma: 220
Drury, Evelyn: 127, 128, 164
Drury, Frank (d. 1921): 128
Drury, Frank (d. 1962): 220
Drury, Harriett Moore: see "Moore, Harriett"
Drury, Inez Furman: see "Furman, Inez"
Drury, Lucille Anne: 129, 130, 131
Drury, Lynn G.: 128
Drury, Mary Messenger Kepner: see "Messenger, Mary"
Drury, Mary T.: 128, 129, 131, 132, 222, 231
Drury, Paul: 20, 121, 129, 130, 131, 132, 176
Drury, Richard: 12, 13, 15, 220, 260
Drury, Theresa Lundergun: see "Lundergun, Theresa"
Drury and Son: 20, 129
DuBois, Nancy: 283
DuBois, Roy: 283
Duga, Beverly: 344
Duger, Blanche: 70
Duger, Henry: 70
Dunbar, Emma: 125, 187, 188, 189
Dunn, Bridget: 221
Durbin, Fred: 291
E.W. Catchpole & Sons: 178
Earle, Harry: 35
Earle, Mary: 35
Earle, William: 35
Early, Ann: 244, 245
Early, Constance Rendell: see "Rendell, Constance"
Early, Robert Rainey: 245
Eaton, Olive Ruth: 183
Edelman, Clyde: 131
Edmonds, Jean Dennis: see "Dennis, Jean"
Edmonds, Lee Jr.: 116
Edwards, Beverly Wiltsie: see "Wiltsie, Beverly"
Edwards, Clarence Everett: 135, 136
Edwards, Dennis Alan: 133, 134
Edwards, Dennis: 134
Edwards, Derrick: 134
Edwards, Dianne: 136
Edwards, Donald Edward: 132, 133, 135, 137
Edwards, Donald Philip: 132, 133, 134
Edwards, Frances Dapolito: see "Dapolito, Frances"
Edwards, Gloria: 134
Edwards, Grace Benedict: see "Benedict, Grace"

Edwards, Harry Lauder: 15, 135, 136
Edwards, Helen Shepherd: see "Shepherd, Helen"
Edwards, Irene Briggs: see "Briggs, Irene"
Edwards, Jean Brown: see "Brown, Jean"
Edwards, Jennie Vanderwinckel: see "Vanderwinckel, Jennie"
Edwards, Joan Kathleen: 136
Edwards, Keith: 136
Edwards, Kim: 134
Edwards, Lois Margaret: 136
Edwards, Margaret Barrett: see "Barrett, Margaret"
Edwards, Marion Ruth: 20, 63, 135, 136, 354
Edwards, Mark (mother: Jean): 134
Edwards, Mark (mother: Ruth): 136
Edwards, Mildred Anna: 137
Edwards, Myron Adelbert: 135
Edwards, Paul: 134
Edwards, Peter: 134
Edwards, Ronald: 132, 133, 134
Edwards, Ruth Bagshaw: see "Bagshaw, Ruth"
Edwards, Sandra Kay: 133, 134
Edwards, Thomas: 134
Edwards, Tracy: 134
Edwards, Troy: 134
Edwards, Warren Grant: 15, 135, 136
Edwards, Warren Llewellyn: 66, 133, 134, 135, 136
Edwards, Wende Cahill: see "Cahill, Wende"
Edwards, William: 136
Eidman, Clyde: 70
Eidman, Lena: 70
Eldman, Clyde: 194
Ellinwood, Kenneth R.: 15
Elmhurst, Eleanor: 287
Elwood, (Chloe) Edna: 345, 346
Elwood, Alzadah: 345
Emery, Elizabeth: 309
Emery, Walter: 59
Empey, Becky Baker Connelly: see "Baker, Becky"
Empey, Scott: 298
Engel, Lois Olive: 128
Engert, Clara: 300
Epworth League Institute: 24, 45, 59, 175, 205, 213, 283
Evans, David H.: 233
Evans, Mary: 233
Everett, Edith: 198
Everett, John H.: 15
Everett, Walter: 15
Ewing, Ethel Harris Hill Skinner: see "Harris, Ethel"
Ewing, Roger S.: 297
Exter, Julia: 167
Facer, Betty: 351
Facer, Daisy: 218
Facer, Debby: 218
Facer, Donald Frederick: 218

Facer, Nancy Leaird: see "Leaird, Nancy"
Failey, Alta: 240
Failey, Florence Daniels: see "Daniels, Florence"
Failey, Harris: 240
Failey, Ida: 240
Failey, Julia: 240
Failey, Leona Irene: 133, 239, 240, 241, 295
Failey, William: 239, 240
Fairbanks, Louise Rebecca: 179
Fanning, Joel: 316
Farnam, Mildred: 68, 69, 70, 72
Farnam, Stanley: 70
Farnsworth, Bernard "Tommy" "Bernie": 20, 80, 137, 138, 139, 140, 356
Farnsworth, Bernard J.: 138
Farnsworth, Craig A.: 138, 139, 140
Farnsworth, John William: 20, 84, 139, 141
Farnsworth, Josephine: 58, 75, 143, 144, 145
Farnsworth, Mary Camilla: 140
Farnsworth, Myrtle Brown: see "Brown, Myrtle"
Farnsworth, Sylvia Demaris: see "Demaris, Sylvia"
Farnsworth, Virginia Jewell: see "Jewell, Virginia"
Farnsworth, William D.: 140
Farnsworth and Son Funeral Directors: 20, 137, 139, 140
Farnsworth Museum: 139, 171, 356
Farrow, Barbara Marie: 69, 70
Farrow, Jay D.: 69
Farrow, Minnie Lapp: see "Lapp, Minnie"
Favreau, Alice: 141
Favreau, Caroline Brecht: see "Brecht, Caroline"
Favreau, Carrie E.: 141, 142, 143, 279
Favreau, Edmond: 141
Favreau, Ernest E. (d. 1916): 141, 142
Favreau, Ernest H. (d. 1964): 141, 142, 143, 279
Favreau, Ernest H. Jr. (d. 1999): 141, 142, 143, 279
Favreau, Harriett Alice: 142
Fenk, George Harrison: see "Fink, George Harrison"
Fennell, Anne Wood: 313, 314
Ferguson, Clara: 186
Ferguson, Ethel Della: 77, 78
Ferkes, Erminie Catchpole: see "Catchpole, Erminie"
Ferkes, James: 90
Fikes, Charles E.: 15
Finch, Anne Gilkey: see "Gilkey, Anne"
Finch, Frank: 352
Finch, Keith: 352
Fink, Christopher Christian: 146
Fink, Donald C.: 147
Fink, Edna: 75, 143, 145
Fink, Eva: 58, 143, 145
Fink, Franklin: 58, 75, 143, 145, 147, 218
Fink, Franziska Homeman: see "Homeman, Franziska"
Fink, George Harrison: 146, 147, 168
Fink, Gilman H.: 147

Fink, Grace Lorena: 146
Fink, Greta: 75, 76, 77, 143, 144, 145
Fink, Harold: 147
Fink, Hazel: 147
Fink, Henry: 147
Fink, Ida Wolf: see "Wolf, Ida"
Fink, Josephine Farnsworth: see "Farnsworth, Josephine"
Fink, Julia: 75, 99, 143, 144, 145
Fink, Maude Miner: see "Miner, Maud"
Fink, Mildred: 147
Fink, Nettie Hart: see "Hart, Nettie"
Firra, Eva: 222
Fischette, Mary: 174
Fish, Virginia Quereau: see "Quereau, Virginia"
Fish, William Cornelius: 270
Fisher, Carrie Dillingham Aldrich: see "Dillingham, Carrie"
Fisher, Maryette "Mary": 254, 255
Fisher, Rachel Biedick Marshall: see "Biedick, Rachel"
Fisher, Susan Mary: 23, 226
Fisher, Virginia Quereau: see "Quereau, Virginia"
Fisher, William (d. 1896): 224
Fisher, William C. (d. 1948): 42
Fleming, Lillian: 247
Flood, (Marie) Jane: 43, 229, 278, 298, 300, 301, 302, 303, 343
Flood, Arthur: 300
Flood, Clara Engert: see "Engert, Clara"
Flood, Elizabeth "Bet": 300
Flood, Gilbert "Gib": 275, 278
Flood, John "Jack": 300
Flood, John: 300
Foisia, Francis Kirky: see "Kirky, Francis"
Foisia, Jay Charles: 93
Foisia, Lenard Carlton: 93, 95
Foisia, Lyle: 95
Foisia, Madeline: 93, 95
Foote, Effie Boyd: see "Boyd, Effie E."
Foote, George N.: 268
Forbush, Elizabeth "Bessie" Pauline: 212
Forbush, Paulina Weston Prince: see "Prince, Paulina"
Foreback, Frances "Effie": 94
Forgham, Richard: 66
Fornier, Charles: 244
Foster, Celia: 151
Fowler, Ann Sours: see "Sours, Ann Eliza"
Fowler, Bertha Louisa: 58, 60, 61
Fowler, Cecile Mae: 204, 205
Fowler, Charles Gillett: 147
Fowler, Dewitt Clinton Sr.: 147
Fowler, Etta Bargy: see "Bargy, Etta"
Fowler, Floyd Edward: 147
Fowler, Harry: 149
Fowler, Kenneth Charles: 147, 289

Fowler, Phoebe Gillett: see "Gillett, Phoebe"
Fowler, Ruth E.: 89, 147
Fowler, William Henry: 61
Fowler, Wray: 15
Fox, Albert Henry "Bert": 148, 157
Fox, Albert Leo: 148
Fox, Arloa Belle Powell: see "Powell, Arloa Belle"
Fox, Charles: 148
Fox, Clark M.: 149, 150
Fox, Dora Perkins: see "Perkins, Dora"
Fox, Dora Ticknor: see "Ticknor, Dora"
Fox, Fred: 149
Fox, George H: 149
Fox, George Washington: 148
Fox, Lawrence: 160
Fox, Lewis: 148
Fox, Mary Goetzman: see "Goetzman, Mary"
Fox, Maude Baker: see "Baker, Maude"
Fox, May Lincks: see "Lincks, May"
Fox, Mildred Putney: see "Putney, Mildred"
Fox, Minnie Cutting: see "Cutting, Minnie"
Fox, Rebecca Myers: see "Myers, Rebecca"
Frank Noyes Coal and Feed: 22
Franklin, Charles A. Jr.: 323
Franklin, Jean Ann Van Hout: see "Van Hout, Jean Ann"
Fraser, (Arthur) Roy: 210
Fraser, Caroline Converse: see "Converse, Caroline"
Fraser, Donald H.: 211
Fraser, Harold R.: 211
Fraser, Harold: 210
Fraser, Helen Kalbfleisch: see "Kalbfleisch, Helen"
Fraser, Leola Snyder: see "Snyder, Leola"
Fraser, Leon A.: 211
Fraser, Peter Charles: 210
Frazier, James Charles: 338
Fremouw, Elizabeth Pieternella: 323
French, Celia Elizabeth: 151, 152, 153, 155
French, Celia Foster: see "Foster, Celia"
French, Elizabeth van de Putte: see "Van de Putte, Elizabeth"
French, Ernest: 211
French, Frank B.: 151
French, Mark Leonard: 151, 152, 154
French, Mary Ann: 333
French, Myrtle: 60, 151, 184, 211
French, Ruth: 151
Fromholzer, Cheryl: 236
Fromholzer, Debra: 236
Fromholzer, Joan McOmber: see "McOmber, Joan"
Fromholzer, Robert: 236
Fromholzer, Susan: 236
Frymer, Paul: 305
Fuller, Gary: 341
Fuller, Marjorie Westfall: see "Westfall, Marjorie"

Fuller, Sharon: 341
Fuller, Thomas: 341
Furguson, Elizabeth "Betty": 209
Furman, Dorothy: 129, 130
Furman, Inez: 121, 129, 130, 176, 198
Furman, Jeanne: 130
Furman, Leland: 129
Furman, Marilyn: 130
Furman, Mary: 130
Furman, Mathilda Rothang: see "Rothang, Mathilda"
Furman, Norris: 129, 130
Furman, Wilbur: 130
Furman, Winona: 130
Gable, Clark: 230, 231
Gaffield, Maria: 262, 264, 265
Gage, Dorothy H.: 156, 157, 158, 162
Gage, Edna: 47
Gage, Edwin: 156
Gage, Frederick William: 155
Gage, Harold John: 155
Gage, Hattie Davis: see "Davis, Hattie"
Gage, Henry M.: 156, 157, 222, 290
Gage, Ida Miller: see "Miller, Ida"
Gage, Lydia Syron: see "Syron, Lydia"
Gage, Margaret Dawson: see "Dawson, Margaret M."
Gallery, Helen: 307
Galloway, (Russell) Vincent: 158, 291
Galloway, Betty Jean: 158, 159
Galloway, Elizabeth Countryman: see "Countryman, Elizabeth"
Gardner, Carl: 159
Gardner, Ella: 259, 260
Gardner, Floyd: 159
Gardner, Grace Sherman: see "Sherman, Grace"
Gardner, Henry: 159
Gardner, William: 159
Garlic, Ruth Thomas: see "Thomas, Ruth"
Garlic, Traver H.: 159, 160, 161, 229, 248, 249, 265
Garlick, Charles: 151
Garlick, Frances Edith: 33, 34
Garlick, Franklin: 33, 34
Garlick, Henry: 33
Garlick, Sally: 33
Garlick's General Store: 8, 9
Garton, Abram: 64
Garton, Dorothy: 101, 102
Garton, Emily Boughton: see "Boughton, Emily Jane"
Garton, George (d. 1875): 64
Garton, George (d. 1944): 54, 101, 102
Garton, Ida: 64
Garton, Lena: 54, 100, 101, 102
Garton, Mattie: 102
Garton, Maude: 20, 53, 54, 97, 102, 197
Garton, Ross: 102
Garton, Sarah: 64

Gary, Donald: 135
Gary, Tracy Edwards: see "Edwards, Tracy"
Gaver, Pauline: 336
General Storage and Ice Co.: see "Cold Storage"
Gent, David: 15
Genung, Mary: 148
George W. Marshall & Sons Feed Co.: 223
Gerber, Anna Eliza Warner: see "Warner, Anna Eliza"
Gerber, Charles: 61
Ghent, Harold S.: 15, 162, 163
Ghent, Hazel Steitler: see "Steitler, Hazel"
Ghent, Joseph: 162, 163
Gilder, John: 15
Gilfilian, Blanche: 72
Gilfilian, Earl: 263
Gilfilian, Gertrude "Gertie": 106, 108
Gilfilian, Henry: 108
Gilfilian, Lucille: 72
Gilfilian, Nellie: 108
Gilfilian, Sedate Corey: see "Corey, Sedate E."
Gilfilian, William J.: 108
Gilkey, Anne: 352
Gill, James: 15
Gillett, Asahel: 39
Gillett, Harvey: 39
Gillett, Isaac: 38, 39
Gillett, John: 39
Gillett, Mabel: 104
Gillett, Orsen: 104
Gillett, Phoebe: 147
Gillett, Sally: see "Sellick, Sally"
Gillette, Claude Coe: 161, 164, 165
Gillette, Darwin: 84
Gillette, Frieda Machholz: see "Machholz, Frieda"
Gillette, Jeanette Doremus: see "Doremus, Jeanette"
Gillette, Marjorie: 164
Gillette, Pearl Agnes Hackett: 84
Gillette, Richard: 164
Gillette, Russell Dowd: 74
Gilmore, (Elizabeth) Mae: 162
Gilmore, Jane Alice: 158, 159, 161, 162, 214
Gilmore, John Alexander: 162
Gilmore, John Elton: 162
Giovine, Carmella: 329
Glanzel, Elsie: 267
Glen, Helen: 112
Godkin, Bernadine Burse: see "Burse, Bernadine"
Godkin, Claire: 36, 336
Godkin, Clarence G.: 335
Godkin, Donald: 335
Godkin, Elizabeth Van Pelt: see "Van Pelt, Elizabeth Frances"
Godkin, Elizabeth: 333, 334
Godkin, Ethel: 333, 334, 335
Godkin, Fred: 333, 334

Godkin, Harold W.: 335
Godkin, Inez Mae: 333, 334, 335
Godkin, Jan Kurt: 336
Godkin, Jeanette Sarsnett: see "Sarsnett, Jeanette"
Godkin, Katheryn Lynn: 336
Godkin, Louella "Ella" Ditton: see "Ditton, Louella"
Godkin, Mary Ammerman: see "Ammerman, Mary"
Godkin, Mary Ann French: see "French, Mary Ann"
Godkin, Millie Pitcher: see "Pitcher, Millie"
Godkin, Milton: 335
Godkin, Myrna: 333, 334, 335
Godkin, Pauline Gaver: see "Gaver, Pauline"
Godkin, Richard Creig: 336
Godkin, Robert: 335
Godkin, Ruth Porter: see "Porter, Ruth"
Godkin, Samuel Jr.: 333, 334, 335
Godkin, Samuel: 333, 334
Godkin, Steven: 336
Godkin, Thomas Henry Jr.: 333
Godkin, Valentine "Bus" Grove: 15, 123, 336
Godkin, Ward: 123, 333, 334, 335, 336
Goetzman, Mary: 148
Goldstein, Cynthia Roney: see "Roney, Cynthia"
Goldstein, Diane Kelley: see "Kelley, Diane Elaine"
Goldstein, Jerold: 103
Goldstein, Robert: 279
Goodrich, Sherman: 238
Goodsell, Lloyd: 15
Goodsell, Merrial: 15
Gordon, Lena: 30, 222, 269, 270, 271
Goss, Ella: 33
Gould, Bessy Mae: 200, 204, 253
Grady, Catherine "Kittie": 220, 221, 222
Grady, Frances "Fannie" Clark: see "Clark, Frances"
Grady, Thomas J.: 221
Graham, Arch: 166
Graham, Florence Lovejoy: see "Lovejoy, Florence"
Graham, Nelson: 165, 280
Graham, Susan E. "Susie": 165, 166, 167, 178, 211, 230
Grasiosa, Mildred: 318
Gray, Albion Mintonoye (d. 1945): 167, 168, 169, 170, 171, 172
Gray, Albion: 15
Gray, Alvin M.: 168
Gray, Charles Andrew: 21, 66, 167, 168, 169, 170
Gray, Doris: 167, 168, 169
Gray, Eleanor: 167, 168, 169
Gray, Elizabeth: 168
Gray, George: 15
Gray, George Otis: 170
Gray, John Martin: 21, 66, 168, 170
Gray, John Russell: 170
Gray, Lena Shaver: see "Shaver, Sarah"
Gray, Mabel Campbell: see "Campbell, Mabel M."
Gray, Marian: 167
Gray, Mary Quereau: see "Quereau, Mary"
Gray, Otis Albion: 66, 139, 168, 169, 170, 171, 275, 356
Gray, Sarah Shaver: see "Shaver, Sarah"
Gray, Sarah Smalley: see "Smalley, Sarah"
Gray Brothers Hardware: 10, 21, 167, 168, 170
Green, Frances: 160, 228
Green, Leo: 15
Green, Lucy Groves Vincent: see "Groves, Lucy"
Green, Milton R. Jr.: 327
Green, Vinnie Thomas: see "Thomas, Vinnie"
Green, William M.: 316
Greenwood, Addie: 194
Griffin, (Michael) Frank: 132
Griffin, Mary Drury Jacqui: see "Drury, Mary T."
Grinnals, Clara Bell: 220
Grinnels, Bessie: 128
Griswold, Barbara Mae: 249, 250
Groat, Anna Buttaccio: see "Buttaccio, Anna C."
Groat, Darlene Marie: 174
Groat, David N.: 15, 172, 173, 174
Groat, Elaine: 172, 175
Groat, Erwin: 173
Groat, Floyd J.: 15, 20, 172, 173, 174, 231
Groat, Gladys: 172, 173
Groat, Grace: 173
Groat, Karolyn DeLeys: see "DeLeys, Karolyn"
Groat, Linda Anne: 174
Groat, Loretta Johnston: see "Johnston, Loretta"
Groat, Marian: 173
Groat, Maude Milliman: see "Milliman, Maude"
Groat, Mary Fischette: see "Fischette, Mary"
Groat, Paul: 172, 173
Groat, Russell Jerry: 20, 172, 173, 174
Groat, William (d. 1953): 172, 231
Groat, William Raymond: 172, 173
Groat, Yvonne Marshall Bates: see "Marshall, Yvonne"
Grove, Frank: 92
Groves, Lucy: 326
Guernsey, Carrie: 68
Guidone, Anthony J.: 324
Guidone, Sandra Kay Van Hout: see "Van Hout, Sandra"
Guino, Barbara Hoskins: see "Hoskins, Barbara"
Guino, Joseph: 258
Guth, Edwin F.: 312
Guth, Lila Stone: see "Stone, Lila"
Guthrie, Alice: 176, 177
Guthrie, Beatrice Washburn: see "Washburn, Beatrice"
Guthrie, Cecille Mary: 58, 177
Guthrie, Cleon: 15, 177
Guthrie, Freda Mae: 129, 175, 176, 267
Guthrie, George: 175
Guthrie, Gerald: 15, 45, 129, 176, 177

Guthrie, Graydon: 129, 175, 176, 267
Guthrie, Larry Cleon: 177
Guthrie, Lulu Mettler: see "Mettler, Lulu"
Guthrie, Lyle: 15, 175, 176, 177
Guthrie, Maurice: 175
Hackney, Leonard: 26
Hadley, Mary Bowen Kenan: see "Bowen, Mary"
Haleus, Glenwood: 15
Hall, Alice Catchpole: see "Catchpole, Nancy Alyssa"
Hall, Audrey: 146
Hall, Beta: 146
Hall, Charles A.: 211
Hall, David: 146
Hall, Harvey: 15
Hall, Helen: 90
Hall, Iva Betts: see "Betts, Iva"
Hall, Kathleen: 146
Hall, Lance: 146
Hall, M.C.: 22
Hall, Perthena Keller: see "Keller, Perthena"
Hall, Robert E.: 90
Hall, Robert K.: 90
Hall, Ruth Edna: 211
Hall, Wilmer C.: 146
Halterman, William: 192
Hamm, Arlene: 318
Hamm, Calvin: 15
Hamm, Jennie Caroline: 61
Hand, Lucy: 107
Hansen, Marguerite: 207
Harder, Alice Favreau: see "Favreau, Alice"
Harder, Arlene: 141
Harder, Howard L.: 141
Harder, Richard: 141
Harper, Albert Fremont: 177
Harper, Anna Lovejoy: see "Lovejoy, Anna"
Harper, Bertha: 266
Harper, Chelsea Damon: 177, 287, 319
Harper, Cora Welch: see "Welch, Cora"
Harper, Dale: 179
Harper, David W.: 178
Harper, Dorothy: 179
Harper, Elaine Sullivan: see "Sullivan, Elaine"
Harper, George: 178
Harper, Janet: 3, 179, 180, 181, 182, 277, 346
Harper, Jessie: 178
Harper, Louise Fairbanks: see "Fairbanks, Louise"
Harper, Lydia Elaine: 177
Harper, Marvin (d. 1975): 177, 178
Harper, Marvin David Jr. (d. 1995): 178, 179
Harper, Marvin III: 179
Harper, Mary Cahoon: see "Cahoon, Mary"
Harper, Mary Moore: see "Moore, Mary"
Harper, Nina Sidler: see "Sidler, Nina Marguerite"
Harper, Roscoe Ladu: 179

Harrington, Bertha: 261
Harrington, James LaVerne: 338
Harrington, Mary: 189
Harrington, Myron: 189
Harris, Ethel: 294, 296, 297
Harris, Gladys Newkirk: see "Newkirk, Gladys"
Harris, Gregory H.: 236
Harris, Harriett "Hattie" Anna: 61, 62, 101, 237
Harris, Horatio "Ray": 182, 183
Harris, Howard: 232, 235, 236
Harris, Jeanette Burley: see "Burley, Jeanette"
Harris, John Watson: 183
Harris, Laura: 222, 254, 264, 297
Harris, Mary Eliza: 210
Harris, Neva Monroe: see "Monroe, Neva"
Harris, Olive Eaton: see "Eaton, Olive"
Harris, Ralph: 182, 183
Harris, Zaida: 183
Harris & Winchell Meat Market: 9, 21, 168, 339, 342
Harrison, Betty Ann: 183, 184
Harrison, Doris Helen: 183, 184
Harrison, Eva Mae: 130, 183, 184
Harrison, Helen Kalbfleisch Fraser: see "Kalbfleisch, Helen"
Harrison, William Henry: 183, 184, 211
Harrison, William Richard: 184
Harry Quereau General Store: 22
Hart, Nettie Mae: 146, 147
Hartley, Donald: 91
Hartman, (Ruth) Shirley: 43, 85, 86, 89, 90, 91
Hartman, Lulu Rifenberg: see "Rifenberg, Lulu"
Hartman, Raymon: 85
Havert, Margaret: 113, 114
Haviland, Norman: 16
Hawkes, Agnes Jeanette "Jennie": 234
Hay, Edward: 21
Hayes, Barton: 16
Hayes, Luna Lee: 338
Head, Elizabeth: 45
Hebert, Alice: 126, 229
Heck, Margaret C. "Maggie": 102, 206
Heifer, Patricia: 347
Hellman, Rebecca: 304
Hendershot, Cynthia: 186
Hendershot, Dora Carnell: see "Carnell, Dora"
Hendershot, Elizabeth "Bess" Brown: see "Brown, Elizabeth"
Hendershot, Herbert: 69, 185, 186
Hendershot, Kathryn Barnes: see "Barnes, Kathryn"
Hendershot, Lester Lee: 185, 186, 187
Hendershot, Raymon Lee: 185, 187
Hendershot, Raymond: 310
Hendershot, Susan Smith: see "Smith, Susan"
Henecke, Betty: 16
Hess, Mary Elizabeth: 282, 283

Hetzke, Mildred: 161, 214, 264
Hewson, Hannah: 82, 191, 219
Hill, Alyce: 162
Hill, Arlo B.: 189, 190
Hill, Arthur: 187
Hill, Eliott G.: 188
Hill, Ethel Harris: see "Harris, Ethel"
Hill, Flora Sidler: see "Sidler, Flora"
Hill, Frank: 22, 59, 66, 121, 145, 187, 190, 270, 271, 296, 306
Hill, Gilbert B.: 124, 125, 187, 188, 259, 340
Hill, Harriett Seager Dodds: see "Seager, Harriett"
Hill, John: 22, 66, 187, 190
Hill, Lillian: 161, 271
Hill, Lydia Doremus: see "Doremus, Lydia"
Hill, Margery Elizabeth: 48, 296, 297, 298
Hill, Mary Ellen: 269
Hill, Mattie Allen: see "Allen, Mattie"
Hill, Richard: 188
Hill, Roy J.: 296
Hill, Ruth Weeks: see "Weeks, Ruth"
Hill, Thomas: 189
Hill, William B.: 187, 189, 190
Hills, Alice Alden: 212
Hilts, Earl: 82, 190, 191, 192, 219
Hilts, Inez Carpenter Little: see "Carpenter, Inez"
Hoad, Edna: 113
Hoad, Henry: 103
Hoad, William: 113
Hodom, Arleen Whalen: see "Whalen, Arleen"
Hodom, Donald: 60
Hodom, Lyndia: 61
Hoff, Grant: 21, 176, 193
Hoff, Helen H.: 193
Hoff, Mary C.: 193
Hoff, Mary: 193
Hoff's Service Station: 21, 193
Hoffman, Darleen: 168, 169
Hoffman, Eleanor Gray: see "Gray, Eleanor"
Hoffman, George E.: 167, 168, 169
Hoffman, Gray: 168, 169
Hoffman, Julia Exter: see "Exter, Julia"
Hoffman, Seymour Horatio: 167
Hojack Line: 7, 21, 194, 311, 355
Hollebrandt, Cora: 154
Home and Foreign Missionary Society: 25, 60, 66, 96, 110, 169, 173, 213, 222, 241
Homeman, Franziska Catherine: 146
Hookway, Marjorie: 313, 314
Hoople, Gordon: 171
Hoople, Howard: 171, 208
Hoople, Phyllis: 171
Hopkins, Bruce W.: 328
Hopkins, Edith Wolf: see "Wolf, Edith"
Hopner, Elizabeth: 5

Hoppe, Elizabeth "Eliza": 84
Hoppel, Christina Klein: see "Klein, Christina"
Hoppel, Frederick: 126
Hoppel, Pearl Frances: 126, 127
Horn, Bertha Reeder: see "Reeder, Bertha"
Horn, Christian: 195
Horn, Earl R.: 193, 194, 195, 196
Horn, Edna Warren: see "Warren, Edna"
Horn, Elizabeth Godkin: see "Godkin, Elizabeth"
Horn, Grace Anderson: see "Anderson, Grace"
Horn, Helen I.: 334
Horn, Lincoln: 16, 194, 195, 198
Horn, Lorenzo: 195, 196
Horn, Milton V.: 334
Horn, Robert F.: 334
Horn, Sharon Lee: 195
Horn, Vera E.: 334
Horn, Wesley E.: 334
Horn, Alfred W.: 334
Horning, Linda: 324
Hornsby, Robert: 328
Horton, Mary: 130
Hoskins, Allen: 258
Hoskins, Barbara: 258
Hoskins, Doris: 258
Hoskins, Eugene: 258
Hoskins, Helen Penner: see "Penner, Helen"
Hoskins, Kathleen: 258
Hoskins, Kenneth: 257
Hoskins, Leonard: 257, 258
Hoskins, Margaret: 258
Hoskins, Nancy: 258
Hoskins, Robert: 258
Hotchkiss, Calvin: 227
Hotchkiss, Ruth Webers: see "Webers, Ruth"
Householder, Clara: 105
Howell, Bertha Harper: see "Harper, Bertha"
Howell, Kermit: 266
Howes, George: 108
Howes, Nellie Gilfilian: see "Gilfilian, Nellie"
Hoyez, Ron: 126
Hubbard, Alice: 212
Hubbard, Allen: 212
Hubbard, Arthur E.: 212
Hubbard, Arthur Jr.: 212, 213
Hubbard, Elizabeth "Bessie" Forbush: see "Forbush, Elizabeth"
Hubbard, Frederick: 16
Hubbard, Mabel Sterling: 212, 213
Huckle, Donald Robert: 48
Huckle, Marjorie Baker: see "Baker, Marjorie"
Huhak, Andrea: 45
Huhak, Linda Aldrich: see "Aldrich, Linda"
Huhak, Timothy: 45
Hume, Richard: 134

Hume, Sandra Edwards: see "Edwards, Sandra"
Hunt, Lynford W.: 241
Hunt, Sandra Mills: see "Mills, Sandra"
Hunter, Marie: 279, 280
Hutchings, Arthur Thomas: 196, 197
Hutchings, Edith Everett: see "Everett, Edith"
Hutchings, Glen Frank: 16, 101, 197, 198
Hutchings, Helen Spink: see "Spink, Helen"
Hutchings, Jessie Brown: see "Brown, Jessie"
Ingersoll, George W.: 256
Ingraham, Sam: 256
Jacques, (George) Gordon: 198, 199, 200, 201, 204, 205
Jacques, (Martha) Nathalie Mitchell: see "Mitchell, Nathalie"
Jacques, (William) Mallette: 200, 201, 203, 204, 205, 253
Jacques, Anna Nicholas: see "Nicholas, Anna"
Jacques, Bessy Gould: see "Gould, Bessy Mae"
Jacques, Cecile Fowler: see "Fowler, Cecile "
Jacques, Eugene L.: 198, 199, 205
Jacques, Florence Helene: 200
Jacques, George H.P.: 203
Jacques, James G.: 198, 199, 205
Jacques, Jean Malcolm: 202, 203, 205, 229
Jacques, John Mitchell: 198, 199, 205
Jacques, John Raymond: 200, 201, 203, 204
Jacques, John: 201
Jacques, Karen: 200
Jacques, Montefort Lloyd: 201
Jacques, Pieter: 205
Jacques, Ronald: 200, 204
Jacques, S. Frederica Mallette: see "Mallette, S. Frederica"
Jacques, William: 199, 200, 201, 202, 203, 204, 205
Jacqui, Mary Drury: see "Drury, Mary T."
Jacqui, Robert Elsworth: 132
James, Alfred: 166
James, Anna: 166
James, William: 107
Jeffers, Georgia: 200, 247
Jeffers, Ralph: 165
Jenks, Alice Marie: see "Cook, Alice Marie"
Jenks, Charles: 234
Jenks, Ina Ripley Cook: see "Ripley, Ina"
Jensen, Edra: 206
Jensen, John: 72, 206
Jensen, June: 206
Jensen, Marvin: 206
Jensen, Shirley: 206
Jewell, Blanche McHuron: see "McHuron, Blanche"
Jewell, Charles J.: 137, 138
Jewell, Dorothy: 138
Jewell, Edwin: 137, 138
Jewell, Virginia: 137, 138, 139

Johns, Gail: 329
Johnson, Benjamin: 221
Johnson, Carol Ann: 99
Johnson, David: 34
Johnson, Esther "Etta": 272
Johnson, Jane "Jennie": 34
Johnson, Lois Patricia: 99
Johnson, Mabel: 83, 84
Johnson, Mary: 284
Johnston, Loretta: 173
Johnston, Margaret: 161
Jones, A.W.: 247
Jones, Alfred: 167, 178
Jones, Gay A.: 316
Jones, Martha "Mattie": 227
Jones, Nellie: 167
Jones, Rena: 344
Joseph H. Ghent Barber Shop: 21, 163
Juffs, Clarence: 84, 176
Kalbfleisch, George E.: 16
Kalbfleisch, Helen: 183, 184, 211
Kalbfleisch, Myrtle French: see "French, Myrtle"
Kalbfleisch, Richard: 184
Kashiwada, Yasu: 105
Keefe, Joseph: 167
Keeler, Grace: 166
Keller, Elizabeth "Libby": 339
Keller, Perthena: 211
Kelley, Diane Elaine: 103
Kelley, Dorothy Davis: see "Davis, Dorothy Jean"
Kelley, Elizabeth Godkin Horn: see "Godkin, Elizabeth"
Kelley, Louis B.: 334
Kelley, Raymond G.: 102
Kelley, Raymond Jr.: 102, 103
Kelley, Ruth Curtis: see "Curtis, Ruth"
Kellicutt, Margaret: 64
Kellogg, Bertha: 16
Kellogg, Lloyd: 16
Kemp, Dorothy Maria: 206
Kemp, Edith: 206
Kemp, Grace Irene: 206
Kemp, Mary Elizabeth: 206
Kemp, Robert Samuel: 206
Kemp, Virginia Ruth: 206
Kenan, Mary Bowen: see "Bowen, Mary"
Kenan, Patricia "Patsy": 43, 207, 208
Kenan, Raymond Hadley: 43, 52, 68, 206, 207, 208, 211, 240
Kenan, Robert C.: 207
Kenan, Theresa O'Donnell: see "O'Donnell, Theresa"
Kenan, Thomas Francis: 207
Kendrot, Diane: 330
Kendrot, Faith Vincent Sherman: see "Vincent, Faith"
Kendrot, Jack: 330
Kendrot, Jim: 330

Kendrot, John P.: 330
Kennedy, William: 286
Kepner, (Ida) June: 128
Kepner, Eugene Alexander: 128
Kepner, Harvey W.: 128, 164
Kepner, Mary Lou: 128
Kepner, Mary Messenger: see "Messenger, Mary"
Kester, Donald: 16
Kidder, Mary Eliza: 275, 278
Kimpland, George: 208
Kimpland, Lena: 33, 208
Kinny, Mary: 16
Kirky, Francis Sarah: 93, 95
Kise, Leonard: 16
Kistner, Ellen Louise: 122
Kitchen, (Lillie) Belle: 54, 55, 189, 243, 287
Kitchen, Eva: 49, 50
Kitchen, Matthew: 50
Kitchen, Olive Atwater: see "Atwater, Olive"
Klein, Christina: 127
Klippel, Robert: 164
Knapp, Addie Brown: see "Brown, Addie"
Knapp, Beverly Richardson: see "Richardson, Beverly"
Knapp, Carl: 210
Knapp, Cheryl Ann: 210
Knapp, Elizabeth Furguson: see "Furguson, Elizabeth"
Knapp, Florence Zapf: see "Zapf, Florence"
Knapp, Frederick C.: 65, 208, 209, 210
Knapp, Harold L.: 210, 211
Knapp, Ivan: 16
Knapp, Leola Snyder Fraser: see "Snyder, Leola"
Knapp, Leon E.: 210, 211, 212
Knapp, Mary Elizabeth: 217
Knapp, Nellie Watt: see "Watt, Nellie"
Knapp, Perthena Keller Hall: see "Keller, Perthena"
Knapp, Richard Daley: 210
Knapp, Willis G. Jr.: 208, 209
Knapp, Willis G. Sr.: 67, 208, 209
Knepka, Earl G.: 16
Knox, Pearl: 98, 100
Koch, Marian: 84
Koehler, Richard: 16
Koney, Brent: 351
Koney, Phyllis Yancey: see "Yancey, Phyllis"
Koney, Vickie: 351, 352
Koney, Victor William: 350, 352
Kotouc, Mary Louise: 302
Ladies' Aid Society: 25, 169, 199, 249, 283
Ladies' Guild: 25, 65, 110
Laffalot Minstrel Show: 10, 11
Laird, Adelia May "Ada": 340
Laird, Ed: 288
Laird, Eliza Snell: see "Snell, Eliza Jane"
Laird, Frances "Fanny" Rebecca: 259, 339, 340, 342, 343

Laird, John Ellis: 339
Lake, David: 106
Lake, Laura Merrell: see "Merrell, Laura"
Lake, Phoebe: 106
Lamb, (Henry) Addison: 96, 97
Lamb, Almira: 298, 305
Lamb, Clyde: 96
Lamb, Cora: 96, 97
Lamb, Della Thomas: see "Thomas, Della"
Lamb, Dorcas Weeks: see "Weeks, Dorcas"
Lamb, Eliza "Jennie" McQueen: see "McQueen, Eliza"
Lamb, Elizabeth Hopner: see "Hopner, Elizabeth"
Lamb, George R.: 316
Lamb, Helen Vanatta: see "Vanatta, Helen"
Lamb, Isaac Jr.: 38
Lamb, Isaac: 5, 6, 38, 97, 299, 305
Lamb, John William: 5
Lamb, Minnie: 39, 55, 66, 95, 96
Lamb, Myron John: 96
Lamb, Peter: 39
Lamb, Sarah "Sally" Stanley: see "Stanley, Sarah"
Lamb's Corners: 5, 6, 7, 38, 39, 97
Lamo, Anna D.: 96
Lander, Louise: 247, 248, 249, 279
Langford, Frances L.: 124
Langford, John Cosyn: 124
Langford, Margaret Bertha: 124, 125
Langley, Lillian: 55, 56, 166, 167, 211, 252
Langley, Margaret Brisbin: see "Brisbin, Margaret"
Langley, Samuel: 55
Lanich, Clarence Ivan: 335
Lanich, Clarence L.: 335
Lanich, Dorothy: 335
Lanich, Inez Godkin: see "Godkin, Inez"
Lansing, George H.: 106
Lansing, Ida Bell: 106
Lansing, Josephine Emma Osborn: see "Osborn, Josephine"
Lape, Asher M.: 16
Lape, Homer: 16
Lape, Mahlon: 16
Lapp, Albert: 261
Lapp, Bertha Harrington: see "Harrington, Bertha"
Lapp, Catherine E.: 261, 262
Lapp, Edward: 104
Lapp, Gordon: 16
Lapp, Lydia: 105
Lapp, Mathias Elias Jr.: 104, 261
Lapp, Mathias Elias Sr.: 104
Lapp, Maude: 103, 104, 105
Lapp, Minnie: 69
Lapp, Samantha Wood: see "Wood, Samantha"
Larocque, Marie Desneige: 321
Latham, (William) Arthur Swaby Jr.: 21, 212, 213
Latham, Alice Hills: see "Hills, Alice"

Latham, Mabel (later Mabelle) Hubbard: see "Hubbard, Mabel"
Latham, William Arthur Swaby Sr.: 212
Latham's Pharmacy: 21, 212, 213
Latosky, Clara: 153
Lauder, Agnes Mae: 342
Laurette, Peter: 218
Laurette, Shirley Leaird: see "Leaird, Shirley"
Laurette, Kimberlee: 218
Lauster, Graydon D.: 310
Lauster, LaRue Spade: see "Spade, LaRue"
Lauster, Marie: 310
Lauster, Marsha: 310
Lauster, Maureen: 310
LaVere, Bruce R.: 16
Lawrence, (Anna) Grace Crane: see "Crane, (Anna) Grace"
Lawrence, (Mary) Elizabeth Tellier: see "Tellier, (Mary) Elizabeth"
Lawrence, Donald: 162, 214, 215, 342
Lawrence, Elizabeth: 215
Lawrence, Estella Peck: see "Peck, Estella"
Lawrence, Henry: 22, 214, 215, 216
Lawrence, John: 215
Lawrence, Margaret "Maggi": 215
Leadley, (Allen) Douglas: 260
Leadley, (Lina) Marguerite Phillips: see "Phillips, (Lina) Marguerite"
Leadley, Helen Palmer: see "Palmer, Helen"
Leadley, Martha: 260
Leadley, Morgan: 260
Leadley, Phillip Duane: 260
Leadley, Ralph M.: 260
Leaird, Anna Campbell: see "Campbell, Anna"
Leaird, Betty Jean: 217, 218
Leaird, Charles (d. 1972): 105, 217
Leaird, Charles Moses (d. 1948): 216, 217, 218
Leaird, Doris: 217
Leaird, Dorothy Shaver: see "Shaver, Dorothy"
Leaird, Esther: 217
Leaird, Etta Thompson: see "Thompson, Etta"
Leaird, George John: 217
Leaird, George William: 217, 218
Leaird, Jean Peters: see "Peters, Jean"
Leaird, Lorie: 218
Leaird, Nancy Anne: 217, 218
Leaird, Pamela: 218
Leaird, Ruby: 217
Leaird, Sandy: 218
Leaird, Shirley Mae: 217, 218
Leaird, Stanley: 217
Leasure, Clara Ida: 346
LeBlanc, (Joseph) Isadore: 321
LeBlanc, Laura: 320, 321, 322
LeBlanc, Marie Desneige Larocque: see "Larocque, Marie Desneige"
Lee, Carl: 16
Lee, George: 163
Leewood, David: 298
Leewood, Pauletta Baker: see "Baker, Pauletta"
LeFavor, William: 64
Legg, Hulda: 265
Lenihan, Suzette: 122
LeVal, Elizabeth "Betty": 191
Lewis, Anna Lenora: 84, 140
Lewis, Lloyd Byron: 140, 219
Lewis, Maude Silliman: see "Silliman, Maude"
Lincks, May Mary: 148
Lindauer, Bonnie Vernoy: see "Vernoy, Bonnie"
Lindauer, Dawn: 326
Lindauer, Douglas: 326
Lindauer, Mark: 326
Lindauer, Pamela: 326
Lingl, John: 67
Lingl, Mary Ellen Boyd: see "Boyd, Mary Ellen"
Literary Club: 31, 66, 125, 160, 199, 204, 214, 253, 259, 263, 268, 270
Little, Catherine Joyce: 190, 191, 192
Little, Charles: 219
Little, Fletcher N.: 191, 219
Little, Gaye: 219
Little, Gladys Thelma: 191
Little, Inez Carpenter: see "Carpenter, Inez"
Little, Iona Van Amburg: see "Van Amburg, Iona"
Little, James: 190, 191, 192
Little, Jane Louise: 191
Little, Richard James: 192
Little, Russell Elvin: 191, 192
Little, Sarah E.: 315, 316
Little, Sylvia Monteith: see "Monteith, Sylvia"
Little, Willis Ray: 191, 192, 219
Looke, Charles: 220
Looke, Maud: 220
Loomis, Amos "Plumb": 255
Lord, Emma Drury: see "Drury, Emma"
Lovejoy, Anna: 178
Lovejoy, Celia: 62
Lovejoy, Elvira: 311
Lovejoy, Florence: 165, 166
Loveless, David: 16
Loveless, Elnathan J.: 16
Loveless, Ernest: 94
Loveless, Frank E.: 147
Loveless, Nettie Hart Fink: see "Hart, Nettie"
Lowe, Ellen: 76
Ludwig, Emil J.: 16
Luffman, Ada Merrill: see "Merrill, Ada"
Luffman, Alda Chloe: 287, 288, 289, 290, 291
Luffman, George Leroy: 288
Luffman, Mary McIntyre: see "McIntyre, Mary"

Luncheon Club: 31, 161, 166, 252
Lundergun, Bridget Dunn: see "Dunn, Bridget"
Lundergun, Catherine "Kittie" Grady: see "Grady, Catherine"
Lundergun, Dora Satterlee: see "Satterlee, Dora"
Lundergun, James: 220, 221, 222, 223
Lundergun, Michael: 221
Lundergun, Theresa: 129, 130, 131, 132, 221, 222, 223
Lundergun, William "Will": 112, 132, 221, 222, 223, 268, 283
Lunkenheimer, Charles Faye: 94
Lyman, Charles: 16
Lyman, George: 157
Lyman, Rose Brown: see "Brown, Rose"
Lyman, William: 353
Lynch, Fred: 340
Lynch, Inez Van Hout: see "Van Hout, Inez"
Lynch, Thomas: 324
MacDougall, Donnie: 130
MacDougall, Kathryn Washburn: see "Washburn, Kathryn"
MacDougall, Raymond: 130, 176
Machan, Katharyn: 303
Machholz, Frieda Louise: 161, 164
Mallette, Lestina Tanner: see "Tanner, Lestina"
Mallette, S. Frederica: 201, 203, 204
Mallette, William Smith: 201
Maloy, Anne Fennell: see "Fennell, Anne"
Maloy, George Roland: 314
Maloy, Nancy: 314
Maloy, Susanne: 314
Manion, Kathleen: 108
Mark, Emma: 296
Mark, Margaret May: 81, 294, 296
Market Basket: 21, 47, 48, 176, 344
Marriott, Doris Mae: 236, 237, 238
Marriott, Ellen Kistner: see "Kistner, Ellen"
Marriott, Fannie Marshall: see "Marshall, Fannie"
Marriott, Helen Margaret: 236, 237, 238, 239
Marriott, Luella Nesbitt: see "Nesbitt, Luella"
Marriott, Orlo "Bud": 122
Marriott, Ronald: 120, 122
Marriott, William H.: 110, 238
Marsh, Joel C.: 16
Marshall, (George) Clifford: 225, 230
Marshall, Charlotte McOmber: see "McOmber, Charlotte"
Marshall, Edwin E.: 16
Marshall, Ellinor "Ella" Redman: see "Redman, Ellinor"
Marshall, Fannie R.: 110, 238
Marshall, George William (d. 1938): 66, 224, 225, 226, 228, 230
Marshall, George: 156

Marshall, Gertrude: 224, 225
Marshall, Glenn: 226
Marshall, Harold J.: 226
Marshall, Ina Stevens: see "Stevens, Ina"
Marshall, Jack: 176
Marshall, Lawrence: 226
Marshall, Leona: 226
Marshall, Lila Tod Smith: see "Smith, Lila Tod"
Marshall, Lloyd Marion: 21, 35, 131, 160, 205, 224, 225, 226, 227, 228, 229, 230
Marshall, Marion T.: 224
Marshall, Melvin: 238
Marshall, Olive Gertrude: 225, 226, 228
Marshall, Paul: 72, 99, 176, 238, 239
Marshall, Rachel Biedick: see "Biedick, Rachel"
Marshall, Ruth Webers: see "Webers, Ruth"
Marshall, Scott: 23
Marshall, Shirley: 226
Marshall, Susan M. Fisher: see "Fisher, Susan"
Marshall, William Gilman: 23, 221
Marshall, William Marion: 23, 226
Marshall, William: 224
Marshall, Yvonne Carolyn: 132, 205, 226, 227, 228, 229, 230, 231
Marshall BioResources: see "Marshall Farm"
Marshall Farm: 23
Martin, Cathleen C.: 307
Maunder, Betty Jane: 16
Maust, John: 267
May, Charles Cook: 232, 233, 234
May, Geraldine: 232, 235
May, Joan: 232, 235
May, Kathleen: 232, 235
May, Mary Evans: see "Evans, Mary"
May, Norma: 232, 235
May, Porter: 233
May, Renee Francine "Fran" Mitchell: see "Mitchell, Renee"
Maynard, Earl: 50
Maynard, Iva Moore: see "Moore, Iva"
Mayo, Sarah Millie: 345
Mayo, Thomas: 345
McBooks Bookstore: 303, 304
McCall, Margaret: 222
McCarthy, Donald: 16
McDorman, Patricia Joan: 272
McHugh, Miriam: 161
McHuron, Blanche: 137, 138
McIntryre, Mary: 288
McKay, Claudia Arlene: 76, 145
McKay, Ellen Lowe: see "Lowe, Ellen"
McKay, G. Isabel Brown: see "Brown, G. Isabel"
McKay, Linda: 76
McKay, Russell Jr. "Rusty": 76, 145
McKay, Russell Martin: 76, 145

McLaury, Jennie M.: 33
McMullen, Hilda Anna: 41, 42
McOmber, Charlotte Alice: 99, 101, 238, 239
McOmber, Donald Hiram: 236, 237, 238
McOmber, Doris Marriott: see "Marriott, Doris"
McOmber, Gary Paul: 239
McOmber, Harriett "Hattie" Harris: see "Harris, Harriett "Hattie""
McOmber, Helen Margaret Marriott: see "Marriott, Helen Margaret"
McOmber, Janet Stark: see "Stark, Janet"
McOmber, Joan Lucille: 236, 238
McOmber, Paul Ross: 72, 236, 237, 238, 239, 291
McOmber, Ross H.: 237
McQueen, C.E.: 316
McQueen, Eliza "Jennie": 97
McQueen, Emily: 77
McQueen, Helen Lucy: 162
McQueen, Leon C.: 16
McQueen, Milton D.: 16
McQueen, Ruth: 192
McQueen, Suzanne: 3, 91, 192
McWharf, Bernice Briggs: see "Briggs, Bernice"
McWharf, Laura O'Donnell: see "O'Donnell, Laura"
McWharf, Randy: 70
McWharf, Raymond "Ray": 70
McWharf, Robert: 70
McWharf, Tammie Sue: 70
Mead, Jack S.: 324
Mead, Wreatha Van Hout: see "Van Hout, Wreatha"
Meone, Nettie Julia Gardner: 268
Merrell, Katharine: 119
Merrell, Laura Louisa: 106
Merrill, Ada Marie: 288
Merrill, Henry: 275, 278
Merrill, Mary "Estella": 66, 80, 90, 91, 111, 163, 184, 208, 214, 231, 275, 277, 278, 279, 280
Merrill, Mary Eliza Kidder: see "Kidder, Mary Eliza"
Mertz, Jane: 351
Merz, Pearl Agnes Hackett Gillette: see "Gillette, Pearl"
Messenger, Bertha: 164
Messenger, Ida Seager: see "Seager, Ida"
Messenger, Lula "Lulu": 164, 265, 266
Messenger, Mary J.: 127, 128, 164, 197, 354
Messenger, Walter L.: 128, 164
Messinger, Lula: see "Messenger, Lula"
Metcalfe, Marian: 264
Methodist Youth Fellowship: 25, 184, 213, 293, 325
Mettler, Lulu: 175
Mierke, Dorothy Claus: see "Claus, Dorothy"
Mierke, Howard "Dick": 92, 93
Mierke, Lewis: 92
Mierke, Minnie: 92
Mikeltish, Julianna: 162
Miles, Ann Janette "Nettie": 75

Miles, Mabel: 255, 256
Miles, Orlie: 278
Miller, Eva Harrison: see "Harrison, Eva"
Miller, Ida: 156
Miller, Ronald K.: 184
Milliman, Maude: 172, 173, 231
Mills, Bradley Harris: 241
Mills, Bruce: 239, 241
Mills, Cyril: 323
Mills, Donald Lynn: 239, 241
Mills, Doris Vanderzille: see "Vanderzille, Doris"
Mills, Elery Sterling: 133, 176, 239, 240, 242, 295
Mills, Ethel: 242
Mills, Franklin: 243
Mills, Geraldine Williams: see "Williams, Geraldine"
Mills, Glenn Arthur Jr.: 241, 242
Mills, Glenn Arthur Sr.: 84, 240, 242
Mills, Jacqueline: 241
Mills, Joyce Vandewinckel: see "Vandewinckel, Joyce"
Mills, Laura Chappell: see "Chappell, Laura"
Mills, Leona Failey: see "Failey, Leona"
Mills, Mary "Lena" Moyer: see "Moyer, Mary Magdalena"
Mills, Onnalee Van Steen: see "Van Steen, Onnalee"
Mills, Patricia Ann: 242
Mills, Robert Francis: 242
Mills, Robert James: 240, 242, 243
Mills, Russell: 242-3
Mills, Sandra: 240, 241
Miner, Ada Ruth: 55
Miner, Belle: see "Kitchen, Lillie Belle"
Miner, Celia Foster French: see "Foster, Celia"
Miner, Dorthea: 54, 55, 197, 243, 287, 297
Miner, Edward A.: 16
Miner, James Odell: 54, 243, 287
Miner, John: 151
Miner, Lillie Bell Kitchen: see "Kitchen, Lillie Belle"
Miner, Maud: 147
Miner, Ruth: 243, 287
Minot, Josephine: 167
Mitchell, Allan Dickerman: 16, 109, 243, 244, 245, 291
Mitchell, Ann Early: see "Early, Ann"
Mitchell, Barnard: 71
Mitchell, Becky: 245
Mitchell, Berenice Dickerman: see "Dickerman, Berenice"
Mitchell, Bernice: 243, 244
Mitchell, Charles: 328
Mitchell, D.P.: 157
Mitchell, Dorothy Wolf: see "Wolf, Dorothy"
Mitchell, Eunice: 70, 71, 121
Mitchell, Fanny Quereau: see "Quereau, Fanny"
Mitchell, George II ("Duke"): 244, 245
Mitchell, George Johnson: 66, 243, 244
Mitchell, George Jr.: 244

Mitchell, Heather: 245
Mitchell, Jean: 243, 244
Mitchell, Jessie E.: 246
Mitchell, Josephine: 66, 243, 244
Mitchell, Mary: 244
Mitchell, Nathalie: 198, 199, 200, 205
Mitchell, Renee Francine "Fran": 232, 234
Mitchell, Robert: 245
Mitchell, Roxie Wood: see "Wood, Roxie"
Mitchell, Sally Ann: 71
Mitchell, Susan Bruner: see "Bruner, Susan"
Mock, Leah Grace: 55, 309, 310
Monroe, Bertha: 183, 192
Monroe, Emil: 183
Monroe, Flora Mae: 95
Monroe, Irene: 183, 192
Monroe, Muriel: 183
Monroe, Neva: 182, 183, 247
Monroe, Nora: 183
Monteith, Sylvia: 191
Moore, Charles: 121
Moore, Colleen: 101
Moore, Eva Kitchen: see "Kitchen, Eva"
Moore, Harriett L.: 128
Moore, Helen: 246
Moore, Henry: 281
Moore, Iva: 50
Moore, Joseph: 246, 268
Moore, Lucy: 246
Moore, Mary: 177, 178
Moore, Meda M.: 49, 50, 51
Moore, Nettie: 246
Moore, Robert: 246
Moore, William H.: 50
Morey, Charlotte: 283
Morey, Dorothy Marie: 55
Morey, Ethel: 42
Morey, John: 82
Morgan, John: 16
Morris, Florence: 91
Morris, George: 91
Morton, Bruce: 98
Morton, Virginia Dagle: see "Dagle, Virginia"
Moses, Anna Mary: 282
Moyer, Mary Magdalena "Lena": 240, 242, 243
Mudge, Frederick: 297
Mudge, Jennie Owens: see "Owens, Jennie"
Muhl, Maud Almyra: 66, 313, 314
Muhl, Philip: 314
Mundy, (Anna) Lavada: 351, 352
Munger, James: 284
Munger, Mary Jean Satterlee: see "Satterlee, Mary Jean"
Munson, Abner: 247
Munson, Artemus Miles: 247
Munson, Daisy Florence: 247
Munson, Helen Ana: 104, 247
Munson, Sarah Cartman: see "Cartman, Sarah"
Munson, Warren: 247
Murdock, Belle Brecht: see "Brecht, Belle"
Murphy, Gordon: 258
Murphy, Larry: 258
Murphy, Nancy Hoskins: see "Hoskins, Nancy"
Murray, Frederick R.: 16
Murray, John: 16
Murray, Ruthmary: 16
Myers, Rebecca: 149
Myers, Sabra A.: 308
Nattress, Adella Skinner: see "Skinner, Adella (d. 2005)"
Nattress, Jane: 297
Nattress, Roy Kenneth Jr.: 297
Nattress, Roy Kenneth: 297
Nesbitt, Luella P.: 80, 120, 122
Nesbitt, Mae Adams: see "Adams, Mae"
Nesbitt, Wallace: 80, 122
Neufligier, Elizabeth: 151, 152, 153, 154
New York Central Railroad: 2, 4, 7, 21, 311, 312, 320
Newberry's chain department store: 9
Newbury, Ruth: 74
Newkirk, Gladys: 182
Nicholas, Anna: 201
Nickolette, Alice: 347
Niles, Howard F.: 16
Norris, Albert: 16
Norris, Alberta: 153
Norris, Charles O.: 16
Norris, E.F.: 16
Norris, Thomas: 16
North Rose Central School (NRCS): 1, 10, 11, 35, 45, 46, 47, 51, 63, 69, 71, 72, 74, 79, 86, 87, 90, 91, 101, 112, 118, 119, 121, 122, 123, 126, 127, 133, 137, 138, 139, 140, 145, 152, 153, 156, 157, 161, 162, 174, 175, 179, 184, 186, 193, 194, 195, 199, 205, 209, 214, 218, 223, 232, 237, 239, 241, 244, 245, 249, 258, 272, 274, 287, 288, 291, 293, 297, 322, 329, 332, 340, 341, 346, 347, 350, 351, 352, 353, 355
North Rose Chemical Company: 29, 120, 182, 252, 332
North Rose Cold Storage Company: 21, 22, 230, 287
North Rose Fire Co.: 51, 237
North Rose Fire Department: 9, 13, 29, 30, 48, 52, 72, 90, 113, 140, 176, 182, 222, 238, 240, 248, 250, 265, 270, 289, 301, 332, 350, 351
North Rose Home Bureau: 28, 60, 76, 90, 99, 132, 144, 186, 197, 200, 207, 249, 265, 318
North Rose Hook and Ladder Company: 29, 182, 252
North Rose Inn: 288
North Rose Masons: 2, 8, 10, 28, 29, 43, 86, 138, 176,

194, 204, 248, 286, 318, 356
North Rose Methodist Church: 8, 25, 26, 27, 36, 46, 54, 55, 59, 72, 84, 92, 96, 102, 114, 128, 157, 176, 182, 197, 199, 202, 203, 204, 209, 212, 222, 223, 226, 250, 264, 268, 269, 270, 283, 286, 287, 291, 301, 302, 306, 325, 326, 344, 347, 351, 356
North Rose Methodist Episcopal Society: 263
North Rose Pharmacy: 284
North Rose Presbyterian Church: 8, 26, 27, 48, 64, 65, 66, 76, 90, 108, 110, 124, 125, 127, 139, 144, 183, 188, 213, 218, 240, 241, 312, 318, 340, 356
North Rose Presbyterian Church Mission Society: 318
North Rose Railroad Company: 356
North Rose Supply Company: 22, 214, 216
Notoriety Bookstore: 303
Noyes, Andrea: 250
Noyes, Barbara Griswold: see "Griswold, Barbara"
Noyes, Diane Curran Bramer: see "Curran, Diane"
Noyes, Donald Frank: 249
Noyes, Eileen: 249, 265
Noyes, Frank M.: 22, 26, 160, 161, 176, 247, 248, 279
Noyes, Louise Lander: see "Lander, Louise"
Noyes, Richard "Dick" Walter: 247, 248, 249, 250
NRCS Alumni Association: 51, 126, 153, 324
O.A. Skutt Company: 2, 20, 22, 34, 55, 63, 64, 75, 77, 79, 80, 82, 86, 92, 100, 102, 103, 109, 122, 143, 148, 182, 278, 283, 294, 298, 299, 313, 314, 322, 342, 343, 345, 353, 356
O'Dell, Cindy Lee: 273
O'Dell, Claude W.: 273
O'Dell, Donald Edward: 273
O'Dell, Grace Stevens: see "Stevens, Grace"
O'Dell, Russell: 273
O'Dell, Shirley Reed: see "Reed, Shirley"
O'Dell, Tracy: 273
O'Donnell, Laura M.: 70
O'Donnell, Theresa Frances: 43, 68, 206, 207, 208, 211
O'Hara, William: 324
O'Hara, Wreatha Van Hout: see "Van Hout, Wreatha (d. 2024)"
O'Keefe, Frank: 111, 112
O'Keefe, Marian Dean: see "Dean, Marian"
O'Loughlin, Ethel: 30
Oaks, Charles: 22, 125, 246
Oaks, Hazel: 250
Oaks, Katherine: 161
Oaks, Marilla Gene: 250
Oaks, Miriam Ellen: 250
Oaks, Seth: 22, 208, 250, 266
Oaks and Son: 22
Ogden, Patricia Kenan: see "Kenan, Patricia"
Ogden, Thomas: 208
Old, Doris A.: 239

Oliver, Ann: 222
Oliver, Frank: 222
Olmsted, Laverne: 114
Ontario Shore Lodge 29 (Wolcott) of the IOOF: 29, 65
Order of the Eastern Star: 2, 29, 46, 54, 64, 66, 86, 90, 105, 125, 161, 162, 169, 173, 176, 177, 188, 194, 223, 268, 306
Ormsby, Dell: 238
Osborn, Josephine Emma: 106
Osgood, Aora: 250
Osgood, Dorothy: 251
Osgood, Ray: 250, 340
Osgood, Ruth: 251
Otto, Mary Ruffino: 92
Oviedo, Enrique: 245
Oviedo, Heather Mitchell: see "Mitchell, Heather"
Oviedo, Stella Elizabeth: 245
Owens, Jennie: 297
Pahl, Mary Louise: 274
Pahl, Reginald: 273, 274, 275
Pahl, Ruth Vincent: see "Vincent, Ruth"
Pahl, Sadie Savage: see "Savage, Sadie"
Painter, Benjamin: 251
Painter, Ida: 251
Palmer, Dorothy Shaver Leaird: see "Shaver, Dorothy"
Palmer, George Washington: 251
Palmer, Helen: 260
Palmer, Henry: 218
Pankratz, Earl: 16
Pardwin, John F.: 251
Pardwin, Myrtle: 251
Park, Roswell: 286
Parkhurst, Alta Baldridge: see "Baldridge, Alta"
Parks, Pearl Lilhan: 309
Parlantieri, Andrew Joseph: 78
Parlantieri, Shirley Bullock: see "Bullock, Shirley"
Parslow, Ella Adelaide: 76, 109, 110
Parslow, George: 110
Partrick, Grace Burns: see "Burns, Grace"
Partrick, Harry E.: 166, 167, 200, 204, 214, 229, 252, 253, 301
Partrick, Josephine: 229
Partrick, Nora: 253
Pascoe, Doris Catchpole: see "Catchpole, Doris"
Patchen, Rick: 95
Payne, Frankie: 315
Payne, Harry: 84, 129, 222, 253, 264, 340
Payne, Laura Harris: see "Harris, Laura"
Peck, Dean: 216
Peck, Elwood: 216
Peck, Estella: 216
Peck, Martha Salter: see "Salter, Martha"
Penner, Frank: see "Beebe, Frank"
Penner, Garrison "Gary": 254, 255, 256, 257
Penner, Hazel: 255, 256, 257

Penner, Helen Marie: 256, 257, 258
Penner, Jay G. Jr.: 256
Penner, Jay G.: 255, 256
Penner, Joseph Yates: 254, 255
Penner, Lena: 254, 255, 256, 257, 258
Penner, Mabel Miles: see "Miles, Mabel"
Penner, Maryette Fisher: see "Fisher, Maryette"
Penner, Miles E.: 256
Penner, Minnie Willis: see "Willis, Minnie"
Penner, Nina Belle: 37, 255, 257
Penner, Robert P.: 256
Penner, Ross D.: 256
Penner, Willis K.: 256
Pepperdine, Carrie Dillingham Aldrich: see "Dillingham, Carrie"
Pepperdine, John Robert: 41, 42, 66
Perkins, Dora: 149, 150
Perkins, George Harvey: 149
Perkins, George: 149
Perkins, John: 149
Perkins, Martha York: see "York, Martha"
Perkins, Sarah Weatherly: see "Weatherly, Sarah"
Perkins, Sarah: 149
Pete Skinner Barber Shop: 22, 296
Peters, Grace: 258
Peters, Jean: 218
Peters, John: 258
Peters, Nancy: 259
Peters, Wesley: 258
Peters, Zoie Camp: see "Camp, Zoie"
Pettit, Lucretia Matilda: 103, 104
Phelps, Bertha (d. 1980): 259
Phelps, Bertha Cottrell (d. 1974): see "Cottrell, Bertha"
Phelps, Earl William: 116
Phelps, Edward (d. 2011): 259
Phelps, Edward F. (d. 1974): 259
Phelps, Ella: 259
Phelps, Glen E.: 116
Phi Kappa Pi: 25, 48, 54, 63, 92, 114, 157, 161, 166, 173, 182, 222, 223, 249, 264, 268, 353
Phillips, (Lina) Marguerite: 260
Phillips, Clayton I.: 344
Phillips, Ella Gardner: see "Gardner, Ella"
Phillips, Elmer: 259
Phillips, Esther: 84, 196, 344
Phillips, Marion: 197, 259, 260
Phillips, Mary: 82
Phillips, Rena Jones: see "Jones, Rena"
Pierse, Elizabeth W.: 59
Pierse, Lida May: 58, 59, 60, 61
Pierse, Merlin: 59
Pierse, Minnie: 60
Pierse, William: 60
Pierson, Albert "Bert": 157
Pierson, Donald Robert: 184

Pierson, Doris Harrison: see "Harrison, Doris"
Pierson, Harold: 26
Pierson, Jeanette: 347
Pierson, Kristine: 184
Pierson, Media W.: 157
Pierson, Steven: 184
Pimms Hotel: 8
Pitcher, Benjamin: 150
Pitcher, Charles David: 146
Pitcher, Edith: 336
Pitcher, Frances Belle: 146
Pitcher, Grace Fink: see "Fink, Grace"
Pitcher, Jean Eloise: 146
Pitcher, Marjorie Elizabeth: 146
Polvino, Suzanne McQueen: see "McQueen, Suzanne"
Poole, Carolyn: 130
Poole, Catherine Lapp: see "Lapp, Catherine"
Poole, Cheryl Lee: 262
Poole, Clara Shipley: see "Shipley, Clara"
Poole, Elaine VandenBout: see "VandenBout, Elaine"
Poole, Gary: 356
Poole, Joyce: 262
Poole, Lucille Drury: see "Drury, Lucille"
Poole, Nancy Ann: 262
Poole, Olen Wayne: 131
Poole, Oscar H.: 261
Poole, Priscilla Reynolds: see "Reynolds, Priscilla"
Poole, Wade Grant: 261, 262, 272
Poole, Wade L. "Mike": 261, 262
Poole, William: 261
Poole, Thelma Edith: 290
Porter, Evelyn "Eva" Andrus: see "Andrus, Evelyn"
Porter, George Spencer: 66, 262, 263
Porter, Lloyd: 105
Porter, Maude: 263
Porter, Mildred C.B.: 263
Porter, Pauline: 46, 47, 262, 263, 264
Porter, Ruth: 105, 335
Powell, Alice Waldorf: see "Waldorf, Alice"
Powell, Arloa Belle: 148, 279
Powell, Celia: 155
Powell, Charles: 16, 154, 155
Powell, Cora: 154
Powell, Edward: 267
Powell, Elsie Glanzel: see "Glanzel, Elsie"
Powell, Emma Bullock: see "Bullock, Emma"
Powell, George Henry: 164, 176, 249, 265, 266
Powell, Gerald E.: 164, 176, 197, 265, 266, 267
Powell, Gray D.: 16
Powell, James H.: 148
Powell, John Carl: 267
Powell, Lula "Lulu" Messenger: see "Messenger, Lula"
Powell, Luther: 154
Powell, Myrtle Dobbin: see "Dobbin, Myrtle"
Powell, Nolan: 12, 13, 16

Powers, Fremont: 240
Powers, Rodney: 240
Pratt, Martha: 245
Preston, Olive Streitle: see "Streitle, Olive"
Preston, Roy: 85
Price, Carol: 45
Priebe, Anna M.: 113
Priebe, Charles M. Sr.: 113
Priebe, Florence: 113
Priest, Esther Cashady: see "Cashady, Esther"
Priest, Gorman: 85
Prince, Charlotte R. S.: 213
Prince, Paulina Weston: 212
Proseus, Allan: 108
Proseus, Harry: 16
Proseus, Katherine Satterlee: see "Satterlee, Katherine"
Pulver, Bertha Messenger: see "Messenger, Bertha"
Pulver, Homer: 164
Putnam, Elizabeth: 26
Putnam, Horace: 26
Putnam, M. Donald: 16
Putney, Mildred: 160
Quereau, (James) William: 268, 269
Quereau, Ann: 308
Quereau, Dewitt Raymond: 308
Quereau, Elias (father: John): 308
Quereau, Elias (father: Josue): 307
Quereau, Elliott R.: 66, 308
Quereau, Fanny: 308
Quereau, Florence Boyd: see "Boyd, Florence"
Quereau, Frank: 66, 101, 170, 270, 306
Quereau, George Henry: 269
Quereau, Henrietta Bean: see "Bean, Henrietta"
Quereau, Henrietta: 9, 10, 26, 43, 44, 204, 230, 253, 270, 271
Quereau, Henry Newton "Harry": 9, 22, 222, 229, 268, 269, 270, 271, 307, 308
Quereau, James William Jr.: 269
Quereau, John: 308
Quereau, Joshua: 308
Quereau, Josue: 307
Quereau, Katherine Hill: 269
Quereau, Lena Gordon: see "Gordon, Lena"
Quereau, Margaret: 308
Quereau, Mary Belle: 66, 170
Quereau, Mary Dowd: see "Dowd, Mary (d. 1931)"
Quereau, Mary Ellen Hill: see "Hill, Mary Ellen"
Quereau, Nellie Smart: see "Smart, Nellie"
Quereau, Phoebe Ryder: see "Ryder, Phoebe"
Quereau, Ross Watson: 268, 269, 307, 308
Quereau, Ruth: 66
Quereau, Sabra Anna: 30, 66, 306, 307, 308
Quereau, Sabra Myers: see "Myers, Sabra"
Quereau, Virginia: 269, 270, 271

Quereau, William (d. 1860): 308
Quereau, William (d. 1927): 308
Quereau General Store: 9, 10, 22, 61, 168, 269, 270, 307
Quest's End: 303
Quinlan, Gertrude: 108
Quinlan, Vincent: 108
Raney, Hazel Dean Balch: see "Dean, Hazel"
Raney, James: 112
Raney, Nancy: 112, 130
Ransley, Charles: 16
Rawden, Maxine Clingerman: see "Clingerman, Maxine"
Rawden, Robert: 241
Raymer, Clifford: 16
Rebekah Utopia Lodge No. 400: 30, 48, 54, 61, 76, 81, 99, 112, 123, 144, 176, 182, 183, 265, 295, 315, 318, 353
Rebekahs: see "Rebekah Utopia Lodge No 400"
Redman, Celia: 224
Redman, David: 224
Redman, Eleanor: 257
Redman, Ellinor Fidelia "Ella": 26, 30, 66, 224, 225, 226, 228, 230, 307
Redman, George: 224
Redman, Lafayette: 224
Redman, Ossian: 224
Redman, Sarah Fidelia: 224, 225
Reed, Daniel: 272
Reed, Ethel: 234
Reed, Iva Baldwin: see "Baldwin, Iva"
Reed, Joanne: 272
Reed, Lucille Esther: 271, 272
Reed, Patricia McDorman: see "McDorman, Patricia"
Reed, Paul (mother: Patricia): 272
Reed, Paul (mother: Viola): 272
Reed, Robert: 272
Reed, Shirley Jane: 271, 272, 273
Reed, Viola Alford: see "Alford, Viola"
Reed, Walter David Jr.: 261, 271, 272
Reed, Walter Waywood: 272
Reed, William A. "Bill": 16, 271, 272
Reeder, Bertha Alice: 195, 196
Reilly, Helen Mary: 112
Rendell, Constance: 245
Reuning, Christopher: 181
Rexer, Esther: 45
Reyn, Edward: see "Yancey, Edward"
Reyn, Lena: 73, 348, 349
Reyn, Theodore: 349
Reyn, William: 349
Reynolds, Priscilla Ann: 261
Reynolds, Thora Marie: 332
Rhodes, Charles G.: 273, 274
Rhodes, Gertrude Savage: see "Savage, Gertrude"

Rice, William: 289, 290
Rich, Alice Amanda: 66, 85, 89
Richardson, Albert "Bert": 75, 76, 144, 145
Richardson, Alice Guthrie: see "Guthrie, Alice"
Richardson, Alice Waldorf Powell: see "Waldorf, Alice"
Richardson, Betty: 209
Richardson, Beverly Jane: 209
Richardson, Bruce: 177
Richardson, Catherine Pauline: 144
Richardson, Donald: 16
Richardson, Doris Chalupa: see "Chalupa, Doris"
Richardson, Ethel Ross: see "Ross, Ethel"
Richardson, Eugene: 144
Richardson, Franklin: 144
Richardson, Julia Fink: see "Fink, Julia"
Richardson, Lillian: 266
Richardson, Lloyd Merton: 144, 246
Richardson, Maurice: 267
Richardson, Maynard Leo: 144
Richardson, Paul (wife: Betty): 209
Richardson, Paul (wife: Julia): 99
Richardson, Ralph: 176
Riesdorph, Carl A.: 98
Riesdorph, Darlene: 99
Riesdorph, John: 99
Riesdorph, Josephine Bulson: see "Bulson, Josephine"
Riesdorph, Mildred: 98, 99, 100
Rifenberg, Lulu: 85
Riggle, Carol: 335
Riggs, Charles: 257
Riggs, Francis Edith Garlick: see "Garlick, Francis Edith"
Riggs, Frank: 33
Riggs, Glenn David: 33, 34
Riggs, Marie Wilkinson: see "Wilkinson, Marie"
Rings, Edwin: 16
Ripley, Ina: 234
Roberts, Aki Takeuchi: see "Takeuchi, Aki"
Roberts, Andrea L.: 302
Roberts, James "Jim": 302, 304
Roberts, John M. "Jack": 281, 302, 303
Roberts, John M. Jr: 302, 304
Roberts, Marilyn Skutt: see "Skutt, (Joan) Marilyn"
Roberts, Mary Louise Kotouc: see "Kotouc, Mary Louise"
Roberts, Myrtle: 228
Roberts, Tania Marie: 302
Robinson, Agnes: 332
Robinson, Archer: 315
Robinson, Benjamin: 315
Robinson, Daniel: 315
Robinson, Doris: 332
Robinson, Elsie: 315
Robinson, Frederick (father: Daniel): 315
Robinson, Frederick: 16

Robinson, Leslie: 315
Robinson, Lottie: 315
Robinson, Margaret: 332
Robinson, Samuel: 315
Robinson, Virginia Collier: see "Collier, Virginia"
Roe, Alfred S.: 5
Rogers, Rufus: see "Ball, George H. Jr."
Rolfe, Irene Monroe: see "Monroe, Irene"
Rolfe, William: 192
Roney, (Judson) Merrill: 16, 279, 280
Roney, Adelbert: 278
Roney, Beth: 279
Roney, Charles: 279
Roney, Cynthia: 279
Roney, Diane Marie: 279
Roney, Donald: 279
Roney, Flora: 279
Roney, Frank (mother: Rose): 279
Roney, Frank F. Jr.: 275, 277, 279
Roney, Frank Fiero: 66, 94, 207, 211, 237, 278, 279
Roney, Gordon Heyd: 279
Roney, Gordon Jr.: 279
Roney, Jean Ellen: 279
Roney, Jimmy: 279
Roney, John: 279
Roney, Josephine Turk: see "Turk, Josephine"
Roney, Kathleen: 279
Roney, Lee Albert: 279
Roney, Lincoln Merrill: 279
Roney, Marie Hunter: see "Hunter, Marie"
Roney, Mary "Estella" Merrill: see "Merrill, Mary "Estella""
Roney, Mary: 278
Roney, Nancy Russell: see "Russell, Nancy"
Roney, Rebecca: 279
Roney, Rick: 279
Roney, Robert: 279
Roney, Rose Conway: see "Conway, Rose"
Rosa, Edna Fink: see "Fink, Edna"
Rosa, George: 145
Rosa, Kenneth: 145
Rosary Society: 27, 132
Rose, Lela: 263
Rose, Lena: 66
Rose Baptist Church: 27, 83, 163, 214, 325, 351
Rose Fire Department: 332
Rose Free Methodist Church: 152, 192
Rose Grange, no. 1051: 29, 83, 125, 165, 191, 301
Rose Masonic Lodge: 123, 125, 160, 197, 245, 270, 301, 306
Rose Neighborhood Sketches: 5
Rose Public Health Committee: 29, 51, 215
Ross, Ethel Marie: 144
Rotach, Beth: 74
Rotach, Brian: 74

Rotach, Darren Duane: 74
Rotach, Frank: 74
Rotach, John D.: 16
Rotach, Joyce Yancey: see "Yancey, Joyce"
Rotach, Keith: 74
Rotach, Mary: 74
Rotach, Richard F.: 16, 74
Rotach, Sherry Lou: 74
Roth, Charles: 168
Roth, Eleanor Gray Hoffman: see "Gray, Eleanor"
Rothang, Mathilda: 129
Rounds, Eunice: 77
Rowe, Mary Elizabeth: 147
Rupert, Mary Brown Spade: see "Brown, Mary Ethel"
Rupert, Sidney J.: 308
Russell, Flora: 278
Russell, Nancy Cynthia: 279
Ryan, Kim Edwards: see "Edwards, Kim"
Ryan, Robin: 134
Ryder, Phoebe: 308
Salter, Edward Adrian: 22, 54, 65, 66, 280
Salter, Evelyn: 166
Salter, Leon Jay: 22, 231, 280, 281, 282
Salter, Martha Jane: 66, 166, 197, 254, 279
Salter, Myrta Ball: see "Ball, Myrta"
Salter, Thelma Brede: see "Brede, Thelma"
Salter Canning Company: 2, 22, 37, 49, 54, 59, 76, 82, 89, 98, 100, 102, 124, 133, 156, 172, 173, 174, 183, 184, 197, 220, 223, 236, 237, 242, 246, 254, 257, 258, 259, 262, 273, 274, 275, 280, 281, 282, 286, 287, 294, 298, 308, 309, 315, 318, 319, 321, 326, 327, 346
Salter Hose and Chemical Company: 30, 110, 160, 331, 332, 353
Sanderson, Shirley: 234
Saner, Louise: 192
Santoli, Antonia: 133
Sarsnett, Jeanette: 334
Satterlee, Benjamin H.: 222, 223, 283
Satterlee, Benjamin Jr.: 223
Satterlee, Bertha Monroe: see "Monroe, Bertha"
Satterlee, Delia Wright: see "Wright, Delia"
Satterlee, Dora Elizabeth: 222, 223, 268, 283
Satterlee, Dorothy Baker: see "Baker, Dorothy"
Satterlee, Eugene "Gene": 282, 283, 284
Satterlee, Gladys Jean: 81, 284
Satterlee, Harold Jr.: 284
Satterlee, Harold: 16, 283, 284
Satterlee, Kate: 34, 35, 36
Satterlee, Katherine "Katie": 161, 223, 283
Satterlee, Luranda Smith: see "Smith, Luranda"
Satterlee, Mae Thomas: see "Thomas, Mae"
Satterlee, Mary Jean: 284
Satterlee, Mary Johnson: see "Johnson, Mary"
Satterlee, Russell: 16, 81, 283, 284, 295

Satterlee, Samuel: 284
Satterlee, Uriah: 35, 283
Sattler, Alberta Norris: see "Norris, Alberta"
Sattler, Celia French: see "French, Celia"
Sattler, Charles: 153
Sattler, John Charles: 153
Saturday Night Club: 31, 130
Savage, Gertrude: 273, 274
Savage, Jeanette "Jane": 274
Savage, Sadie: 273, 274
Sawyer, S. Nelson: 316
Scalzo, Grace: 126
Schmeiser, William: 16
Schmidt, Edward William: 191
Schmidt, Gladys Little Adams: see "Little, Gladys"
Schopfer, Jim: 86, 87
Schopfer, Lynda Catchpole: see "Catchpole, Lynda"
Schultz, George Lee: 173
Schultz, Gladys Groat: see "Groat, Gladys"
Schultz, Roy: 173
Schuyler, Leaon N.: 16
Schwab, Anna Boll: see "Boll, Anna"
Schwab, Julius: 69
Schwarz, Ellen Seelye: see "Seelye, Ellen"
Schwarz, Eugene: 293
Scullion, Raymond E.: 16
Seager, (David) Munson: 188
Seager, Ada: 285, 286, 287
Seager, Alta Candace: 92, 285, 286, 324
Seager, Alvie: 98, 100
Seager, Bertha: 285, 286
Seager, Bub: 292
Seager, Candace Bumpus: see "Bumpus, Candace"
Seager, Catherine Cronk: see "Cronk, Catherine"
Seager, Earl Asher Washington: 285, 286, 287
Seager, Emma Dunbar: see "Dunbar, Emma"
Seager, Emma Sprong: see "Sprong, Emma"
Seager, Ernest: 285
Seager, Esther Louise: 97, 98, 100
Seager, Fanette "Nettie": 189
Seager, George: 285, 286
Seager, Harriett: 124, 125, 187, 188, 189
Seager, Ida: 128, 163, 164
Seager, Ila V.: 73
Seager, Kenneth: 285
Seager, Luna: 97
Seager, Maude: 285
Seager, Pearl Knox: see "Knox, Pearl"
Seager, Sarah: 54, 166
Seager, Shelia: 179
Seager, Wayne: 285
Seager, Wesley: 285
Seager, Winifred: 285
Searles, J.W.: 278
Sears, Lawrence: 16

Sebring, James W.: 16
Seely, William A.: 16
Seelye, Ada: 288
Seelye, Alda Luffman: see "Luffman, Alda"
Seelye, Carol Linda: 290, 292
Seelye, Carson Luffman: 22, 288, 289, 290, 291, 292
Seelye, Dorr Frank: 22, 26, 288, 289, 290, 291, 292
Seelye, Edith Chaddock: see "Chaddock, Edith"
Seelye, Ellen Ann: 26, 291, 293
Seelye, Ernest Osgood: 288
Seelye, Frank Ernest: 22, 139, 287, 288, 289, 290, 291, 292
Seelye, James D.: 291, 293
Seelye, Nedra Armstrong: see "Armstrong, Nedra"
Seelye, Virginia: 293
Seelye Apartments: 288
Seelye Ladder Co.: 19, 22, 47, 238, 288, 290, 291, 292
Sellick, Sally: 38, 39
Sew-and-Sew Club: 31, 129, 176
Shading, Earl: 16
Shaughnessy, Mary: 328
Shaver, Arloa: 171, 298
Shaver, Cassius Martin: 171
Shaver, Charlotte Beckett: see "Beckett, Charlotte"
Shaver, Dorothy Louise: 217, 218
Shaver, Mary Elizabeth Knapp: see "Knapp, Mary Elizabeth"
Shaver, Sarah Selena "Lena": 30, 66, 169, 170, 171, 172
Shaver, William H.: 217
Shear, Genevieve Lanola: 47, 264, 320
Shear, Margaret: 293
Shear, Steven: 293
Sheffield, Judson: 288
Shepard, Fred: 278
Shepherd, Helen Agnes: 135
Sherman, Caroline Beam: see "Beam, Caroline"
Sherman, Donald: 16
Sherman, Dorothy Garton: see "Garton, Dorothy"
Sherman, Faith Vincent: see "Vincent, Faith"
Sherman, Gail: 330
Sherman, Gary: 330
Sherman, Gerald Michael: 330
Sherman, Glen: 330
Sherman, Grace: 159
Sherman, Jefferson Albert: 99, 100
Sherman, Leon A.: 330
Sherman, Lori: 330
Sherman, Mark: 330
Sherman, Mildred Riesdorph Darling: see "Riesdorph, Mildred"
Sherman, Orin Henry: 99
Sherman, Rebecca: 330
Sherman, Ronald: 330
Sherman, Rose Bushey: see "Bushey, Rose"

Sherman, Roy: 101
Shi, Wen-long: 180, 181
Shipley, Carol Seelye: see "Seelye, Carol"
Shipley, Clara: 261
Shipley, Olan: 290, 292
Shipley, Sonia Michelle: 292
Shipley, Thelma Poole: see "Poole, Thelma"
Shipley, Warren: 290
Shippers, Elizabeth Hermenet: 119
Shippers, Ida DeRuischer: see "DeRuischer, Ida"
Shippers, Isaac J.: 119
Shippers, Melvin Stanley: 119
Shortsleeve, Henry: 102
Shortsleeve, Jessie: 102, 103
Shortsleeve, Lucy Day: see "Day, Lucy"
Shortsleeve, Ted: 103
Shove, Marguerite: 257
Showers, Nelson: 321
Sidler, Albert: 293
Sidler, Arthur: 16
Sidler, Flora: 30, 66, 187, 270, 271, 306
Sidler, George: 16
Sidler, Harry: 293
Sidler, Lawrence: 16, 294
Sidler, Lena: 293
Sidler, Nina (d. 2016): 293
Sidler, Nina Marguerite (d. 1918): 178
Sigel, Mildred: 273
Sigma Society: 27, 76, 125, 144, 145, 183, 188, 318, 340
Silliman, Maude: 140
Sisson, Francis: 266
Skinkle, Emery: 16
Skinkle, Grant: 16
Skinner, (Francis) Mark: 81, 157, 294, 295, 296, 297
Skinner, (Marion) Boyce "Bud": 81, 294, 295, 296
Skinner, Adella (d. 1911): 296
Skinner, Adella Mae "Della" (d. 2005): 296, 297
Skinner, Cheryl: 295
Skinner, Christine: 295
Skinner, Dale: 81, 295
Skinner, Dean: 81, 295
Skinner, Delphine: 296
Skinner, Ethel Harris Hill: see "Harris, Ethel"
Skinner, Francis Marion "Pete": 22, 81, 294, 296, 297
Skinner, Francis Marion Sr.: 296
Skinner, Leona Burns: see "Burns, Leona"
Skinner, Margaret Mark: see "Mark, Margaret"
Skinner, Maude Conklin: see "Conklin, Maude"
Skinner, Neil: 295
Skinner, Robert "Bob": 295
Skinner, Ronald "Ronnie": 295
Skinner, Ronald B. Jr.: 295
Skinner, Tammy M.: 295
Skinner, Virginia Conrow: see "Conrow, Virginia"

Skinner, Wayne: 296
Skutt, (Joan) Marilyn: 3, 43, 152, 171, 281, 298, 301, 302, 303
Skutt, (Orin) Watson: 169, 229, 298, 299, 300, 302
Skutt, A. (Alexander) Gray: 22, 32, 43, 64, 86, 152, 160, 229, 240, 278, 298, 299, 300, 301, 302, 307
Skutt, Alexander G.: 167, 168, 301, 302, 303, 304
Skutt, Almira Lamb: see "Lamb, Almira"
Skutt, Arloa Shaver: see "Shaver, Arloa"
Skutt, Daniel: 304
Skutt, Doris Lee: 300
Skutt, Ethan B.: 304
Skutt, Jane Flood: see "Flood, (Marie) Jane"
Skutt, Jonathan: 298, 304, 305
Skutt, Judith Ruth: 300
Skutt, Orin Alexander: 21, 157, 280, 298
Skutt, Orrin: 298, 304, 305
Skutt, Ruth Town: see "Towne, Ruth"
Smalley, Sarah Elizabeth: 167, 168, 170
Smart, Nellie: 66, 170, 192, 270, 306
Smart, William: 191, 192
Smith, (George) Arthur: 306, 307
Smith, (William) Howard: 306, 307
Smith, Agnes Clingerman: see "Clingerman, Agnes"
Smith, Alice: 116
Smith, Cathleen Martin: see "Martin, Cathleen"
Smith, Charles: 307
Smith, Chester R.: 17
Smith, Clark: 307
Smith, Corinne Isabel: 116
Smith, Donald: 17
Smith, Edmond Franklin: 94
Smith, Edwin L.: 230
Smith, Elizabeth: 307
Smith, Elmira: 186
Smith, Emma: 95
Smith, Frank: 17
Smith, Frederic: 307
Smith, Gerald: 307
Smith, Harold: 17
Smith, Helen Gallery: see "Gallery, Helen"
Smith, Herbert Watson: 66, 306, 307
Smith, Irving: 17, 72
Smith, James: 307
Smith, Jennifer: 295
Smith, Lila Stafford: see "Stafford, Lila"
Smith, Lila Tod: 230
Smith, Lizbeth: 307
Smith, Lois Johnson: see "Johnson, Lois"
Smith, Luranda: 223
Smith, Phyllis: 347
Smith, Ralph: 17
Smith, Raymond: 99
Smith, Sabra Quereau: see "Quereau, Sabra Anna"
Smith, Sally: 307
Smith, Susan: 185
Smith, Thelma Grace: 94
Smith, Wallace: 307
Smith, Wilbur L.: 17
Snell, Eliza Jane: 339, 340
Snyder, Esbon Blackmer: 210
Snyder, Leola Nancy: 210, 211
Snyder, Mary Trummonds: see "Trummonds, Mary"
Sodus Church of the Epiphany: 27, 130, 132
Sodus Cold Storage: 22, 351, 355
Sommer, Eva: 89
Sours, Ann Eliza: 61
Sower, Vincent: 16
Sozio, Beverly Wiltsie Edwards: see "Wiltsie, Beverly"
Sozio, Thomas: 134
Spade, Frank Benjamin: 308, 309
Spade, Frederick Levi: 16, 309
Spade, Judy: 310
Spade, LaRue Aileen: 309, 310
Spade, Leah Mock: see "Mock, Leah"
Spade, Leo A.: 310
Spade, Leo S.: 17, 309, 310
Spade, Marion "Harry": 17, 55, 309, 310
Spade, Martha Jane: 310
Spade, Mary Ethel Brown: see "Brown, Mary Ethel"
Spade, Mary Hendershot: see "Hendershot, Mary"
Spade, Pearl Lilhan Parks: see "Parks, Pearl"
Spade, Robert H.: 310
Spade, Violet Younker: see "Younker, Violet"
Spencer, Agnes: 234
Spiller, Bonnie Vernoy Lindauer: see "Vernoy, Bonnie"
Spiller, Fredrick: 326
Spink, Helen: 198
Sprague, Mattie Bumpus: see "Bumpus, Mattie"
Sprong, Emma Mariah: 285
Stafford, Lila: 230
Stanley, Joseph: 119
Stanley, Kathleen DeRuischer: see "DeRuischer, Kathleen"
Stanley, Sarah "Sally": 5
Stanton, Elizabeth Hannah: 40, 123
Star Market: 341
Stark, Doris Old: see "Old, Doris"
Stark, Garry Austin: 239
Stark, Janet Ruth: 239
Starlight Club: 31, 176, 267
Stauch, John: 274
Stauch, Ruth: 274
Stechow, Ora: 208
Steele, Jacqueline: 354
Steitler, Hazel Mae: 162, 163
Stevens, Grace Irene: 273
Stevens, Ina: 23
Stevenson, Eleanor: 252, 253
Stevenson, Stanley Eugene: 338

Steves, Mary Shaughnessy: see "Shaughnessy, Mary"
Steves, Mary: 328
Steves, Nelson R.: 328
Stickles, Bertha Della: 78
Stickles, Eunice Carrie: 159
Stickles, Fidelia A.: 78
Stickles, Nelson: 78
Stimers, Frederick: 33
Stimers, Maude Torrey Abbott: see "Torrey, Maude"
Stokes, Charles: 335
Stokes, Elizabeth Ditton: see "Ditton, Elizabeth"
Stokes, William E.: 60
Stolte, Anna Whalen: see "Whalen, Anna"
Stolte, William: 60
Stone, Alison Connon Green: 51
Stone, B.R.: 222
Stone, Earl Lewis: 51
Stone, Elvira Lovejoy: see "Lovejoy, Elvira"
Stone, Homer: 310, 311, 312, 313
Stone, Isabel "Belle": 311
Stone, Lyle N.: 311
Stone, Verna E.: 311, 312, 313
Stone, Virginia: 51, 52, 155
Stone, Warren J.: 311
Stoutenger, Carrie Guernsey: see "Guernsey, Carrie"
Stoutenger, Joel: 68
Stoutenger, Mary: 68, 69, 70, 72, 73
Straut, William C.: 17
Streitle, Benjamin: 84
Streitle, Elizabeth Hoppe: see "Hoppe, Elizabeth"
Streitle, Esther Cashady: see "Cashady, Esther"
Streitle, Olive: 84, 85
Strong, Millicent Sarah: 47, 48
Stubley, Arlene: 313
Stubley, Elizabeth: 313
Stubley, Ethel Van Sicklen: see "Van Sicklen, Ethel"
Stubley, George: 171
Stubley, Perry: 313, 323
Stubley, Rodney: 313
Sullivan, Elaine: 179
Swart, Ann Quereau: see "Quereau, Ann"
Sweet, Job: 46
Sweet, Mary Eliza: 46
Swift, Caroline "Carrie": 106, 107
Syron, Lydia Jane: 155
Syron, Myrtle Bond: see "Bond, Myrtle"
Syron, Roy Sloan: 155
Taft, Chester W.: 17
Taft, Clifford: 17
Taft, Weldon: 17
Takeuchi, Aki: 304
Tanner, Lestina: 201
Taylor, Dottie Towne: see "Towne, Dorothy"
Taylor, Fred: 256
Taylor, Jonnie Kay: 196

Taylor, Kathryn: 196
Taylor, Rodney: 158
Teeple, Harold: 17
Tellier, (Mary) Elizabeth: 153, 214, 215, 314, 342
Tellier, Ann: 314
Tellier, David W.: 342
Tellier, Ellen: 215, 216, 314
Tellier, Eugene "Toby" Hugh Jr.: 342
Tellier, Eugene Hugh: 314, 341, 342, 343
Tellier, Harry Adrian: 66, 313, 314
Tellier, Harry Jr.: 314
Tellier, Jane Winchell: see "Winchell, (Elizabeth) Jane"
Tellier, John "Jack" Marvin: 342
Tellier, Martha: 314
Tellier, Maud Muhl: see "Muhl, Maud"
Tellier, Mildred Vanderwall: see "Vanderwall, Mildred"
Tellier, Stephen R. "Tex": 343
Tellier, Susan Katherine: 342
Tellier, Zachary: 343
Terbush, Dick: 290
Terbush, Hazel Armstrong: see "Armstrong, Hazel"
Terbush, LaVerne: 47, 48, 289, 290
Terry, Anna: 71, 120, 284
Thayer, Laurence E.: 17
The Clyde Herald: 34, 45, 46
The Glad Tidings Church: 24, 25, 191
The Lake Shore News: 3, 13, 33, 45, 94, 101, 245, 342, 351
The Lyons Republican: 3, 342
The Voices of Wayne County: 10
The Wayne County Herald Eagle: 3
Thomas, Charlotte Morey: see "Morey, Charlotte"
Thomas, Della: 315, 316, 317
Thomas, Diane: 26
Thomas, Edwin D.: 282, 283
Thomas, Elsie Robinson: see "Robinson, Elsie"
Thomas, Eva: 315, 316
Thomas, Frankie Payne: see "Payne, Frankie"
Thomas, Frankie: 315
Thomas, Fred: 161
Thomas, George E.: 315, 316
Thomas, George F.: 17
Thomas, Jerome E.: 315, 316
Thomas, John (d. 1931): 161
Thomas, John: 17
Thomas, Katherine Oaks: see "Oaks, Katherine"
Thomas, Mae Elizabeth: 71, 282, 283, 284
Thomas, Mary Elizabeth Hess: see "Hess, Mary Elizabeth"
Thomas, Merritt: 51
Thomas, Philip Sr.: 283
Thomas, Reva: 26
Thomas, Ruth: 159, 160, 161, 229
Thomas, Sarah A.: 315
Thomas, Sarah Little: see "Little, Sarah"

Thomas, Sue: 26
Thomas, Vinnie L.: 315, 316
Thomas, William: 161
Thompson, (James) Ross: 105
Thompson, Addie Cahoon: see "Cahoon, Addie"
Thompson, Cecile Aldrich: see "Aldrich, Cecile"
Thompson, Clara Householder: see "Householder, Clara"
Thompson, Elaine: 319
Thompson, Ernest "Ernie": 317, 318
Thompson, Etta: 217, 218
Thompson, Eunice: 267, 317
Thompson, Frank: 105, 234, 317
Thompson, Harriet Aldrich: see "Aldrich, Harriet"
Thompson, Ida Anna: 317
Thompson, Katherine Day: see "Day, Katherine"
Thompson, Leslie Edwin: 17, 260, 318, 319
Thompson, Mary Jane: 105
Thompson, Orin Albert: 318, 319
Thompson, Richard Day: 105
Thompson, Russell: 267, 317
Thompson, Yasu Kashiwada: see "Kashiwada, Yasu"
Thursday Club: 2, 31, 84, 132, 157, 182, 222
Tibbitts, Josephine: 47
Ticknor, A.J.: 150
Ticknor, Dora: 150
Todd, Hollis: 214
Todd, Thelma: 214
Toles, Orson H.: 17
Torrey, Annah L.: 33
Torrey, George D.: 33
Torrey, Maude: 33
Town, Milton L.: 17
Town of Rose Historical Society: 38, 120, 139, 163, 181, 215, 346, 356
Towne, Anna Lewis: see "Lewis, Anna"
Towne, C. Eugene: 140, 157, 158, 319
Towne, Charlotte H. "Lottie": 158, 319
Towne, Dorothy Gage: see "Gage, Dorothy"
Towne, Dorothy Lee "Dottie": 158
Towne, Lynne Seelye: 158
Towne, Norris Eugene: 140, 158
Towne, Norris Seelye "Red": 157, 158
Towne, Ruth Lee: 169, 300
Tracy, Robert "Bob": 44
Triska, Bill: 122
Triska, Janet Adams: see "Adams, Janet"
Trummonds, Mary: 210
Turbush, Frank: 335
Turk, Josephine: 278
Turner, Franklin: 17
Tyron, Arthur: 285
Tyron, Grace: 285
Tyron, Maude Seager: see "Seager, Maude"
Tyron, Ruth: 285

Urbanik, Jadwiga "Hattie": 273
Usher, Carol Yancey: see "Yancey, Carol"
Usher, Gloria: 74
Usher, Joan: 74
Usher, John W.: 74
Usher, Ruth Newbury: see "Newbury, Ruth"
Usher, Samuel: 74
Usher, Wiliam: 74
Valentine, Bert: 340
Valentine, Elizabeth: see "Van Pelt, Elizabeth Frances"
Valentine, Frank: 123, 335
Valentine, Genevieve Shear: see "Shear, Genevieve"
Valentine, George: 340
Valentine, Ida Abbott: see "Abbott, Ida"
Valentine, Jackson: 320
Valentine, Laural: see "Van Pelt, Elizabeth Frances"
Van Amburg, Iona Mae: 192, 219
Van de Putte, Abraham: 151, 153
Van de Putte, Clara Latosky: see "Latosky, Clara"
Van de Putte, Elizabeth: 151, 152, 153, 154
Van de Putte, William: 153
Van den Broek, Adriaan: see "VandenBrook, Adrian"
Van der Lijcke, Herbert: see "Vanderlyke, Herbert"
Van Deusen, Lawrence: 137
Van Deusen, Mildred Edwards: see "Edwards, Mildred"
Van Deusen, Richard: 137
Van Deusen, Robert: 137
Van Duyne, Donald: 235
Van Duyne, Geraldine May: see "May, Geraldine"
Van Duyne, Glenn: 235
Van Duyne, Gregory: 235
Van Duyne, Lynne Anne: 235
Van Eden, Cora Hollebrandt: see "Hollebrandt, Cora"
Van Eden, Elizabeth Neufligier Van de Putte Vandenbrook: see "Neufligier, Elizabeth"
Van Eden, Jacob: 154
Van Hoff, Carl C.: 321, 322
Van Hoff, Charles L.: 320, 321
Van Hoff, Corwin Charles: 320, 321, 322
Van Hoff, Julia U.: 320
Van Hoff, Laura LeBlanc: see "LeBlanc, Laura"
Van Hoff, Lorraine Arlene: 321, 322
Van Hout, Bonnie Lou: 324
Van Hout, Donna Fay: 322, 324
Van Hout, Elsie Vanderlyke: see "Vanderlyke, Elsie"
Van Hout, Florence Borden: see "Borden, Florence"
Van Hout, Gloria Behm: see "Behm, Gloria"
Van Hout, Herbert L.: 322, 323
Van Hout, Inez: 77, 324
Van Hout, Jacob: 62, 323
Van Hout, Jean Ann: 322, 323
Van Hout, Jeffrey Lloyd "Bud": 324
Van Hout, Lloyd: 62, 322, 323
Van Hout, Sandra Kay: 322, 323
Van Hout, Wreatha (d. 2024): 324

Van Hout, Wreatha E. (d. 1982): 323
Van Patten, Earl: 168
Van Pelt, Elizabeth Crawford: see "Crawford, Elizabeth"
Van Pelt, Elizabeth Frances: 36, 123, 335, 336
Van Pelt, John Grove: 123
Van Sicklen, Ethel: 313, 323
Van Steen, Jacob: 241
Van Steen, Lottie: 241
Van Steen, Onnalee: 241
Vanatta, Helen: 96
VandenBout, Elaine: 261
VandenBrook, Adrian: 153, 154
VandenBrook, Elizabeth Neufligier Van de Putte: see "Neufligier, Elizabeth"
Vanderlyke, Elizabeth Fremouw: see "Fremouw, Elizabeth"
Vanderlyke, Elsie: 62, 322, 323
Vanderlyke, Herbert: 323
Vanderwall, Mildred: 314
Vanderwinckel, Jennie Elodie: 136
Vanderzell, Frank: 113
Vanderzell, Inez: 113, 114
Vanderzell, Margaret Havert: see "Havert, Margaret"
Vanderzell, Pearl: 114
Vanderzell, Raymond: 114
Vanderzille, Doris: 323
Vanderzille, John: 323
Vanderzille, Marie Beck: see "Beck, Marie"
Vanderzille, Richard Lloyd: 323
Vanderzille, Wreatha Van Hout: see "Van Hout, Wreatha E."
Vandewinckel, Joyce Marie: 241
Vanhout, Clayton G.: 265
Vanhout, Daniel: 265
Vanhout, Hulda Legg: see "Legg, Hulda"
Vanhout, Maria Gaffield: see "Gaffield, Maria"
VanLare, Maria Frances: 114
VanPatten, James J.: 17
Vernoy, Alta Seager: see "Seager, Alta"
Vernoy, Bonnie: 324, 325, 326
Vernoy, Hugh Houston: 92, 286, 324
Vernoy, Leon Seager: 92, 286, 324, 325, 326
Vernoy, Olive Ruth: 286
Vernoy, Thelma Claus: see "Claus, Thelma"
VerStraete, Joyce Poole: see "Poole, Joyce"
VerStraete, William "Bill": 262
Video Ithaca: 304
Vincent, (David) Kenneth: 326, 329, 330
Vincent, Albert LeRoy: 326, 327, 328, 329
Vincent, Alexander: 326
Vincent, Carol Ann: 328
Vincent, Claude R.: 327
Vincent, Curtis E.: 17, 327, 328
Vincent, Dale E.: 326, 330

Vincent, David: 330
Vincent, Donald: 326, 329
Vincent, Esther Woods: see "Woods, Esther"
Vincent, Ethel Curtis: see "Curtis, Ethel"
Vincent, Faith: 326, 330
Vincent, Fred Alexander: 326, 327, 330
Vincent, Frederick: 17, 326, 327, 329
Vincent, Gail Johns: see "Johns, Gail"
Vincent, Harry: 330
Vincent, James J.: 329
Vincent, Kathleen: 330
Vincent, Leslie: 330
Vincent, Lucy Groves: see "Groves, Lucy"
Vincent, Marie: 329
Vincent, Mary Steves: see "Steves, Mary"
Vincent, Richard: 330
Vincent, Rita: 329
Vincent, Rose Divincenzo: see "Divincenzo, Rose"
Vincent, Ruth: 274
Vincent, Virginia: 329
Vincent, Vivian Edith: 327, 328, 345
Vollmer, Elaine Thompson: see "Thompson, Elaine"
Vollmer, John: 319
Wadsworth, Grace: 330
Wagner, Earl Frederick Henry: 98
Wagner, Esther Seager: see "Seager, Esther"
Wagner, Lorraine: 97, 98
Wahl, Carol Johnson: see "Johnson, Carol"
Wahl, Lawrence: 99
Waldorf, Alice Theresa: 176, 197, 266, 267
Waldorf, Glen: 332
Waldorf, Guy Dillow: 266
Waldorf, Lillian Richardson: see "Richardson, Lillian"
Waldorf, Ralph: 17
Waldron, Anna: 49, 50
Walhizer, Andrew G.: 83
Walhizer, Anna May: 82, 83
Walhizer, Earl: 83
Walhizer, Elizabeth: 83
Walhizer, Flora: 83
Walhizer, George Washington: 83
Walker, Hank: 181
Wallace, Caroline: 347
Walsh, John W.: 230
Walsh, Lila Smith: see "Smith, Lila Tod"
Walter, George: 255
Wambold, Carl: 235
Wambold, Carla: 235
Wambold, Michael: 235
Wambold, Norma May: see "May, Norma"
Ward, Catherine Carnell: see "Carnell, Catherine"
Ward, Clyde: 186
Ward, George: 186
Warden, Elizabeth: 315
Wardwell, Arlo Hill: see "Hill, Arlo"

Wardwell, Horace M.: 190
Wardwell, Marilyn: 190
Wardwell, Maxine: 190
Warner, Anna Eliza: 61
Warner, Bertha Fowler: see "Fowler, Bertha"
Warner, Esther Bancroft: see "Bancroft, Esther"
Warner, Truman Dare: 61, 211
Warner, Woodworth: 61
Warren, Addie Greenwood: see "Greenwood, Addie"
Warren, Avery: 194
Warren, Edna Mae: 194, 195
Warren, Paul: 194
Washburn, Beatrice: 176, 177, 331
Washburn, Betty Jean Leaird: see "Leaird, Betty Jean"
Washburn, Carol: 218
Washburn, Clinton: 331
Washburn, Donna: 218
Washburn, Grace: 98
Washburn, James Oliver: 218
Washburn, Jeffrey: 218
Washburn, June: 105
Washburn, Kathleen: 218
Washburn, Kathryn: 130, 176, 330
Washburn, Linda: 218
Washburn, Patricia Dawn: 218
Watson, E.W.: 247
Watson, Thomas: 282
Watt, George Gray: 210
Watt, Mary Harris: see "Harris, Mary Eliza"
Watt, Nellie: 210
Wayne, Laura Pitcher Harris: 129
Weatherly, Sarah: 149
Weber, Elizabeth: 232
Weber, Maria: 251
Webers, Julius: 227
Webers, Martha Jones: see "Jones, Martha"
Webers, Ruth: 166,167, 205, 226, 227, 228, 229, 230, 231
Weed, Alice Hebert: see "Hebert, Alice"
Weed, Gary: 139
Weed, Norma: 126
Weed, Oscar: 126, 160, 229, 230, 240
Weed, Richard: 17
Weeks, A.J.: 327
Weeks, Agnes Robinson: see "Robinson, Agnes"
Weeks, Barbara: 332
Weeks, Dawn: 332
Weeks, Dorcas Anna: 96
Weeks, Earle R.: 331, 332
Weeks, Edith Elizabeth: 57
Weeks, Edward A.: 331
Weeks, Harriett "Hattie": 331, 332
Weeks, Hazel Boyle: see "Boyle, Hazel"
Weeks, Russell O.: 331, 332
Weeks, Ruth: 188

Weeks, Sharon: 332
Weeks, Thora Reynolds: see "Reynolds, Thora"
Weiland, Albert D.: 333, 334, 336
Weiland, Edith Pitcher: see "Pitcher, Edith"
Weiland, Louella "Ella" Ditton Godkin: see "Ditton, Louella"
Weiss, Karen: 38, 39
Weiss, Ken: 38, 39
Welch, (Joseph) Donald: 229, 337, 338
Welch, Christina: 179
Welch, Cora Permillie "Millie": 179
Welch, Donald: 21
Welch, Harold J.: 338
Welch, Mary J.: 337
Welch, Olive Briggs: see "Briggs, Olive"
Welch, Russell Thomas: 338
Welch, Thomas B.: 22, 338
Wellman, H.E.: 278
Wells Dodds Nursery: 22, 125, 188
Wemelsfelder, Marna "Mary" Dinah: 115
Wera, Irene: 321
Wera, Louis: 321
Westfall, Marjorie: 341
Whalen, Anna Mae: 60
Whalen, Arleen: 60, 61
Whalen, Gertrude Bly: see "Bly, Gertrude"
Whalen, James Thomas: 59, 60
Whalen, Kathleen: 60, 61
Whalen, Mary A.: 59, 60
Whalen, Ruth: 60, 61
Whalen, Thomas: 60
Whelan, Midge McOmber: see "McOmber, Midge"
Whitcomb, Beth: 216
Whitcomb, Ellen Tellier: see "Tellier, Ellen"
Whitcomb, James N.: 216
Whitcomb, Jonathan P.: 216
Whitcomb, Lynn: 216
Whitcomb, Matthew: 216
Whitcomb, Newell "Chip": 216
Whitcomb, Newell "Newt": 215, 216
Whitcomb, Timothy H.: 216
Whittier, Kathleen May: see "May, Kathleen"
Whittier, Robert: 235
Wigfield, Catherine Little: see "Little, Catherine"
Wigfield, Joyce: 192
Wigfield, Raymond: 192
Wigfield, Richard Earl: 192
Wigfield, Ronnie: 192
Wilber, Bessie E.: 232, 233
Wilcox, Alta Failey: see "Failey, Alta"
Wilcox, Diane: 240
Wilcox, Harold: 240
Wilcox, Larry: 240
Wilcox, Richard: 240
Wilkinson, Cornelius: 255, 256

Wilkinson, Hazel Penner: see "Penner, Hazel"
Wilkinson, Marie Pauline: 256, 257
Willey, Betty: 78
Williams, Charles Benjamin: 138
Williams, Charles: 266
Williams, Dick: 244
Williams, Dorothy Jewell: see "Jewell, Dorothy"
Williams, Francis Sisson: see "Sisson, Francis"
Williams, Geraldine: 241, 242
Williams, Jeffrey: 138
Williams, Kent Barry: 138
Willis, Minnie: 254, 255, 256, 257
Wilson, (William) Clark: 225, 226, 228, 240
Wilson, Benjamin Harrison: 338
Wilson, Bernice: 196
Wilson, Charles "Charlie": 17, 98
Wilson, Hayes: 17
Wilson, I. Laverne: 21
Wilson, Lorraine Wagner: see "Wagner, Lorraine"
Wilson, Luna Hayes: see "Hayes, Luna"
Wilson, Marjorie: 338
Wilson, Mary Ann: 26
Wilson, Olive Marshall: see "Marshall, Olive"
Wilson, Richard Marshall: 17, 225
Wilson, William Clark Jr.: 225
Wiltsie, Beverly: 134
Winchell, (Elizabeth) Jane: 314, 340, 341, 342, 343
Winchell, Caroline: 339
Winchell, Dora: 341
Winchell, Elizabeth "Libby" Keller: see "Keller, Elizabeth"
Winchell, Frances "Fanny" Laird: see "Laird, Frances"
Winchell, George: 41, 66, 340
Winchell, Gladys: 341
Winchell, Hazel Jane: 341
Winchell, Irving: 178
Winchell, John: 339
Winchell, Leone Bush: see "Bush, Leone"
Winchell, Marian S.: 340
Winchell, Marjorie Westfall Fuller: see "Westfall, Marjorie"
Winchell, Marvin W. Jr.: 340, 341, 343
Winchell, Marvin Webster Sr.: 20, 182, 320, 339, 340, 341, 342, 343
Winchell, Minnie Boyd: see "Boyd, Minnie"
Winchell, Richard "Dick" Marvin: 341
Winchell, Victor: 341
Winchell, Virginia Rae: 339, 342
Winchell, William R.: 339
Winkworth, C.T.: 203
Winters, Anna Lewis Towne: see "Lewis, Anna"
Winters, John A.: 140
Wirth, Charles D.: 17
Wise, Beverly Duga: see "Duga, Beverly"
Wise, Demaris "Dee": 344

Wise, Esther Phillips: see "Phillips, Esther"
Wise, Francis S.: 344
Wise, Kathelyn A.: 344
Wise, Marion: 344
Wise, Philip "Gordon": 344
Wise, Robert "Bruce": 344
Wise, Robert B. "Robbie": 344
Wise, Samuel: 21, 26, 48, 81, 84, 187, 344
Wolcott Grange, no. 348: 29, 144
Wolcott St. Mary Magdalene Catholic Church: 27, 130, 131, 132
Wolf, Dorothy: 328, 345
Wolf, Edith: 328, 345
Wolf, George B.: 328
Wolf, George O'Neil: 328, 345
Wolf, Ida Belle: 146
Wolf, Vivian Vincent: see "Vincent, Vivian"
Wolven, (Chloe) Edna Elwood: see "Elwood, (Chloe) Edna"
Wolven, Elisha Sheridan: 345
Wolven, Ernest Thomas: 345, 346
Wolven, Jeanette Ernestine: 345, 346
Wolven, Joyce Edna: 345, 346, 347
Wolven, Sarah Mayo: see "Mayo, Sarah"
Women's Society of Christian Service: 27, 44, 51, 54, 64, 96, 161, 167, 169, 173, 223, 249, 264, 344
Wood, Arden T.: 17
Wood, Catherine M.: 154
Wood, Dorothy: 346
Wood, Emma: 192
Wood, Joseph: 245
Wood, Marion: 192
Wood, Martha Pratt: see "Pratt, Martha"
Wood, Pauline: 192
Wood, Roxie Ann: 245
Wood, Samantha: 104
Wood, Wallace K.: 154
Woods, Esther Zornow: 330
Woods, Harry: 330
Woods, Pauline: 330
Worden, Leonard: 108
Worden, Nancy: 192
Wright, Brendon: 168
Wright, Charles: 168
Wright, Delia: 35, 283
Wright, Doris Gray: see "Gray, Doris"
Wright, James: 168
Wright, Lynn O.: 168, 169
Wright, M.E.: 59
Yancey, Anna Mundy: see "Mundy, Anna"
Yancey, Anne Gilkey: see "Gilkey, Anne"
Yancey, Benjamin Alvin: 23, 73, 74, 194, 347, 348, 349, 350, 351, 352
Yancey, Boyce Robert: 74, 347, 348, 352
Yancey, Carol Janice: 71, 73, 74

Yancey, Daniel: 73, 348, 349
Yancey, Dawn: 351
Yancey, Debbie: 351, 352
Yancey, Delene: 351
Yancey, Donald B.: 17, 74, 347, 348, 351, 352
Yancey, Donna: 351, 352
Yancey, Edward: 348, 349
Yancey, Eva Briggs: see "Briggs, Eva"
Yancey, Joyce Miriam: 71, 73, 74
Yancey, Lena Reyn: see "Reyn, Lena"
Yancey, Magdalene Briggs: see "Briggs, Magdalene Elizabeth"
Yancey, Nelson: 349
Yancey, Paula: 72, 74, 347, 348, 352
Yancey, Peter: 348
Yancey, Phyllis: 74, 347, 348, 350, 351, 352
Yancey, Theodore M.: 73, 74, 349
Yates, Kenneth Walter: 72
Yates, Leroy: 17, 134
Yates, William Edward: 72
Yetman, George: 279
Yetman, Nancy Russell Roney: see "Russell, Nancy"
York, Martha: 149, 150
Yost, Louise: 342
Yost, Mary Roney: see "Roney, Mary"
Young, Ada Miner: see "Miner, Ada"

Young Married Couples' Anniversary Club: see "Anniversary Club"
Youngman, Bruce: 115
Youngman, David: 115
Youngman, Graydon Allen: 114, 115
Youngman, James: 115
Youngman, Julia: 115
Youngman, Maria VanLare: see "VanLare, Maria"
Youngman, Molly DeBack: see "DeBack, Molly"
Youngman, William Abraham Arthur: 114
Younker, Violet: 310
Zaborowski, Edward: 272, 273
Zaborowski, Jadwiga "Hattie" Urbanik: see "Urbanik, Jadwiga"
Zaborowski, Lucille Reed: see "Reed, Lucille"
Zaborowski, Stanley: 273
Zapf, Florence: 67, 208, 209
Zapf, George H.: 67
Zapf, Huldena: 64, 67, 209
Zapf, Irene: 67, 209
Zapf, Wallace: 67, 209
Ziegler, Henry Van Allen "Van": 63, 352, 353, 354
Ziegler, Katherine: 62, 63, 64, 354
Ziegler, Louise Lucille: 20, 63, 80, 353, 354
Ziegler, Mabel Brown: see "Brown, Mabel"

www.ingramcontent.com/pod-product-compliance
Lightning Source LLC
Chambersburg PA
CBHW052008070526
44584CB00016B/1660